Andrew Greasley
Simulating Business Processes for Descriptive, Predictive and Prescriptive Analytics

Andrew Greasley

Simulating Business Processes for Descriptive, Predictive and Prescriptive Analytics

—

ISBN 978-1-5474-1674-5
e-ISBN (PDF) 978-1-5474-0069-0
e-ISBN (EPUB) 978-1-5474-0071-3

Library of Congress Control Number: 2019937567

Bibliographic information published by the Deutsche Nationalbibliothek
The Deutsche Nationalbibliothek lists this publication in the Deutsche Nationalbibliografie;
detailed bibliographic data are available on the Internet at http://dnb.dnb.de.

© 2019 Andrew Greasley
Cover image: Matveev_Aleksandr/iStock/Getty Images and PonyWang/E+/Getty Images
Typesetting: Integra Software Services Pvt. Ltd.
Printing and binding: CPI books GmbH, Leck

www.degruyter.com

Preface

Analytics has received much interest in recent years reflecting the opportunities presented by approaches such as machine learning. Many of the techniques of analytics have been used for some time, often classified using the term *artificial intelligence* (AI), but the recent increase in the availability of data has led to an upsurge in the use and capability of analytic techniques. Computer simulation is now in widespread use as a tool to look into the future and test designs. In fact, simulation is now an essential element in technological development and is an important way in which what is called the scientific method, how discoveries are made, can be employed. While simulation has a vast area of application, this text will focus on the use of simulation to analyze business processes.

This book uses the term *analytics* in two ways. Firstly, analytics can be considered in terms of outcomes that represent an approach to the measurement of performance. Analytic outcomes can be categorized into three types: descriptive analytics describes what is happening in order to understand, predictive analytics shows us what will be happening for different future scenarios in order to plan and prescriptive analytics recommends what should be happening in order to achieve our aims. The ability of simulation to study the current and future behavior of business processes and provide a course of action makes it an ideal tool for all three types of analytic outcomes. Secondly, analytics can be used as a term to represent the processing of large data sets (often termed *big data*) using statistical techniques such as machine learning. In terms of an analysis approach, analytics can be defined as a data-driven method which uses large data sets to develop predictive algorithms and is contrasted with the model-driven method of simulation. As a model-driven approach, simulation uses domain knowledge (knowledge of people who understand how the system works) to move from the real system to a simplification termed the *conceptual model*. The conceptual model is then implemented on a computer using simulation software. This enables us to "run" the model (simulate) into the future, thus providing a descriptive, predictive and prescriptive analytic capability.

The text will explain the use of simulation and analytics for analysis, show how to undertake a simulation study and provide a number of case studies to demonstrate the use of simulation in a business setting to undertake descriptive, predictive and prescriptive analytics. Chapter 1 introduces the three main areas covered of simulation modelling, business processes and analytics. The model-driven approach of simulation and the data-driven approach of analytics are covered and the relationship between the two is defined. Chapter 2 covers how business processes can be redesigned and performance measured. Chapter 3 covers the first main stage in simulating business processes which entails defining the conceptual model which is a simplification of the real business process. Chapter 4 discusses the conversion of the conceptual model into a computer model using simulation modelling software. A simple example is used to demonstrate the steps involved. Chapter 5 covers the interpretation of the simulation model results. Due to the variability inherent in the simulation model output this requires the use of statistical analysis. Chapters 6–19 aim to show the potential of simulation and provide guidance on how it can be used by the presentation of a number of manufacturing and service case study examples.

Andrew Greasley
January 2019

Acknowledgments

I would like to recognize the contributions from many individuals to the contents of this book and the case studies in Part 2. I would specifically like to thank Anand Assi, Yucan Wang, David Smith, Melissa Venegas Vallejos, Chris M. Smith, Emmanuel Musa, Stuart Barlow, Emmanuel Thanassoulis, Chris Owen and John S. Edwards.

I would also like to thank Steve Hardman for his support and Jeffrey M. Pepper and Jaya Dalal at De Gruyter.

About the Author

Andrew Greasley lectures in Simulation Modeling and Operations Management at Aston Business School, Birmingham, UK. He has taught in the UK, Europe, and Africa at a number of institutions. Dr. Greasley has over 100 publications with 13 books including *Operations Management*, Wiley; *Operations Management: Sage Course Companion*, Sage; *Simulation Modeling for Business*, Ashgate; *Business Information Systems*, Pearson Education (co-author); and *Enabling a Simulation Capability in the Organisation*, Springer Verlag. He has provided a simulation modeling consultancy service for 30 years to a number of companies in the public and private sectors including ABB Transportation Ltd. (now Bombardier), Derbyshire Constabulary, GMT Hunslet Ltd., Golden Wonder Ltd., Hearth Woodcraft Ltd., Luxfer Gas Cylinders Ltd., Pall-Ex Holdings Ltd., Rolls Royce Ltd. (Industrial Power Group), Stanton Valves Ltd., Tecquipment Ltd., Textured Jersey Ltd., and Warwickshire Police.

Contents

Preface —— V

Acknowledgments —— VII

About the Author —— VIII

Part 1: Understanding Simulation and Analytics

Chapter 1 Analytics and Simulation Basics —— 3

Chapter 2 Simulation and Business Processes —— 52

Chapter 3 Build the Conceptual Model —— 67

Chapter 4 Build the Simulation —— 110

Chapter 5 Use Simulation for Descriptive, Predictive and Prescriptive Analytics —— 154

Part 2: Simulation Case Studies

Chapter 6 Case Study: A Simulation of a Police Call Center —— 195

Chapter 7 Case Study: A Simulation of a "Last Mile" Logistics System —— 206

Chapter 8 Case Study: A Simulation of an Enterprise Resource Planning System —— 214

Chapter 9 Case Study: A Simulation of a Snacks Process Production System —— 230

Chapter 10 Case Study: A Simulation of a Police Arrest Process —— 239

Chapter 11 Case Study: A Simulation of a Food Retail Distribution Network —— 249

Chapter 12 Case Study: A Simulation of a Proposed Textile Plant —— 259

Chapter 13 Case Study: A Simulation of a Road Traffic Accident Process —— 271

Chapter 14 Case Study: A Simulation of a Rail Carriage Maintenance Depot —— 280

Chapter 15 Case Study: A Simulation of a Rail Vehicle Bogie Production Facility —— 289

Chapter 16 Case Study: A Simulation of Advanced Service Provision —— 298

Chapter 17 Case Study: Generating Simulation Analytics with Process Mining —— 308

Chapter 18 Case Study: Using Simulation with Data Envelopment Analysis —— 321

Chapter 19 Case Study: Agent-Based Modeling in Discrete-Event Simulation —— 325

Appendix A —— 336

Appendix B —— 337

Index —— 338

Part 1: Understanding Simulation and Analytics

Chapter 1
Analytics and Simulation Basics

Organizations need to provide goods and services that meet customer needs such as low price, fast delivery, wide range and high quality. In order to do this, these organizations operate as complex systems with many internal parts interacting with an external environment that is ever changing in response to forces such as technological advances. Because of this increasing complexity, organizations require tools that can help them both understand their current business processes and plan for future changes in response to their internal and external environment. This book is about the how simulation modeling of business processes for descriptive, predictive and descriptive analytics can attempt to explain behavior and thus help make decisions in the face of an uncertain future. Figure 1.1 shows these three areas in context and also shows how they work together.

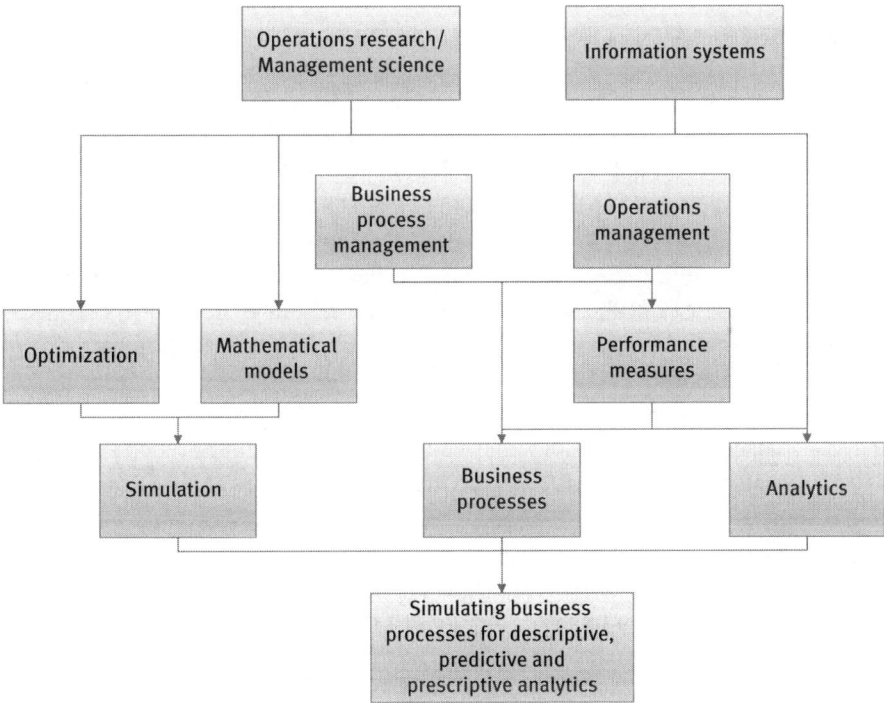

Figure 1.1: Simulating business processes for descriptive, predictive and prescriptive analytics.

Simulation can take many forms, but the type of simulation that is the focus of this text is based on a mathematical model that can implemented on a computer.

These models can be used to represent a simplified version of a real system in order to aid its understanding and to provide a prediction of its future behavior. The use of models allows us to overcome the drawbacks of predicting future behavior with the real system which can be costly, time-consuming, unfeasible while testing many design options and in some cases dangerous for safety critical systems. In order to determine the "best" option for future actions, we may use optimization techniques. Both mathematical modeling and optimization techniques fall under the areas of operations research as the focus on business applications has expanded management science. These terms are often used interchangeably or under the umbrella terms operations research/management science (OR/MS). Optimization may also come under the information systems area when the optimization is enabled by program code in the form of machine-learning algorithms.

The type of simulation can vary and so can its application range into physics, chemistry, biology and many other areas. This text is focused on the application of simulation to analyze processes within business organizations. The process perspective is associated with the area of operations management, which considers the transformation of materials, information and customers into goods and services. This transformation is undertaken by processes that require the allocation of resources such as people and equipment. Business process management (BPM) is a discipline that is focused on the use of business processes as a way of improving organizational performance. Deriving and using process performance measures is a key aspect of both operations management and BPM. In operations management performance is often measured using the metrics of cost, quality, speed, flexibility and dependability. These measures not only provide an indication of performance but the identification and pursuit of a subset of these measures provide a way of connecting the strategic direction of the company with its operational decisions.

Analytics or business analytics can be seen as incorporating the use of modeling and statistics from OR/MS and information systems capabilities such as the storage of big data in order to transform data into actions through analysis and insights in the context of organizational decision making. A key part of analytics is the use of performance measures to assess business performance.

Analytics is usually associated with the use of large data sets termed *big data* and computer programs running algorithms to process that data in what is known as data-driven analysis. This text is focused on the use of a model-driven approach using simulation to analyze business processes to produce analytic outcomes. So before describing simulation in more detail, the data- and model-driven perspectives for the analysis of business processes will be covered. This analysis will include the possibility of combining the data- and model-driven approaches.

Data- and Model-Driven Analysis

In the context of analyzing organizational business processes, analytics can be classified into the following:

Descriptive Analytics
- This is the use of reports and visual displays to explain or understand past and current business performance.
- Descriptive data-driven reports often contain statistical summaries of metrics such as sales and revenue and are intended to provide an outline of trends in current and past performance. Model-driven techniques are often used for descriptive analysis in the context of the design of new products and processes when little current data exists.

Predictive Analytics
- This is the ability to predict future performance to help plan for the future.
- Data-driven models often do this by detecting patterns or relationships in historical data and then projecting these relationships into the future. Model-driven approaches use domain knowledge to construct a simplified representation of the structure of the system that is used to predict the future.

Prescriptive Analytics
- This is the ability to recommend a choice of action from predictions of future performance.
- Data-driven models often do this by recommending an optimum decision based on the need to maximize (or minimize) some aspect of performance. Model-driven approaches may use optimization software to try many different scenarios until one is found that best meets the optimization criteria.

A *data-driven* modeling approach aims to derive a description of behavior from observations of a system so that it can describe how that system behaves (its output) under different conditions or scenarios (its input). Because they can only describe the relationship between input and output, they are called descriptive models. One approach is to use *pattern recognition* as a way to build a model that allows us to make predictions. The idea of pattern recognition is based on learning relationships through examples. Pattern recognition is achieved through techniques such as associations, sequences, classification and clustering of the data. These techniques are implemented in models that use equations, logical statements and algorithms to find the patterns. In essence, this approach produces a model that imitates real behavior based on past observations of that behavior termed a *descriptive model*. This imitation can be achieved by defining a relationship that relates model input to model output. Generally, the more data (observations) that can be used to form the description, the more accurate the description will be and thus the interest in big data analytics that uses large data sets. Machine learning uses a selection of learning algorithms that use large data sets and a desired outcome to derive an algorithm that can be used for descriptive, predictive and prescriptive analytics.

A model-driven modeling approach aims to explain a system's behavior not just derived from its inputs but through a representation of the internal system's structure. The model-driven approach is a well-recognized way of understanding the world based on a systems approach in which a real system is simplified into its essential elements (its processes) and relationships between these elements (its structure). Thus in addition to input data, information is required on the system's processes, the function of these processes and the essential parts of the relationships between these processes. These models are called explanatory models as they represent the real system and attempt to explain the behaviour that occurs. This means that the effect of a change on design of the process can be assessed by changing the structure of the model. These models generally have far smaller data needs than data-driven models because of the key role of the representation of structure. For example, we can represent a supermarket by the customers that flow through the supermarket and the processes they undertake—collecting groceries and paying at the till. A model would then not only enable us to show current customer waiting time at the supermarket tills (descriptive analytics) but also allow us to change the design of the system such as changing the number of tills and predict the effect on customer waiting time (predictive analytics). We can also specify the target customer waiting time based on the number of tills required (prescriptive analytics). However most real systems are very complex—a supermarket has many different staff undertaking many processes using different resources—for example, the collection and unpacking of goods, keeping shelves stocked, heating and ventilation systems, etc. It is usually not feasible to include all the elements of the real system, so a key part of modeling is making choices about which parts of the system should be included in the model in order to obtain useful results. This simplification process may use statistics in the form of mathematical equations to represent real-life processes (such as the customer arrival rate) and a computer program (algorithm) in the form of process logic to represent the sequence of activities that occur within a process.

> **Simulation for Descriptive, Predictive, and Prescriptive Analytics**
>
> Simulation is not simply a predictive or even a prescriptive tool but can also be used in a descriptive mode to develop understanding. Here the emphasis is not necessarily on developing accurate predictive models but on using the simulation model to help develop theories regarding how an organizational system works. In this role simulation is used as an experimental methodology where we can explore the effect of different parameters by running the simulation under many different conditions. What we do is start with a deductive method in which we have a set of assumptions and test these assumptions and their consequences. We then use an experimental method to generate data which can be analyzed in an inductive manner to develop theories by generalization of observations. In fact the simulation analyst can alternate between a deductive and inductive approach as the model is developed.

Data-Driven Analysis Techniques

In general terms, there are many analysis techniques that can be considered as data-driven techniques including regression analysis, econometric modeling, time series experiments and yield management. However, data-driven techniques considered here are most often associated with big data analytics. These techniques relate to those that are used for the analysis on large-scale data sets termed *big data*. A brief description follows of each of the main categories of big data-driven analytics techniques.

Data Mining

In a general sense, data mining can be defined as identifying patterns in complex and ill-defined data sets. Particular data mining techniques include the following:
- Identifying associations involves establishing relationships about items that occur at a particular point in time (e.g., what items are bought together in a supermarket).
- Identifying sequences involves showing the order in which actions occur (e.g., click-stream analysis of a website).
- Classification involves analyzing historical data into patterns to predict future behavior (e.g., identifying groups of website users who display similar visitor patterns).
- Clustering involves finding groups of facts that were previously unknown (e.g. identifying new market segments of customers or detecting e-commerce fraud).

There are various categories of mining depending on the nature of the data that is being analyzed. For example, there is *text mining* for document analysis and *web mining* of websites.

Machine Learning

Machine learning uses an iterative approach for the analysis of prepared training and test sample data in order to produce an analytical model. Through the use of iteration, learning algorithms build a model that may be used to make predictions. This model may be in the form of a mathematical equation, a rule set or an algorithm. Thus, machine learning does not refer to actual learning by a machine (computer) but the use of algorithms that through iteration provide an ability to predict outcomes from a data set. The main steps involved in machine learning are preprocessing of the data set, creation of a training set (usually 80% of the data) and a test set (usually 20% of the data) and selection of a learning algorithm to process the data.

Supervised machine learning relates to learning algorithms that build models that can be used to make predictions using *classification* and *regression* techniques while unsupervised machine learning relates to identifying similar items using *clustering* techniques. In supervised machine learning, our training data sets have values for both our input (predictor) and output (outcome) variables that are known to us so that we can use classification techniques such as support vector machines (SVMs) and regression techniques such as linear regression, decision trees (DTs) and neural networks for prediction. In unsupervised learning our training data sets have values for our input (predictor) variables but not for our output (outcome) variables so this approach involves examining attributes of a data set in order to determine which items are most similar to one another. This clustering function can be achieved using techniques such as K-Means algorithms and neural networks. In addition to the categories of supervised and unsupervised machine learning, Reinforcement Learning is a subfield of machine learning that uses learning algorithms that explore options and when they achieve their aim, deduce how to get to that successful endpoint in the future. A reinforcement approach can be implemented by the use of a reward and penalty system to guide a choice from a number of random options. Simulation is particularly relevant for this type of machine learning as it can provide a virtual environment in which the reinforcement training can take place safely and far quicker than in a real system.

Some examples of machine learning algorithms used are:
- Association rules mining uses a rules-based approach to finding relationships between variables in a data set.
- DTs generate a rule set that derive the likelihood of a certain outcome based on the likelihood of the preceding outcome. DTs belong to a class of algorithms that are often known as *CART* (classification and regression trees). *Random forest DTs* are an extension of the DT model in which many trees are developed independently and each "votes" for the tree that gives the best classification of outcomes.
- SVMs are a class of machine-learning algorithms that are used to classify data into one or another category.
- k-Means is a popular algorithm for unsupervised learning that is used to create clusters and thus categorize data.
- Neural networks or artificial neural networks represent a network of connected layers of (artificial) neurons. These mimic neurons in the human brain that "fire" (produce an output) when their stimulus (input) reaches a certain threshold. They have recently become a popular approach due to the development of the backpropagation algorithm which makes it possible to train multi-layered neural networks. Multilayered neural networks have one or more intermediary ("hidden") layers between the input and output layers to enable a wider range of functions to be learnt. Neural networks with more than two hidden layers are generally known as deep neural networks or deep learning systems.

> **Simulation vs Machine Learning for Prediction**
>
> The model-driven approach of simulation requires the model builder to understand causations and codify them in the model. The model then permits prediction by running the model into the future—simulation. Machine Learning's great promise is by using a data-driven approach it can generate algorithms that may provide predictions. However there are a number of challenges for the Machine Learning approach when used for prediction
> - Although the prediction algorithm is generated, the learning algorithm and training method must be devised to enable this. This task can be challenging.
> - We often do not understand how the prediction algorithm has arrived at its prediction. Thus algorithms based on approaches such as neural networks are "black box" and are thus difficult to validate.
> - The data used to train and test the algorithm is based on a fixed period of time (i.e. a sample) and thus may not cover all required learning examples—this is termed incompleteness.
> - There is a need to distinguish natural variation in the data from changes in the data due to rare or infrequent behavior not representative of typical behavior—this is termed noise
> - As the context of the prediction widens the number of potential variables impacting on the prediction increases vastly. Thus there is a need for increasingly massive data sets to cover the "state space" of the effects of these variables.

Process Mining

The use of process mining involves obtaining and extracting event data to produce an event log and transforming the event log into a process model termed *process discovery*. The process model can then be used to check conformance of the system with the process design and to measure the performance of the process. In terms of event log construction, the data required to make an event log can come from a variety of sources including collected data in spreadsheets, databases and data warehouses or directly from data streams. The minimum data required to construct an event log consists of a list of process instances (i.e., events), which are related to a case identification number and for each event a link to an activity label such as "check ticket." Activities may reoccur in the event log, but each event is unique and events within a case need to be presented in order of execution in the event log so that casual dependencies can be derived in the process model. It is also usual for there to be a timestamp associated with each event in the event log. Additional attributes associated with each event may also be included such as the association of a resource required to undertake the event and the estimated cost of the event.

Once we are satisfied that the process model does provide a suitable representation of behavior, then we can use the model in a normative mode and judge discrepancies in terms of deviations from the ideal behavior shown by the model. Undesirable behavior is when deviations occur due to unwanted actions (for example, not obtaining authorization for a purchase) and desirable deviations occur when actions occur that are outside normal parameters but show flexibility in meeting the process objectives (for example, providing additional customer service). Conformance checking of processes against a normative model is a major use of process mining. In addition to conformance checking, process mining can be used to assess performance across a number of dimensions by providing additional information in the event log, which is subsequently incorporated into the process model. For example, performance can be reviewed by associating resources to the people undertaking the activities. The interactions between people can be mapped in a social network to provide an organizational perspective. In addition, a cost perspective can be achieved by associating costs with activities.

Visual Analytics

The basic idea of visual analytics is to present large-scale data in some visual form, allowing people to interact with the data to understand processes better. In order to facilitate better understanding of data, software that provides a visual representation of data is available in the form of applications such as spreadsheets, dashboards and scorecards. In conjunction with their statistical and forecasting capabilities, spreadsheets are particularly useful at providing graphical displays of trends such as sales for analysis by an organization. To meet the needs of managers who do not use computers frequently, a graphical interface, called a *dashboard* (or a *digital dashboard*), permits decision makers to understand statistics collated by an organization. A dashboard display is a graphical display on the computer presented to the decision maker, which includes graphical images such as meters, bar graphs, trace plots and text fields to convey real-time information. Dashboards incorporate drill-down features to enable data to be interrogated in greater detail if necessary. Dashboards should be designed so that the data displayed can be understood in context. For example, sales figures can be displayed against sales figures for the previous time period or the same time period in the previous year. Figures can also be compared against targets and competitors. For example, quality performance can be benchmarked against best-in-class competitors in the same industry. The visual display of data can also be used to show the amount of difference between performance and targets both currently and the trend over time. Visual indicators, such as traffic lights, can be used to show when performance has fallen below acceptable levels (red light) is a cause for concern (amber light) and is acceptable (green light).

While dashboards are generally considered to measure operational performance, scorecards provide a summary of performance over a period of time. Scorecards may be associated with the concept of the balanced scorecard strategy tool and examine data from the balanced scorecard perspectives of financial, customer, business process and learning and growth.

Data Farming

Data farming is the purposeful generation of data from computer-based models, including simulation models. Large-scale simulation experiments can be initiated by varying many input variables, examining many different scenarios or both. Data farming offers the possibility of using simulation to generate big data, with the advantage that the data generated is under the control of the modeler. However, the implementation of data farming may require the use of simulation software with a relatively fast execution speed.

> **People Analytics**
>
> Some of the pitfalls around data driven analytics are shown by the use of people analytics in organizations. People analytics deals with perceptual data and data based on intangible variables rather than the factual data used in finance for example. Historically data on people within a business has been used for applications such as workforce modeling in order to match the supply of people and skills to planned workload. Performance measurement of people has also taken place in the context of the business itself. However the use of big data to drive analytics has seen the development of people analytic models that provide measurement based on data gathered on a massive scale. The idea is that the sheer scale of data will improve the accuracy of the analytical process and allow "fact-based" decisions to be made on people at the individual level. However as Cathy O'Neil (2016) found, the complexity of people has led to a number of pitfalls with the use of people analytic methods, including:
>
> Proxy measures are used to attempt to measure complex human behaviors that may not be an accurate representation.
>
> The algorithms have inbuilt feedback loops that reinforce the assumptions of the model leading to self-fulfilling results.
>
> There is inbuilt bias by model builders reflecting their viewpoint on people's behaviors.
>
> There is a lack of transparency of the workings of the models leading to a lack of knowledge around the limitations of the results of the models and a lack of accountability regarding the model's validity.

Model-Driven Analysis Techniques

Model-driven analysis techniques use a model that can be defined as a simplified representation of a real system that is used to improve our understanding of that real system. The representation is simplified because the complexity of most systems means that it is infeasible to provide all details of the real system in the model. Indeed, the simplification process actually benefits understanding, where it allows a focus on the elements of the system that are relevant to the decision. For this reason, a model should be as simple as possible, while being valid, in order to meet its objectives. The modeling process thus involves deciding what is relevant and should be included in the model to meet the aims of the current investigation.

The model then provides information for decision making that can be used to make predictions of real-world system behavior (Figure 1.2).

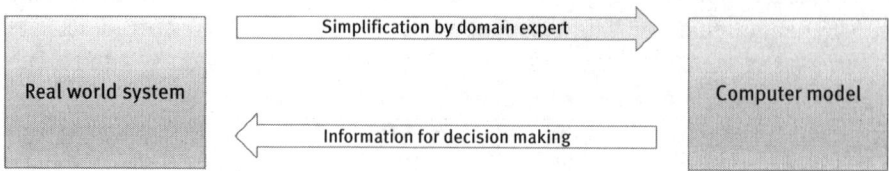

Figure 1.2: The modeling process.

There are many different approaches to modeling, but mathematical models represent a system as a number of mathematical variables (termed *state variables*) with mathematical equations used to describe how these state variables change over time. An important distinction between mathematical models is the classification between static (fixed in time) or dynamic (change over time), with dynamics systems being modeled using a continuous or discrete approach (Figure 1.3).

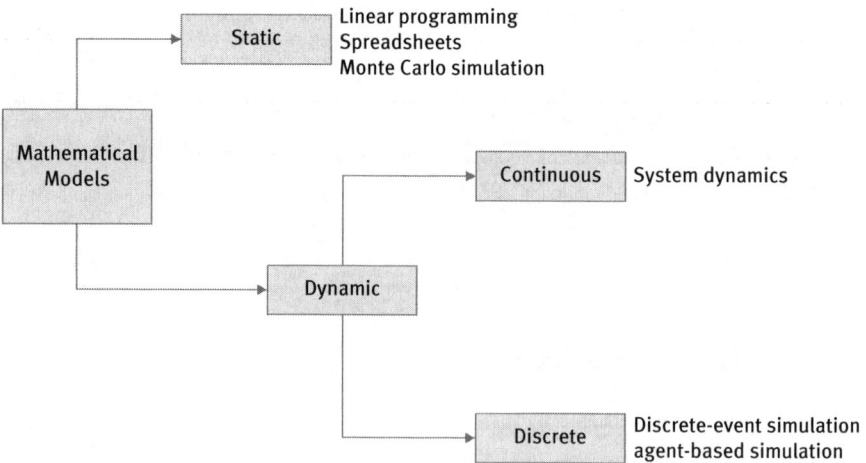

Figure 1.3: Categories of mathematical models.

Static Mathematical Models

Static models include the use of a computer spreadsheet, which is an example of a numerical static model in which relationships can be constructed and studied for different scenarios. Another example of a static numerical model is the Monte Carlo simulation method. This consists of experimental sampling with random numbers and deriving results based on these. Although random numbers are being used, the problems that are being solved are essentially determinate. The Monte Carlo method is widely used in risk analysis for assessing the risks and benefits of decisions. Linear programming is a modeling technique that seeks defined goals when a set of variables and constraints are given. A linear programming technique is data envelopment analysis (DEA), which is a method for calculating efficiency. DEA can be used as a benchmarking tool to generate a score that indicates the relative distance of an entity to the best practices so as to measure its overall performance compared with its peers. This overall performance measured by DEA can be manifested in the form of a composite measure that aggregates individual indicators. Chapter 18 shows how DEA may be used in conjunction with simulation.

Dynamic Mathematical Models

A dynamic mathematical model allows changes in system attributes to be derived as a function of time. A classification is made between continuous and discrete model types. A discrete system changes only at separate points in time. For example, the number of customers in a service system is dependent on individual arrivals and departures of customers at discrete points in time.

Continuous systems vary over time; for example, the amount of petrol in a tanker being emptied is varying continuously over time and is thus classified as a continuous system. In practice most continuous systems can be modeled as discrete and vice versa at different levels of detail. Also, systems will usually have a mixture of both discrete and continuous elements. In general, continuous models are used at a high level of abstraction, for example, investigating cause-and-effect linkages in organizational systems, while discrete models are used to model business processes. The system dynamics (SD) approach is described as an example of a continuous mathematical model, while discrete-event simulation (DES) is described as a discrete mathematical modeling approach.

Simulation

Simulation is a particular kind of dynamic modeling in which the model (usually represented on a computer) is "run" forward through (simulated) time. This book is focused on the use of simulation in an organizational context to measure business process performance. In order to use simulation, we must represent a theory of how the organization works (conceptual model) and transform that into

a procedure that can be represented as a computer program (simulation model). Simulation has an experimental methodology in that we can explore the effect of different parameters by running the simulation under many different conditions. From these observations, we can refine our theory about how the organization works and can make predictions about how it might work in the future. Thus simulation can be used to:
- Understand past and current behavior of business processes (descriptive analytics).
- Predict the future behavior of business processes (predictive analytics).
- Recommend action based on the future behavior of business processes (prescriptive analytics).

The Need for Simulation When Studying a Dynamic System

When studying organizational systems we are studying a dynamic system—one that changes over time and reacts to its environment and thus shows both structure and behavior. This means that the model must also be dynamic and it can be represented by a mathematical equation, a logical statement (such as a series of if-then statements) or as a computer program (in the form of an algorithm). There are two aspects of dynamic systems are addressed by simulation:

Variability

Most business systems contain variability in both the demand on the system (e.g., customer arrivals) and in durations (e.g., customer service times) of activities within the system. The use of fixed (e.g., average) values will provide some indication of performance, but simulation permits the incorporation of statistical distributions and thus provides an indication of both the range and variability of the performance of the system. This is important in customer-based systems when not only is the average performance relevant, but performance should also not drop below a certain level (e.g., customer service time) or customers will be lost. In service systems, two widely used performance measures are an estimate of the maximum queuing time for customers and the utilization (i.e., percentage time occupied) for the staff serving the customer. If there is no variability, there will be no queues as long as the arrival rate is less than or equal to the service time. However, Figure 1.4 shows that the higher the variability, the higher the average queue length for a given utilization. It is difficult to eliminate variability entirely, so it is recommended to try to keep utilization (of staff and equipment) below 80%.

Variability can be classified into customer-introduced variability and internal process variability. Customer-introduced variability includes factors such as the fact that customers don't arrive uniformly to a service and customers will require different services with different service times. Also not all customers appreciate the same thing in a service; some like self-service and some do not. In addition customer-introduced variability can arise from internal processes within the organization such as variability in staff performance (this includes both variability between different people's performance and variability in process performance by one person over time). Variability can also be caused by equipment and material variations.

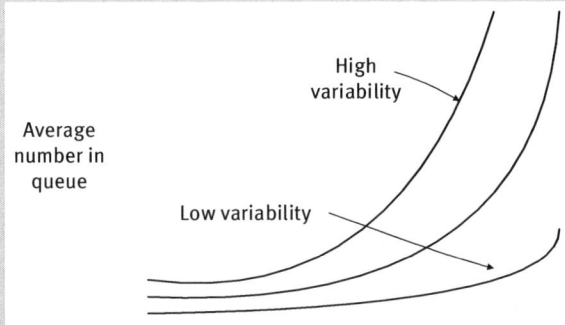

Figure 1.4: Average number in queue against average utilization.

Interdependence

Most systems contain a number of decision points that affect the overall performance of the system. The simulation technique can incorporate statistical distributions to model the likely decision options taken. Also the "knock-on" effect of many interdependent decisions over time can be assessed using the model's ability to show system behavior over a time period.

To show the effect of variability on systems, a simple example will be presented. An owner of a small shop wishes to predict how long customers wait for service during a typical day. The owner has identified two types of customer, who have different amounts of shopping and so take different amounts of time to serve. Type A customers account for 70% of custom and take on average 10 minutes to serve. Type B customers account for 30% of custom and take on average 5 minutes to serve. The owner has estimated that during an 8-hour day, on average the shop will serve 40 customers. The owner then calculates the serve time during a particular day:

Customer A = 0.7 × 40 × 10 minutes = 280 minutes
Customer B = 0.3 × 40 × 5 minutes = 60 minutes
Therefore, the total service time = 340 minutes and gives a utilization of the shop till of 340/480 × 100 = 71%

Thus, the owner is confident that all customers can be served promptly during a typical day. A simulation model was constructed for this system to estimate the service time for customers. Using a fixed time between customer arrivals of 480/40 = 12 minutes and with a 70% probability of a 10 minutes service time and a 30% probability of a 5 minutes service time, the overall service time for customers (including queuing time) has a range of between 5 and 10 minutes and no queues are present in this system.

Service Time for Customer (minutes)
Average   8.5
Minimum   5
Maximum   10

However, in reality customers will not arrive, equally spaced at 12-minute intervals, but will arrive randomly with an average interval of 12 minutes. The simulation is altered to show a time between arrivals following an exponential distribution (the exponential distribution is often used to mimic the behavior of customer arrivals) with a mean of 12 minutes. The owner was surprised by the simulation results:

Service Time for Customer (minutes)
Average   17
Minimum   5
Maximum   46

The average service time for a customer had doubled to 17 minutes, with a maximum of 46 minutes!

The example demonstrates how the performance of even simple systems can be affected by randomness. Variability would also be present in this system in other areas such as customer service times and the mix of customer types over time. Simulation is able to incorporate all of these sources of variability to provide a more realistic picture of system performance.

Deterministic and Stochastic Models

Another way of classifying models is between deterministic and stochastic models. A deterministic model does not represent uncertainty and so for a given set of conditions and parameters will always produce the same outcome. This implies that given a well enough detailed snapshot of a system we should be able to forecast the system's dynamic behavior perfectly. Thus these types of models are analytically tractable and may be expressed as mathematical formulae. Stochastic models include some random components such as variable demand rate or variation of processing rates due to natural variability. The inclusion of stochasticity typically makes even simple models intractable but increases their realism. This is because few systems show no variation over time or can be perfectly understood and measured. However a stochastic model only allows us to quote a probability of a future prediction.

The Role of Simplification in Data-Driven and Model-Driven Analysis

In order to be used for prediction, both data- and model-driven analysis methods need to simplify the real world in order to reduce complexity.

In the area of data-driven machine learning, the terms overfitting and underfitting are used to describe the simplification process. Overfitting is when the learning algorithm "tries too hard" to fit the data, approximating nearly all the points in the data set. This means there is a lack of generalization and the algorithm only explains behavior that directly derives from the training data. In this case, any noise such as missing or incorrect data in the test data set will cause a misleading prediction. The algorithm will produce a number of different mistakes, termed high variance. Underfitting is when the algorithm is "not trying hard enough" to fit the data, leading to the same mistakes repeated, termed high bias. This means there is too much generalization and the algorithm predicts behavior that does not derive from the training data. The solution to overfitting is to try a less flexible learning algorithm or to obtain more data. The solution to underfitting is to try a more flexible learning algorithm or try a different learning algorithm. The issue of simplification in machine learning is about guiding the learning algorithms to provide a balance between underfitting and overfitting the data, which is a difficult task.

> In the area of model-driven simulation, simplification is about providing a specification for a conceptual model that contains a suitable level of detail to meet the predictive needs of the model. Too little simplification will lead to an overly complex model, which may hinder understanding of the effects being studied. Too much simplification will lead to inaccurate results as important elements of the system that have an effect on the predictive metrics of interest have been omitted from the model. In data-driven machine learning, the simplification process is coded into the design of the learning algorithm by the data scientist, whereas in model-driven simulation the simplification process is achieved using the domain knowledge of the modeler. Both approaches need careful application of the model and interpretation of model results by personnel with the requisite technical (quantitative) and domain knowledge (qualitative) skillsets.

Data- and Model-Driven Analysis with Simulation and Analytics

So far we have defined data- and model-driven approaches to the analysis of business processes. Analytics is categorized as a data-driven approach and simulation is categorized as a model-driven approach. There are instances, however, of the use of analytics techniques that are driven by data generated from a model that will be termed *model-driven analytics* and simulations that are data driven, termed *data-driven simulation*.

Simulation and analytics and thus each of these combinations attempt to codify the real world into a computer model that can be used for understanding and prediction of the real system. This reality will usually be based on knowledge of only a part of all the data that exists (or ever existed) about the real system. The relationship between data-driven, model-driven, analytics and simulation is presented in this context. Figure 1.5 shows how the four combinations of simulation and analytic analysis can be represented by four types of reality that reflect their different emphasis in terms of the use of a subset of all the data that exists that is related to a system.

	Data-driven	Model-driven
Analytics	Selected reality Data (raw)	Farmed reality Data (simulated)
Simulation	Digital reality Data (analyzed)	Simplified reality Data (sampled)

Figure 1.5: Data- and model-driven analysis with simulation and analytics.

The categories in Figure 1.5 cover the following:
- Data-driven analytics techniques that use *raw data* to learn from the past to represent a *selected reality* based on the variables and observations included. This is the data-driven approach described earlier and is represented by analytics techniques such as data mining, machine learning and process mining. Data-driven analytics represent a selected reality in that no matter how large the data sets used for analysis they will only present a selected view of all the data generated by a process over time.
- Model-driven simulation techniques that use *sampled data* from the past to represent a *simplified reality*. This is the model-driven approach described earlier and is represented by the technique of simulation. This is termed a *simplified reality* as the modeling process employs a simplification of reality by removing elements that are not considered relevant to the study objectives.
- Data-driven simulations that use *analyzed data* to drive simulation to provide a *digital reality*. These applications allow data, which may be processed through analytic techniques such as process mining, data mining and machine learning, to advance the capability of simulation model development and experimentation. The use of a data-driven approach to provide model-building capabilities and thus enable recoding of the model to reflect the actual state of a system is a particularly important advance represented by the use of applications such as digital twins. This is termed *digital reality* as the approach is used to construct a real-time digital replica of a physical object.
- Model-driven analytics that use *simulated data* to drive analytics techniques to provide *a farmed reality*. This enables simulation to be used for training and testing machine-learning algorithms and facilitating the use of analytic techniques for future system behaviors and for systems that do not currently exist. This is termed a *farmed reality* in reference to the term data farming, which refers to the use of a simulation model to generate synthetic data.

Data-Driven Simulation

Usually a simulation model will take some time to develop with a custom model built for each application and collection of data over a period of time by methods such as observation and interviews with personnel involved in the process. This relatively long development time and use of historical data can limit the use of simulation to medium- to long-term decisions based on steady-state operation. To enable simulation for short-term operational decision making, there is a need for continuous updating of both the data that is used by the model and in some instances of the model itself.

This can be now be achieved in a number of ways including:
1. The use of historical process data from factories such as those provided using the manufacturing execution systems (MES) standard to provide automated collection and faster updating of data values to configure a simulation model.

2. Real-time information on the status of machines and production schedules in the factory to provide automated model regeneration to reflect changes in the physical system as they occur.
3. Data from the simulation model used in conjunction with machine-learning analytics to flow back to the physical system to control its actions.

All three of these options could be referred to as data-driven simulations and their use should be based on the complexity of the system being modeled and the objectives of the simulation study. In terms of the use of historical process data, MES systems are used to track and control production systems and provide a scheduling capability. For example, the Simio simulation software package provides facilities to extract data directly from an MES and build and configure a Simio model from that data. Simio includes a feature to auto-create model components and their properties based on the contents of the imported tables, which can then be used to build complete models from external data. These models would normally provide a base model, which could then be refined if necessary. This option thus provides the ability to generate a model much faster than traditional simulation approaches.

Digital Twins

The term *digital twin* is used to refer to a data-driven simulation that makes use of real-time data flows and requires a number of components which together in a manufacturing context are implemented in a Smart Factory. These components include:
- Data infrastructure such as the internet of things (IoT) to provide data collection through sensors and data connection through the internet.
- Machine-learning techniques to provide an analytics capability.
- Robotics to provide automated control.

Digital twins can be categorized by the level of data integration between the simulation and real-world object counterpart and by the organizational scope of the simulation.

In terms of the level of data integration there are three possible levels of integration between the simulation and its real-world object counterpart. When there is no automated data exchange between the simulation and real-world object, when there is an automated one-way data flow from the real-world object which leads to a change in state of the simulation and when data flows are fully integrated in both directions. Digital twins require a two-way data flow to provide a control capability to take action in response to predicted behavior. Corrective actions are often implemented using analytics techniques based on machine-learning algorithms that provide appropriate methods of process control actuation. The development of digital twins with fully integrated data flows in both directions is complex and is still in its infancy.

In the context of the organization, the scope of a digital twin can be at the product, process and enterprise level.

Digital Twins of Products

This type of digital twin relates to the emulation of physical objects such as machines, vehicles, people and energy. They can be considered as an extension of computer-aided design (CAD) and computer-aided engineering systems, which capture data that can then be used to detect issues and generate information that can be used to improve performance. They often have a focus on improving the efficiency of product life-cycle management, which is important for successful product-as-a-service business models. Digital twins allow monitoring of multiple products and resources in different operating conditions and different geographic locations.

Digital Twins of Processes

These emulate processes over time and so require a dynamic simulation engine based on methods such as DES covered in this book. Depending on the application, process data may be collected in real time or near real time. Near real-time collection either allows for a delay for data processing or collects data at set time points and may provide greater feasibility in execution.

Digital Twins of Enterprises

At the enterprise level, the objective of a digital twin is to capture the business-operating model for control and management purposes. Enterprise digital twins can be implemented by using multiple digital twins that are in use at the process level. Applications include connection of the digital twin to an enterprise resource-planning system in order to improve factory scheduling.

By combining the classification of digital twins by level of data integration and organizational scope we can see that the concept covers a wide range of applications. Figure 1.6 shows that a key consideration between these different applications is the complexity implied in the application, with a full digital twin of the enterprise representing the most complex.

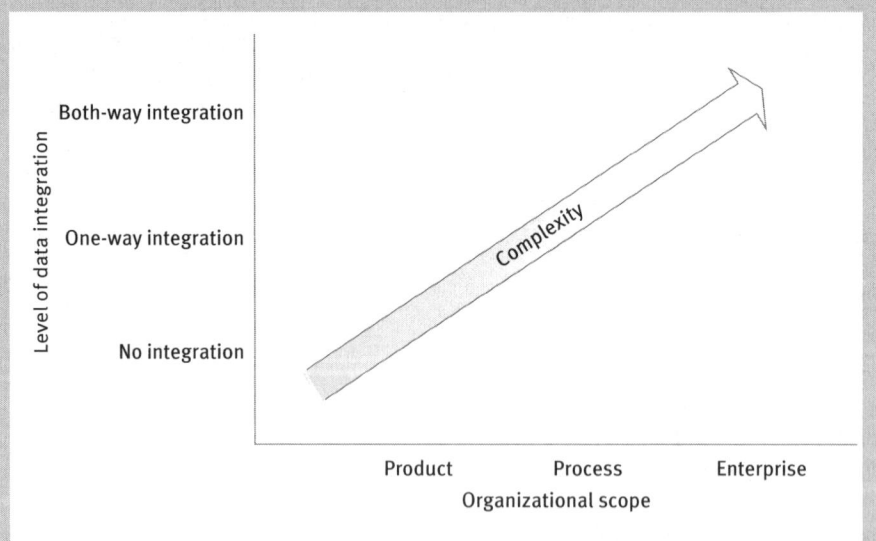

Figure 1.6: Level of data integration and organizational scope of a digital twin.

An Example of a Digital Twin

An example of the use of data-driven simulation combined with machine learning is for predictive maintenance for a welding machine. Here a simulation provides a virtual representation in real time of the manufacturing process through data connections over the IoT. The current status of the welding machine is known by the digital twin. A machine-learning algorithm is used to provide a prediction of the remaining useful life of the manufacturing equipment based on its current usage and historical data of the process. The digital twin can be run into the future and predict machine failure based on its current status and scheduled future usage. The digital twin can then communicate back to the equipment to instigate a maintenance operation at the appropriate time. The digital twin thus provides an intelligent and automated predictive maintenance capability.

Model-Driven Analytics

One use for simulation is to generate data to train and test machine-learning algorithms. For example, in scheduling manufacturing systems, a simulation can be used to randomly generate combinations of control attributes (such as work-in-progress and utilization). The simulation can then compare the scheduling performance of the trained machine-learning-based algorithms and further traditional scheduling rules such as shortest process time. Using simulation in this way offers the possibility of its use for training algorithms for current and planned systems and for systems that do not currently exist.

The categories in Figure 1.5 cover data-driven analytics techniques that use raw data to learn from the past to represent a selected reality based on the variables and observations included; and model-driven simulation techniques that use sampled data from the past to represent a simplified reality. The predictive capabilities of both of these approaches are limited by the transient nature of organizational processes. No matter how large the dataset used in a data-driven approach it may not describe a future behavior owing to changes in the system causing that behavior. This will occur at least until the new behavior has been incorporated into the data provided to the learning algorithms. For model-driven approaches no matter how large the model we may not incorporate a future behavior owing to the simplified representation of the model, at least until we have recoded the model to incorporate the cause of that behavior. Two further categories are shown in Figure 1.5, data-driven simulation that use data from analytics to drive simulation to provide a digital reality; and model-driven analytics that use data from simulation to drive analytics techniques to provide a farmed reality. In terms of data-driven simulation, practitioners need to take into account the limitations of the data-driven approach in terms of the use of historical data to represent the future of a transient system. In terms of model-driven analytics simulation, here the limitation is based around the use of a sampled dataset that is a simplification of the raw data generated by the real system.

A barrier to the combined use of simulation and analytics is the different backgrounds and skillsets of simulation and analytics practitioners. Simulation practitioners typically combine the technical knowledge required to undertake simulation such as model building and statistical methods with an understanding of an application domain such as manufacturing or healthcare. In a business setting analytics may be undertaken by teams consisting of data scientists with data, statistical and IT skills, business analysts with deep domain knowledge and IT professionals to develop data products. Many simulation practitioners began their simulation careers coding models in simulation languages such as SIMAN and using languages such as FORTRAN for file processing. However in the light of the development of drag and drop interfaces in such tools as Arena, recent users may find it a particular challenge to adapt to the need for coding when developing a machine learning algorithm in Matlab, R or Python. One way of addressing this issue may be to emphasize the need for training of simulation practitioners in data science techniques and the adoption of a multi-disciplinary approach to research and training.

Comparing the Use of Model-driven Simulation and Data-driven Analytics for Prediction

Simulation and analytics techniques such as machine learning represent two different perspectives on how we can attempt to predict the future. Simulation applies our domain knowledge to define a relationship between cause and effect which is codified in a conceptual model. Machine Learning applies our domain knowledge to the design of a learning algorithm that uses statistics to generate an algorithm that defines a relationship between cause and effect. Both methods require abstraction methods to simplify reality to produce a relationship between cause and effect that is generalizable in different applications. In simulation a model-driven approach requires the definition of the model scope and level of detail in order to meet the simulation objectives. Validation is achieved by significance tests of a comparison between the real and simulated system. In machine learning a data-driven approach is required which limits what is termed the state-space; the number of attributes and number of possible outcomes for the learning algorithm. Validation is achieved by significance tests of a comparison between the training and test data. The advantage of simulation may be that it codifies within the model the relationship between cause and effect. The statistical approach of machine learning can only provide a correlation for prediction. As is often quoted correlation is not causation, we cannot use the strength of correlation between observed and predicted data to infer that a model's prediction is valid. We may also have issues with the use of correlation as a measure in itself. For example if a model systematically under or over-predicts by a roughly constant amount, no matter how large, then the correlation will be unaffected. Also if there is a lag in the timing of the prediction the correlation will be low, even if the magnitude of the prediction is reasonably accurate. Finally very different data can give exactly the same correlation co-efficient and the use of visual inspection of model outcomes is recommended. Despite this however correlation analysis may provide all the information we need and we may even take our correlation as a sign of causation in certain circumstances. Also we may be attempting to predict aspects such as human behavior that may be difficult or impossible to codify in a simulation model.

Combining Simulation and Analytics

When undertaking simulation and analytics in combination the following approaches are possible. For data-driven simulation, a non-integrated approach involves the use of analytics to process input data for further use in a simulation model. For example, machine learning algorithms can be used to generate decision trees that can be codified within the simulation which then runs independently of the analytics application. An integrated approach embeds the analytics techniques within the simulation model. One approach is to "call" previously trained algorithms from the simulation during runtime. However in order for the context of the simulation and analytics algorithms to be synchronized it may be necessary to undertake training of algorithms simultaneously with each simulation run. This can be undertaken during the warmup period of the simulation (before execution of the main simulation experiment) or during the simulation run itself through the use of real-time data streams such as may be used by a digital twin. For model-driven analytics applications the simulation can either generate data files that are subsequently used by the analytics application or in an integrated approach provide the environment around which the analytics application operates. An example of this approach could be the use of simulation to provide the transport environment in which the analytics algorithms are trained to direct delivery vehicles.

Types of Simulation

There follows a brief overview of the three main simulation approaches, namely, SD, agent-based simulation (ABS) and DES. The three methods have their own philosophies, communities of users and main areas of application.

System Dynamics (SD)

SD is a modeling technique that was originally developed by Professor Jay Forrester when it was known as *industrial dynamics*. In SD models, stocks of variables are connected together via flows. SD has been used extensively in a wide range of application areas, for example, economics, supply chain, ecology and population dynamics to name a few. SD has a well-developed methodology in that the main stages and phases of the construction of a model are defined. SD attempts to describe systems in terms of feedback and delays. Negative feedback loops provide a control mechanism that compares the output of a system against a target and adjusts the input to eliminate the difference. Instead of reducing this variance between actual output and target output, positive feedback adds the variance to the output value and thus increases the overall variance. Most systems consist of a number of positive and negative feedback cycles, which make them difficult to understand. Adding to this complexity is the time delay that will occur between the identification of the variation and action taken to eliminate it and the taking of that action and its effect on output. What often occurs is a cycle of overshooting and undershooting the target value until the variance is eliminated. The SD concept can be implemented using computer software such as Stella II. A system is represented by a number of stocks (also termed *levels*) and flows (also termed *rates*). A stock is an accumulation of a resource such as materials and a flow is the movement of this resource that leads to the stock rising, falling or remaining constant. A characteristic of stocks is that they will remain in the system even if flow rates drop to zero and they act to decouple flow rates. An example is a safety stock of finished goods which provides a buffer between a production system which manufactures them at a constant rate and fluctuating external customer demand for the goods. An SD flow diagram maps out the relationships between stocks and flows. In Stella II, resource flows are represented by a double arrow and information flows by a single arrow. Stocks are represented by rectangles. Converters, which are used for a variety of tasks such as combining flows, are represented by a circle. Figure 1.7 shows a simple SD model in Stella II format.

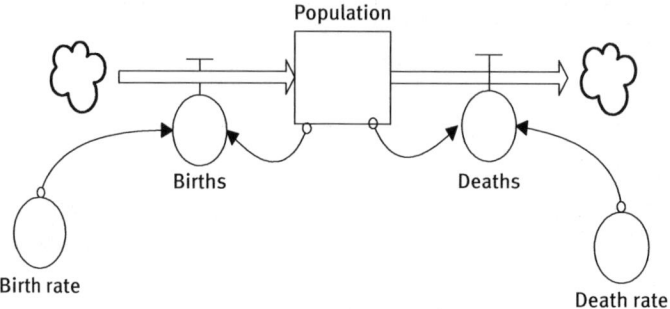

Figure 1.7: System dynamics diagram for population model.

Once the diagram is entered, it is necessary to enter first-order difference equations that compute the changes of a time-slice represented by the time increment *dt*. At the current time point (*t*) the stock value Lev(*t*) is calculated by the software as follows:

Lev(*t*) = Lev (*t*–*dt*) + (InRate–OutRate) * *dt*

This equation translates to the current stock value is a function of the previously calculated stock value plus the net flow over the time interval since the last calculation. For a population model, the following equation could be used to express the POPULATION stock value.

POPULATION (*t*) = POPULATION (*t*-*dt*) + (BIRTHS$_{dt}$–DEATHS$_{dt}$) * *dt*

One difference in the approach of SD compared to the discrete-event approach can be demonstrated by an example of a simulation of a new product development process. Here the discrete-event approach is able to model each customer purchase (rather than the quantity sold during a time period) and thus model individual purchase decisions through the ability of DES to carry information regarding each entity (customer) in the system. Also queuing behavior derived from demand exceeding supply requires the use of the discrete-event method. Thus, rather than as a substitute for the discrete-event method, SD can be seen as a more complementary technique particularly suited for analyzing overall cause-and-effect linkages in human systems.

Agent-Based Simulation (ABS)

The use of agents in the design of simulation models has its origins in complexity of science and game theory. Agents are components in a system (for example, a person or an organization) that have a set of rules or behavior that controls how they take in information, process that information and effect change on their environment. ABS refers to the study of the behavior of agents from the bottom up. This means that agent behaviors are defined, and then the agents are released into the environment of study. The behavior of the agents then emerges as a consequence of their interaction. In this sense, the system behavior is an emergent property of the agent interactions and the main source of structural change in the system itself is in the form of the relationship between the agents. ABS has been applied across a wide area, for example, economics, human behavior, supply chains, emergency evacuation, transport and healthcare. A particular class of agent-based systems termed *multiagent simulations* are concerned with modeling both individual agents (with autonomy and interactivity) and also the emergent system behavior that is a consequence of the agent's collective actions and interactions.

> **Cellular Automata**
>
> Cellular automata are simple agent-based systems that consist of a number of identical cells that are arranged in a grid usually in the form of a rectangular or 3D cube structure. Each cell may be in one defined state (such as "on" or "off") that is determined by a set of rules that specify how that state depends on its previous state and the states of the cell's immediate neighbors. The same rules are used to update the state of every cell in the grid. Thus, the technique is best used to model local interactions, which are governed by rules that are homogeneous in respect to the cell population. Most types of agent-based systems now have actors that are freed from their cells with the ability to perform autonomous and goal-directed behavior.

Discrete-Event Simulation (DES)

DES takes a process view of the world and individual entities can be represented as they move between different resources and are processed or wait in queues. It is hard to estimate the number of global users of DES, but there is little doubt that of the three types of simulation outlined here, DES has the largest user base. Evidence for this is provided by the biannual simulation survey carried out by *OR/MS Today*, which demonstrates the wide range of applications for which DES has been used. The main areas of application are manufacturing, supply chain and logistics, military and more recently healthcare. DES is concerned with the modeling of systems that can be represented by a series of events. The simulation describes each individual event, moving from one to the next as time progresses. When constructing a DES, the system being simulated is seen as consisting of a number of entities (e.g., products, people) that have a number of attributes (e.g., product type, age). An entity may consume work in the form of people or a machine, termed a *resource*. The amount and timing of resource availability may be specified by the model user. Entities may wait in a queue if a resource is not available when required. The main components of a DES are as follows:

- Event—an instantaneous occurrence that may change the state of the system.
- Entity—an object (e.g., material, information, people) that moves through the simulation activating events.
- Attribute—a characteristic of an entity. An entity may have several attributes associated with it (e.g., component type).
- Resource—an object (e.g., equipment, person) that provides a service to an entity (e.g., lathe machine, shop assistant).

For a DES, a system consists of a number of objects (entity) that flow from point to point in a system while competing with each other for the use of scarce resources (resource). The approach allows many objects to be manipulated at one time by dealing with multiple events at a single point in time. The attributes of an entity may be used to determine future actions taken by the entities. In DES time is moved forward in discrete chunks from event to event, ignoring any time between those events. Thus, the simulation needs to keep a record of when future events will occur and activate them in time order. These event timings are kept on what is termed as the *simulation calendar* that is a list of all future events in time order. The simulation calendar is also known as the future event list. The simulation executes by advancing through these events sequentially. When an event has been completed, the simulation time—stored as a data value called the simulation clock—is advanced in a discrete step to the time of the next event. This loop behavior of executing all events at a particular time and then advancing the simulation clock is controlled by the control program or executive of the simulation. There are three main methods of executive control.

In an *event-based* simulation, future events are scheduled on an event list. In the first phase of the approach, the executive program simply advances the simulation clock to the time of the next event. At the second phase, all events at that particular clock time are then executed. Any new events that are derived from these events are added to the simulation calendar. When all events have been executed at the current time, the executive program advances the simulation clock to the time of the next event and the loop repeats. The simulation continues until no events remain on the simulation calendar or a termination event is executed.

The *activity-based* approach works by scanning activities at a fixed time interval and activities that satisfy the necessary conditions are immediately scheduled. Unlike the event-based approach, the activity scanning method does not require event lists to be maintained. However, the method is relatively inefficient and therefore slow because of the number of unnecessary scans that are needed when no events may be occurring. Also an event may be scheduled between two consecutive scans and thus will not be activated at the correct time.

Most commercial software uses the *process-based* approach, which allows the user to enter a program in a more intuitive flowchart format. The simulation program is built as a series of process flowcharts that detail the events through which a class of entity will pass. The use of entity attributes allows decision points to be incorporated into the flowchart, providing alternative process routes for entity classes.

A popular method of control is the *three-phase approach* that combines the event- and activity-based methods. The three phases are shown in Figure 1.8 and described as follows:

- The "A" *phase* involves advances the simulation clock to the next event time. The simulation calendar is inspected and the clock jumps directly to the event with the time closest to the current simulation clock time. The clock is held constant during the three phases until the next "A" phase.
- The "B" *phase* involves execution of all activities whose future time is known (i.e., bound events). The simulation takes all bound events that are due to occur at the current simulation time from the calendar and executes them. The execution of bound events may cause further events to occur. These are placed on the simulation calendar to be activated at the appropriate time.
- The "C" *phase* involves execution of all activities whose future time depends on other events (i.e., conditional events termed C-events). For each "C" phase, all conditional events are checked to see if the conditions determining whether they can be executed are met. If the conditions are met, the conditional event is executed. The execution of a C-event may cause other C-event conditions to be met. For this reason the C-events are repeatedly scanned until all C-event conditions are not met at this time point.

In general, bound events are events such as the end of a process when time can be predicted by simply adding the current simulation time to the process duration. Conditional events are occurrences that are dependent on resource availability whose future timing can not be predicted (e.g., a customer awaiting service at a bank). The three-phase approach simply scans all conditional events after the bound events have been executed to check if the simulation state allows the

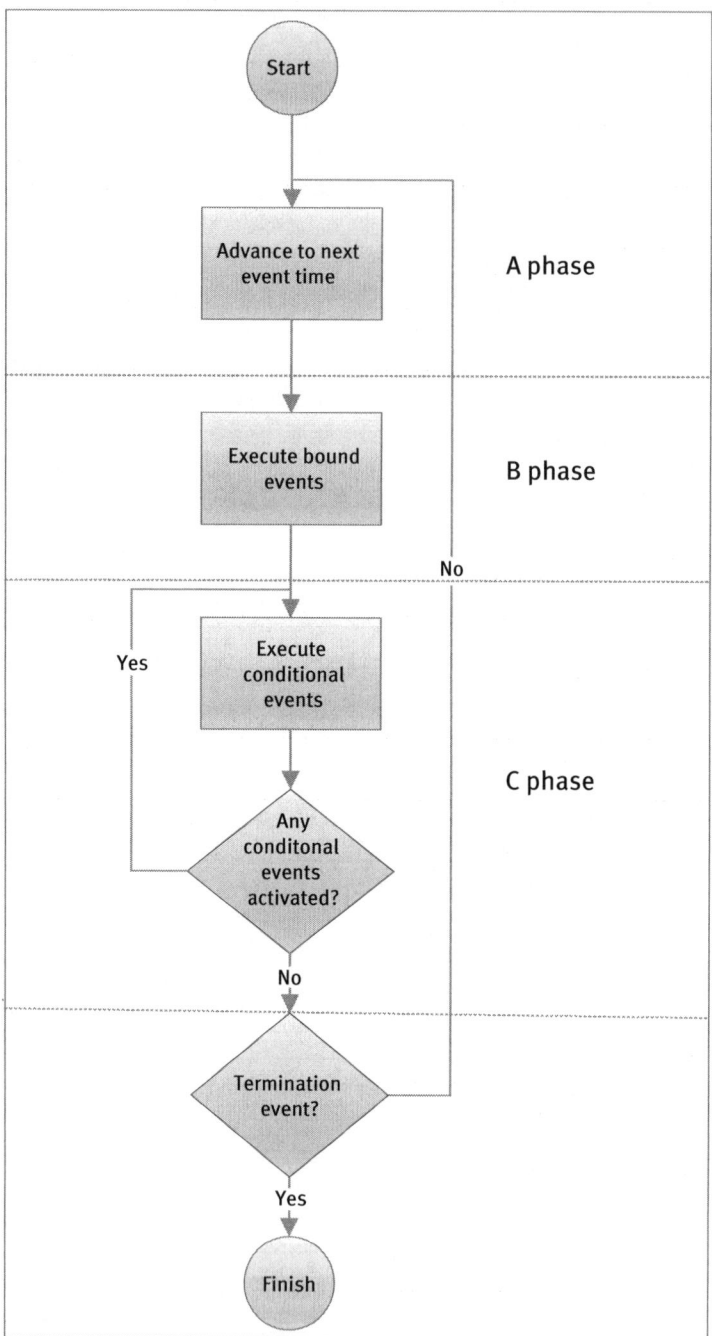

Figure 1.8: The three-phase executive.

conditional event to take place. The operation of the three-phase discrete-event method can be shown by studying the actions of the next event mechanism on the simulation clock.

Figure 1.9 illustrates the next-event time advance approach. Arrival times (A1, A2, ...) and service times (S1, S2, ...) will normally be random variables taken from a suitable distribution. The discrete-event system operates as follows. The simulation clock advances to the first event at time 8. This is an arrival event (A1) where an entity arrives at the resource. At this time the resource is available ("idle") and so is immediately serviced for 16 time units (S1). During this period, the server status is set to "busy." The simulation calculates the service completion time (C1) of 24 units and inserts an event on the calendar at that time. At time 20, a second entity arrives (A2). Because the server is currently in the "busy" state, the entity waits at the server queue until the server becomes available. At each future event, the status of the server is checked using a conditional (C) event. At time 24 the first entity completes service (C1) and thus changes the server status from "busy" to "idle." Entity 2 will now leave the queue and commence service, changing the server status back from "idle" to "busy." The completion time is calculated as the current time + service time (24+12 = 36) and a completion event is entered on the calendar at this time. At time 30, entity 3 arrives (A3). Again, the server is busy so the entity waits at the server queue. At time 36, the second entity completes service (C2) and entity 3 can now leave the queue and commence service. The simulation continues until a termination state is reached. The time in the system for each entity can be calculated by the addition of the queuing time and service time (Table 1.1).

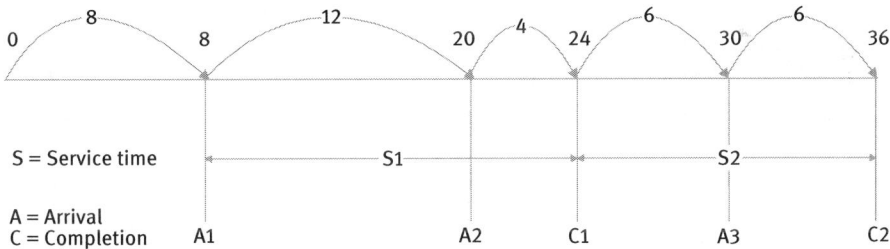

Figure 1.9: Operation of the three-phase approach.

Table 1.1: Queue and Service Times for Entities.

Entity	Queue Time	Service Time	System Time
1	0	16	16
2	4	12	16

This demonstrates how the next-event time mechanism increments the simulation clock to the next (in time order) event on the calendar. At this point the system status is updated and future event times are calculated. The time between each advance will vary depending on the pattern of future events.

> **Hybrid Simulation: Combining SD, ABS and DES**
>
> Hybrid simulation refers to the combined used of two or more of the techniques of SD, ABS and DES in a simulation study. Hybrid Simulation is intended to enable a suitable modeling approach to different aspects of the problem and avoid complicated model constructs (known as workarounds) or oversimplification to achieve a valid model. A hybrid simulation study can be achieved by the following.
>
> Developing multiple models that exchange data between them. An example is the use of an SD model that exchanges customer flow data with an ABS that is modeling individual customer behavior.
>
> Using different models for different stages of the simulation study. "A systems thinking study" in Chapter 3 is an example of the use of system dynamics to understand the causes around the behavior of a system that was modeled using DES.
>
> A combination of the approaches in a single model. The AnyLogic software package provides a multimethod modeling platform that allows the three approaches to be combined. For example, a supply chain can be modeled using DES to model business processes with each element of the supply chain at the same time an agent with attributes such as supplier choice, orders and shipments.

Using Simulation to Model Human Behavior

The modeling of people is becoming increasingly important in the design of business processes. Thus to provide a realistic basis for decision support, people's behavior will need to be included in simulation models if they are to be effective tools. Many of the systems that we would like to understand or improve involve human actors, either as customers of the system or as people performing various roles within the system. Modeling passive, predictable objects in a factory or a warehouse, however, is very different from trying to model people. Modeling people can be challenging because people exhibit many traits to do with being conscious sentient beings with free will. Human beings can be awkward and unpredictable in their behavior and they may not conform to our ideas about how they should behave in a given situation. This presents a practical challenge to model builders, i.e. when and how to represent human behavior in our simulation models. In some situations, the role of human behavior in the model may be small and may be simplified or even left out of the model. In other cases, human behavior may be central to the understanding of the system under study and then it becomes important that the modeler represents this in an appropriate way.

Figure 1.10 presents an overview of potential methods of modeling people who are identified and classified by the level of detail (termed *abstraction*) required to model human behavior. Each approach is given a *method name* and *method description* listed in the order of the level of detail used to model human behavior. The overview recognizes that the incorporation of human behavior in a simulation study does not necessarily involve the coding of human behavior in the simulation model itself. It is the combination of the simulation model used in conjunction with the user of that model that will provide the analysis of human behavior required and so this may be achieved by an analysis ranging from solely by the user to the detailed modeling of individual human behavior in the simulation model itself. Thus, the methods are classified into those that are undertaken *outside the model* (i.e., elements of human behavior are considered in the simulation study, but not incorporated in the simulation model), and those that incorporate human behavior within the simulation model, termed *inside the model*. Methods inside the model are classified in terms of a *world view*. Model abstraction is categorized as macro, meso or macro in order to clarify the different levels of detail for methods "inside

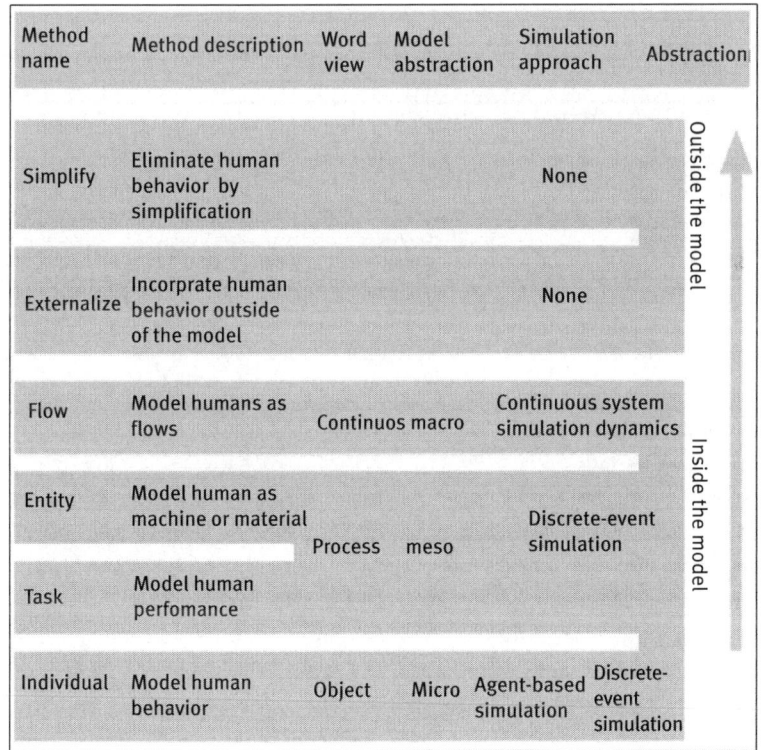

Figure 1.10: Methods of modeling human behavior in a simulation study.

the model." The framework then provides a suggested *simulation approach* for each of the levels of detail.

The methods of modeling human behavior shown in Figure 1.10 are now described in more detail.

Simplify (Eliminate Human Behavior by Simplification)

This involves the simplification of the simulation model in order to eliminate any requirement to codify human behavior. This strategy is relevant because a simulation model is not a copy of reality and should only include those elements necessary to meet the study objectives. This may make the incorporation of human behavior unnecessary. It may also be the case that the simulation user can utilize their knowledge of human behavior in conjunction with the model results to provide a suitable analysis. Actual mechanisms for the simplification of reality in a simulation model can be classified into omission, aggregation and substitution and will be considered under the topic of conceptual modeling (Chapter 3).

Externalize (Incorporate Human Behavior Outside of the Model)

This approach involves incorporating aspects of human behavior in the simulation study, but externalizing them from the simulation model itself. For example, the "externalize" approach to represent human decision making is to elicit the decision rules from the people involved in the relevant decisions and so avoid the simplification inherent when codifying complex behavior. Analytic techniques such as machine learning and neural networks can be interfaced with the simulation and be used to provide a suitable repository for human behavior.

Flow (Model Humans as Flows)

At the highest level of abstraction inside the model, humans can be modeled as a group which behaves like a flow in a pipe. In the case of the flow method of modeling human behavior, the world view is termed *continuous* and the model abstraction is termed *macro*. The type of simulation used for implementation of the flow method is usually the SD technique. The *flow* approach models humans at the highest level of abstraction using differential equations. The level of abstraction, however, means that this approach does not possess the ability to carry information about each entity (person) through the system being modeled and is not able to show queuing behavior of people derived from demand and supply. Thus, the simulation of human behavior in customer-processing applications, for example, may not be feasible using this approach.

Entity (Model Human as a Machine or Material)

This relates to a mesoscopic (meso) simulation in which elements are modeled as a number of discrete particles whose behavior is governed by predefined rules. One way of modeling human behavior in this way would mean that a human would be either a resource, such as a unit of equipment that is either "busy" or "idle." Alternatively modeling a human as an entity would mean that they would undertake a number of predetermined steps, such as the movement of material in a manufacturing plant. This approach can be related to the process world view, which models the movement of entities through a series of process steps. The *entity* approach models human behavior using the process world view to either represent people by simulated machines (resources) and/or simulated materials (entities). This allows the availability of staff to be monitored in the case of resources and the flow characteristics of people, such as customers, to be monitored in the case of entities.

Task (Model Human Performance)

This method models the action of humans in response to a predefined sequence of tasks and is often associated with the term human performance modeling. Human performance modeling relates to the simulation of purposeful actions of a human as generated by well-understood psychological phenomenon, rather than modeling in detail all aspects of human behavior not driven by purpose. The task approach can be related to the process world view and mesoscopic (meso) modeling abstraction level that models the movement of entities, in this case people, through a series of process steps. The task approach is implemented using rules governing the behavior of the simulation attributes of human behavior. These attributes may relate to factors such as skill level, task attributes such as length of task and organizational factors such as perceived value of the task to the organization. Two assumptions of simulation models are seen as particular barriers to modeling knowledge workers. The first is that all resources are assumed to belong to pools where any worker within the pool has the ability to carry out the task. Secondly there is an assumption that once a task is initiated it will be completed. In DES people can be represented as entities, rather than resource pools, which enable work on a task to be segmented into sessions. At the end of each session, work priorities are reassessed and work continues either on the same tasks if priorities have not changed or on an alternative task. Thus, the *task* approach attempts to model how humans act without the complexity of modeling the cognitive and other variables that lead to that behavior.

Individual (Model Human Behavior)

This method involves modeling how humans actually behave based on individual attributes such as perception and attention. The approach is associated with an object world view where objects are not only self-contained units combining data and functions, but are also able to interact with one another. The modeling approach can be termed *microscopic* (*micro*) and utilizes either the discrete-event or ABS types. The approach can use cognitive models for modeling human behavior at an individual level. This approach is implemented by assigning numerical attributes, representing various psychological characteristics, to the model entities (people). These characteristics could include patient anxiety, perceived susceptibility, knowledge of disease, belief about disease prevention, health motivation and educational level for a medical application for example. The *individual* approach attempts to model the internal cognitive processes that lead to human behavior. A number of architectures that model human cognition have been developed. However, the difficulty of implementation of the results of studies on human behavior by behavioral and cognitive researchers into a simulation remains a significant barrier. There is a debate about the suitability of DES to model human behavior but a solution could be the use of DES software to implement agent-based models (see Chapter 19).

> **The Use of ABS and DES to Model Human Behavior in Practice.**
>
> A review undertaken by the author of published work (covering the period 2005–2015) that reported on the use of ABS and DES found the following:
>
> In terms of overall applications, ABS dominates the modeling of people over DES with 90% of publications.
>
> The level of ABS publications rose to a consistently higher level since 2008.
>
> The majority of ABS applications (73%) were shown to be in the crowd and evacuation categories, which can be considered as a special category of application. ABS uses a bottom-up approach to modeling where control mechanisms are embedded in the individual agents and an overall behavior emerges from the individual decisions taken. Agent-based software generally includes a visual spatial display to allow this behavior to be observed at an aggregate or "crowd" level. It may be that the study of crowd behavior is particularly suited to the bottom-up and visual display features of the agent-based technique, although there are instances of the use DES for crowd and evacuation applications.
>
> The balance between techniques used when crowd and evacuation applications are excluded is more balanced with ABS covering 70% and DES 30%. This implies both techniques present a viable option in modeling people, but more work is required to ascertain the appropriateness of the two techniques in different contexts when behavioral modeling is required.
>
> The main barriers to further use of the techniques to model human behavior are found in terms of data collection requirements and the difficulty of validation.

The DES method will now be adopted for the remainder of this book for descriptive, predictive and prescriptive analytics. Thus DES will now be referred to as simulation.

Enabling a Simulation Capability in the Organization

The use of simulation is both a technical issue involving model development and analysis and a process of the implementation of organizational change. This section discusses technical issues such as the selection of simulation software and organizational issues such as the selection of personnel and the acquisition of resources required to provide the capability to undertake a simulation project. It is important that the full costs of introducing simulation are considered, including user time and any necessary training activities. The potential benefits of simulation must also be estimated. One of the reasons simulation is not used more widely is the benefits from change, undertaken as a result of a simulation study can be difficult to quantify.

However, simulation may not always be the appropriate tool. Also for providing a positive cost/benefit analysis, it should be compared to alternative approaches for solving the problem. Solutions such as spreadsheet analysis and the use of analytical methods may be faster and cheaper. It may be that the organization lacks the infrastructure to provide the necessary data required by the simulation model. Finally some aspects of the organization, such as human behavior and social interactions, may be too complex to represent as a model.

The steps in introducing simulation in the organization are outlined as follows:
1. Select a simulation sponsor
2. Estimate the benefits of simulation
3. Estimate the costs of simulation
4. Select the simulation software

1. Select a Simulation Sponsor

If the organization has not utilized the simulation method previously, then it may be necessary to assign a person with responsibility for investigating the relevance and feasibility of the approach. This person will ideally have both managerial understanding of the process change that simulation can facilitate and knowledge of data collection and statistical interpretation issues, which are required for successful analysis. The development of training schemes for relevant personnel should be investigated, so the required mix of skills and experience is present before a project is commenced. It may be necessary to use consultancy experience to guide staff and transfer skills in initial simulation projects.

2. Estimate the Benefits of Simulation

Often the use of simulation modeling can be justified by the benefits accruing from a single project. However, due to the potentially high setup costs in terms of the purchase of simulation software and user-training needs, the organization may wish to evaluate the long-term benefits of the technique across a number of potential projects before committing resources to the approach. This assessment would involve the simulation project sponsor and relevant personnel in assessing potential application areas and covering the following points:

- Do potential application areas contain the variability and time-dependent factors that make simulation a suitable analysis tool?
- Do the number and importance of the application areas warrant the investment in the simulation technique?
- Is there existing or potential staff expertise and support to implement the technique?
- Are sufficient funds available for aspects such as software, hardware, training and user time?
- Is suitable simulation software available that will enable the required skills to be obtained by staff within a suitable timeframe?
- Will sufficient management support in the relevant business areas be forthcoming in the areas of the supply of data and implementation of changes suggested by the technique?
- Are there opportunities for integration with other process improvement tools such as activity-based costing?
- Does the level of uncertainty/risk in change projects increase the usefulness of simulation as a technique to accept change and increase confidence in implementing new practices?

Although not always easy to do, simulation can be treated just like any other investment and its desirability measured by the level of the return on investment (ROI) it can provide. One way to do this is to estimate the potential savings made by the analysis of a problem using simulation as opposed to alternatives such as a spreadsheet analysis. When making substantial investment decisions, the detailed information contained in simulation results that take into account variability in the system are likely to prove their worth over the static analysis of a spreadsheet. For example, a client may wish to know the quantity of equipment required when planning a new manufacturing plant to meet a certain output capacity. If each unit of capacity costs £500,000, then £25,000 expenditure on a simulation to obtain the right amount of capacity represents a high ROI for simulation. Savings might also be estimated by the reduction in cost elements such as increased staff efficiency or a reduction in the use of inventory. Improvements in other aspects of performance such as speed and flexibility will need to be translated into monetary terms in order for the ROI benefit to be estimated. Also note that the cost reduction when undertaking a process improved using simulation will be cumulative over time. The longer time period the process is used the higher the cumulated savings and better the cost/benefit ratio of using simulation will become.

In addition, in an ROI calculation, there are other intangible benefits that can be considered. For example, the simulation study process requires a detailed approach to system design that can increase understanding of how the business works, which may lead to improvements. This benefit may be achieved at the conceptual modeling stage without the need to build the simulation model. Another aspect is that the simulation animation facilities can also increase understanding of processes and be used as a marketing tool to demonstrate capability. Even if the simulation results do not lead to changes in policy, the simulation can increase the confidence that planned actions will lead to certain outcomes and so can be seen as a risk management tool.

> **An Example of the Benefit of Using Simulation**
>
> Chapter 12 shows the use of simulation to test the design of a proposed textile manufacturing plant. Here the emphasis is on ensuring sufficient resources are provided to meet a target for plant output. The tasks required in the textile plant were well understood and a spreadsheet analysis provided an estimate of what resources were required for a target production level for a particular product mix. However a more detailed investigation was required to ensure the operation of the plant would indeed meet the required level of performance. This is because of the variability in demand and process duration and interdependence between the stages of the manufacturing process can lead to unused capacity at certain points in time and over-allocated capacity at other times leading to queues. Simulation was able to provide a detailed study of the textile manufacturing process and thus ensure that the operational details were addressed at the design stage rather than waiting for issues to arise during implementation and operation.

3. Estimate the Costs of Simulation

The main areas to consider in terms of resource requirements when implementing simulation are as follows:

Software

Most simulation software has an initial cost for the package and an additional cost for an annual maintenance contract that supplies technical support and upgrades. It is important to ensure that the latest version of the software is utilized as changes in software functionality can substantially enhance the usability of the software and so reduce the amount of user development time required.

Hardware

Most software runs on a PC under Windows (although software for other operating systems is available). Specifications for PC hardware requirements can be obtained from the software vendors.

Staff Time

This will be the most expensive aspect of the simulation implementation and can be difficult to predict, especially if simulation personnel are shared with other projects. The developer time required will depend on the experience of the person in developing simulation models, the complexity of the simulation project and the number of projects it is intended to undertake. Time estimates should also factor in the cost of the time of personnel involved in data collection and other activities in support of the simulation team.

Training

To successfully conduct a simulation modeling project, the project team should have skills in the following areas:

General skills for all stages of a simulation project
- Project management (ensure project meets time, cost and quality criteria)
- Awareness of the application area (e.g., knowledge of manufacturing techniques)
- Communication skills (essential for the definition of project objectives and data collection and implementation activities)

Skills relevant to the stages of the simulation study
- Data collection (ability to collect detailed and accurate information)
- Process analysis (ability to map organizational processes)
- Statistical analysis (input and output data analysis)
- Model building (simulation software translation)
- Model validation (ability to critically evaluate model behavior)
- Implementation (ability to ensure results of study are successfully implemented)

In many organizations, it may be required that one person acquires all these skills. Because of the wide ranging demands that will be made on the simulation analyst, it may be necessary to conduct a number of pilot studies in order to identify suitable personnel before training needs are assessed. Training is required in the steps in conducting a simulation modeling study as presented in this text, as well as training in the particular simulation software that is being used. Most software vendors offer training in their particular software package. If possible, it is useful to be able to work through a small case study based on the trainees' organization in order to maximize the benefit of the training. A separate course of statistical analysis may be also be necessary. Such courses are often run by local university and college establishments. Training courses are also offered by colleges in project management and communication skills. A useful approach is to work with an experienced simulation consultant on early projects in order to ensure that priorities are correctly assigned to the stages of the simulation study.

A common mistake is to spend too long on the model-building stage before adequate consultation has been made, which would achieve a fuller understanding of the problem situation. The skills needed to successfully undertake a simulation study are varied and one of the main obstacles to performing simulation in-house is not cost or training but the lack of personnel with the required technical background. This need for technical skills has meant that most simulation project leaders are systems analysts, in-house simulation developers or external consultants rather than people who are closer to the process such as a shop-floor supervisor. However, the need for process owners to be involved in the simulation study can be important in ensuring on-going use of the technique and that the results of the study are implemented.

4. Selecting the Simulation Software

Historically simulations were built on general-purpose computer languages such as FORTRAN, C and C++. Later languages such as Java were employed and there are also implementations using the Visual Basic for Applications language to employ the technique on a spreadsheet platform (Greasley, 1998). There are also a number of specialist computer languages developed specifically for constructing simulation models including SIMAN, SIMSCRIPT, SLAM and GPSS. However, for most applications for decision making in an organizational setting, the use of Windows-based software, sometimes referred to as *visual interactive modeling systems*, are employed. These software packages include Arena, Simio, AnyLogic, Witness, Simul8 and the Tecnomatix Plant Simulation. These packages are based on the use of graphic symbols or icons that reduce or eliminate the need to code the simulation model. A model is instead constructed by placing simulation icons on the screen, which represent different elements of the model. For example, a particular icon could represent a process. Data is entered into the model by clicking with a mouse on the relevant icon to activate a screen input dialog box. Animation facilities are also incorporated into these packages. For most business applications, these systems are the most appropriate, although the cost of the software package can be high. These systems use graphical facilities to enable fast model development and animation facilities. However, these systems do not release the user from the task of understanding the building blocks of the simulation system or understanding statistical issues.

When selecting simulation software, the potential user can read the software tutorial papers from the Winter Simulation Conference available at www.informs-cs.org/wscpapers.html, which provide information about the available software.

Additional information can be obtained from both vendor representatives (especially a technical specification) and established users on the suitability of software for a particular application area.

Vendors of simulation software can be rated on aspects such as:
- Quality of vendor (current user base, revenue, length in business)
- Technical support (type, responsiveness)
- Training (frequency, level, on-site availability)
- Modeling services (e.g. consultancy experience)
- Cost of ownership (upgrade policy, runtime license policy, multiuser policy)

A selection of simulation software supplier details is listed in Table 1.2.

Table 1.2: Simulation Software Vendors.

Vendor	Software	Web Address
SIMUL8 Corporation	Simul8	www.simul8.com
Adept Scientific	Micro Saint Sharp	www.adeptscience.co.uk/products/mathsim/microsaint
ProModel Corporation	ProModel	https://www.promodel.com/products/ProModel
Lanner Group Ltd.	Witness Horizon	https://www.lanner.com/en-gb/technology/witness-simulation-software.html
Siemens PLM	Tecnomatix	www.plm.automation.siemens.com/global/en/products/tecnomatix/
The AnyLogic Company	AnyLogic	www.anylogic.com
Simio LLC	Simio	www.simio.com
Rockwell Software Inc.	Arena	www.arenasimulation.com

Simulation software can be bought in a variety of forms including single-user copies and multiuser licenses. Some software allows "run-time" models to be installed on unlicensed machines. This allows the use of a completed model, with menu options that allow the selection of scenario parameters. However, run-time versions do not allow any changes to the model code or animation display. It is also possible to obtain student versions (for class use in universities) of software that contain all the features of the full licensed version but are limited in some way such as the size of the model or have disabled save or print functions. The two packages used within this book are Arena and Simio.

Simulation is associated with planning and scheduling software. Here schedules can be analyzed using a probabilistic analysis incorporating variability to estimate the underlying risks associated with the schedule. Risk measures generated can include the probability of meeting defined targets with as well as expected, pessimistic and optimistic results. Commercial software includes Dropboard (by Systems Navigator, www.systemsnavigator.com/dropboard) and planning and scheduling with Simio

Enterprise (by Simio LLC, www.simio.com/software/production-scheduling-software.php).

Tools such as Visio (by Microsoft, www.microsoft.com) can be used to develop the simulation process map, which can then be imported into simulation software such as Arena or Simio to form the basis of the simulation model. Tools such as AutoCAD (www.autodesk.co.uk) can be used to create background schematics and drawing that can be imported into simulation software such as Arena and Simio.

There is also optimization software associated with simulation. Of the commercial software available, one of the most popular is the OptQuest software (by OptTek Systems Inc, www.opttek.com).

A selection of process mining software that has been used with simulation is provided in Table 1.3.

Table 1.3: Process Mining Software Vendors.

Vendor	Software	Web Address
Open-Source (Eindhoven University of Technology)	ProM	www.promtools.org
Fluxicon BV	DISCO	https://fluxicon.com/disco
Minit	Minit	https://www.minit.io

A selection of machine-learning software that has been used with simulation is provided in Table 1.4.

Table 1.4: Machine-Learning Software vendors.

Vendor	Software	Web Address
RapidMiner	RapidMiner	https://rapidminer.com
IBM	IBM SPSS Modeler	https://www.ibm.com/products/spss-modeler
MathWorks	MatLab	https://uk.mathworks.com/products/matlab.html
Open-Source (R Foundation)	R	https://www.r-project.org
Viscovery	Viscovery SOMine	https://www.viscovery.net/somine
Open-Source (University of Waikato)	Massive Online Analysis (MOA)	https://moa.cms.waikato.ac.nz

Simulation Application Areas

Simulation modeling is a flexible tool and is capable of analyzing most aspects of an organization. The two main areas of operations are in the design and management of processes. In terms of design, simulation has an obvious role in the testing of system designs for systems that do not yet exist. Simulation can also be used for the design of existing systems where it can be used to assess a number of design options without disruption to the real system. One of the advantages of thoroughly testing processes at the design stage is that errors found at this stage will generally be much more costly to rectify at later stages of installation and operation. Simulation is often used to assess large capital investments such as for equipment and plant, where it can reduce the risk of implementation at a relatively small cost. Simulation can also be used in the management of business processes. For example a service operation may wish to ensure continued good customer service whilst meeting increased demand. Making decisions around aspects such as staffing levels and job priorities to meet increased demand requires the ability to predict changes in these areas on performance. Simulation can be used to provide a predictive capability to help make better decisions and ensure future service levels are maintained.

To ensure the maximum value is gained from using the technique it is necessary to define the areas of the organization that are key to overall performance and select feasible options for the technique in these areas. Some examples of simulation use are given below with reference to decision areas that are applicable to simulation analysis and to the case studies included later in this book.

Manufacturing Systems (Chapters 9, 12, 15)

In order to remain competitive manufacturing organizations must ensure their systems can meet changing market needs in terms of product mix and capacity levels whilst achieving efficient use of resources. Because of the complex nature of these systems with many interdependent parts, simulation is used extensively to optimize performance. Design decision areas in manufacturing include estimating required resource capacity, layout design, bottleneck analysis, machine setup time reduction, implementation of automation and production lead time estimation. Management decision areas in manufacturing include estimating batch size, determining parts sequencing, workforce scheduling and assessing preventative maintenance policies.

Service Systems (Chapters 6, 10, 13, 14, 16)

The productivity of service sector systems has not increased at the rate of manufacturing systems and as the service sector has increased the potential increase in productivity from improving services has been recognized. The use of methodologies to streamline service processes has many parallels in techniques used in manufacturing for many years. Simulation is now being used to help analyze many service processes to improve customer service and reduce cost. For example the emphasis on performance measures in government services such as health care has led to the increased use of simulation to analyze systems and provide measures of performance under different configurations. Design decision areas include customer queuing time estimation, layout planning, service capacity planning. Management decision areas include staff scheduling, customer service priorities, emergency planning.

Supply Chain Management Systems (Chapters 7, 11)

Supply chains systems are a network of activities that entities flow through from raw materials supply to production, distribution and then retail to the customers. The supply chain should aim to minimize costs whilst maintaining service levels. Supply chains will incorporate transportation systems such as rail and airline services as well as internal systems such as automated guided vehicles (AGVs) which can be analyzed using simulation. Many simulation software packages have special facilities to model track-based and conveyor type systems and simulation is ideally suited to analyze the complex interactions and knock-on effects that can occur in these systems. Design decision areas include supply chain structure, process redesign, supplier selection, facilities and capacity planning, supply chain integration, the Bullwhip Effect, reverse logistics, replenishment control policies, supply chain optimization, cost reduction, system performance, inventory planning and management and customer service levels.

Information Systems (Chapter 8)

Simulation is used to predict the performance of the computerization of processes. This analysis can include both the process performance and the technical performance of the computer network itself, often using specialist network simulation software. Design decision areas include the effects of automation by IS systems on customer service levels, estimating IS capacity requirements to meet customer transaction volumes and designing client-server systems.

Determining the Level of Usage of the Simulation Model

The objective of the simulation technique is to aid decision making by providing a forum for problem definition and providing information on which decisions can be made. Thus, a simulation project does not necessarily require a completed computer model to be a success. At an early stage in the project proposal process, the analyst and other interested parties must decide the role of the model-building process within the decision-making process itself. Thus in certain circumstances, the building of a computer model may not be necessary. However, for many complex interacting systems (i.e., most business systems), the model will be able to provide useful information (not only in the form of performance measures, but also indications of cause-and-effect linkages between variables), which will aid the decision-making process. The focus of the simulation project implementation will be dependent on the intended usage of the model as a decision-making tool (Table 1.5). As the level of usage moves from a stand-alone to an integrated tool for decision making, the focus moves toward a data-driven approach that allows for real-time and adaptable models.

Table 1.5: Levels of Usage of a Simulation Model.

	Level of Usage				
	Problem Definition	Demonstration	Scenarios	On-going Decision Support	Real-Time Integrated
Level of development	Process map	Animation	Experimentation	Decision support system	On-going decision support
Level of interaction	None	Simple menu	Menu	Extended menu	Automated
Level of integration	None	Stand-alone	Stand-alone Excel files	Integrated company database	Fully integrated as a digital twin
Analytic outcome	None	Descriptive	Predictive and prescriptive	Predictive and prescriptive	Prescriptive

The levels of usage categories are defined as follows:

Problem Definition

One of the reasons for using the simulation method is that its approach provides a detailed and systematic way of analyzing a problem in order to provide information on which a decision can be made. It is often the case that ambiguities and inconsistencies are apparent in the understanding of a problem during the project proposal formulation stage. It may be that the process of defining the problem may provide the decision makers with sufficient information on which a decision can be made. In this case, model building and quantitative analysis of output from the simulation model may not be required. The outcome from this approach will be a definition of the problem and possibly a process map of the system.

Demonstration

Although the decision makers may have an understanding of system behavior, it may be that they wish to demonstrate that understanding to other interested parties. This could be to internal personnel for training purposes or to external personnel to demonstrate capability to perform to an agreed specification. The development of an animated model provides a powerful tool in communicating the behavior of a complex system over time. An example of this could be a train manufacturer who is bidding for the manufacture of a number of train carriages. Associated with this contract is the delivery of a train maintenance service. If the company has experience in train manufacturing, they can demonstrate this to the client. If the company has no experience in delivering train maintenance operations, they can develop a simulation of a proposed train maintenance operation with animation to demonstrate capability to the client. These models are associated with a descriptive capability to help understanding.

Scenarios

The next level of usage involves the development of a model and experimentation in order to assess system behavior over a number of scenarios. The model is used to solve a number of predefined problems but is not intended for future use. For this reason, a menu system allowing change of key variables is appropriate. The simulation may use internal data files or limited use of external data held in spreadsheets. These models are associated with a predictive capability for scenario analysis and if used to direct action with a prescriptive capability.

On-going Decision Support

This option provides decision support for a number of problems over time and requires that the model be adapted to provide assistance to new scenarios as they arise. The extended menu system will need to provide the ability to change a wider range of variables for on-going use. The level of data integration may require links to company databases to ensure the model is using the latest version of data over time. Animation facilities should be developed to assist in understanding cause-and-effect relationships and the effect of random events such as machine breakdowns. The technical hardware and software capability issues relevant to an integrated system need to be addressed at the project proposal stage to ensure a successful implementation. If it is envisaged that the client will perform modifications to the simulation model after delivery, then the issue of model reuse should be addressed. Reuse issues include ensuring that a detailed model code documentation is supplied and detailed operating procedures are provided. Training may also be required in model development and statistical methods. In general, this type of simulation will be largely data driven, with most of the data held external to the model in spreadsheets and company databases. These models are associated with a predictive and prescriptive analytics capability.

Real-Time Integrated

Here the model automatically adapts in response to real-time data. The purpose of these models should be distinguished from a traditional simulation application in that they are real-time adaptive models that work on historical and current data to provide a replication of the real system for applications such as digital twins. These models will often be able to direct actions automatically in the real system and so are associated with a prescriptive analytics capability.

Simulation Project Management

The use of simulation to address an organizational issue can be approached as a project activity and the ideas of project management can be employed in order to manage the resources and skills needed to implement a simulation analysis. In order to successfully use simulation, a structured process must be followed. This section aims to show that simulation is more than just the purchase and use of a software package, but a range of skills are required by the simulation practitioner or team. These include project management, client liaison, statistical skills, modeling skills and the ability to understand and map out organizational processes.

First, an important aspect of the project management process is identifying and gaining the support of personnel who have an interest in the modeling process. The simulation developer(s) in addition to the technical skills required to build and analyze the results from a model must be able to communicate effectively with people in the client organization in order to collect relevant data and communicate model results. Roles within the project team include the following:
- *Client*—sponsor of the simulation project—usually a manager who can authorize the time and expenditure required.
- *Model User*—Person who is expected to use the model after completion by the modeler. The role of the model user will depend on the planned level of usage

of the model. A model user will not exist for a problem definition exercise, but will require extended contact with the developer if the model is to be used for on-going decision support to ensure all options (e.g., menu option facilities) have been incorporated into the design before handover.
- *Data Provider*—Often the main contact for information regarding the model may not be directly involved in the modeling outcomes. The client must ensure that the data provider feels fully engaged with the project and is allocated time for liaison and data collection tasks. In addition, the modeler must be sensitive to using the data providers time as productively as possible.

The project report should contain the simulation study objectives and a detailed description of how each stage in the simulation modeling process will be undertaken. This requires a definition of both the methods to be used and any resource requirements for the project. It is important to take a structured approach to the management of the project as there are many reasons why a project could fail. These include the following:
- The simulation model does not achieve the objectives stated in the project plan through a faulty model design or coding.
- Failure to collect sufficient and relevant data means that the simulation results are not valid.
- The system coding or user interface does not permit the flexible use of the model to explore scenarios defined in the project plan.
- The information provided by the simulation does not meet the needs of the relevant decision makers.

These diverse problems can derive from a lack of communication, leading to failure to meet business needs to technical failures, such as a lack of knowledge of statistical issues in experimentation, leading to invalid model results. For this reason, the simulation project manager must have an understanding of both the business and technical issues of the project. The project management process can be classified into the four areas of estimation, scheduling/planning, monitoring and control, and documentation.

Estimation

This entails breaking down the project into the main simulation project stages and allocating resources to each stage. The time required and skill type of people required are along with the prerequisite for access to resources such as simulation software. These estimates will allow a comparison between project needs and project resources available. If there are insufficient resources available to undertake the project, then a decision must be made regarding the nature of the constraints on the project. A *resource-constrained* project is limited by resources (i.e., people/software) availability. A *time-constrained* project is limited by the project deadline. If the project deadline is immovable, then additional resources will need to be acquired in the form of additional personnel (internal or external), overtime or additional software licenses. If the deadline can be changed, then additional resources may not be required as a smaller project team may undertake the project over a longer time period.

Once a feasible plan has been determined, a more detailed plan of when activities should occur can be developed. The plan should take into account the difference between effort time (how long someone would normally be expected to take to complete a task) and elapse time that takes into account availability (actual time allocated to project and the number of people undertaking the task) and work rate (skill level) of people involved. In addition, a time and cost specification should be presented for the main simulation project stages. A timescale for the presentation of an interim report may also be specified for a larger project. Costings should include the cost of the analyst's time and software/hardware costs. Although an accurate estimate of the timescale for project completion is required, the analyst or simulation client needs to be aware of several factors that may delay the project completion date. The most important of these factors is to ensure that appropriate members of the organization are involved in the simulation development. The simulation provides information on which decisions are made within an organizational context, so involvement is necessary for interested parties to ensure confidence and implementation of model results. The need for clear objectives is essential to ensure the correct system components are modeled at a suitable level of detail. Information must also be supplied for the model build from appropriate personnel to ensure that important detail is not missing and false assumptions regarding model behavior are not made. It is likely that during the simulation process, problems with the system design become apparent that require additional modeling and/or analysis. Both analyst and client need to separate between work for the original design and additional activity. The project specification should cover the number of experimental runs that are envisaged for the analysis. Often the client may require additional scenarios tested, which again should be agreed at a required additional time/cost.

Scheduling/Planning

Scheduling involves determining when activities should occur. Steps given in the simulation study are sequential, but in reality they will overlap—the next stage starts before the last one is finished—and are iterative, e.g., validate part of the model, go back and collect more data, model build, validate again. This iterative process of building more detail into the model gradually is the recommended approach but can make judging project progress difficult.

Monitoring and Control

A network plan is useful for scheduling overall project progress and ensuring on-time completion, but the reality of iterative development may make it difficult to judge actual progress.

Documentation

Interim progress reports are issued to ensure that the project is meeting time and cost targets. Documents may also be needed to record any changes to the specification agreed by the project team. Documentation provides traceability. For example, data collection sources and content should be available for inspection by users in future in order to ensure validation. Documentation of all aspects of the model is also needed such as coding and the results of the simulation analysis.

Benefits and Limitations of Simulation

In summary the benefits and limitations of simulation are now outlined.

Benefits of Simulation

- Provides capability for descriptive analysis

Often an outcome of undertaking a simulation study is that the structured approach to problem solving can lead to a better understanding of system behavior. This can come from activities such as bringing together data collected from various disparate sources within the organization and building a process map to provide an overview of the relationships between process elements. The understanding gained at the conceptual modeling stage may negate the need for model development.

- Provides capability for predictive analysis

Simulation helps to minimize the risk involved when predicting future behavior. It does this by dealing with uncertainty inherent in the behavior of business systems. Rather than provide a single prediction of future behavior simulation allows for comparison between different future scenarios to provide an indication of the level of risk and sensitivity of the predictions.

– Provides capability for prescriptive analysis

By completing multiple scenario analysis, either manually or automatically using optimization software, simulation allows a "best" course of action to be recommended. The parameters that define the scenarios can take into account contextual factors that constrain design choices so that only feasible solutions are provided.

- Simulation can address issues at the design stage, before the new system exists, so that problems that might have appeared later (with greater time and cost) are dealt with.
- Simulation can help convert strategic aims into reality by providing specific workable implementations of change at an operational level.

Limitations of Simulation

- The skillset for simulation may not be available, especially in small and medium-sized enterprises. Simulation requires a varied skillset including domain knowledge, statistics, process analysis and simulation software skills across an individual or a team.
- Establishing a capability in simulation can be expensive in terms of items such as the initial costs of simulation software and staff training.
- The cost of a simulation project may not be warranted by the decision. If a cost-benefit approach is used the payback from a better informed decision using simulation must substantially outweigh the costs of the simulation study. However non-financial benefits of better decisions (such as generating customer demand through better designed services) are often overlooked.
- A simulation project may take too long to be useful for a decision. Consultancy organizations can be used to provide a faster team approach to simulation development at a higher cost.
- Simulation analysis often ignores the human element in system performance. However the increased interest in behavioral factors in operations management and operations research has increased interest in incorporating human behavior in models.
- Commercial simulation software lacks integration with analytics techniques such as machine learning and process mining.
- The benefits of simulation are not maximized leading to its underuse. Chapter 15 provides an example of how use as a "one-off" technique, a lack of skills transfer and a lack of communication in the organization can limit the benefits of the simulation approach.
- Simulations, like analytic techniques, are algorithms executed as computer programs that map input data to output data and as such cannot actually create new knowledge. What they can do is provide us with new information or

information presented in a new way that may lead us to the new knowledge we need to solve a problem.
- When used for prediction simulation is about the reduction of aleatory uncertainty (uncertainty due to system variability); actual prediction of the future in terms of business processes is impossible due to epistemic uncertainty (uncertainty due to lack of knowledge of system behaviour).

Chapter 2
Simulation and Business Processes

This chapter is focused on the use of simulation to analyze processes within business organizations. The process perspective is associated with the area of operations management that considers the transformation of materials, information and customers into goods and services (Figure 2.1). This transformation is undertaken by processes that require the allocation of resources such as staff and facilities.

Business process management is a discipline that focuses on the use of business processes as a way of improving organizational performance. Deriving and using process performance measures is a key aspect of both operations management and business process management. This section will outline a range of performance measures that can be used to measure process performance, cover the use of tools for documenting the process design and describe methods for process improvement.

The task of designing processes should be undertaken in a structured manner and the steps involved can be described as follows:
1. Identify opportunities for process improvement.
2. Document the process design.
3. Redesign the process.

1 Identify Opportunities for Process Improvement

In order to identify where performance improvement should take place, it is necessary to compare the performance against a performance standard. This standard can be internal to the organization such as comparing against previous performance or against targets for future performance. Internal targets are often based on a comparison between past financial and sales performance and targets for future performance. The advantage of these measures is that they are widely used and comparable across organizations and use data that are readily available. However, they may be of limited value in identifying why performance is above or below the target value. External targets include comparison to competitor performance, best practice or "best-in-class" performance or market requirements. External performance targets have the advantage of providing a comparison of performance against competitors operating in similar competitive markets. This approach is often termed *benchmarking*. There now follows a discussion of traditional economic performance measures, the balanced scorecard, the five strategic performance measures of operations management, process performance measures and activity-based costing.

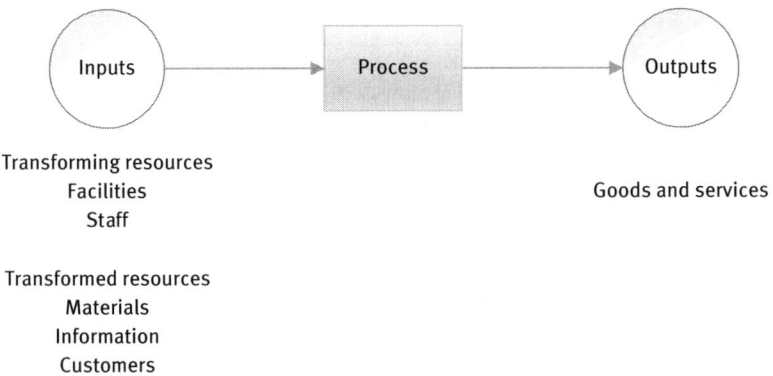

Figure 2.1: The process perspective of operations management.

Traditional Economic Performance Measures

Traditional performance measures have focused on indicators such as productivity. Productivity divides the value of the output by the value of the input resources consumed:

Productivity = output/input

Productivity is used at both the organizational and national level as a comparative measure of performance. From the equation it can be seen that productivity can be increased by either increasing the output without a proportionate increase in the input or by decreasing the input without a proportionate decrease in the output. Although productivity provides an indication of the level of utilization of resources, it can be difficult to find appropriate input and output parameters for the calculation, and the measure also fails to consider performance from a wider viewpoint encompassing customer and other stakeholder needs. Another performance measure is efficiency:

Efficiency = actual output/effective capacity

Efficiency is defined as a measure of the use of capacity remaining after the loss of output due to planned factors such as maintenance and training. In other words, efficiency relates to the use of a resource in terms of availability. However, a high level of efficiency does not necessarily imply that resources are being used effectively in improving the overall performance. Effectiveness can be defined as the extent to which the output of a process meets the requirements of its customers. This is more difficult to measure quantitatively than productivity or efficiency. In service operations, effectiveness is often measured by surveys of customer satisfaction. However, customer satisfaction will be dependent on the perceptions and expectations of individual customers. Other indicators of effectiveness could be sales volume and sales margin figures for products and services.

The Balanced Scorecard

Another approach to performance measurement has been the use of the balanced scorecard. The balanced scorecard approach is an attempt to incorporate the interests of a broader range of stakeholders through performance measures across four perspectives of financial, customer, business process, and learning/growth. The idea of the scorecard is to provide managers with multiple perspectives of the goals that need to be met for organizational success. Although designed for performance measurement at a strategic level, its relevance to operations is that it provides a direction for the organization that will impact on and be impacted by operations. The balanced scorecard also provides a way of translating strategy into action. It does this by translating performance measures at a strategic level into operational performance measures.

The case study at the end of this chapter shows how strategic targets on individual performance at a UK Police Service were translated into measurements at an operational level.

The Five Strategic Performance Measures of Operations Management

From the area of operations management comes the five strategic performance measures of quality, speed, dependability, flexibility and cost. Two models that use these measures to identify where performance should be improved are as follows.

The Hill methodology (Hill and Hill, 2012) is based on market requirements. The concepts of "order winning" and "qualifying factors" are used to distinguish between those factors that directly contribute to winning business and those that are necessary to qualify for the customer's consideration between a range of products/services. Its importance is that while it may be necessary to raise performance on some qualifying factors to a certain level in order to be considered by the customer, a further rise in the level of performance may not achieve an increase in competitiveness. Instead competitiveness will depend on raising the level of performance of different "order-winning" factors. Because these factors are critical to winning customers, they are translated into the five performance measures mentioned earlier.

The second model of Slack et al. (2019) uses a combination of market and competitive factors and two dimensions—importance and performance—to help prioritize performance measures. The relative importance of a competitive factor is assessed in terms of its importance to internal or external customers using a nine-point scale. The degrees of order winning, order qualifying and less important customer viewed competitive factors are measured on this scale. The next step ranks the relative performance of a competitive factor against competitor achievement. A nine-point performance scale (rating from consistently better than the nearest competitor to consistently worse than most competitors) is used for each performance measure. This indicates what customers find important in achieved performance when compared with that of competitor performance.

Once key performance areas have been identified using the above-mentioned models, the performance measures can provide both an indication of performance that can be derived from customer requirements and can be used to align the physical resources and management systems of the company's operations. Thus, the pursuit of a subset of these measures provide a way of connecting the strategic direction of the company with its operational decisions. For example, if key metrics are identified as speed and cost, then investments in resources such as customer-processing technology should improve these aspects of performance.

An additional aspect regarding the five performance measures is that there is both an external benefit in improving performance within a performance area and an internal benefit in terms of reducing cost in that area. For example, improving quality performance not only means higher customer satisfaction but also reduces internal cost through a reduction in the need to rectify mistakes. This shows the potential of replacing strategies that rely on immediate cost cutting, which might achieve short-term savings by lowering the costs of inputs such as staff and equipment into the process, but risks lowering the capability of the process to meet customer needs.

Although simulation is usually associated with operational measurement—it can actually be used to measure performance across all five of the strategic performance measures of speed, cost, quality, dependability and flexibility. Table 2.1 shows links to case studies that focus on the different performance measures.

Process Performance Measures

Simulation is mostly associated with the measurement of processes at the operational level and a number of these measures are found in the reports provided by simulation software. These include:

Flow Time. The time taken to undertake the steps in a process. This can also be referred to as throughput time. This can relate to the speed performance metric for delivering goods and services to customers.

Queue Time. The time taken between being ready to be processed and the resource undertaking the processing to become available and processing to commence. This can be related to speed for a manufacturing process in which the aim

Table 2.1: Business Process Performance Measures.

Performance Measure	Description	Case Study
Speed	How fast can we do it?	Chapter 6 Meeting response times
Cost	How much will it cost?	Chapter 10 Identifying and reducing cost
Quality	Can we meet the specification?	Chapter 14 Ensuring customer service quality
Dependability	Can we delivery to a time slot every time?	Chapter 7 Ensuring on-time delivery to customers
Flexibility (service)	Can we introduce a new service design?	Chapter 8 Responding to customer service requirements
Flexibility (volume)	Can we adjust our output level?	Chapter 9 Ensuring a response to unexpected events

is to minimize the proportion of flow time that is queue time. In a service operation we need to minimize queue time to ensure customer service quality.

Resource Utilization. The time that a resource is in operation as a proportion of total time. This can be related to the cost performance metric for staff and equipment.

Cost. Most simulation software allows cost to be estimated by defining usage cost rates and idle cost rates in the model. Some resources may also incur a fixed cost with each entity handled which may be defined as a cost per use. Simulation is an ideal tool to implement the concept of Activity-Based Costing (ABC) which is covered in the next section.

Chapter 4 will provide further information on the performance measures reported by simulation software.

Activity-Based Costing

Cost is traditionally calculated by estimating in terms of staff, facilities and materials which are the resources that are required for the input and transformation processes in an operation. However, the way these costs are allocated to products and services is often arbitrary. For example, the actual costs of producing a product in a factory where hundreds of other products are also being made are dependent on an accurate allocation of direct costs (staff, equipment and material costs directly connected to the product) and indirect costs (for example, overhead such as factory space, energy, administration and central staffing costs). The aim of performance measurement is to identify where cost is being incurred within an operation, so improvement efforts can be focused in the correct areas. As an alternative to the usual overhead-based costing methods, activity-based costing

provides a way of allocating costs to manufacturing and service activities in order that a company can determine how much it costs to make a certain product or deliver a service. In *activity-based costing* (ABC) there are three main drivers of cost: the cost driver, the resource driver and the activity driver.
– The cost driver relates to the amount of resources needed to perform an activity and can be reduced by, for example, redesigning the process.
– The resource driver relates to the type of resources needed for an activity and can be reduced, for example, by using different personnel, information technology or equipment.
– The activity driver relates to the number of times the process occurs and can be reduced, for example, by training to improve the reliability of a process.

The cost assignment view of ABC allocates costs to activities by identifying resource drivers, which determine the cost of resources, and activity drivers, which determine the use of these resources. The process view of ABC provides information about the effort needed for the activity (called *the cost driver)* and provides performance measures of the outcome of the activities. The cost assignment view can be used to reduce the activity cost by either reconfiguring the resources needed for an activity (resource driver) or reducing the amount of resource required (activity driver). The process view provides a link between the inputs needed to perform an activity (cost driver) and the outputs required by the internal or external customer of that activity (performance measure). Thus, an investigation of a combination of resource drivers, activity drivers and cost drivers for an activity can improve performance of the process by identifying why cost has been incurred.

Chapter 10 shows the advantages of being able to identify where cost is being incurred.

2 Document the Process Design

The identification of activities in a current process design is a data-collection exercise using methods such as examination of current documentation, interviews and observation. In order to provide a framework for the design and improvement of service processes, the documentation techniques of process mapping and service blueprinting can be used.

Process Mapping

A document of the process can be created by the use of a process map, also called *a flow chart*, which is a graphical representation of the elements that make up a process. This is a useful way of understanding any business process and showing the interrelationships between activities in a process. This can help in identifying and fixing problems with the process, assisting the development of new processes and comparing the design of similar processes. For larger projects, it may be necessary to represent a given process at several levels of detail. Thus, a single activity may be shown as a series of sub-activities on a separate diagram. Process maps are useful in a number of ways. For example, the procedure of building a process map helps people define roles and see who does what. The process map can also serve as the first step in using simulation as it identifies the processes and decision points required to build the model. More details on the use of process maps are given in Chapter 3.

Service Blueprinting

Let's consider a case where a service consists of a number of sub-processes that are not linked and the service "output" is a number of customer–employee interactions. In this case, the process design may first focus on the design of the customer–employee interactions and then identify external performance measures such as customer satisfaction. To assist in the analysis of customer–employee interactions, the process maps can be extended to show how a business interacts with customers. One system is a flow chart (termed *a* service *blueprint*) that structures the process activities on either side of a customer's "line of visibility" (Figure 2.2). The activities above the line are visible to the customer and those below the line are operations that the customer does not see. Activities above the line of visibility are subdivided into two fields separated by the "line of interaction"; this divides activities undertaken by the customer and the service provider. In the case of below the line of visibility, a "line of internal interaction" separates the activities of front-line personnel who carry out setting-up actions prior to service provision (not in view of the customer) and support personnel who contribute materials or services required for the provision of the service. Finally, the "line of implementation" separates support activities from management activities such as planning, controlling and decision making. Figure 2.2 shows an example of a service blueprint for a restaurant.

The objective of the service blueprint is that it not only charts the service process flow (from left to right) as does a process map but also shows the structure of the service organization on the vertical axis, showing relationships between, for example, internal customers, support staff and front-line providers. In particular, the diagram aims to highlight the interactions between the customer and process where customer services can be affected. The diagrams can also be used as a design tool to determine staffing levels, job descriptions and selection of equipment and as a control tool to identify gaps in service provision through the analysis of fail points. Fail points are potential service system shortfalls between what the service delivers and what the targeted customers have been led to expect.

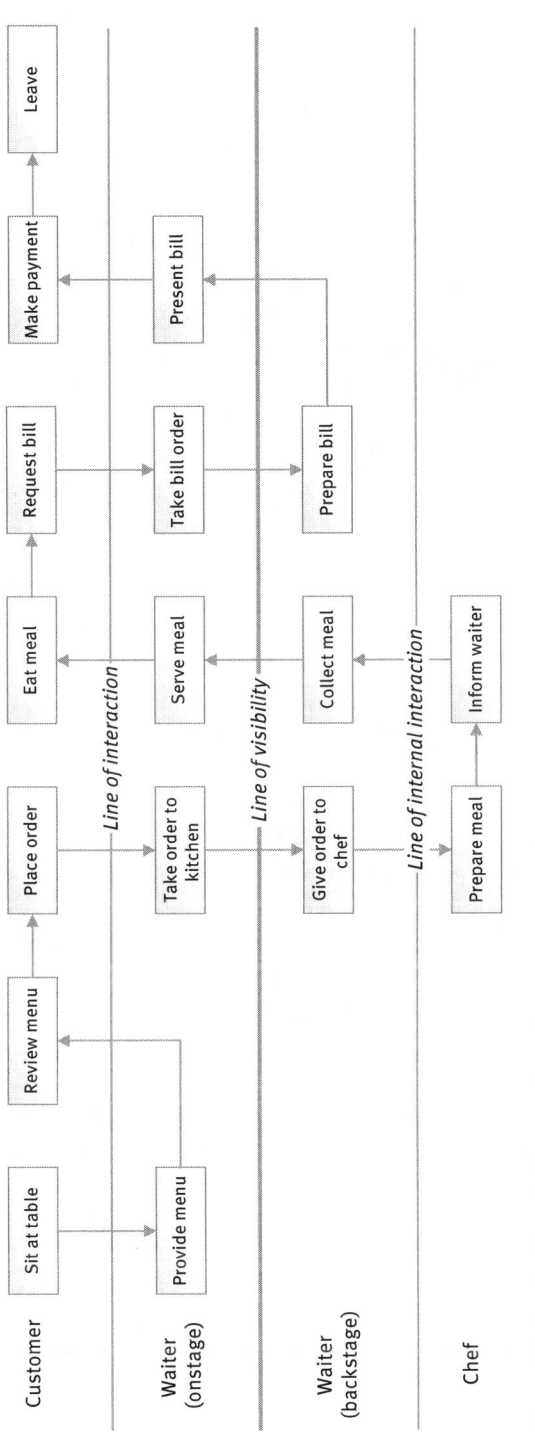

Figure 2.2: Service blueprint for a restaurant.

3 Redesign the Process

There are many ways in which a process can be redesigned to meet particular objectives, and so it is necessary to generate a range of innovative solutions for evaluation. Three approaches that can be used to generate new ideas are as follows:

Generating new designs through brainstorming
This approach offers the greatest scope for radical improvements to the process design but represents a risk in the implementation of a totally new approach. A deep understanding of the process is required so that the design will be feasible.

Modifying existing designs
This approach is less risky than a blue-skies approach, but may mean that the opportunity for a radical improvement in process design is missed.

Using an established "benchmark" design
This approach applies the idea of identifying the best-in-class performer for the particular process in question and adopting that design. Disadvantages with this approach may be that the process design of the best-in-class performer may not be available or the context of the best-in-class performer may not match the context for the new design.

The process map or service blueprint provides an overall view of the current or expected process design, and this should be used so that an overall view is taken when process design options are generated. This helps to ensure that design solutions proposed in a specific area do not have a detrimental effect in other areas of the process and thus affect the overall process performance. The design of service processes in particular is a key factor in meeting the needs of the customer. The process incorporates employees, customers and facilitating goods in a dynamic manner that may be undertaken differently each time, according to the demands of the individual customer.

Peppard and Rowland (1995) provide a number of areas for the potential redesign of processes under the headings of eliminate, simplify, integrate and automate (ESIA) (Table 2.2).

It will be necessary to reduce the number of design alternatives generated and this can be achieved by a rating scheme that scores each design solution against key performance dimensions such as response time and cost of operation. The outcome of this analysis will be a reduced number of design solutions, which can then be subjected to a more detailed analysis using simulation.

The following case study shows the use of performance measures at a strategic level, using the balanced scorecard to link them to operational process measures.

Table 2.2: ESIA Areas for Potential Redesign.

Eliminate	Simplify	Integrate	Automate
Over-production	Forms	Jobs	Dirty
Waiting time	Procedures	Teams	Difficult
Transport	Communication	Customers	Dangerous
Processing	Technology	Suppliers	Boring
Inventory	Problem areas		Data capture
Defects/failures	Flows		Data transfer
Duplication	Processes		Data analysis
Reformatting			
Inspection			
Reconciling			

Source: Peppard and Rowland (1995).

Case Study: Process Improvement at a UK Police Service

The nature of the police service as a service industry means that a central task is the management and deployment of human resources (HR). As part of a re-engineering study covering all aspects of police duties, an investigation of the HR division and its information technology infrastructure was undertaken. A particular area selected for redesign was the sickness and absence process located in the HR division. The following steps were undertaken in the process improvement exercise:

1. Identify Opportunities for Process Improvement
2. Document the Process Design
3. Redesign the Process

Step 1: Identify Opportunities for Process Improvement

Critical success factors (CSFs) can provide a guide to determine "what needs doing well" in order to implement a strategy and fulfill the organizational vision. The CSF can be placed within the four perspectives of the balanced scorecard, which provides a balanced set of performance indicators to reflect the views of the wide range of stakeholder groups involved. A balanced scorecard can be constructed at the organizational or departmental level at which a focused strategy can be adopted. The CSFs for the HR organization were based on the strategic plan developed by the police service at a divisional level. The objectives were then passed to the heads of the various departments within the HR division (for example, head of personnel or head of training) for discussion. The CSFs are listed in Table 2.3.

Table 2.3: CSF and the Balanced Scorecard Perspectives.

Perspective	Critical Success Factor
Innovation and learning	*Increase individual performance* This CSF needs positive improvement and measures to improve individual performance. For example, health and welfare of staff, rewards/penalties, attract quality applicants, retain staff, staff relations, development and training of staff.
Business process	*Increase effectiveness of strategic management* This CSF will provide accurate management information on which the strategic development and policies and decisions are based. For example, improve service to the public, develop policies, support and advise on organizational change, and enable empowerment.
	Improve staff communications This CSF will ensure that staff are better informed of and are aware of new legislation, policies and procedures, where to obtain relevant management information and expert advice and set up procedures to enforce policies particularly those mandated by legislation or otherwise.
Stakeholder/customer	*Meet legislative requirements* Failure to meet this CSF will result in penalties including financial and dismissal. For example, EC regulations, health and safety, police regulations, employment legislation, etc.
	Increase effectiveness of force in its delivery to external customers This CSF will require HR to provide accurate management information to the force on which the force can base both strategic and tactical responses to the needs of external customers and agencies.
	Increase effectiveness in delivery to internal customers This CSF will require HR to provide accurate management information and professional advice to heads of departments and line managers (all levels) on which heads of departments and line managers can base both strategic and tactical responses to the needs of their own staff and other internal customers.
Financial	*Improve value for money (of HR to the organization)* This CSF will require HR management to develop strategic and tactical plans and policies to guide strategic development of all HR aspects to make the most effective use of resources and systems to provide a high-quality service.

Step 2: Document the Process Design
In order to identify activities within the sickness and absence process, the technique of process mapping was used. This involved interviewing personnel and observation of the relevant process. The analysis showed the interrelationships between activities and identifies the elements and roles involved in process execution.

Once the process mapping has been completed, it is necessary to prioritize the process elements, which will be allocated resources for improvement. The following example presents a measurement system developed in conjunction with this service. The system consists of a two-dimensional marking guide based on the impact of the process on the CSF determined in the balanced scorecard review and an assessment of the scope for innovation (the amount of improvement possible) to the current process design. Processes that are strategically important and offer the largest scope for improvement are prioritized under this model. The marking guide marks each process on a scale of 0–5 against two measures of *impact*—the extent to which the achievement of the CSF depends on the process and *innovation*—the extent of the change required to the process in order to meet the CSF. The marking guides for each measure are listed in Tables 2.4 and 2.5.

Table 2.4: Impact (External Perspective) Marking Guide.

Mark	Impact (External Perspective) Marking Guide
0	This individual process has minimal or no effect on the individual CSF.
1	This individual process is dependent on another process in order for it to have an effect on this CSF.
2	This individual process has a marked influence on this CSF.
3	The individual process has substantial impact on whether another process can maximize its beneficial effects on this CSF.
4	The individual process has substantial influence on this CSF.
5	The individual process is a critical part of being able to achieve the individual CSF.

In terms of the balanced scorecard, the impact measure relates to the achievement of the CSF from the stakeholder/customer and financial (external) perspectives of the balanced scorecard. The innovation measure relates to the amount of change required from the innovation, learning and internal business process) perspectives Figure 2.3).

Each process element is scored (0–5) against each CSF for the impact and innovation measures. The score for each measure is multiplied to provide a composite

Table 2.5: Innovation (Internal Perspective) Marking Guide.

Mark	Innovation (Internal Perspective) Marking Guide
0	This process can not be improved for this CSF.
1	This process achieves its objective but could be improved even further.
2	This process achieves its objective but could be improved by review of both automation and process improvement.
3	This process does not effectively achieve all its objectives and could be improved by review of both automation and process improvement.
4	The process exists and functions but needs substantial alteration to meet its objectives.
5	The process either does not exist or only partially exists and fails to meet any objectives.

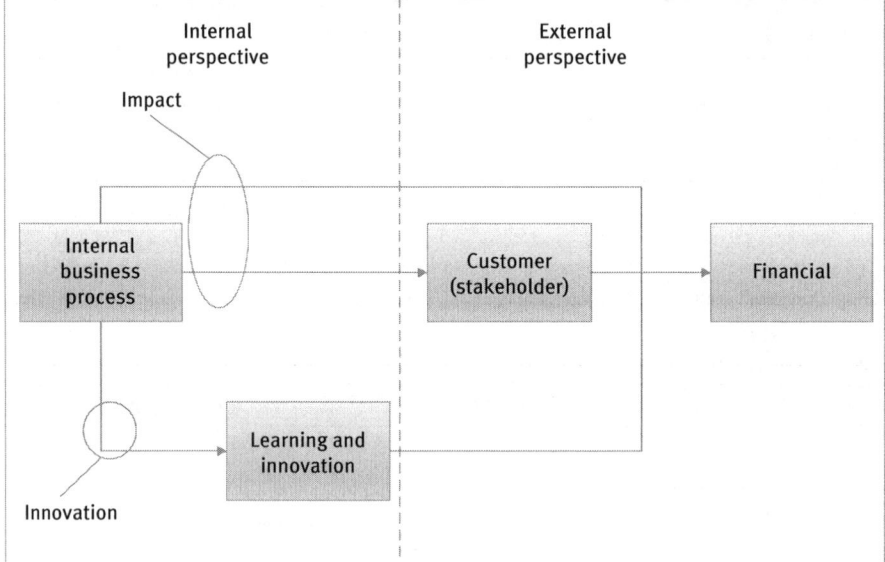

Figure 2.3: Relationship between the scoring systems and the balanced scorecard perspectives.

score (0–25) for each CSF. An overall composite score for each process is calculated by adding the composite score for each CSF. A spreadsheet sorted by composite score identifies a priority list of processes for improvement (Figure 2.4).

Step 3: Redesign the Process

Once suitable processes have been identified for improvement, the next stage is to redesign these processes to improve their performance. In the case of the "sickness and absence" process, this involved integration of the present 30 separate process maps into a single process. Some duplication of activities was found, primarily due

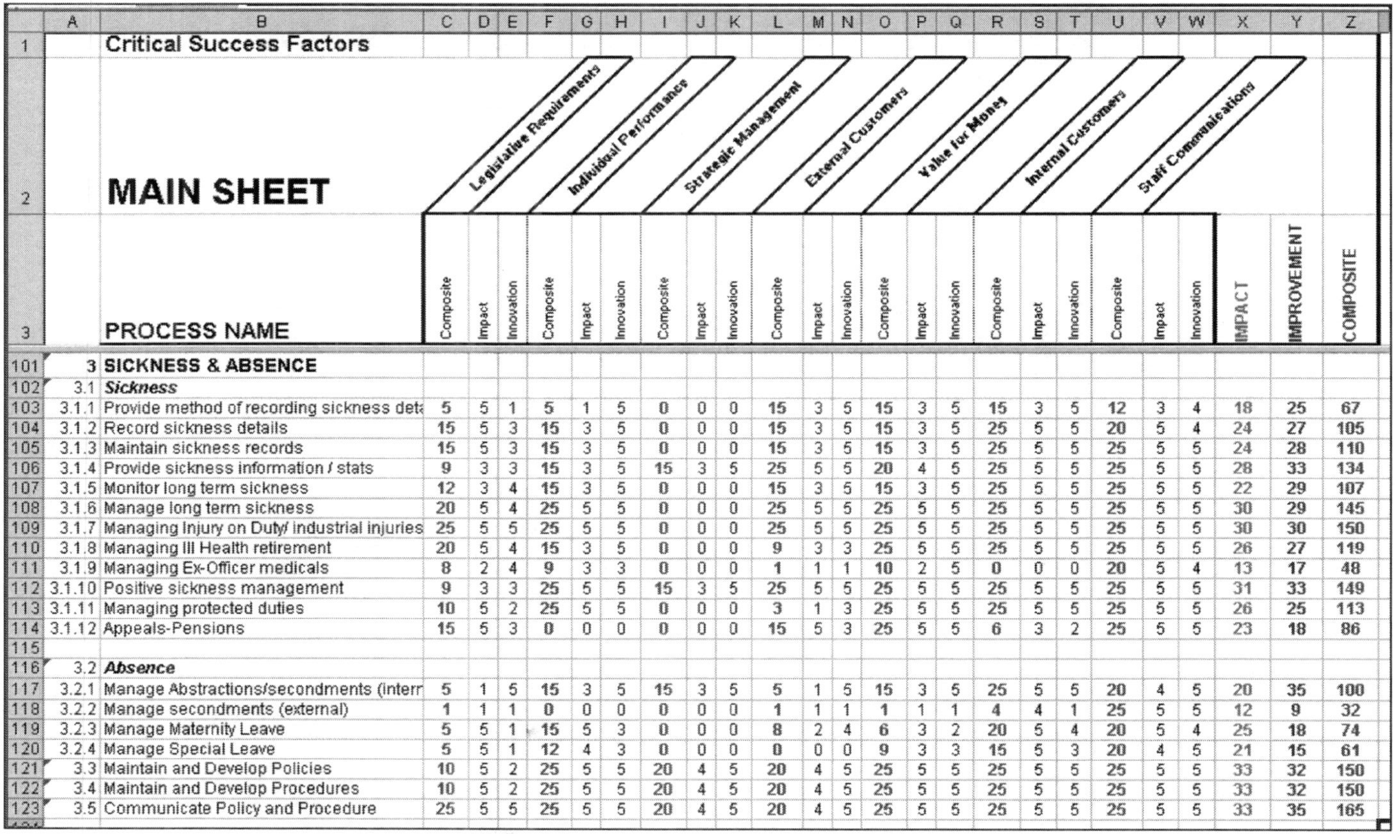

	A	B	C	D	E	F	G	H	I	J	K	L	M	N	O	P	Q	R	S	T	U	V	W	X	Y	Z
1		Critical Success Factors																								
2		MAIN SHEET	Legislative Requirements			Individual Performance			Strategic Management			External Customers			Value for Money			Internal Customers			Staff Communications					
3		PROCESS NAME	Composite	Impact	Innovation	Composite	Impact	Innovation	Composite	Impact	Innovation	Composite	Impact	Innovation	Composite	Impact	Innovation	Composite	Impact	Innovation	Composite	Impact	Innovation	IMPACT	IMPROVEMENT	COMPOSITE
101	3	**SICKNESS & ABSENCE**																								
102	3.1	***Sickness***																								
103	3.1.1	Provide method of recording sickness det	5	5	1	5	1	5	0	0	0	15	3	5	15	3	5	15	3	5	12	3	4	18	25	67
104	3.1.2	Record sickness details	15	5	3	15	3	5	0	0	0	15	3	5	15	3	5	25	5	5	20	5	4	24	27	105
105	3.1.3	Maintain sickness records	15	5	3	15	3	5	0	0	0	15	3	5	15	3	5	25	5	5	25	5	5	24	28	110
106	3.1.4	Provide sickness information / stats	9	3	3	15	3	5	15	3	5	25	5	5	20	4	5	25	5	5	25	5	5	28	33	134
107	3.1.5	Monitor long term sickness	12	3	4	15	3	5	0	0	0	15	3	5	15	3	5	25	5	5	25	5	5	22	29	107
108	3.1.6	Manage long term sickness	20	5	4	25	5	5	0	0	0	25	5	5	25	5	5	25	5	5	25	5	5	30	29	145
109	3.1.7	Managing Injury on Duty/ industrial injuries	25	5	5	25	5	5	0	0	0	25	5	5	25	5	5	25	5	5	25	5	5	30	30	150
110	3.1.8	Managing Ill Health retirement	20	5	4	15	3	5	0	0	0	9	3	3	25	5	5	25	5	5	25	5	5	26	27	119
111	3.1.9	Managing Ex-Officer medicals	8	2	4	9	3	3	0	0	0	1	1	1	10	2	5	0	0	0	20	5	4	13	17	48
112	3.1.10	Positive sickness management	9	3	3	25	5	5	15	3	5	25	5	5	25	5	5	25	5	5	25	5	5	31	33	149
113	3.1.11	Managing protected duties	10	5	2	25	5	5	0	0	0	3	1	3	25	5	5	25	5	5	25	5	5	26	25	113
114	3.1.12	Appeals-Pensions	15	5	3	0	0	0	0	0	0	15	5	3	25	5	5	6	3	2	25	5	5	23	18	86
115																										
116	3.2	***Absence***																								
117	3.2.1	Manage Abstractions/secondments (interr	5	1	5	15	3	5	15	3	5	5	1	5	15	3	5	25	5	5	20	4	5	20	35	100
118	3.2.2	Manage secondments (external)	1	1	1	0	0	0	0	0	0	1	1	1	1	1	1	4	4	1	25	5	5	12	9	32
119	3.2.3	Manage Maternity Leave	5	5	1	15	5	3	0	0	0	8	2	4	6	3	2	20	5	4	20	5	4	25	18	74
120	3.2.4	Manage Special Leave	5	5	1	12	4	3	0	0	0	0	0	0	9	3	3	15	5	3	20	4	5	21	15	61
121	3.3	Maintain and Develop Policies	10	5	2	25	5	5	20	4	5	20	4	5	25	5	5	25	5	5	25	5	5	33	32	150
122	3.4	Maintain and Develop Procedures	10	5	2	25	5	5	20	4	5	20	4	5	25	5	5	25	5	5	25	5	5	33	32	150
123	3.5	Communicate Policy and Procedure	25	5	5	25	5	5	20	4	5	20	4	5	25	5	5	25	5	5	25	5	5	33	35	165

Figure 2.4: Spreadsheet implementation of the scoring system.

to functions included with the sickness process being based both at headquarters and at the divisional level. The redesign improved performance both internally and externally. From an internal balanced scorecard perspective, process efficiency was increased with an estimated saving per sickness/absence event of between 45 and 60 minutes of staff time, representing a significant resource saving that can be redeployed to improve performance. From an external balanced scorecard perspective process effectiveness has been improved by increasing the speed of follow-up checks to absent officers and new innovations such as requiring earlier checks by the police doctor.

In this case, in order that progress is maintained toward strategic objectives, it was considered important to relate performance of the process at an operational level to strategic targets. The "sickness and absence" process is related to the CSF identified in the balanced scorecard initiative of increasing individual performance. At a strategic level, the measurement of staff productivity was chosen with a target to increase availability of police officers by 5%. In order to meet this strategic target, measurements and targets are needed at an operational level. These are derived both from the strategic measure and an understanding of the relevant business process. The measurement chosen for the sickness and absence process was "average days lost per year." The target for this measurement is 11.9 days lost per year per employee for sickness and absence. This benchmark was derived from the national average performance. The current performance was at 14.1 days lost per year per employee (Figure 2.5).

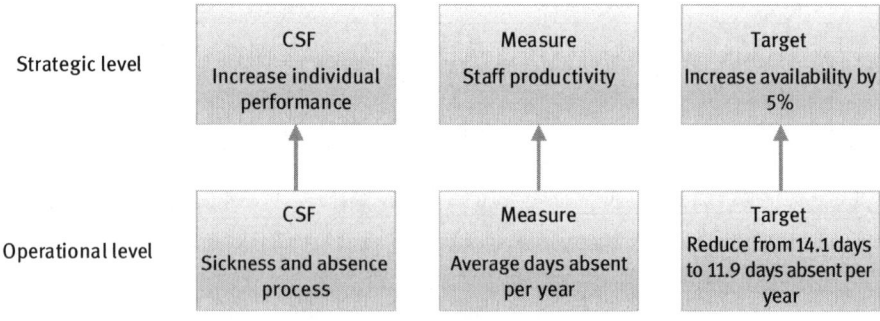

Figure 2.5: Deriving operational measures from strategic objectives.

The case study presents a way of ensuring that the correct processes are identified and redesigned at an operational level in such a way as to support the organization's strategic aims. In addition, a performance measurement system is used to attempt to ensure that the changes implemented do actually achieve the desired effect over time.

Chapter 3
Build the Conceptual Model

The main steps in undertaking a simulation study, considered in this section, are shown in Figure 3.1.

Step 1: Build the Conceptual Model (Chapter 3)
The conceptual model provides a specification for the computer-based simulation model that will be developed in step 2. It does this by providing an outline of the simplification of the real-world system by a domain expert (a person who understands how the system works) into a form that can be represented as a computer model. The conceptual model will be based on an understanding of the problem objectives and the definition of the study objectives. This will allow a definition of the model scope and level of detail and the simplifications and assumptions that are made when forming a description of the real-world system. A process map should provide a medium for obtaining information from a variety of viewpoints regarding the system being organized. In order to prepare for the simulation build (step 2), it is necessary to specify data collection activities in terms of the source of the information and its form, such as documentation, observation and interview. In addition, a specification of the type of statistical analysis used for modeling input data should be made.

Step 2: Build the Simulation Model (Chapter 4)
This step involves implementing the conceptual model specification on a computer using a selected simulation software package. Before the model can be used for analytics it must be verified and validated. Verification involves ensuring that the computer model is a correct representation of the conceptual model developed in step 1. Validation concerns ensuring that the simplifications and assumptions made about the real-world system are acceptable in the context of the simulation study objectives.

Step 3: Use Simulation for Descriptive, Predictive and Prescriptive Analytics (Chapter 5)
This step involves the use of the model to provide information for decision making by studying the effect that changes in the model (termed scenarios) have on performance measures defined in the model. For each scenario, the statistical analysis required should be defined and the use of a terminating or steady-state analysis should be stated. The results of the simulation study should be presented in report form and include full model documentation, study results and recommendations for further studies. An implementation plan may also be specified.

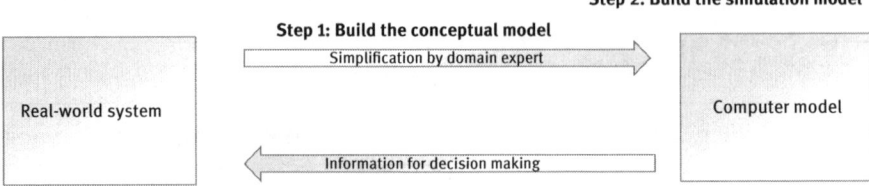

Figure 3.1: Steps in undertaking a simulation study.

When combining simulation with analytic techniques to undertake data-driven simulation and model-driven analytics, the methodology shown in Figure 3.1 is extended as follows (Figure 3.2).

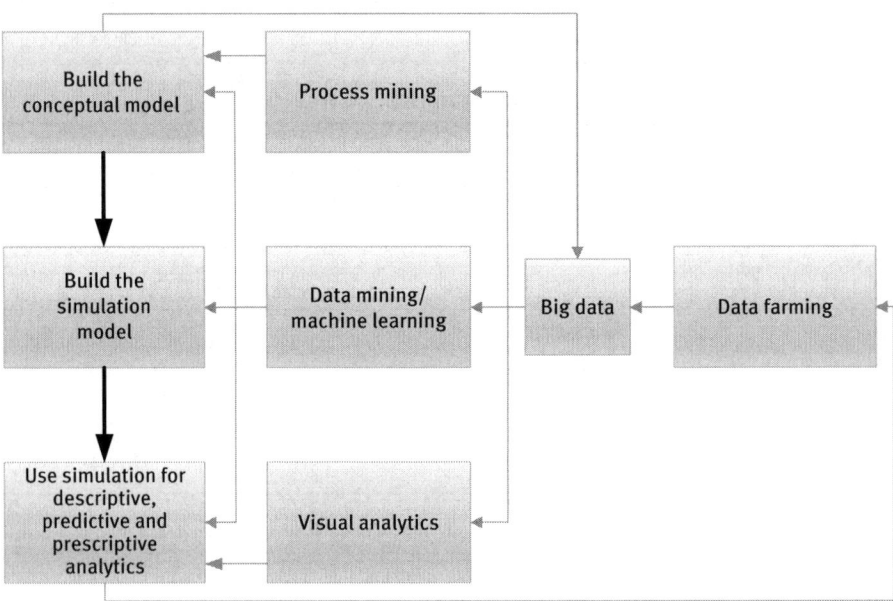

Figure 3.2: Combining simulation with big data analytics.

Figure 3.2 shows the use of the big data analytics techniques of process mining, machine learning and data mining and visual analytics to facilitate stages of the simulation methodology. At the "Build the Conceptual Model" stage process mining can be used to generate a process map. Machine Learning and Data Mining can be used at this stage to cluster data, and machine learning can be used to determine decision logic. At the "Build the Simulation" stage, machine learning algorithms can be used to facilitate digital twins. At the "Use Simulation for Descriptive, Predictive and Prescriptive Analytics" stage, machine learning and data mining can be used to facilitate simulation experimentation, for example, in optimization, and visual analytics is relevant in providing analysis of large-scale simulation experiments through techniques such as clustering. The large data sets required of these techniques are derived at the data collection phase of the "Build the Conceptual Model" stage through sources such as sensors. Alternatively, the simulation can generate large data sets, known as *data farming*.

Although the three main steps in Figure 3.1 and Figure 3.2 are shown as sequential it is important to recognize that the simulation study will be an iterative process. Thus the model building stage may identify areas in the conceptual modeling stage where additional data collection and input modeling are required. Indeed it is normal practice to begin the model building stage before the conceptual modeling stage is complete to minimize development time whilst data collection activities continue. This iterative approach also applies to the final stage when it may transpire that generating the metrics required involves additional work in the conceptual modeling and model building stages. One approach to undertaking a simulation study is to build a simple "prototype" version of the model in order to help define a detailed specification. This prototype can then either be "thrown away" and the simulation study process started afresh or the prototype can be developed and refined based on the new specification.

The following activities for step 1 are now defined. These provide a specification for the computer-based simulation model that will be developed in step 2 (Chapter 4):
- Understand the problem situation
- Define the study objectives
- Define the scope and level of detail
- Process mapping
- Data collection
- Modeling input data

The first two activities of understanding of the problem situation and defining the study objectives provide the context for the development of the conceptual model. This contains a definition of the scope and level of detail of the model and a specification for the process map. In order to build the model, further work is required in terms of a specification for data collection and modeling input data.

Understand the Problem Situation

This step involves the modeler in understanding the context of the problem so that they are able to identify what elements of the real system will be relevant to the model and also the relationship between these elements. Modeling incorporates both information from data collection on aspects such as process durations but also contextual understanding of the problem situation which is needed to conceptualize the system into a simplified representation of a model. This conceptualization enables the model to project into the future and be used for predictive and prescriptive analytics.

Usually the problem situation will differ for each simulation project and will require knowledge of the process being modeled, whether it is a just-in-time (JIT) system in a manufacturing context or a customer call center in the service industry. This will most likely require data collection through discussions with personnel involved in the process and the use of existing documentation. It may be necessary to seek this information from a number of people in order to provide a full picture of the problem. One way of representing this knowledge is to produce a process map of the real system showing the steps involved and the flow of information, materials and people through the system. This can act as a communication device with the client so that an agreement on the outline of the process can be agreed. This process map can form the basis of the conceptual model, which will take into consideration those aspects of the system that require modeling in terms of the study objectives and need for model assumptions and simplifications.

Finally, there may be aspects of the problem in which we are not able to gain an understanding. If these aspects fall within the scope of our investigation we should codify this lack of knowledge in the simulation specification as an assumption of the model. For example, we might assume that workers involved in our process do not increase their productivity through learning or training during the period of the simulation. At this point, we need to obtain agreement with the client on these assumptions and our overall understanding of the problem situation, which is called establishing the model credibility.

In general, simulation is suited to well-structured problems and tends to leave the human aspect of systems aside. For example, the different values, beliefs and interests of people involved in the problem lead to what are called different world views of the problem situation. Also different model builders may well have a different definition of what the real system is (i.e., exhibit bias). Thus, a modeler will produce a model that will differ from another person modeling the same system based on their different knowledge and interpretation of reality. For certain types of problems, the need to take into consideration the human aspects of systems and provide a holistic view of issues has led to the use of approaches such as Soft Systems Methodology and Systems Thinking.

A Systems Thinking Study

A project was undertaken of a discrete-event simulation study of a production planning facility in a gas cylinder manufacturing plant. As the project progressed it became clear that although the discrete-event simulation would solve the objectives of the study in a technical sense, the organizational problem of "delivery performance" would not be solved by the discrete-event simulation study alone. Although discrete-event simulation can incorporate qualitative analysis the systems thinking approach, which involves identifying an archetype that describes the systemic structure of the system and assesses the underlying beliefs and assumptions of the participants, it is found to be a useful addition to the toolkit of the discrete-event simulation practitioner.

The case study company manufactures a range of aluminum gas cylinders for a global market. The cylinders are used in applications such as beverage machines and fire extinguishers. Generally, the demand for cylinders is nonseasonal, with the only predictable demand pattern being the annual seasonal variation of heavy and light (weight of cylinders) mixes, associated with demand for beverage (fizzy drink) cylinders. As the size of the cylinders range from a diameter of 102 to 250 mm, cycle times at the various workstations vary accordingly, that is, the bigger the cylinder, the longer the cycle time. The current method of scheduling production is undertaken using a set of complex sequencing rules, built on experience and workstation performance figures. The quality of the products as well as strong market performance has increased the demand for the company's products. In order to achieve high volumes, both factories suffer from a number of common manufacturing problems, including high levels of Work-in-Progress inventory, long production lead time, moving bottlenecks and poor delivery performance. Principally, cylinders can be grouped into 10 different diameter families, each supporting six separate markets. The smallest design change to a cylinder can necessitate a renaming of the cylinder type. Consequently, over the years, such changes have seen the growth in cylinder designs offered to the customer to the current figure of approximately 250. The effect on production and capacity planning has been that it is now an extremely complex exercise when attempting to schedule the best mix of products for manufacture. Each cylinder is manufactured from a diameter-specific bar of aluminum, which is cut into a billet, machined and then prepared for extrusion. Once extruded, the cylinder has its neck formed and is then heat-treated to age (strengthen) the material. An order-specific internal thread is then machined into the neck followed by a compulsory pressure test sequence. Cylinders are then painted (if requested) and accessories are then fitted. A final internal inspection is then carried out by an outside testing authority before dispatch.

Systems thinking, termed the "fifth discipline" by Senge (2006), is an approach for seeing the structures that underlie complex situations and thus for identifying what causes patterns of behavior. In an organizational setting, it is postulated that there are four levels of the systems view operating simultaneously of events, patterns of behavior, underlying structures and mental models (Maani & Cavana, 2007). Events are reports that only touch the surface of what has happened and offer just a snapshot of the situation. Patterns of behavior look at how behavior has changed over time. Underlying structures describe the interplay of the different factors that bring about the outcomes that we observe, and mental models represent the beliefs, values and assumptions held by individuals and organizations that underlie the reasons for doings things the way we do them. This framework is now used to analyze the case study scenario.

Events
A recurring event was that of missing customer order dates. This was leading to dissatisfied customers and an increasing reliance on a few "strategic" customers who were using their buying power to negotiate price reductions and so reduce profitability.

Patterns of Behavior
Orders are made as per customer demand (i.e., not supplied from stock) and are placed on to the capacity plan over a number of months before the actual order is manufactured. The position of an order in the plan is a result of negotiations between the customer, the sales manager who liaises with the customer and a capacity planner. A senior manager is also involved in "strategic orders," which are deemed to be of particular importance to the company. There is no fixed definition of what makes an order "strategic." The production plan for an order is only

fixed when the order enters the manufacturing process, approximately 7 weeks before delivery to the customer. Because of the wide variety of products offered, the extended amount of time an order is on the capacity plan and the changing capacity situation lead to a great deal of uncertainty in the capacity planning process. In particular, the process of expediting "strategic" orders has led the company to be labeled by many "nonstrategic" customers as unreliable in terms of delivery performance. This behavior has increasingly led to some customers over-ordering or ordering in advance to ensure on-time delivery leading to a capacity plan which overstates the actual capacity requirements. Also due to poor delivery performance some customers have chosen to move to alternative suppliers, which led to an increasing proportion of the output being dedicated to "strategic" customers. This has led to an even greater use of expediting as the "strategic" customers become an ever-increasing proportion of the company's output.

Underlying Structures

One of the tools of systems thinking is system archetypes, which are certain dynamics that recur in many different situations. An archetype consists of various combinations of balancing and reinforcing loops. The "fixes that fail" archetype (Kim, 1992) describes a situation in which a solution is quickly implemented that alleviates the symptom of the problem, but the unintended consequences of the "fix" exacerbate the problem. Over time the problem symptom returns to its previous level or becomes worse. An example of the "fixes that fail" archetype is that of "expediting customer orders" (Figure 3.3).

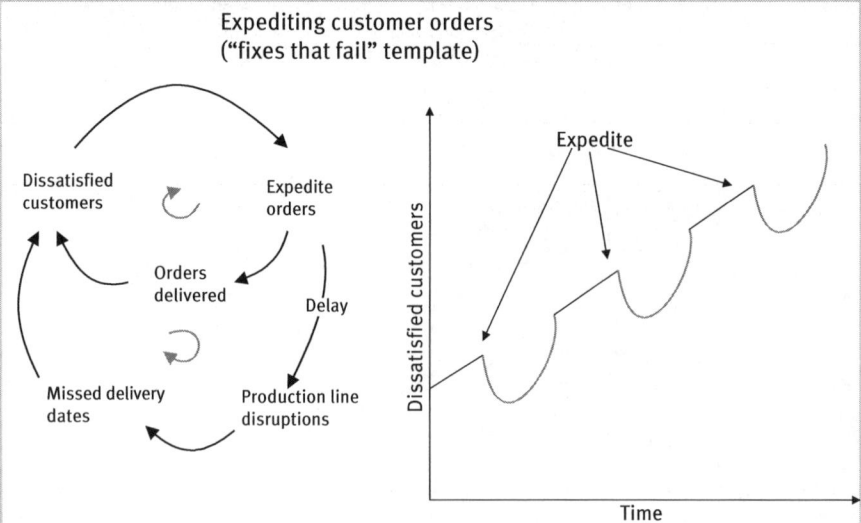

Figure 3.3: Expediting customer orders system archetype.
Source: Kim (1992).

Figure 3.3 shows how in an effort to ensure on-time delivery an order is expedited resulting in a satisfied customer. However, the disruption caused by this policy has led to the need to expedite further orders. A feedback loop is established where more expediting leads to disruptions, resulting in missed delivery dates, which in turn leads to dissatisfied customers and more expediting. This situation occurs because the pain of not doing something right away is often more real and immediate than the delayed negative effects. The situation is exacerbated by the fact that the reinforcing nature of unintended consequences ensures that tomorrow's problems will multiply faster than today's solutions. In other words, solving a problem today will not create another one tomorrow, but will create multiple problems. Breaking the archetype requires the acknowledgment that the fix is merely alleviating a symptom and making a commitment to solve the real problem now. In this case, the idea of "strategic" orders is creating a self-fulfilling prophecy in which eventually all orders will be "strategic." In this situation, the company will supply to fewer and fewer customers, who if they realize their market power can exert substantial pressure on prices and profit margins.

Mental Models
This concerns the most "hidden" level of systems thinking and concerns assumptions, beliefs and values that people hold about the system. In order to investigate these issues, which influence the accuracy of the demand forecast, a questionnaire was administered to 10 sales managers who provide the interface between the customer and the capacity plan. The questionnaire consists of a number of closed questions with space for open-ended comments after the answers. A summary of the outcomes from the questionnaire presented below is codified into three themes:

Theme 1: Changes to the Order Specification
The sales managers report that customers request production space usually within a 12-month period. Eight sales managers request this production space in advance often. Space is usually requested by medium-to-large sized companies. Seven sales managers have experience of customers often or always changing the size and/or delivery date of the order. Up to 3 months' notice is given for this and four sales managers report disruption to other orders when they do change the production schedule to accommodate this. As one sales manager explained,

> *Some of my customers tend to want their delivery postponing when cylinders are due out in two weeks' time. By this time it is too late.*

The reason for making these changes is clear in that eight sales managers report that they gain orders from accommodating these changes while only two claim orders are lost. One reason why customers may do this is that they have a misunderstanding about the production process. According to one sales manager,

> *Some customers still believe cylinders to be "off the shelf".*

Theme 2: Capacity Planning Rules
Nine sales managers always consult the capacity planner before quoting a delivery date and nine sales managers never or rarely are refused space by the capacity planner for the order. Only six sales managers understand the current capacity planning rules, and only five sales managers actually work to these rules. The following quotes underline the current misunderstanding of the capacity planning rules:

> *Don't know if any hard fast rules exist.*
> *Rules changed three times since we started forecasting. Sometimes there is a lot of confusion about what is requested.*
> *Don't know of any rules. The larger customers tend to plan their requirements for the whole year.*

Of the four sales managers who don't understand the rules all agree it would help them in their tasks if they did.

> *Theme 3: Priority Customers*
> All 10 sales managers have priority customers and nine sales managers often or always have priority orders scheduled. The need to satisfy "strategic" customers is underlined by the comment from one sales manager:
>
> > *Companies X, Y and Z more or less always get what they want.*
>
> In summary from a customer perspective, the late changing of orders is accepted as if it was part of the normal "trading" practices with the company. Poor delivery performance has "labeled" the company as unreliable. Consequently, the customers regard themselves as being in a strong bargaining position. Customers prefer to book in advance provisional orders as the lead time is long. Some customers believe the company makes to stock which in reality has never happened.
> Within the company a feeling of confusion exists over the capacity planning rules. The effect of this is that rules are "made up" to suit the needs of the individual with the consequence that order quantities are overbooked, and inquires and reservations are booked as "provisions" for their customers. Nonstandard practices are accepted as normal as this enables some element of control over a system that is poorly understood. Finally, a customer priority system operates in order to ensure what the sales managers consider are the most important customers receive on-time deliveries.
> Senge (2006) states that most people assume cause and effect are close in time and space. Thus, a fixation on short-term events will fail to uncover the longer-term pattern of behavior caused by their actions—in this case the longer-term effect on scheduling stability of short-term expediting decisions. In order to break the cycle, both the belief and assumptions about the planning process had to be addressed and an even greater understanding of the systemic structures was needed in order to understand the relationship between short-term fixes and a longer-term drop in performance. In order to achieve this, meetings were held with the sales managers and use was made of the archetype diagrams and the results of the questionnaire to discuss the effect of the current planning rules. As a result of these meetings, the following policies were agreed:
> - Quotes for delivery times to "strategic customers" would not disrupt the current production plan.
> - Delivery times would be maintained and not brought forward if they caused disruption to the current production plan.
> - Sales to liaise closely with manufacturing to gauge realistic delivery performance.
> - Manufacturing to liaise closely with sales regarding up-to-date production schedule information.
>
> The systems thinking approach provides a framework for understanding why things are happening in the way they are by identifying the structure behind the behavior. The discrete-event simulation approach generally replicates the structure and identifies behavior under a number of scenarios. Thus, a system thinking approach, which involves identifying an archetype that describes the systemic structure of the system and assessing the underlying beliefs and assumptions of the participants, can be a useful addition to the toolkit of the discrete-event simulation practitioner.

Define the Study Objectives

Within a problem area, many different models could be built encompassing different aspects of the problem at different levels of details. The design of the model will reflect that its purpose as a tool is to aid in decision making and so a number of specific study objectives should be derived to achieve this. The study objectives will then provide a guide to the data needs of the model, set the boundaries of the study (scope), the level of modeling detail and define the experimentation analysis required. It is necessary to refine the study objectives until specific scenarios defined by input variables and measures that can be defined by output variables can be specified. General improvement areas for a project are shown in Table 3.1.

Table 3.1: Performance Improvement Approaches.

Performance Improvement Approach	Examples
Change process design	Changes to the process map; routing, decision points and layout by elimination, simplification and automation.
Increase resource availability	Increase in the amount of staff or equipment. Changes to shift patterns. Staff training to increase productivity.
Reduce variability	Moving to a customer appointment system, using preventative maintenance to reduce equipment breakdown, adding products to the product mix to smooth demand, training workers on processes, automating processes.

Many projects will study a combination of the above, but it is important to study each area in turn to establish potential subjects for investigation at the project proposal stage. As well as determining a performance improvement approach the study requires a decision on the performance measures to be used in the study.

The next step is to define more specifically the objectives of the study. For example, a call center may wish to study staffing costs. The objective may be written as follows:

> The simulation model will estimate the staff cost of processing a telephone call to the emergency call center by call type.

From this the simulation analyst can derive the following requirements from the simulation model specification. Important information on model detail (the process for responding to an emergency call), input requirements (demand for each call type) and performance measures required (staffing cost) can be implied from the objective stated. The project proposal should contain a number of objectives at such a level of detail, which allows the simulation analyst to derive an outline model specification upon which an estimate in terms of time and cost can be prepared. For instance, the previous statement requires clarification on the exact nature of the call process. What elements of this process are required for modeling, the initial call handling or should the coordination of the response to the call also be modeled? These factors may require simply additional simulation runs, or major changes to the model design—so an iterative process of redefining model objectives between the analyst and the user is required at this stage.

Define the Scope and Level of Detail

This stage can be considered the most difficult in the design of the simulation model and can be summarized as decisions regarding what should be left out (or included in the model). These decisions are made by defining both the scope and level of detail of the model. The model scope is the definition of the boundary between what is to be included in the model and what is considered external to the specification. The scope will need to encompass aspects of the system that connect the defined input factors (e.g., customer demand) with our output factors (e.g., customer service time).

One way of considering the boundaries or scope of what should be incorporated into the simulation model is to consider the context level of the process being simulated. The decision on what elements at each context level to include should be made by considering the objectives of the study. Four main context levels can be defined moving from a narrow to a wide context.

Entity (instance)

At the entity level the consideration is for a single instance of an entity moving through the process and here the attributes of the entity are considered. For example customers (entities) of different customer types (attribute) may take different process flow paths through the process model.

Process (flow)

At the process level we consider that it is unlikely that a single entity is processed in isolation but many entities may be moving through the process at the same time. This means that how the entity is processed will be determined by its interaction with other entities such as the need to share resources. If insufficient resources are available then entity queuing may occur or the entity process flow may be altered.

Organizational (people)

Here we extend the boundary of the model to include aspects that are not normally covered in simulation studies. At this context level we take account of attributes of people's behavior in the organization and how they will impact the process. This includes people's work priorities, skill levels, teamwork and motivation. Thus at the organizational level consideration is made that people work on a variety of tasks in different ways and how they organize their work and their productivity will affect how they are processed.

External (environment)

Here we consider external factors, for an organizational process this may include customers, suppliers, finance, government actions, weather conditions or any other factors. At the external level there are a number of factors such as supplier actions that may affect the process performance.

Once the model scope has been defined, the next stage is to specify the level of detail of the modeling of components within the scope of our model. In determining the level of detail, the aim is to minimize model complexity while providing a model capable of achieving the project objectives. Model complexity can be considered in terms of the number of components within the model and the amount of connections between them. One reason we wish to minimize complexity is that verification and validation becomes more difficult as the complexity of the model increases. However, if we leave too much out of the model, there is a greater conceptual leap between the conclusions drawn from the model and interpretation in relation to the system. Thus, a model that meets the objectives of the study with the least amount of complexity required would be the ideal solution.

Strategies for reducing model complexity by reducing the level of detail of how we model system components are termed simplifications. Simplifications are distinguished from model assumptions in that simplifications are aspects we choose to simplify to reduce model complexity, whereas assumptions are made to eliminate the need to model aspects of the system we do not fully understand. A key reason for making model simplifications is that the results of the model are easier to interpret since the structure of the model is easier to understand.

Actual mechanisms for the simplification of reality in a simulation model can be classified into omission, aggregation and replacement:
- Omission: omitting aspects of the system from the model. For example, the model may omit staff breaks for meals and presume staff are continuously available. Often machine-based processes are modeled without reference to the human operator they employ.

- Aggregation: merging individual processes into a single process. For example, processes or the work of whole departments may be aggregated if their internal working is not the focus of the simulation study. The model may only consider a customer service process as a whole rather than modeling individual transactions within that process.
- Replacement: replacing complex processes. For example, human processes are often substituted by a "resource" element in a simulation model. This simplifies a human process removing many of the complicating factors of human behavior.

From a modeling perspective, these strategies are useful in reducing model complexity and may be necessary to produce a model within the time and cost constraints of the development. However, there is also a consideration with regard to the perspective of the client of the model. Clients tend to expect every aspect of a process included in the model, and simplification can result in a model that may be too far removed from reality for the client to have confidence in model results. This issue of model credibility requires an interaction between the client and model builder to explain the purpose of the model in terms of assisting decision making rather than an attempt to replicate reality. An important aspect of this is for assumptions and simplifications to be stated explicitly in the simulation report, so that the client is aware of them.

In general, this stage of the simulation study requires the skill and experience of the modeler to decide in the level of model detail required. Practical considerations such as data availability will also need to be taken into account, but the main decisions should be based around the objectives of the simulation study. As a guide it is usually the case that greater detail is required for models that are for predictive and prescriptive analysis than for descriptive purposes.

Finally, it should be remembered that the model will normally be used in conjunction with the model user (client) in order to achieve understanding and make predictions. If this is the case then the level of detail in the model should take into consideration that some aspects of the system understanding can be derived from the user's knowledge and the model can be seen as a tool to support the user's decision making.

> **Model Abstraction**
>
> The term abstraction is used to express that in our model we will represent the essential aspects of the original system but not necessarily in the same form or depth of analysis (termed level of detail). The abstraction process takes place using the following methods:
> Assumptions - these are aspects of the system that are not modeled due to a lack of understanding.
> Simplifications - these are aspects of the system that we partly model to reduce model complexity.
> Out of Scope - these are aspects of the system that are not modeled as they are considered not relevant to the study objectives

Which Model is Best?

One issue with conceptual model building is that even for relatively simple models it becomes apparent that there are many different conceptual models that can be developed to solve a particular task. In instances such as this the analyst might consider how we determine which of these models is best for the task in hand. One approach is termed Occam's razor—if there are multiple models all capable of explaining some phenomena then the most simple model is to be preferred. This does not mean the most simple model is necessarily the best but this represents a pragmatic approach and implies we should start with a simple model and add complexity until it meets our needs rather than start with a detailed model and remove elements from it.

The Context Level and the State Space

As the context level in the process is expanded from entity to process to organizational and to the external context the number of potential variables that can impact the ability to predict increases greatly. This increase in dimensionality or the state space poses challenges for both simulation and analytics. In simulation the use of domain knowledge and the implementation of the methods of abstraction and simplification are used to restrict the number of variables considered in the analysis. This aims to provide both a model and output performance from the model that can be understood by the modeler and client. However the importance of incorporating variables in the organizational context level is increasingly being recognized in order to produce more realistic and valid models. Many organizational variables concern attributes of people, such as motivation or skill level, that are directly or indirectly involved in the process. To address this challenge a range of modeling strategies for modeling human behavior are covered in Figure 1.10. In analytics when using learning algorithms to make predictions the amount of data required increases substantially as the state space increases. For example the use of a learning algorithm to predict the next move in a board game only requires knowledge of the board game itself. A learning algorithm to direct a self-driving vehicle needs to take into consideration many external factors such as road conditions, weather conditions, local road regulations, different driver behaviors, traffic density, etc. This implies a massive data set to provide rules for coping with the many different future states that may occur. One solution may be to use simulation to create the state space within which training of the learning algorithm can occur.

Process Mapping

A useful method for representing the conceptual model that can be used as a basis for the model build stage and provide a communication tool between model developer and client is the use of a process map or a process flow diagram. A process map should be formulated in line with the scope and level of detail defined within the project specification mentioned in this chapter. An essential component of this activity is to construct a diagrammatic representation of the process in order to provide a basis for understanding between the simulation developer and process owner. Two diagramming methods used in discrete-event simulation are activity cycle diagrams and process maps. Activity cycle diagrams can be used to represent any form of simulation system. Process maps are most suited to represent a process interaction view that follows the life cycle of an entity (e.g., customer, product) through a system comprising a number of activities with queuing at each process (e.g., waiting for service, equipment). Most simulation applications are of this type, and the clear form of the process map makes it the most suitable method in these instances.

Activity Cycle Diagrams

Activity cycle diagrams can be used to construct a conceptual model of a simulation, which uses the event, activity or process orientation. The diagram aims to show the life cycles of the components in the system. Each component is shown in either of two states: the *dead* state is represented by a circle and the *active* state is represented by a rectangle (Figure 3.4). Each component can be shown moving through a number of dead and active states in a sequence that must form a loop. The dead state relates to a conditional ("C") event where the component is waiting for something to happen such as the commencement of a service, for example. The active state relates to a bound ("B") event or a service process, for example. The duration of the active state is thus known in advance while the duration of the dead state can not be known, because it is dependent on the behavior of the whole system.

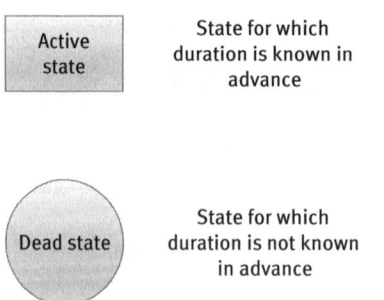

Figure 3.4: Symbols used in activity cycle diagrams.

Figure 3.5 provides an example of an activity cycle diagram for a simplified arrest process.

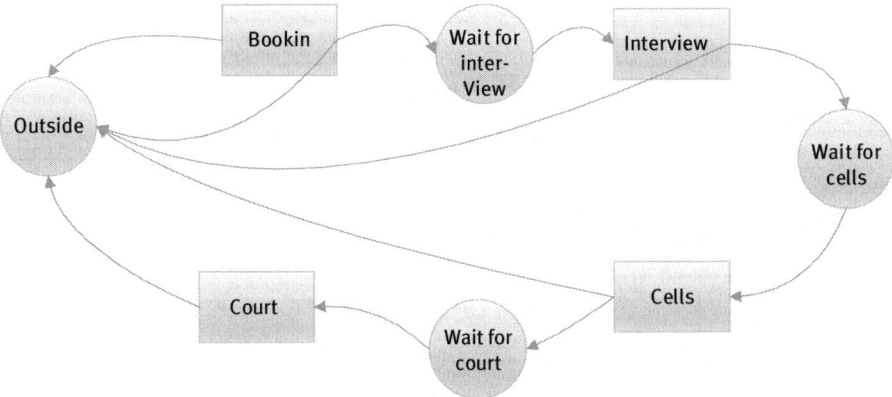

Figure 3.5: Arrest activity cycle diagram.

Process Maps

The construction of a process flow diagram is a useful way of understanding and documenting any business process and showing the interrelationships between activities in a process. Figure 3.6 shows the representations that are used in a simple process flow diagram

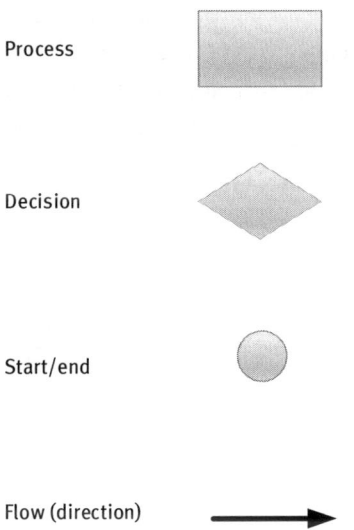

Process

Decision

Start/end

Flow (direction)

Figure 3.6: Symbols used for a process flow diagram.

For larger projects, it may be necessary to represent a given process at several levels of details. Thus, a single activity may be shown as a series of subactivities on a separate diagram. Figure 3.7 shows a process map for a simplified arrest process.

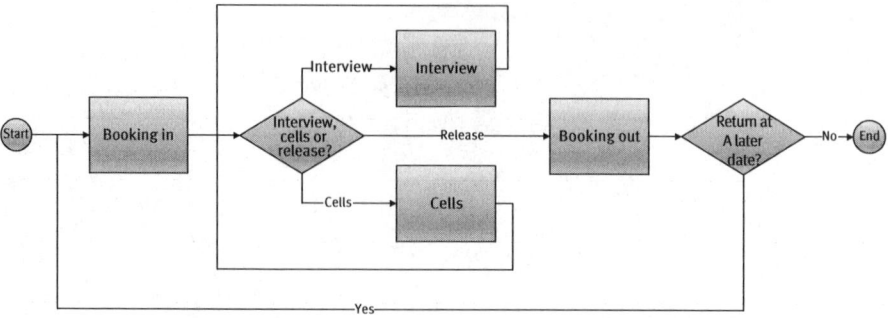

Figure 3.7: Process map of arrest process.

Process Mining

The analytics software of process mining can be used to generate a process map design from raw data that can then be used to build a simulation model. For example, calls to an emergency call service can be logged on arrival and through the process they flow through. Process mining offers the promise of fast construction of representations of complex processes incorporating activities that may not be captured by traditional manual development of the simulation process map. However, process mining does not generally generate a usable process map directly from the event logs but uses a variety of analytic techniques such as inductive mining for abstraction, dealing with issues such as noisy and incomplete data. These approaches abstract events in an automated way that may not capture the required detail to meet the simulation project objectives. Thus, process maps derived using process mining

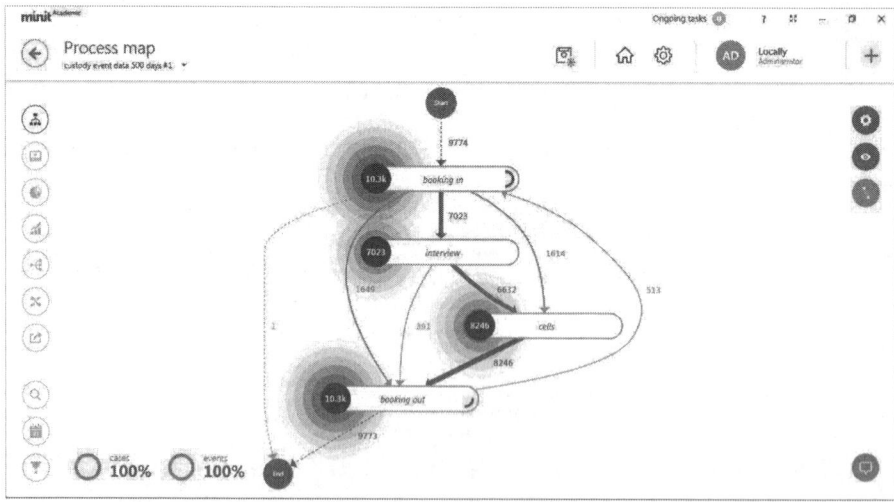

Figure 3.8: Process map generated by process mining software (www.minit.io).

should be cross-checked and validated prior to their use for developing simulation models. See Chapter 17 for the use of process mining software in a simulation study. Figure 3.8 shows a process map generated by the process mining software.

> **Process Mining and Simulation**
>
> The data-driven technique of process mining is intended to discover what actually happens in processes by using data generated by sensors and recording equipment of activities as they occur. This approach can be contrasted with simulation in which an abstraction is used as the basis for the process map. The simulation approach means that the complexities of issues such as human behavior means that they are often removed from the scope of the study. However, removal of these complexities may have a significant effect on the predictive capability of the simulation model. In addition, a mismatch between the actual process behavior and the model behavior can lead to a loss of credibility by the model client.
>
> However, it is important to recognize that data-driven approaches such as process mining do not actually replicate the real system behavior and so to some extent the same issues of validation that occurs with simulation modeling will need to be considered. There are a number of reasons why process mining does not replicate the real system including the issue of scoping (which events that have occurred are included in the analysis) and abstraction level (at what level of detail of events are included in the analysis). There may also be issues with data quality in terms of infrequent behavior that is not representative of the process (termed noise) and insufficient data available to represent the underlying behavior of the process (termed incompleteness).
>
> To address the fact that the data set used in process mining, however large, is a selection that may contain errors, machine learning algorithms are used to process the data. These algorithms must be designed to ensure the resulting process is sufficiently close to the real process (not underfitting) which is termed precision, but not too close that it just replicates the sample (not overfitting) which is termed generalization. It should also provide a good representation of the real system termed fitness and do this with the simplest model possible (simplicity).
>
> Thus, process mining is capable of representing complex process behavior but it is still a simplified representation whose validity is dependent on sufficiently representative data and suitably trained and tested algorithms designed by a data scientist. It should be noted that many process mining software packages simplify the analysis by having built-in algorithms that are not visible to the user and provide flexibility in allowing the user to quickly change between different levels of abstraction. This flexibility of abstraction level would not usually be feasible with a simulation model.

Data Collection

The data collection phase may be a daunting and time-consuming task depending on the complexity of the model and the availability of the data required. A well-defined model specification is vital in providing a realistic assessment of data needs. One of the issues with data collection is the reliance of the simulation analyst on company personnel to collect or provide access to the required data in a timely manner. This will require a clear specification of the data requirements and effective communication with the data providers and if required company management to ensure prioritization is given to this task.

A number of factors will impact on how the data collection process is undertaken including the time and cost constraints within which the project must be conducted. Compromises will have to be made on the scale of the data collection activity and so it is important to focus effort on areas where accuracy is important for simulation results and to make clear assumptions and simplifications made when reporting those results. If it has not been possible to collect detailed data in certain areas of the process, it is not sensible to then model in detail that area. Thus, there is a close relationship between simulation objectives, model detail and data collection needs. If the impact of the level of data collection on results is not clear, then it is possible to use sensitivity analysis to ascertain how much model results are affected by the data accuracy. It may be then necessary to either undertake further data collection or quote results over a wide range.

Two main problems associated with data are that little useful data is available (when modeling a system that does not yet exist, for example) or that the data is not in the correct format.

If no data exist you are reliant on estimates from vendors or other parties, rather than samples of actual performance, so this needs to be emphasized during the presentation of any results. An example of data in the wrong format is a customer service time calculated from entering the service queue to completion of service. This data could not be used to approximate the customer service time in the simulation model as you require the service time only. The queuing time will be generated by the model as a consequence of the arrival rate and service time parameters. In this case, the client may assume that your data requirements have been met and will specify the time and cost of the simulation project around that. Thus it is important to establish as soon as possible the actual format of the data and its suitability for your needs to avoid misunderstandings later. Be sure to distinguish between input data which is what should be collected and output data which is dependent on the input data values. For example, customer arrival times would usually be input data while customer queue time is output data, dependent on input values such as customer arrival rate. However, although we would not enter the data collected on queue times into our model, we could compare these times to the model results to validate the model.

If the required data is not available in a suitable format the analyst must either collect the data or find a way of working around the problem.

As with other stages of a simulation project, data collection is an iterative process with further data collected as the project progresses. For instance, statistical tests during the modeling of input data or experimentation phases of development may suggest a need to collect further data in order to improve the accuracy of results. Also the validation process may expose inaccuracies in the model which require further data collection activities. Thus, it should be expected that data collection activities will be ongoing throughout the project as the model is refined.

In order to amass the data required, it is necessary to use a variety of data sources shown in Table 3.2.

Table 3.2: Sources of Data.

Data Source	Example
Historical records	Diagrams, schematics, schedules
Observations	Time studies, walkthroughs
Interviews	Discussion of process steps
Process owner and vendor estimates	Process time estimates for equipment
Sensors	Timings of events from RFID sensors

Historical Records

A mass of data may be available within the organization regarding the system to be modeled in the form of schematic diagrams, production schedules, shift patterns and so on. This data may be in a variety of formats including paper and electronic (e.g., held on a database). However, this data may not be in the right format, be incomplete or not relevant for the study in progress. The statistical validity of the data may also be in doubt.

Observations

A walkthrough of the process by the analyst is an excellent way of gaining an understanding of the process flow. Time studies can also be used to estimate process parameters when current data is not available.

Interviews

An interview with the process owner can assist in the analysis of system behavior which may not always be documented. Interviews are particularly useful when building understanding of cause-and-effect relationships in the model. This could be regarding aspects such as the interdependencies between processes or codifying conditional decisions. The Delphi procedure may be used to elicit the collective judgment of a panel of individuals rather than that of a single person.

Process Owner/Vendor Estimate

Process owner and vendor estimates are used most often when the system to be modeled does not exist and thus no historical data or observation is possible. This approach has the disadvantage of relying on the ability of the process owner (e.g., machine operator, clerk) to estimate past performance. If possible a questionnaire can be used to gather estimates from a number of process owners and the data statistically analyzed. Vendor information may also be based on unrealistic assumptions of ideal conditions for equipment operation. If no estimates can be made, then the objectives relating to those aspects may need to be changed to remove that aspect of the analysis from the project.

Sensors

Most simulation projects involve manual data collection, where the collection and processing of input data can create a major bottleneck in the modeling process. An alternative approach is the automated generation and collection of data using devices such as RFID and other sensors. Because of the automated nature of the collection large data sets can be quickly amassed, often referred to as *big data*. Technically big data is considered as a data set of at least 1TB but is often used to refer to any large data set. Preparation in terms of IT infrastructure and data compatibility may be required to utilize big data generated by these devices. Real-time simulation applications imply the need for interoperability between simulation software and software applications to provide automated data collection. A standard originating from the area of discrete-event simulation is Core Manufacturing Simulation Data, which is the most implemented standard for data exchange between simulation and other software applications. The standard is incorporated into simulation software such as Arena and ProModel. In terms of data quality, data generated from sensors may also require a cleaning or preprocessing stage. Procedures for cleaning data may need to undertake tasks such as removing typos such as misspelt or joined up words, removing outliers such as out-of-range numeric values and replacing missing values with approximations. Applications of automated data collection in respect of simulation include the generation of event log files for process mining software to generate process maps and data collection for machine learning algorithms that can be used for input modeling, implementing adaptable runtime models and experimentation and analysis.

> **Reducing Uncertainty by Data Collection**
>
> It is useful to consider two types of uncertainty when undertaking data collection. Aleatory uncertainty is the variability which is inherent in the system caused by aspects such as random customer arrivals and variable process times. We are using simulation to address this variability as it cannot be reduced by data collection but data collection in the form of large samples can improve our knowledge about this variability. Epistemic uncertainty is caused by a lack of knowledge about the behavior of the system. This can occur when we are using data collection methods such as reference to historical records or interviews. Here we are aiming to minimize this type of uncertainty in our model by collecting as accurate a data set as possible.

Data Collection When Modeling People

When modeling people as in any model, the level of detail in the model should be based on the study objectives. This can be considered in terms of "does the human behavior affect the goals (output variables) to a sufficient degree that they require consideration in the model?" It may be that when dealing with larger models with complex system dynamics it is difficult to predict whether the inclusion of people's behavior will have a significant effect on overall performance or not. However, as well as the study objectives, there is also a need to consider the effort required to incorporate the modeling of people in the simulation in relation to the gains obtained from doing so. Thus, there should be an evaluation of the modeling impact in terms of cost and workload to introduce these aspects. Thus, it may be decided to use a highly simplified representation of the tasks undertaken by people but determine that the level of abstraction is appropriate for the aims of the study. This trade-off between meeting simulation study objectives against the cost and effort of doing so may be resolved by adjusting the conceptual model specification. However, it is apparent that there are a number of modeling strategies for achieving the required trade-off. Figure 3.9 outlines the modeling approaches of "scenario," "impact" and "individual," where each approach is related to the level of abstraction and data requirements when modeling people's behavior.

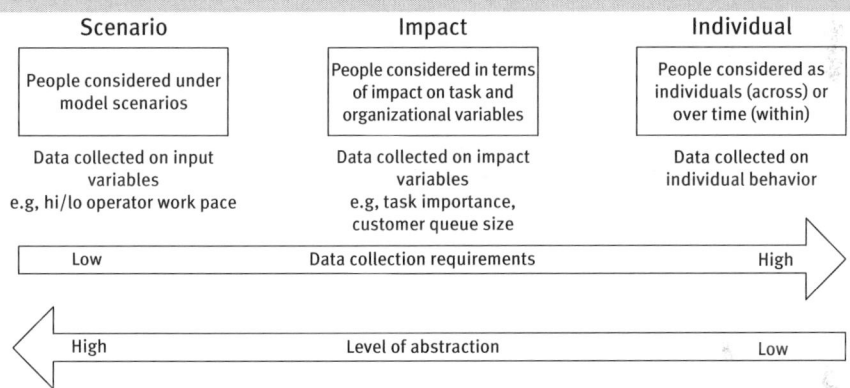

Figure 3.9: Approaches to modeling people's behavior using discrete-event simulation.

The scenario approach considers the effect of people "outside" of the model by observing model results under a range of scenarios. Using this approach people's behavior is codified into a model input variable. For example, worker capacity is set to "normal" or "low" and a scenario run for each value of the variable. The approach is related to studies when data is not available for collection and is treated as an experimental factor rather than a fixed parameter. The remaining approaches to modeling people are termed impact and individual (Figure 3.10) and are implemented "inside" the model.

The effect of people's behavior on system performance can be modeled with the use of impact variables that relate to the task that the person is undertaking or to organizational variables that impinge on a person's performance. Here data collection is required in terms of the impact variable but it is not necessary to collect data on individual behavior regarding the decision of task priority. This approach can reflect organizational policies but if individuals have discretion in their work practices their individual preferences are not reflected using this method. If we do wish to assess the effect of individual characteristics on performance, then we

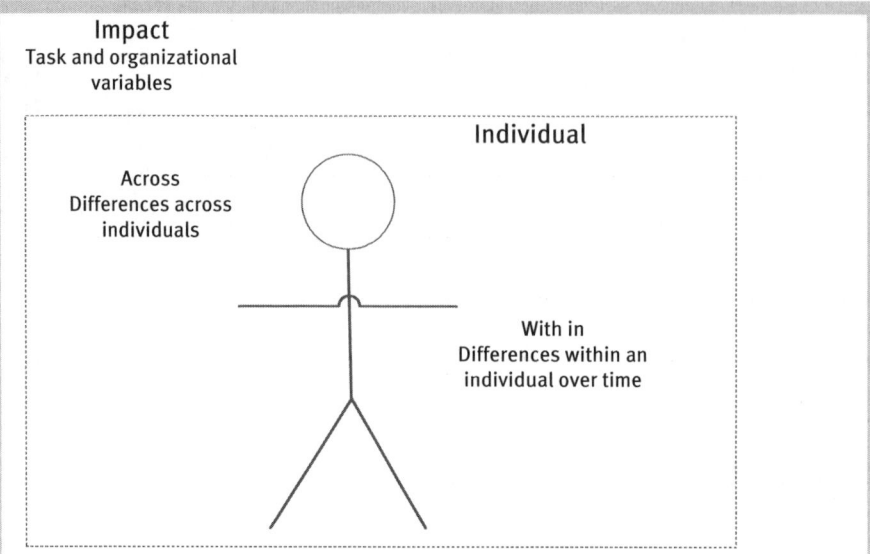

Figure 3.10: Modeling people's behavior "inside" the model by impact and individual approaches.

will need to model these individual differences within the model itself. Using the "individual" approach the characteristics of people are used to distinguish the differences in behavior between different people (termed "across" differences) or differences in behavior of an individual over time (termed "within" differences). An example of an across difference is competence level at an operation which will differ across people. A within difference would be an increase in operating performance of an individual over time such as due to learning.

Modeling Input Data

Modeling input data concerns representing the uncertainty we find in dynamic systems that show variability and interdependence. Modeling input data will be required for the following modeling areas and use the following modeling methods.

Modeling Areas

There are two main modeling areas that require input modeling. First, process logic data is required to represent the processes and enable construction of the process map. This provides us with an outline of what is being performed and defines the design of the *process*. However, to construct the simulation model we need additional information on the *system* regarding the time taken to undertake the processes (process durations), the resources and the availability of those resources required to undertake the processes and the rate of arrival of demand on the processes (Figure 3.11).

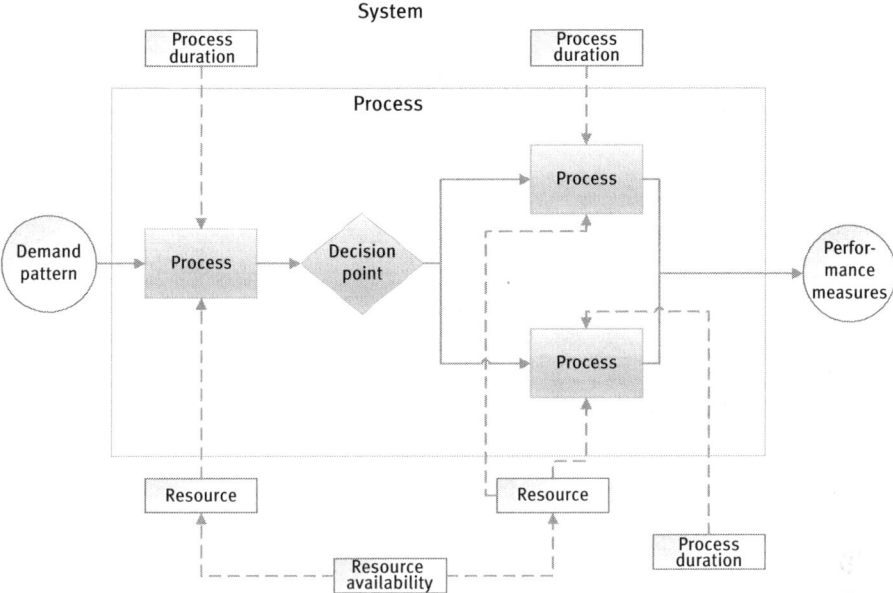

Figure 3.11: Modeling areas within the process and the system.

Data Required for the Process Definition

Process Routing
This is all possible routes through the process or the process flow. The process flow can be of people, materials or information. Data collection may be from observation or discussion with people familiar with the process design. Process mining can be used to derive the process routing.

Decision Points
The logic defining each decision point within the process routing. This is needed to represent branching and merging of the process flow. Decisions can be modeled by conditional (if... then x, else y) rules. Conditional decisions occur when certain defined conditions are satisfied and thus are unpredictable and cannot be known in advance. It may be difficult to codify conditional decisions and so they may be represented by a probability. This represents substituting a cause-and-effect relationship by a distribution based on historical behavior. For a probabilistic decision a sample value is drawn from a continuous, uniform distribution that generates a value between 0 and 1. This means any value is equally likely to occur. For a decision of (0.1,x; 0.5,y; else z) a value generated of 0.76 would lead to a flow following the route defined by the z option.

Data collection for probability values may be by sampling methods while conditional decision rules may be determined by data collection from interviews with personnel involved in decision making. Decision points may also be modeled as other mechanisms such as triggers that activate on an event (e.g., reorder of inventory when levels drop below a defined point).

Additional Data Required for the System Simulation Model

Process Duration
These are durations for all relevant processes, for example, the customer service time at a bank. The process duration does not include the queuing time for the process. Data collection may be by observation or from event logs derived from sensor readings. Processes that do not require a resource are modeled as a delay.

Resource
For processes that do require a resource, the type of resource and the number of units of resource required to operate the process are defined.

Resource Availability
Resource availability schedules for all relevant resources such as people and equipment. Depending on the level of detail this may need to include shift patterns and breakdown events.

Demand Pattern
A schedule of demand "drives" the model. The demand can be in the form of materials, information flows or customers. Demand can be determined through observation for some service systems and analysis of production schedules in manufacturing. The demand pattern or arrival rate is normally represented in the simulation as the "time between arrivals" or interarrival rate. The interarrival time can be calculated by simply recording arrival times and then for each arrival time subtracting the time of the previous arrival.

Process Layout
This covers process routing of material, information and customers and the layout of the location in which this movement takes place. This information can be gathered from observation, documentation or the use of process maps associated with Enterprise Resource Planning (ERP) and workflow systems. The simulation background display and animation can be developed with the use of simulation software draw facilities and the import of graphics files.

Other Elements
Note other fixed or random variables that may need modeling including quantities or levels such as batch sizes, worker absences, the group size of customer arrivals and characteristics of components in the model such as staff skill levels, component sizes and customer types.

Modeling Methods

For the modeling areas previously defined we will normally wish to model the random variation in these areas. Random variables are not undefinable or even unpredictable but vary statistically and are thus probabilistically predictable. This behavior is usually defined by the use of theoretical or empirical distributions. However for each modeling area and depending on the level of detail we require, there are a number of alternative modeling method strategies available. We may also be constrained in our choice of modeling method by the availability and time required for data collection and thus a number of options are now presented. These options include analytical methods and the use of raw data that is sampled (bootstrapping) or used directly (trace).
1. Estimation
2. Theoretical distribution
3. Empirical distribution
4. Mathematical equation
5. Cognitive architectures
6. Analytics
7. Bootstrapping
8. Trace/Event Logs

1. Estimation
If it is proposed to build a model of a system that has not been built or there is no time for data collection, then an estimate must be made. This can be achieved by questioning interested parties such as the process owner or the equipment vendor, for example. A sample size of below 20 is probably too small to fit a theoretical distribution with any statistical confidence although it may be appropriate to construct a histogram to assist in finding a representative distribution. The simplest approach is to simply use a fixed value to represent the data representing an estimate of the mean. Otherwise, a theoretical distribution may be chosen based on knowledge and statistical theory.

Process durations can be simulated using a uniform or symmetric triangular distribution with the minimum and maximum values at a percentage variability from the mean. For example, a mean of 100 with a variability of ±20% would give values for a triangular distribution of 80 for minimum, 100 for mode and 120 for maximum. The normal distribution may be used when an unbounded (i.e., the lower and upper levels are not specified) shape is required. The normal distribution requires mean and standard deviation parameters. When only the minimum and maximum values are known and behavior between those values is not known a uniform distribution generates all values with an equal likelihood.

Statistical theory suggests that if the mean value is not very large, interarrival times can be simulated using the exponential distribution.

The probability values at a decision point can be derived from sample data by simply calculating the number of occurrences within the sample for each decision choice. So a choice for a decision made 24 times out of a sample of 100 observation provides a probability of 0.24.

2. Theoretical Distribution

Deriving a theoretical distribution is the most used modeling input method in simulation. For over 20 data points, a theoretical distribution can be derived. The standard procedure to match a sample distribution to a theoretical distribution is to construct a histogram of the data and compare the shape of the histogram with a range of theoretical distributions. Once a potential candidate is found, it is necessary to estimate the parameters of the distribution which provides the closest fit. The relative "goodness of fit" can be determined by using an appropriate statistical method. The following provides details of some of the potential theoretical distributions that could be used in the matching exercise. Theoretical distributions are classified as either continuous or discrete. Continuous distributions can return any real value quantity and are often used to model arrival times, timing and duration of breakdown events and process durations. Discrete distributions return only whole number or integer values and are used to model decision choices or batch sizes.

Continuous Distributions

Beta: The beta distribution is used in project management networks for process duration. It is most often used when there is limited data available from which to derive a distribution. It can also be used to model proportions such as defective items. The parameters beta and alpha provide a wide range of possible distribution shapes (Figure 3.12).

Gamma/Erlang/Exponential: The Erlang and exponential distributions are a special case of the gamma distribution. The gamma distribution has parameters alpha (shape) and beta (scale), which determine a wide range of distribution shapes. The gamma distribution is used to measure process duration (Figure 3.13).

The distribution is Erlang when the shape (skew) parameter k is an integer (typically values between 2 and 5 are used). The Erlang distribution is used to model several sequential and independent service phases within one distribution when the parameter k is used to represent the number of service phases (Figure 3.14).

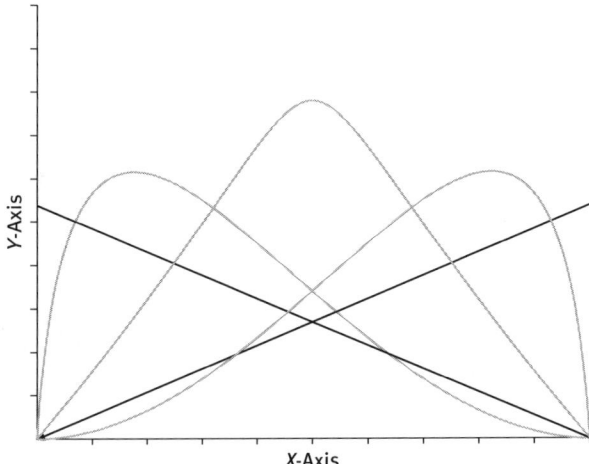

Figure 3.12: Beta (beta, alpha) distribution.

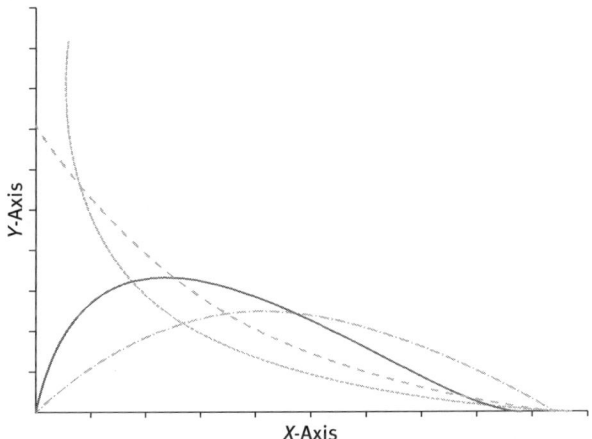

Figure 3.13: Gamma (beta, alpha) distribution.

The exponential distribution is used for independent interarrival events or time between process failures. As such it is often used to represent the interarrival time between customers, where the majority of customer arrivals occur quite close together with occasional long gaps between arrivals (Figure 3.15).

Lognormal: The lognormal distribution is used to model the product of a large number of random quantities. Its shape is similar to the gamma distribution and it can also be used to represent process durations, in particular those that have relatively low amount of variability (Figure 3.16).

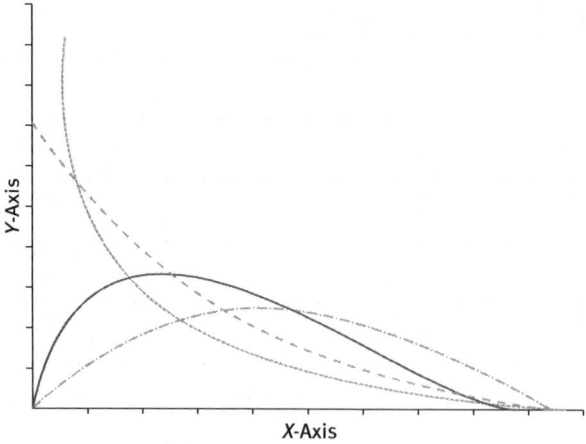

Figure 3.14: Erlang (exp mean, *k*) distribution.

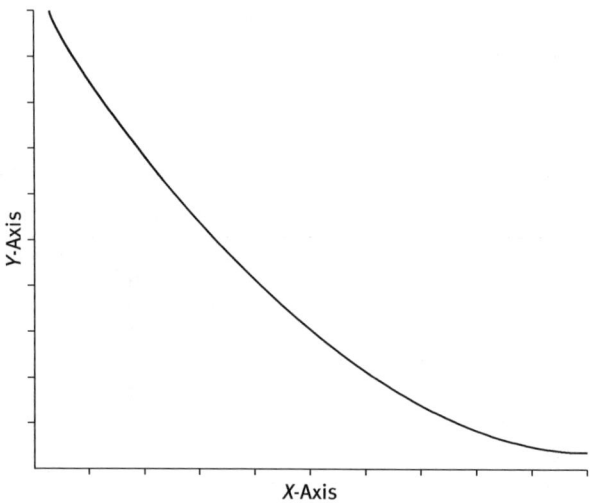

Figure 3.15: Exponential (mean) distribution.

Normal: The normal distribution has a symmetrical bell-shaped curve. It is used to represent quantities that are sums of other quantities using the rules of the central limit theorem. Because the theoretical range covers negative values, the distribution should not be used for positive quantities such as process durations (Figure 3.17).

Triangular: The triangular distribution is difficult to match with any physical process but is useful for an approximate match when few data points are available and the minimum, mode (most likely) and maximum values can be estimated. What can be a useful property of the triangular distribution is that the values it

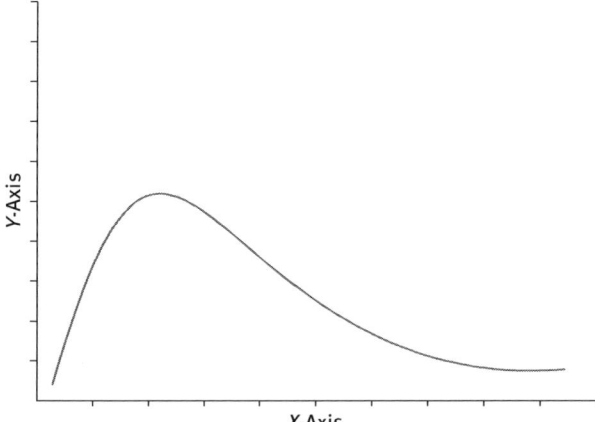

Figure 3.16: Lognormal (log mean, log standard deviation) distribution.

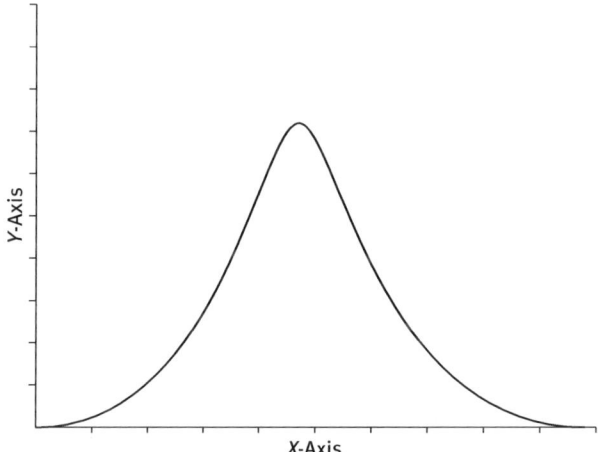

Figure 3.17: Normal (mean, standard deviation) distribution.

generates are bounded by the minimum and maximum value parameters. The mean value is calculated by (minimum + mode + maximum)/3 (Figure 3.18).

Uniform: This distribution has a rectangular shape and specifies that every value between a minimum and maximum value is equally likely. It is sometimes used when only the range (minimum and maximum) values are known and no further information on the distribution shape is available, but a triangular distribution would usually provide a better alternative (Figure 3.19).

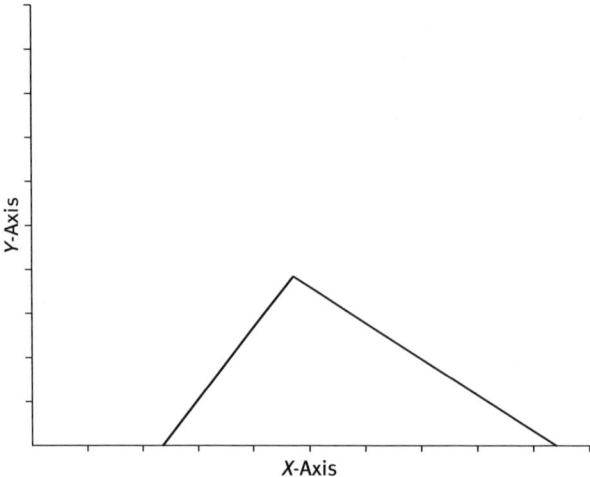

Figure 3.18: Triangular (minimum, mode, maximum) distribution.

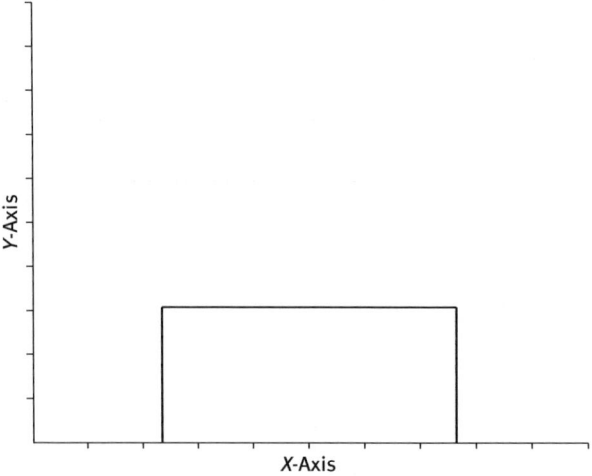

Figure 3.19: Uniform (minimum, maximum) distribution.

Weibull: The Weibull distribution can be used to measure reliability in a system made up of a number of parts. The assumptions are that the parts fail independently and a single part failure will cause a system failure. If a failure is more likely to occur as the activity ages, then an alpha (shape) value of more than one should be used. The distribution can also be used to model process duration (Figure 3.20).

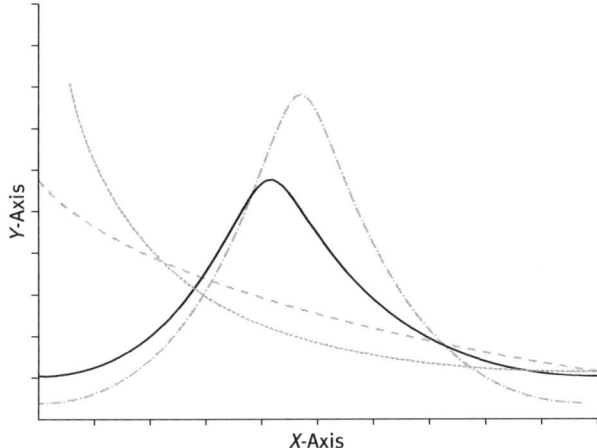

Figure 3.20: Weibull (beta, alpha) distribution.

Discrete Distributions

Binomial: The binomial distribution is used to model repeated independent trials such as the number of defective items in a batch or the probability of error (Figure 3.21).

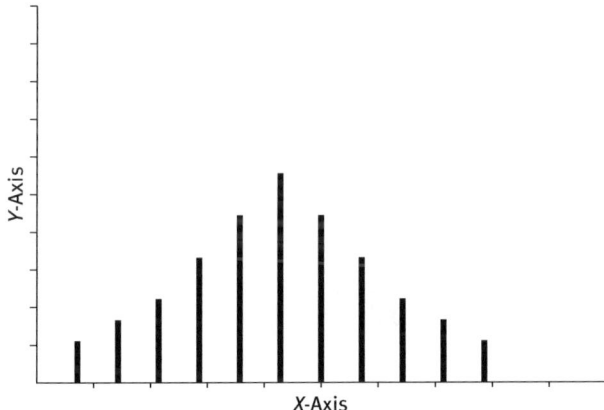

Figure 3.21: Binomial (probability, trials) distribution.

Geometric: The geometric distribution calculates the number of failures before the first success in a sequence of independent trails. An example is the number of items inspected before encountering the first defect (Figure 3.22).

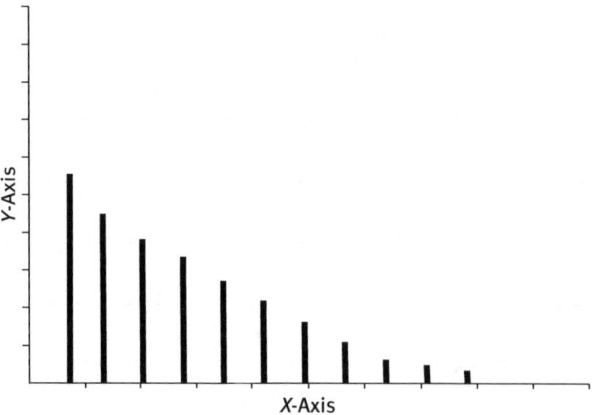

Figure 3.22: Geometric (probability, trials) distribution.

Poisson: The Poisson distribution can model independent events separated by an interval of time. If the time interval is exponentially distributed, then the number of events that occur in the interval has a Poisson distribution. It can also be used to model random variation in batch sizes (Figure 3.23).

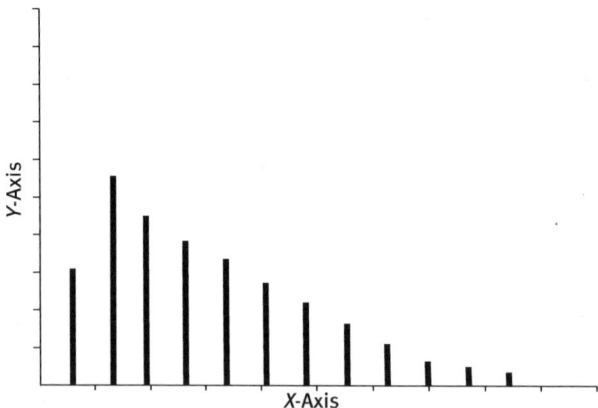

Figure 3.23: Poisson (mean) distribution.

Uniform: The discrete uniform distribution is used to model an event with several equally likely outcomes and thus generates an integer value between the specified minimum and maximum values. It is used when little is known about the data distribution. The uniform distribution exists in continuous form also (Figure 3.24).

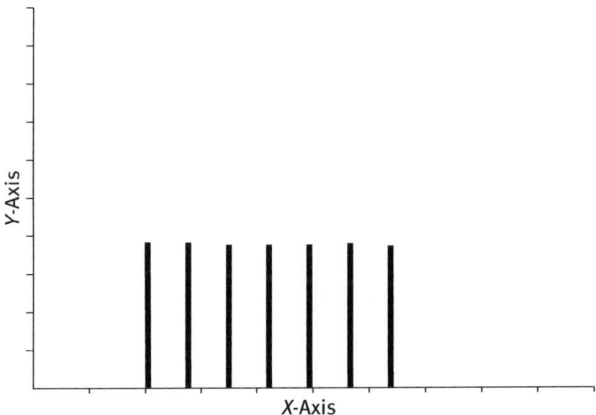

Figure 3.24: Uniform (minimum, maximum) distribution.

Deriving Theoretical Distributions Using Arena

The Arena software (see Chapter 4 for more details) incorporates an "Input Analyzer" software tool (on the Tools menu), which provides facilities to derive theoretical distributions. The procedure is as follows. Say a sample of 100 recordings of a process time in minutes has been made and transferred to a spreadsheet. The spreadsheet is saved as a text file with the name "cust1.dst." The extension ".dst" is used by Arena for data files for the Input Analyzer. In Arena, select the Input Analyzer using the Tools/Input Analyzer option. Select File/New and then select File/Data File/Use Existing. Select the file containing the spreadsheet data and a histogram of the data will be generated. Select the Fit/Fit All option and Arena will display the nearest fit to the data (measured by the minimum square error) from a range of distribution types. Select Window/Fit All Summary for a ranked (best to worst) list of the fit for all the distributions. This list should be used as a guide only as often a number of distributions will show a similar result on this test and the best-fit distribution should not automatically be chosen. Usually the distribution fit tests can be used in an advisory role to provide evidence *against* a choice of distribution made based on the knowledge the modeler has of the real process.

Figure 3.25 shows a plot of the theoretical distribution superimposed on the sample data histogram. Note that the apparent level of fit shown by the graphical display will be dependent on the width of the histogram cells so it may be useful to alter the number of cell divisions to provide a fuller perspective on the fit. A distribution summary report below the histogram provides information of the specification of the theoretical distribution and the goodness of fit with the sample data. Arena calculates the parameters for the chosen distribution type. In this case, the shape and scale parameters for the gamma distribution are given as 17.5 and 1.65, respectively, giving an Arena expression of 1+GAMM(17.5,1.65). The goodness-of-fit information is given with a chi-square analysis providing a p-value of 0.219. For these tests, a higher

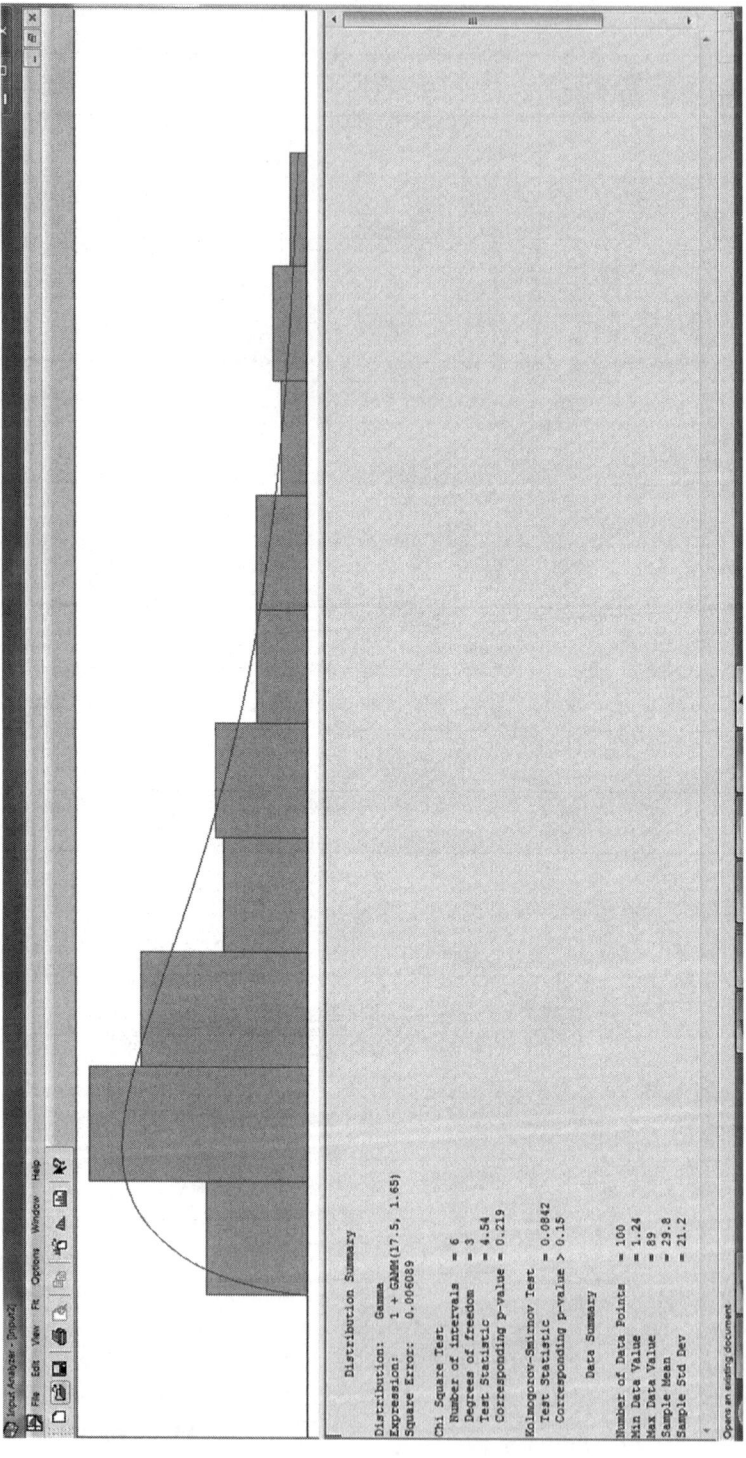

Figure 3.25: Arena Input Analyzer analysis.

p-value indicates a better fit between the collected data and the theoretical distribution formed. A *p*-value of less than around 0.05 indicates a not very good fit, while if the *p*-value is greater than 0.1 then we would have a fair degree of confidence that the theoretical distribution represents the data, assuming that the sample size is sufficient for the test. The Simio v11 simulation software (see Chapter 4 for more details) does not provide distribution fitting capabilities and it is suggested to use third-party packages such as Stat::Fit (www.geerms.com), @RISK (www.palisade.com) and ExpertFit (www.averill-law.com).

Dependent and Nonstationary Processes
When using the above-mentioned distribution fitting procedures, it is important to recognize that they are based on the assumption of independent and identically distributed data. However, this may not always be the case; for example, weekly demand amounts may be partly based on inventory held which is based on previous order amounts. This example requires a time-series model in which the correlations between the observations in the series, termed autocorrelation, is taken into account.

Another issue is when input processes change over time, they are termed nonstationary processes. For example, many arrival patterns such as customer arrivals in service systems vary greatly with time due to outside factors such as lunch breaks and customer behavior and are thus modeled as nonstationary Poisson processes. In order to model this behavior, periods of time when the arrival rate remains constant must be identified (e.g., for each hour of the day) and an arrival rate calculated for each time period per unit of time. It should be noted that simply changing the parameter (e.g., mean) value of the distribution for each time period will generally cause incorrect results and the following method should be used.

i. Determine the maximum arrival rate for all time periods
ii. Generate arrivals using a stationary Poisson process (i.e., exponential distribution between arrivals)
iii. "Thin-out" the arrivals by only allowing them to enter the system with a probability of the arrival rate for the current time period divided by the maximum arrival rate determined in step i.

Nonstationary Processes in Arena
In Arena to enter nonstationary arrival processes in the create block choose the "Time Between Arrivals" Type option as Schedule (Figure 3.26). This creates an arrival schedule, which in this case is named Schedule 1.

For the Schedule module in the spreadsheet view, the schedule "Schedule 1" will appear. Select the type "Arrival" and time units as "Minutes." Click on the duration and a table can be created specifying the arrival rate for each defined time period. An arrival rate specified as a Poisson distribution has been specified for twelve 2-hour time slots for 24 hours of operation (Figure 3.27).

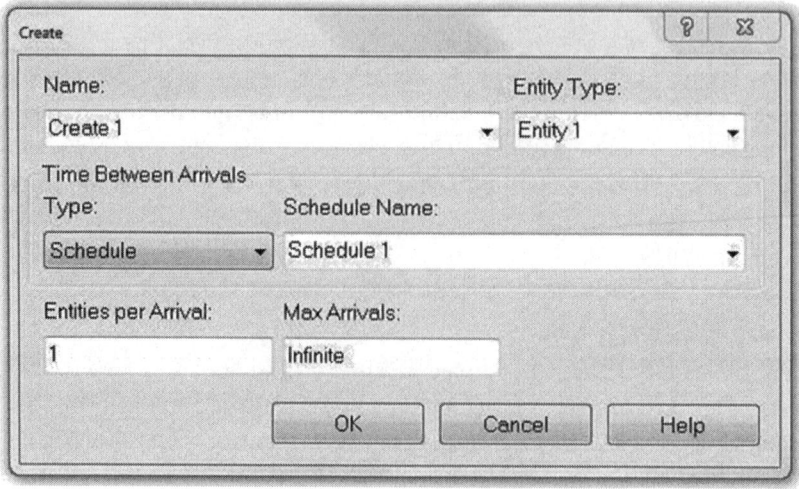

Figure 3.26: Choosing the schedule arrival option in Arena.

3. Empirical Distribution

For more than 200 data points, the option of constructing a user-defined distribution is available. An empirical or user-defined distribution is a distribution that has been obtained directly from the sample data. An empirical distribution is usually chosen if a reasonable fit can not be made with the data and a theoretical distribution.

Constructing an Empirical Distribution with Arena

The Arena Input Analyzer allows both discrete and continuous empirical distributions to be formed using the Fit/Empirical option. In Arena, select the Input Analyzer using the Tools/Input Analyzer option. Select File/New and then select File/Data File/Use Existing. Select the file containing the data and a histogram of the data will be generated. Select the Fit/ Empirical option and Arena will display the empirical distribution as in Figure 3.28.

The distribution is given a list of probabilities and values to return a real-valued quantity. The values given by the Input Analyzer should be used in conjunction with the Arena CONTINUOUS expression. The values are interpreted as follows: 0.048, 7.632 provides a 4.8% chance that the number generated will be between 0 and 7.632. 0.095, 10.263 provides a 4.7% (0.095–0.048) chance that the number generated will be between 7.632 and 10.263 and so on.

4. Mathematical Equation

This approach uses a mathematical equation as a tool for input modeling. Examples of this approach in discrete-event simulation include the following use of analytical equations to compute:

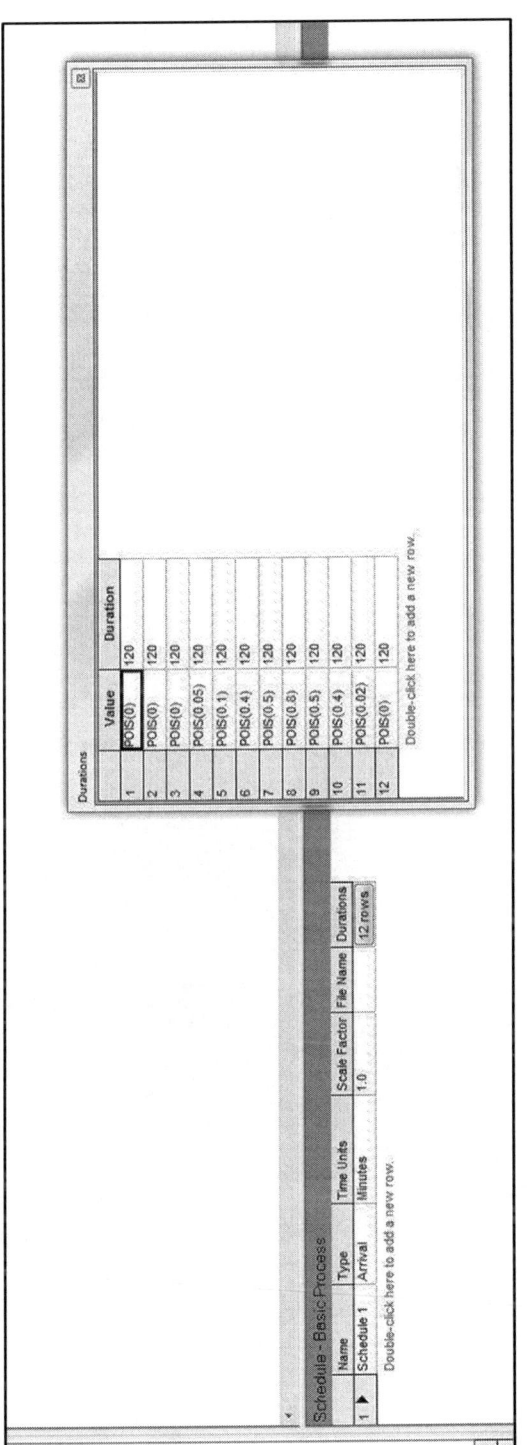

Figure 3.27: Entering nonstationary arrival rates in the Arena schedule block.

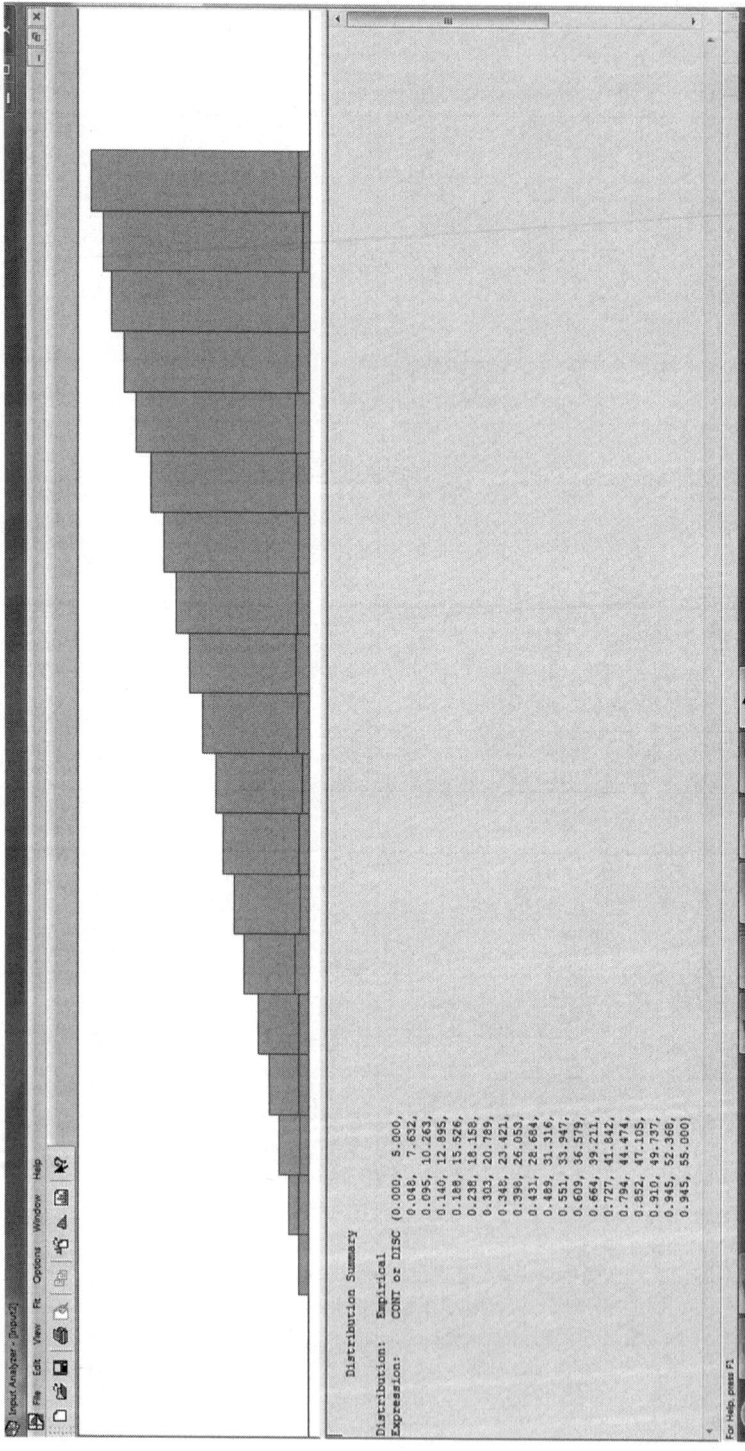

Figure 3.28: Arena Input Analyzer empirical distribution.

- The choice of customer's using self-service or face-to-face hotel check-in facilities
- The shortest path to determine customer movements in a retail store
- Worker performance in terms of job accuracy and job speed
- The selection of tasks from a queue dependent on workload and task importance
- The choice of service provider depending on variables, including queue length for service, distance to the service provider and service process duration.
- The effect of operator fatigue on task duration

The most common use of mathematical equations for input modeling is the use of learning curve equations which predict the improvement in productivity that can occur as experience of a process is gained. If an estimate can be made of the rate at which a process time will decrease due to increased competence over time, then more accurate model predictions can be made. The learning curve is based on the concept that when productivity doubles, the decrease in process time is the rate of the learning curve. Thus, if the learning curve is at a rate of 85%, the second process takes 85% of the time of the first process, the fourth process takes 85% of the second process and the eighth process takes 85% of the fourth and so on. Mathematically, the learning curve is represented by the function

$$Y = ax^b$$

where y represents the process time of the xth process activation, a the initial process time, x the number of process activations and $b = \ln p/\ln 2$. Here $\ln = \log_{10}$ and p is the learning rate (e.g., 80% = 0.8).
Thus for an 80% learning curve:
$b = \ln 0.8/\ln 2 = -0.322$.

To implement the learning curve effect in the simulation, a matrix can be used which holds the current process time for the combination of each process and each person undertaking this process. When a process is activated in the simulation the process time is updated taking into account the learning undertaken by the individual operator on that particular process. The use of the learning curve equation addresses the assumption that all operators within a system are equally competent at each process at a point in time. The log-linear learning curve is the most popular and simplest learning curve equation and takes into account only the initial process time and the workers learning rate. Other learning curve equations can be used, which take into account other factors such as the fraction of machine time that is used to undertake the process.

5. Cognitive Architectures

When attempting to model human behavior in a simulation model the use of cognitive models can be employed. An example is the use of the Psi theory which is a theory about how cognition, motivation and emotion control human behavior. Here task performance can be modeled over time showing how competence oscillates based on experienced success and failure at a new task. This approach provides an alternative to the traditional learning curve effect, which implies a continuous improvement over time without any setbacks in performance due to failures. Another cognitive model that has been used is the theory of planned behavior, which takes empirical data on demographic variables and personality traits and transforms these to attitudes toward behavior, subject norms and perceived behavioral control.

6. Analytics

Analytic techniques are increasingly being used in simulation projects for input modeling, particularly in the area of determining decision logic. Previous work has used association rule mining (ARM) to generate decision rules for patient no-shows in a healthcare service. The ARM method generates a number of rules and a subset of these were embedded as conditional and probability statements in a simulation model. Reinforcement Learning can also be used to determine decision logic. For example if a robot needs to travel between two locations in a factory with obstacles blocking a direct path, a reinforcement learning approach can enable the robot to "learn" an approximate best route to take. This requires the simulation to run a number of learning passes at run time for each movement sequence before the robot movement can commence. For some applications of reinforcement learning the training algorithm can be executed during the warm-up period of the simulation to ensure runtime simulation execution speed is maintained.

For real-time simulation applications decision logic can be coded in languages such as Visual Basic for Applications (VBA). An example here would be VBA algorithms to detect abnormal sensor measurements for a Digital Twin application. In terms of implementing decision rules derived by analytics at simulation time, the choice is to either call an external analytics tool from the simulation system or to transfer or (re-implement) the decision model into the simulation system using its modeling and programming facilities.

Decision trees are one of the few machine learning algorithms that are not a "black box" and it is possible to trace the path by which an outcome is reached. This makes them ideal for input modeling as they can be translated into "if–then" statements for use in the simulation model. Figure 3.29 provides a simple example of a credit application decision tree.

The decision tree can then be directly converted to program code as in Figure 3.30. The rules derived are indicated by the comments to the right of the code.

This program code can then be used in the simulation model, for example, the decision block in the Arena simulation system.

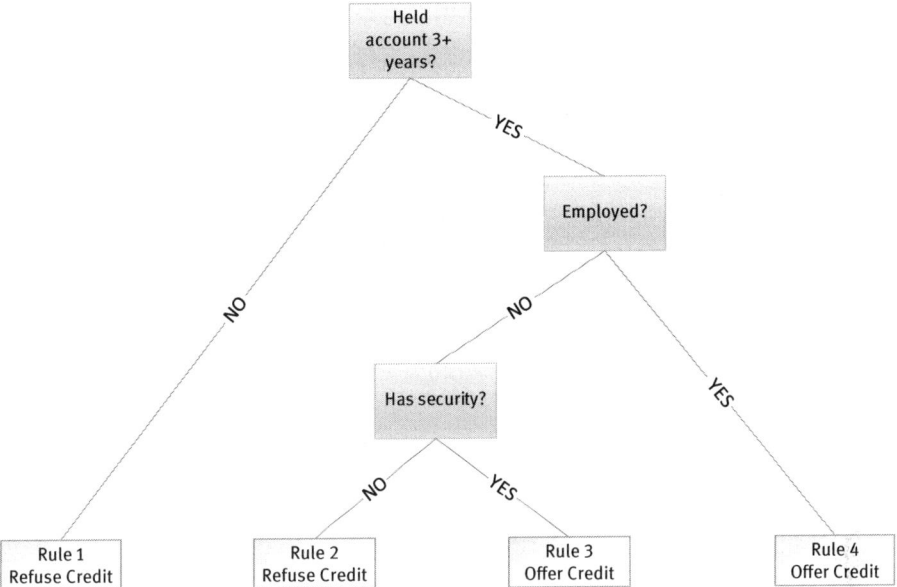

Figure 3.29: Decision tree for credit application.

```
IF Held Account 3+ Years THEN
     IF Employed THEN
             Offer Credit                    {Rule 4}
     ELSE
             IF Has Security THEN
                     Offer Credit            {Rule 3}
             ELSE
                     Refuse Credit           {Rule 2}
             ENDIF
     ENDIF
ELSE
     Refuse Credit                           {Rule 1}
ENDIF
```

Figure 3.30: Program code derived from decision tree.

7. Bootstrapping

This approach involves sampling randomly from raw data which may be held in a table or spreadsheet. This creates a discrete distribution with values drawn from a data set and with their probabilities being generated by the number of times they appear in the data set. This approach does not involve the traditional methods of fitting the data to a theoretical or empirical distribution and thus may be relevant when these methods do not produce a distribution that appears to fit the data acceptably. Also this approach will only generate data values that occur within the sampled data set and so this method benefits from large data sets to ensure that the full range of values that might be generated are present. For example, occasionally large service times may have an important effect on waiting time metrics and so the data set should be large enough to ensure these are represented.

8. Trace/Event Logs

Trace or data-driven simulations use historical process data or real-time information directly. The advantages of a trace or data-driven simulation are that validation can be achieved by a direct comparison of model performance metrics to real system performance over a historical time period. In addition, model credibility is enhanced as the client can observe model behavior replicating real life events. The disadvantages are the need for suitable data availability and the possible restriction in scope derived from a single trace that may not reflect the full variability of the process behavior. Trace simulation is normally used for understanding process behavior (descriptive analytics) and for checking conformance to the "official" process design and cannot be used for predictive analytics such as scenario analysis as it only contains historical data. Trace simulation is similar to process mining which uses historical event logs, although process mining can check conformance of the process map in addition to operational process performance.

Table 3.3 provides guidance on modeling input data:

Table 3.3: Modeling Input Data Methods.

	Disadvantages	Advantages	Comments
Estimation	Lack of accuracy.	May be the only option.	Often used in the development phase before further data collection is undertaken.
Theoretical distribution	No available theoretical distributions may fit data. Generates values outside of the data range which may not be appropriate.	Can "smooth" data to the underlying distribution. Generates values outside of data sampled. For example, rare events at the tail of the distribution which may be missing from a small data sample collected. Compact method of representing data values. Distribution is easy to scale for sensitivity analysis.	Best choice if a reasonable data fit can be made.

Table 3.3 (continued)

	Disadvantages	Advantages	Comments
Empirical distribution	Can not usually generate values outside the range of data (therefore may miss "extreme" values). Difficult to scale for sensitivity analysis.	Provides distribution when no theoretical distribution provides an adequate fit to data.	An option if no theoretical distribution can be fit.
Equation	May require extensive data collection.	Shows relationships that are a consequence of simulated time such as learning effects.	Can be useful for expressing relationships between variables.
Cognitive	Difficult to validate cognitive models.	Attempts to model factors leading to human behavior.	Limited use due to demanding data collection and validation needs.
Analytics	Using some analytic techniques, the logic implemented may not be inspected.	Can employ complex logic processes.	Need for modeler to have analytic skillset.
Bootstrapping	Distributions are derived only from values held in the data set.	Avoids issue of poorly fitted distributions.	Likely to require large data set to ensure coverage of full range of data values.
Trace/Event Logs	Only uses values held in the data set	Replicates reality to check for conformance	Not suitable for prediction.

Chapter 4
Build the Simulation

The model-building process involves using computer software to translate the conceptual model into a computer simulation model that can be "run" to generate model results.

In order to undertake the exercises in this chapter, we require the installation of the Arena simulation software system. This is available as a free download with full functionality but with limited model size at:

https://www.arenasimulation.com/simulation-software-download

The Simio Personal Edition that permits full modeling capability but supports saving and experimentation on only small models that can be downloaded from:

www.simio.com/evaluate.php

The use of the Arena and Simio software systems will be demonstrated using a simple case study of a bank clerk system. Note that the models built in this chapter incorporate probability distributions and so the results you get may differ slightly to those in the text due to random variation. This is to be expected and you can see that the results from the same model run on different simulation software will also vary. This section provides only an introduction to the model-building features of Arena and Simio. For a more detailed coverage of model building, the books in Appendix B are recommended.

The Bank Clerk Simulation

A bank clerk services two types of customer. The time between customer arrivals is exponentially distributed with a mean of 15 minutes for customer type 1 and 10 minutes for customer type 2. The processing time is uniformly distributed between 2 and 6 minutes for type 1 customers and between 4 and 10 minutes for type 2 customers. Performance statistics are required on the average time a customer is in the system, which includes both queue time and service time.

Two versions of the bank clerk systems will be simulated. A single queue system is the one where both types of customers form a queue at a service location staffed by two members of staff. An alternative dual queue system is then modeled. This incorporates a decision rule that directs customers to one of the two service location depending on which location's queue holds the minimum number of customers. Statistical techniques are used to determine if there is a statistically significant difference between the performance of the two systems.

The process map for the single queue bank clerk simulation is shown in Figure 4.1. The two types of customers arrive from outside the system and are processed by one of the two bank clerks. They then leave the system once the process has been completed.

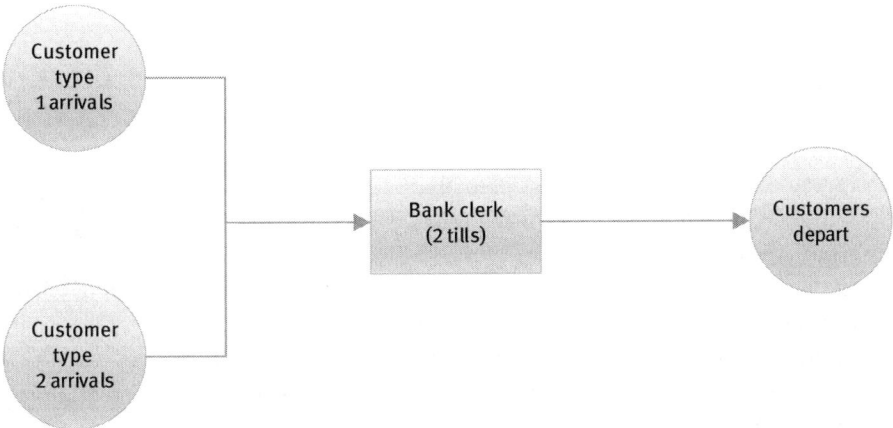

Figure 4.1: Process map of single queue bank clerk simulation.

Building the Bank Clerk Model in Arena

When the Arena system is run, the screen shown in Figure 4.2 should be displayed.

The project bar (to the left of the screen display) contains the modules from which you construct the simulation by dragging them onto the model window. Data can be entered into each module by either double clicking each module to obtain a dialog box or by using the spreadsheet data module window.

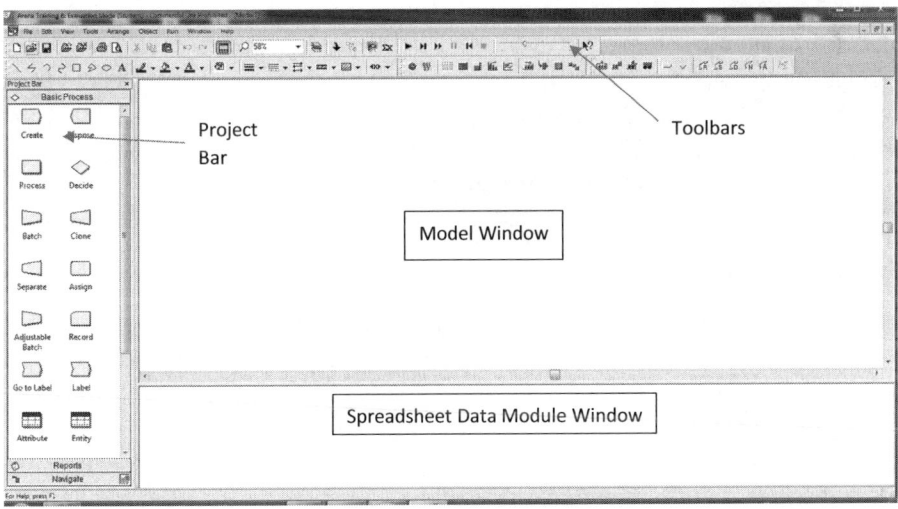

Figure 4.2: Arena BASIC model window.

The four main elements in an Arena simulation are entities, processes, resources and decisions.

Entities

- Entities flow through a network of modules that describe their logical behavior.
- Entities can represent people, materials or information flows in the system being modeled.
- Entities must be created to get them into the model and are disposed of when they leave.
- Entities are distinguished by their attributes.
- Attributes could refer to the characteristics of the people, parts or any other information regarding the entity that can be expressed in numerical form.
- Attributes are useful as their value stays with the entity as it moves through the model and their value can be used at any time by the model.
- Values that are not associated with an individual entity are defined as variables.
- Attributes and variables can be held in an array.

Modeling Entities

Not all entities or entity types in the real system will usually need to be modeled in the simulation. We will often model product types as different entity types if they have different process routes for example, but some product types may be aggregated if they are processed in a similar fashion. Customers may also be grouped into different types if they require directing to resources based on conditional decisions. Customers arriving in groups that are processed as a group may be treated as a single entity within the model. If the customers are processed individually they may be treated as individuals with a small interarrival time to simplify modeling. Alternatively the model software can generate group arrivals by specifying both the interarrival time and batch size of the arrival.

Processes

- Processes represent an activity that takes place over a period of time.
- When an entity arrives at a process, it will try to obtain (seize) the resource necessary to undertake that process.
- If no resource is required for the activity, then the process is modeled as a delay.
- If a resource is required for the activity, then the process is modeled by a seize–delay–release resource procedure.
- If a resource is not available, the entity waits in a queue.

- When the resource is available the length of time the entity uses the resource is the delay.
- The entity releases the resource when processing is complete.

Modeling Processes

Real processes are often merged or grouped into a single modeled process if that provides the detail necessary. Processes that do not consume a resource (such as storage time when the storage resource is not modeled) are represented by a delay. Processes that do consume a resource must request the resources required from a resource pool. Multiple resources may be needed to undertake a process (such as two members of the staff for an interview). The process can not commence until suitable resources are available. Different processes can be assigned priorities over other processes for the use of resources.

Resources

- Resources can be named.
- Have a capacity (number of identical units of this resource).
- Can have a schedule (how many available when).
- Resources can be animated as part of the simulation display.

Modeling Resources

Resources that enable processes can be modeled with either a capacity that varies with time (a schedule) or a fixed capacity. A fixed capacity resource can simply represent a fixed number of staff members who are available to serve any process in the model that requires them. A schedule will alter staff availability in time buckets (for example for 15 minutes) to represent a staff rotation. Resource availability can also be affected by planned maintenance and equipment failures both of which can be modeled by changing the capacity of a resource at the appropriate time. Consumable resources such as energy use may be modeled using variables. Some types of resources are modeled in Arena using transporters for material handling equipment and conveyors.

Decisions

- Decisions control the flow of individual entities.
- Decisions can use either chance or conditional rules to direct flow.
- Chance rules are represented as a percentage.
- Conditional rules are represented as an if–then–else rule.

Modeling Decisions

If conditional rules are understood, then decisions can be modeled in this way. Conditional rules may take any form and be quite complex; for example the rules around scheduling parts in a factory may incorporate many variables. Some of the most used conditional rules include checking the smallest queue for customer service operations, checking resources in turn, and choosing the first resource that is available in a manufacturing option or simply choosing a flow path at random. If conditional rules are not used, then a probabilistic approach is taken based on historical data. Decisions are also required when entities are held in queues. In this case when allocating entities in a queue to a process, various decision rules can be employed, such as the order in which the entity joined the queue; for example the FIFO (first in, first out) rule. In addition an entity attribute value can be set and the decision can be made based on that value. For example, customers assigned as priority customers can jump the queue.

In Arena, the simulation model is represented by Arena modules that are dragged onto the main simulation screen from the project bar (Figure 4.2). Double clicking on these modules generates a menu screen for entry of the data that defines the module parameters. There are many modules available; the descriptions for the main modules for entities, processes, resources and decisions are shown in Figure 4.3 and can be found in the Basic Process panel.

Figure 4.4 shows the modules required for the single queue bank clerk simulation placed on the flowchart view screen. Two create modules are used to generate the two types of bank customers. Two assign modules are used to set the process time for each customer type. A process module is used to represent the bank clerk resource. A dispose module is used to simulate the customers leaving the bank. The modules will automatically connect together to define the relationship between the modules if they are entered on the screen in order from left to right. If the modules are not connected by the connecting lines, they can be connected manually using the connect button ▧ on the toolbar. Click on the connect button and the cursor will change to a cross hair. Then click on the exit point (▶) of the first module and click on the entry point (■) of the module you wish to connect to. The connection will then be made. To remove a connection, click on the connection line to highlight it and press the Del key on your keyboard.

Double click on the create 1 module and the dialog box will appear as in Figure 4.5. For the name parameter, enter customer type 1 arrivals. For the type parameter, select Random(Expo) and for the value parameter enter 15. For units select the minutes option. The module will then create customer arrivals that are exponentially distributed, with a mean of 15 minutes. Press OK to enter the data. Note that the data is also shown in the spreadsheet data module window that provides an alternative way to enter and update the module data. Repeat this for the create 2

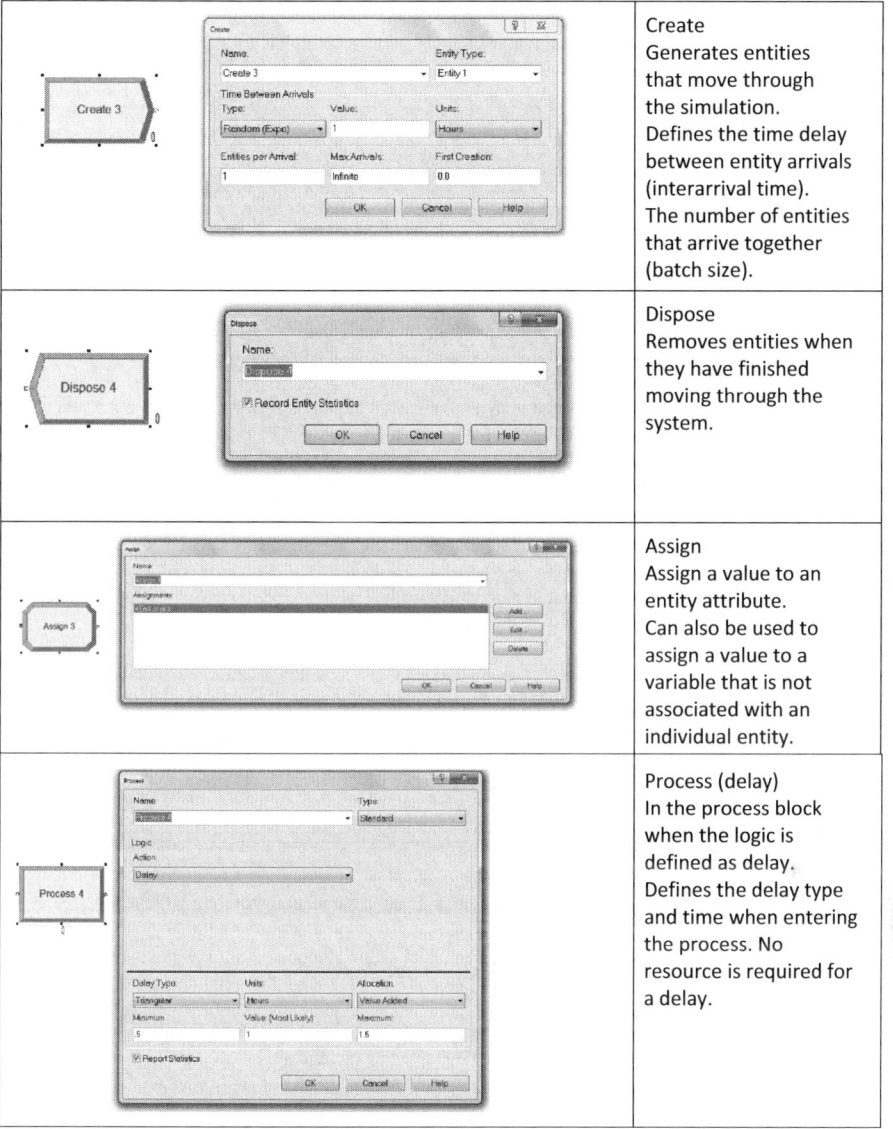

Figure 4.3: Arena Modules.

module, but give it the name customer type 2 arrivals, enter a value parameter of 10, enter units as minutes to give a customer arrival rate with an exponential distribution with a mean of 10 minutes.

Double click on the Assign 1 module and then click on the add button. A dialog box will appear as shown in Figure 4.6. Select attribute for the type parameter. Enter processtime for attribute name and UNIFORM(2,6) for the new value. This sets

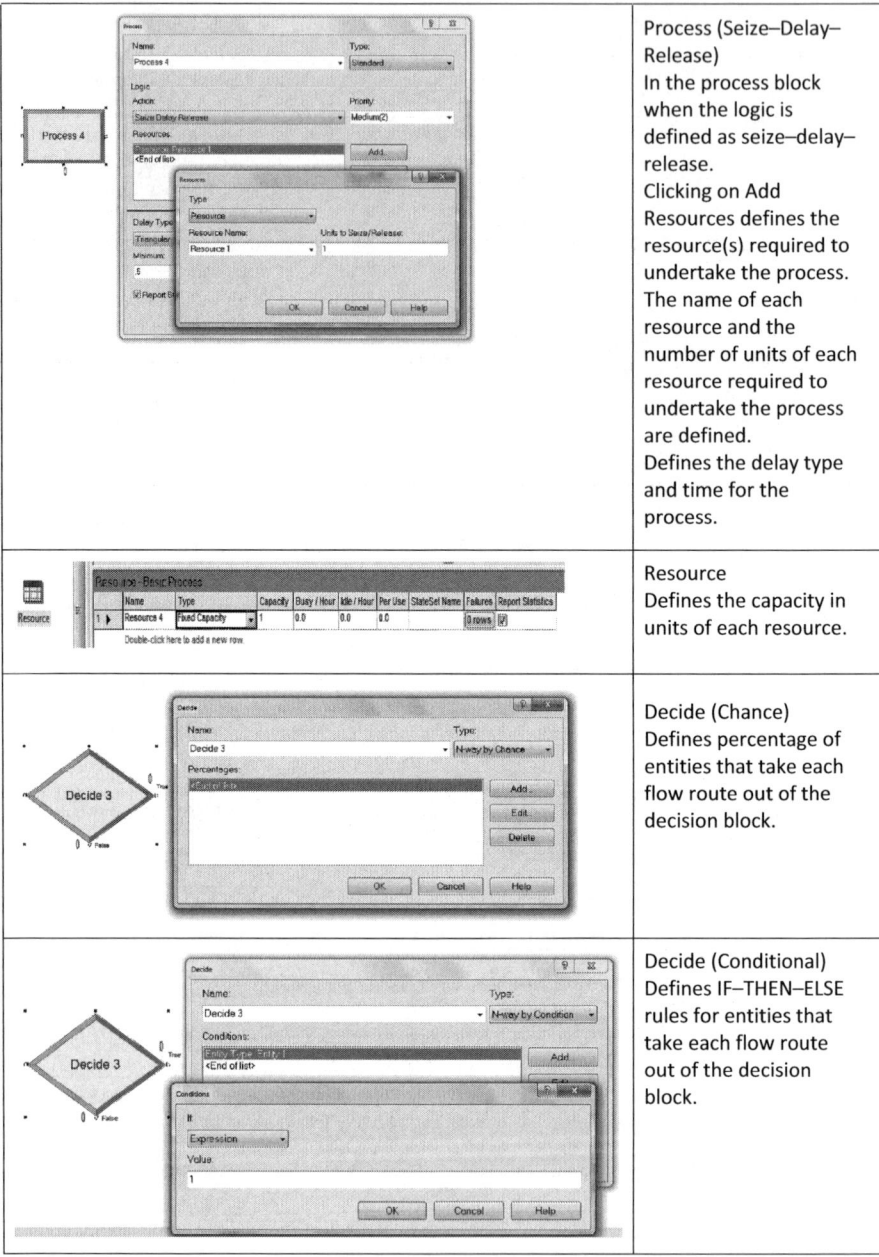

Figure 4.3 (continued)

the attribute value (that is carried with the entity/customer through the simulation) called processtime to a uniform distribution, with a lower bound of 2 minutes and

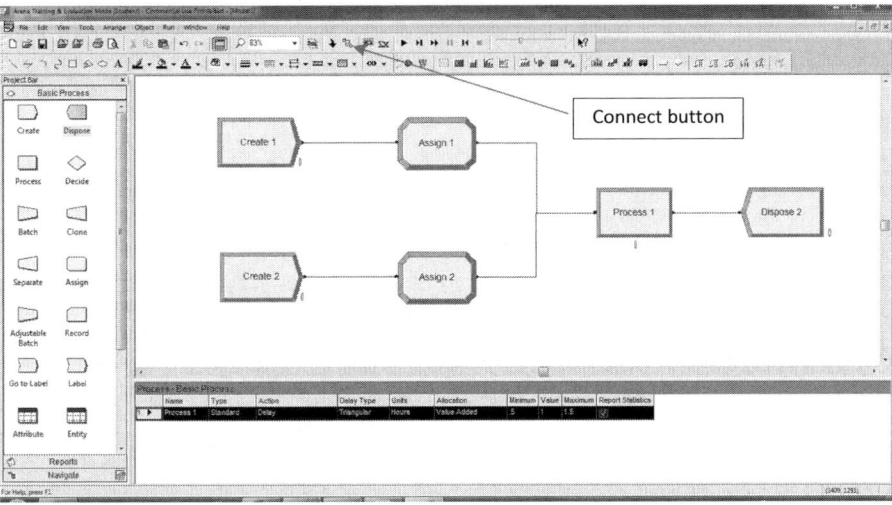

Figure 4.4: Enter the modules on the flowchart view screen.

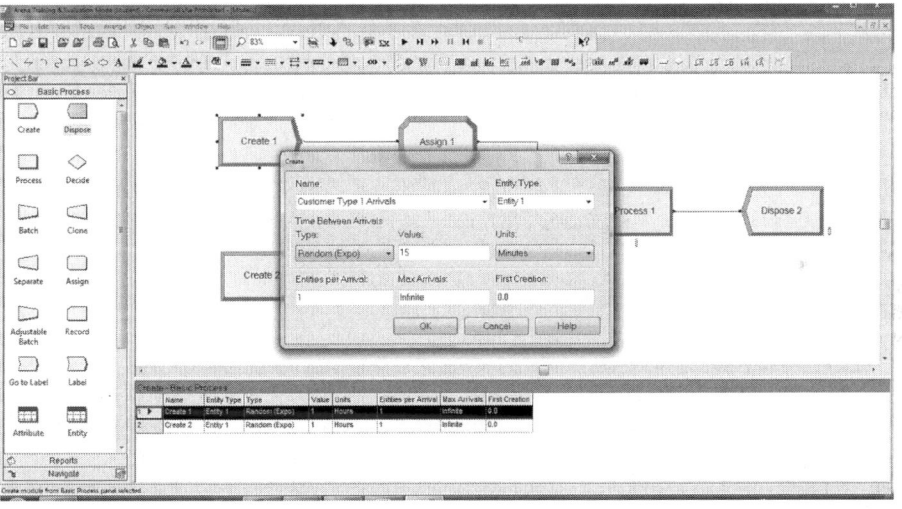

Figure 4.5: Enter the create module parameters.

an upper bound of 6 minutes. Repeat the same for the assign 2 module but set the processtime attribute to UNIFORM(4,10).

The process module can be used to represent a resource such as a machine or a person. In this case, it represents the bank clerk. Double click on the process module to observe the dialog box as shown in Figure 4.7. Set the seize–delay–release option from the action menu. Click on the add button and enter bank clerk for the resource name. Select the constant option for the delay type. Select the units as minutes and

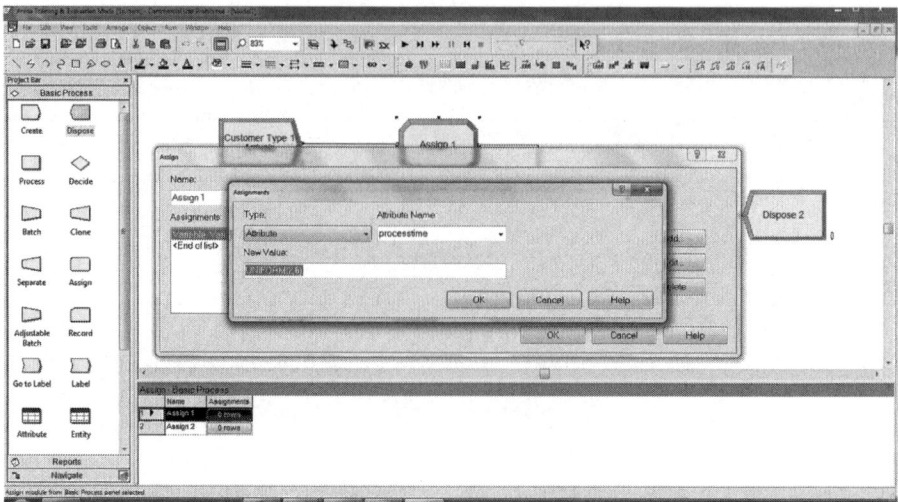

Figure 4.6: Assign the processtime attribute.

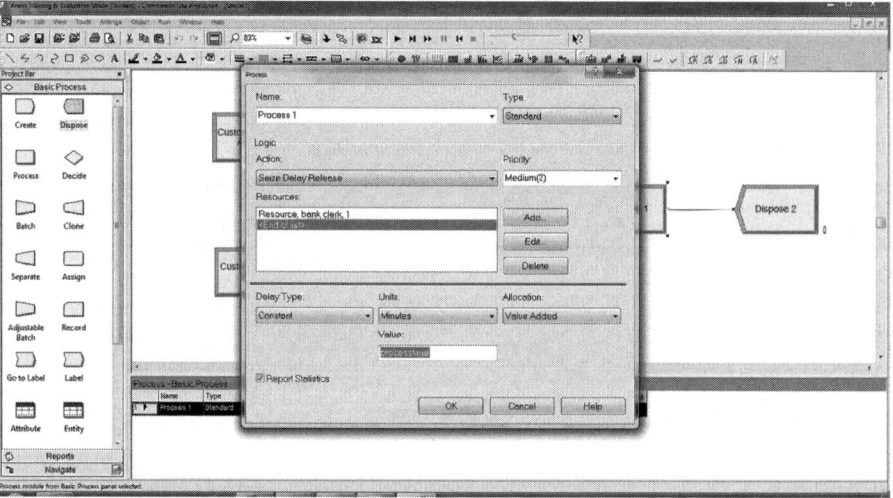

Figure 4.7: Entering the process module parameters.

enter processtime for the value parameter. This sets the process duration as the value assigned to this attribute for each customer type in the previous assign module.

Click on the resource module in the project bar. A spreadsheet view of the currently defined resources should appear in the model window spreadsheet view (Figure 4.8). A bank clerk resource was automatically created when this was entered in the process module. Change the capacity entry from 1 to 2 to fix a maximum capacity level of two bank clerks.

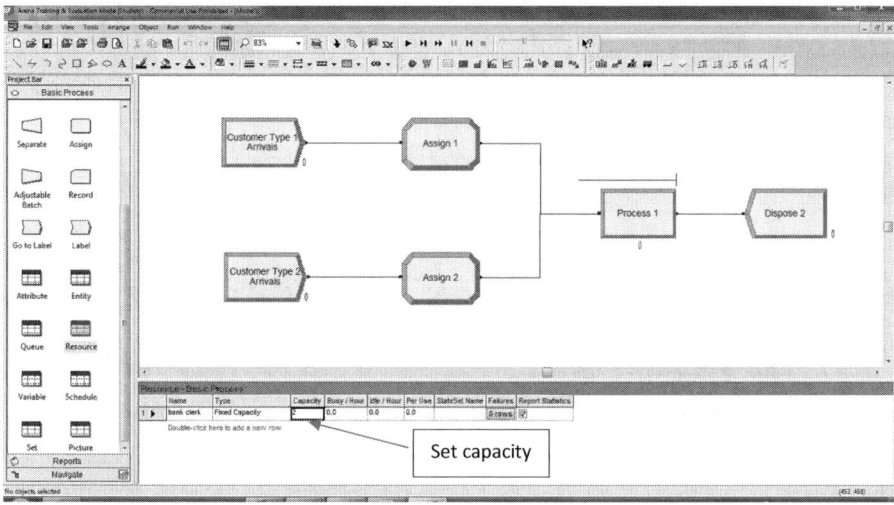

Figure 4.8: Setting the bank clerk capacity.

Select the Run/Setup/Replication parameters option from the menu bar. The dialog box shown in Figure 4.9 should appear. Set the replication length to 480 and all unit entries as minutes.

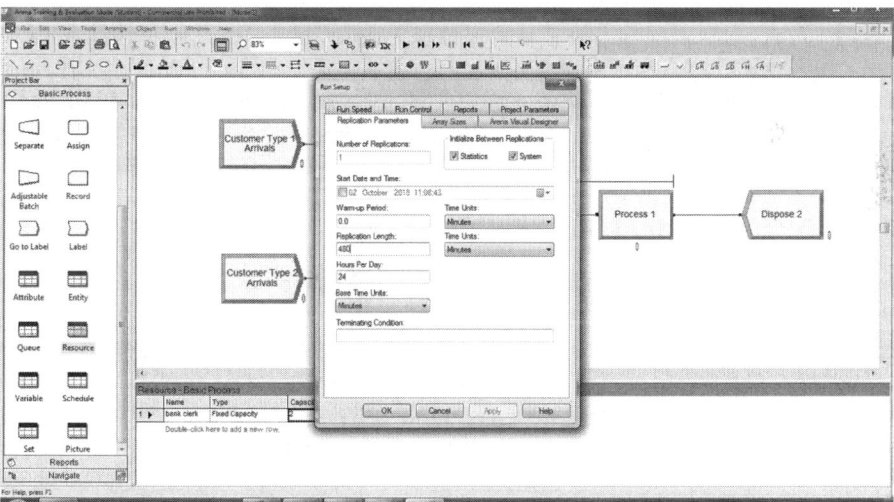

Figure 4.9: Setting the simulation run length.

A variety of reports are available in Arena. In order to provide information on the customer time in the system, select the Run/Setup/Reports option (Figure 4.10). Select the default report as SIMAN Summary Report (.out file).

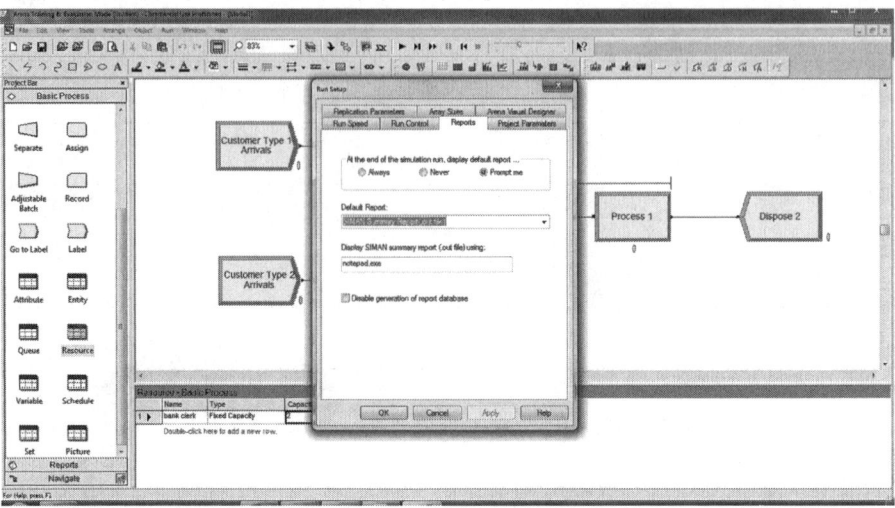

Figure 4.10: Setting the output report format.

Run the model by clicking on the run icon (▶) on the run control toolbar. If there are any errors in your model, a message will appear on the screen, indicating the source of the problem. When you have a functional model, you will see the entities moving through the system as the model runs through time. You can control the speed of the display using the < and > keys. The run can be paused by pressing the Esc key or using the run control toolbar. The simulation can be stopped at any time using the stop icon (■) on the run control toolbar. When the simulation has completed its run, the output report (Figure 4.11) will appear.

Although the report shown in Figure 4.11 is particular to the Arena software, most simulation software will present simulation output data in these categories and so is now explained.

The top of Figure 4.11 reports the replication or run time of the simulation. In this case, this also defines the time over which the output statistics below cover, but the statistics collection period may be defined as less than the runtime if required.

What Arena calls 'Tally variables' are more generally known as observational data. Here, each observation is treated as an individual occurrence and is equally weighted (i.e. the time over which this occurrence happens is not taken into consideration). So for Figure 4.11 to calculate the average time in system (labelled as Entity 1.Totaltime) would entail summing the 70 observations for time in the system and dividing by the number of observations (70). Table 4.1 presents the following observational data by default for the bank clerk simulation.

The next section, Discrete-Change variables, is more generally known as time-weighted or time-persistent data. Here the time over which the occurrence happened is taken into account. To do this the simulation records the current value of

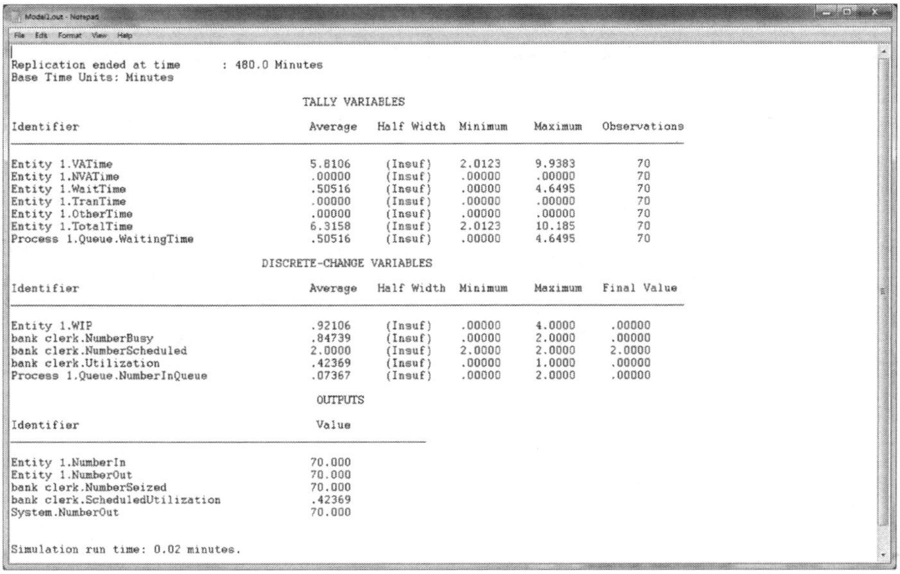

```
Model.Out - Notepad
File  Edit  Format  View  Help

Replication ended at time    : 480.0 Minutes
Base Time Units: Minutes
                              TALLY VARIABLES
Identifier                    Average   Half Width  Minimum   Maximum   Observations

Entity 1.VATime                5.8106   (Insuf)     2.0123    9.9383    70
Entity 1.NVATime                .00000  (Insuf)      .00000    .00000   70
Entity 1.WaitTime               .50516  (Insuf)      .00000   4.6495    70
Entity 1.TranTime               .00000  (Insuf)      .00000    .00000   70
Entity 1.OtherTime              .00000  (Insuf)      .00000    .00000   70
Entity 1.TotalTime             6.3158   (Insuf)     2.0123   10.185     70
Process 1.Queue.WaitingTime     .50516  (Insuf)      .00000   4.6495    70

                          DISCRETE-CHANGE VARIABLES
Identifier                    Average   Half Width  Minimum   Maximum   Final Value

Entity 1.WIP                    .92106  (Insuf)      .00000   4.0000     .00000
bank clerk.NumberBusy           .84739  (Insuf)      .00000   2.0000     .00000
bank clerk.NumberScheduled     2.0000   (Insuf)     2.0000    2.0000    2.0000
bank clerk.Utilization          .42369  (Insuf)      .00000   1.0000     .00000
Process 1.Queue.NumberInQueue   .07367  (Insuf)      .00000   2.0000     .00000

                              OUTPUTS
Identifier                    Value

Entity 1.NumberIn             70.000
Entity 1.NumberOut            70.000
bank clerk.NumberSeized       70.000
bank clerk.ScheduledUtilization  .42369
System.NumberOut              70.000

Simulation run time: 0.02 minutes.
```

Figure 4.11: Arena simulation report.

Table 4.1: Arena Report Tally Variables.

Identifier	Description
Entity 1.VATime	'value added' time that the entity type entity 1 spends in the system. In this model this represents processing, i.e. non-queuing time.
Entity 1.NVATime	'non value added' time. Not defined in this model.
Entity 1.WaitTime	Wait or queuing time
Entity 1.Other Time	Other categories of time. Not defined in this model.
Entity 1.TotalTime	The summation of all time categories. Also termed flow time.
Process 1.Queue.WaitingTime	The time each entity spends in the process 1.queue.

the variable and the last point in time that the variable changed value. When the variable value changes again the variable value is multiplied by the time it was at the value, and then added to the cumulated value for this statistic. If the value of the variable was plotted over time this calculation would represent the area under the plot line. So for Figure 4.11 to calculate the process 1.queue.numberinqueue value would entail recording the time period for each number in queue value and summing these values. Table 4.2 presents the following time-weighted data values by default for the bank clerk simulation (Table 4.3).

Table 4.2: Arena Report Discrete-Change Variables.

Identifier	Description
Entity 1.WIP	The entity Work In Progress (WIP) or number of entities in the system.
Bank.clerk.NumberBusy	The utilization as a proportion of the total number of bank clerks
Bank.clerk.numberscheduled	The number of bank clerks (capacity)
Bank.clerk.utilization	The utilization of a bank clerk
Process 1.queue.numberinqueue	The number of entities in the process 1.queue

The final section named Outputs reports various additional measures by default such as the number of entities entering and leaving the system and measures regarding the bank clerk resource (Table 4.3).

Table 4.3: Arena Report Outputs.

Identifier	Description
Entity 1.NumberIn	The number of entity type entity 1 created
Entity 1.NumberOut	The number of entity type entity 1 disposed
Bank clerk.numberseized	The number of times the bank clerk resource is seized
Bank clerk.scheduledutilization	The utilization of the bank clerk resource
System.numberout	The number of all entity types disposed.

For each identifier the following statistics are defined for observational and time-weighted output measures (Table 4.4). Arena uses the terms as shown for the tally variables. For example, TMAX(process 1.queue.waitingtime) collects the maximum value over a simulation run for the waiting time in the queue named process 1. DAVG(Entity 1.WIP) collects the average value over a simulation run for the work-in-progress or number in the system of entity type entity 1.

Note that the Identifier names for entity types, processes and resources are set in the model. If multiple entity types, processes, queues and resources are defined in the model, then these will automatically be reported on in the simulation output report. Any other elements or variables that require reporting can be included in the summary report. Note also that any variables can be plotted during runtime using the animation facilities of the software.

In the bank clerk simulation, referring to Figure 4.11, the average time in the system for the customer (Entity 1.TotalTime) is given as 5.81 minutes, with a minimum

Table 4.4: Statistics for Arena Tally and Discrete-Change Variables.

Statistic	Description	Tally	Discrete-Change
Average	The average value (time weighted for time-weighted measures)	TAVG	DAVG
Half Width	The half-width of the confidence interval at 95%. A value of Insuf (Insufficient) or Correlated means that the simulation run is not long enough to provide a valid half width estimation.	THALF	DHALF
Minimum	The minimum value recorded during the simulation run	TMIN	DMIN
Maximum	The maximum value recorded during the simulation run	TMAX	DMAX

time of 2.01 minutes and a maximum time of 9.94 minutes. The maximum customer waiting time (Process 1.Queue.WaitingTime) is given as 4.65 minutes. The maximum number of customers in a queue (Process 1.Queue.NumberInQueue) is given as 2. The bank clerk utilization or percentage of busy time (bank clerk.utilization) is given as 0.42 or 42% utilization for each bank clerk. The maximum number of customers in the bank at any one time (Entity 1.WIP) is given as 4 customers and the number of customers (observations) that have passed through the bank in the 480 minutes run time is 70. Thus, this very simple model provides us with a variety of performance measures for our bank clerk system.

The bank clerk simulation will now be expanded to cover the modeling of a decision. In this version of the bank clerk simulation, there are two bank clerks available. On entry to the bank, the customer has a choice of bank clerk, so it will be assumed that they will pick the bank clerk with the queue containing the lowest number of waiting customers. The above scenarios can be represented with a process map as follows (Figure 4.12).

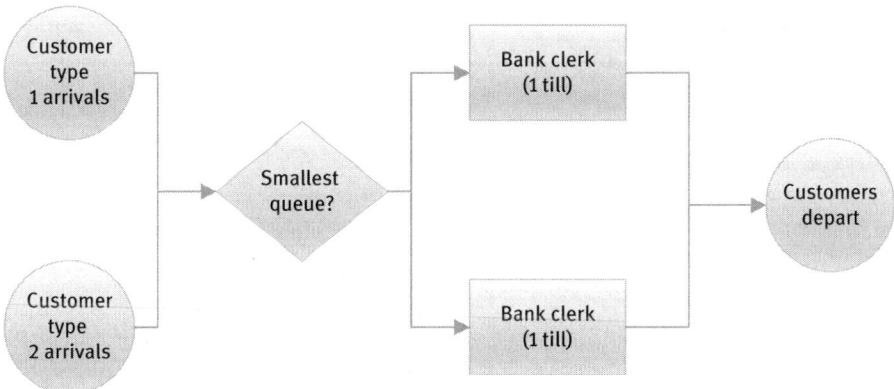

Figure 4.12: Process map of decision-based bank clerk simulation.

To implement the dual queue system, use the single queue model discussed in the previous section and make the following changes. Delete the connecting lines between the assign modules and the process module by clicking on the lines and pressing the Del key on the keyboard. Add a further process module and a decide module. Click on the connect button ■ on the toolbar and connect the additional modules as shown in Figure 4.13.

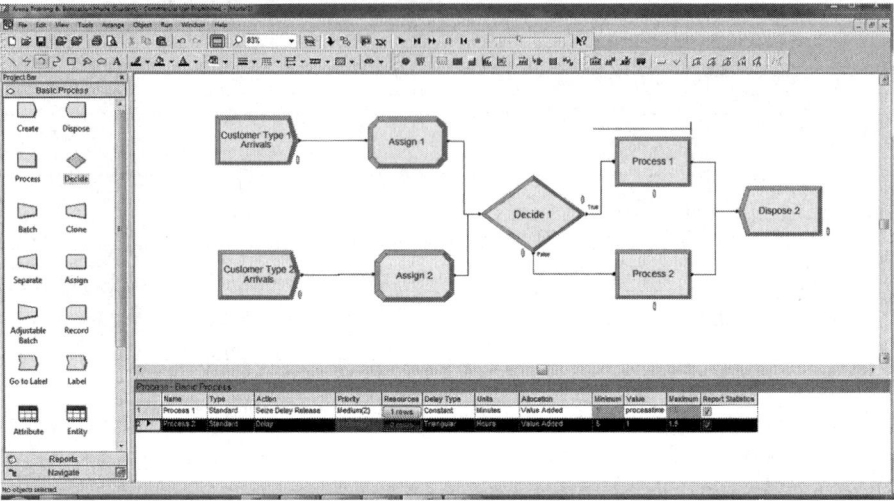

Figure 4.13: Adding the decide and process modules.

The next step is to define the parameters of the two new modules placed on the screen. Arena decisions can be represented by either an If–Then–Else conditional formula ("by Conditional" option) or a probability formula using the "by Chance" option. Double click on the decide module and select two-way "by Condition" as the type parameter. For the If parameter, select Expression. For the value parameter, enter the following expression (Figure 4.14).

NQ(process 1.Queue).LT.NQ(process 2.Queue)

This expression demonstrates the use of a conditional logic statement in Arena. The statement NQ(process 1.Queue) means the number in queue of the queue named process 1.Queue. The logical operator .LT. provides a "less than" comparison. (Further logical operators are .GT. that provides a "greater than" comparison and .EQ. checks for equality.) In this case, the formula compares the number of customers in the queue for process 1 and if this is less than the number in the process 2 queue the condition is True and the entity/customer leaves the decide module on the True route. Otherwise the entity/customer leaves on the False route. In

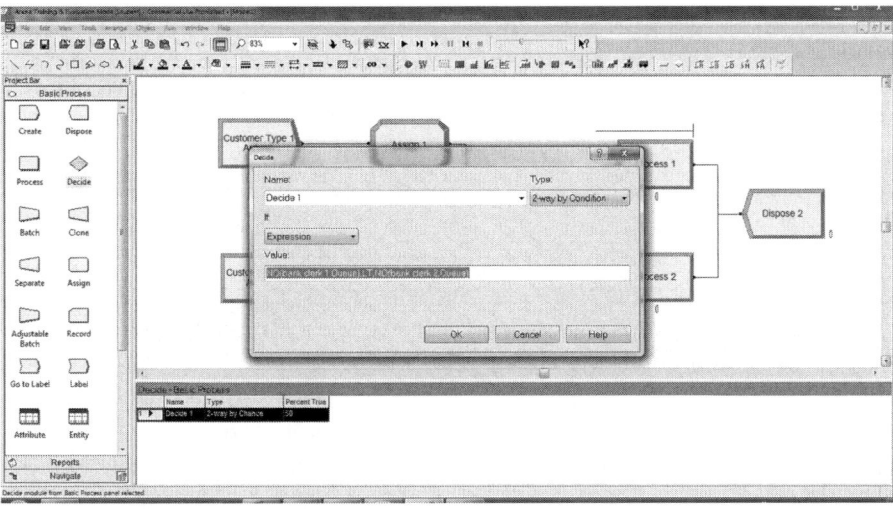

Figure 4.14: Entering the decide module parameters.

this case the True route should connect to process 1 and the False route will connect to process 2.

Finally double click on the process 2 module, select the seize–delay–release option for action and add the resource name bank clerk 2 with a quantity of 1 (Figure 4.15). Select the constant option for the delay type. Select the units as minutes and enter processtime for the value parameter. Finally double click on the process 1 module and change the resource name from bank clerk to bank clerk 1.

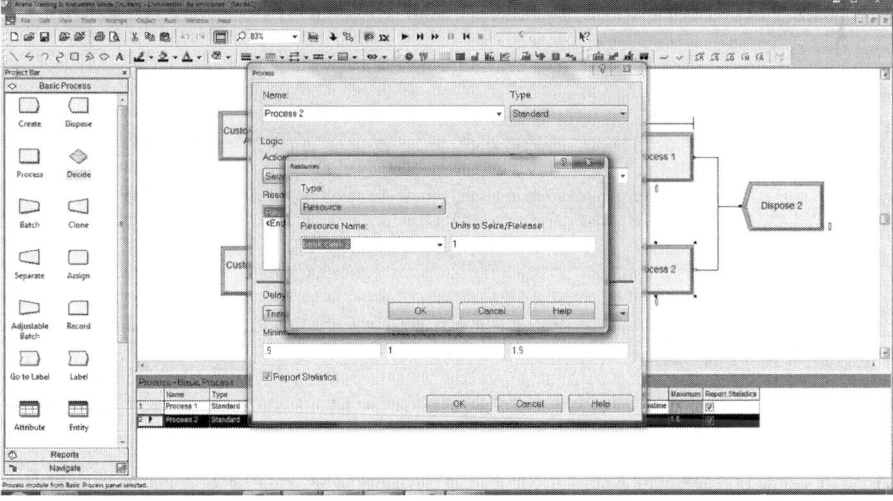

Figure 4.15: Entering the process 2 parameters.

Run the simulation by clicking on the run (►) button on the toolbar. When the simulation has completed, the results screen will be displayed as in Figure 4.16. In this case the average time in system for the customer (Entity 1.TotalTime) is given as 7.62 minutes, with a minimum time of 2.01 minutes and a maximum time of 17.3 minutes. The maximum customer waiting time for process 1 (Process 1.Queue. WaitingTime) is given as 3.01 minutes. The maximum waiting time for process 2 (Process 2.Queue.WaitingTime) is 9.56 minutes. The maximum number of customers in the queue for process 1 (Process 1.Queue.NumberInQueue) is given as 1. The maximum number of customers in the queue for process 2 is given as 2. The bank clerk 1 utilization or percentage of busy time (bank clerk 1. utilization) is given as 0.172 or 17.2% utilization. The bank clerk 2 utilization is given as 0.675 or 67.5% utilization. The maximum number of customers in the bank at any one time (Entity 1.WIP) is given as 5 customers and the number of customers (observations) that have passed through the bank in the 480 minutes run time is 70. Fifty four of these customers have been processed at process 1 and the remaining 16 at process 2.

TALLY VARIABLES

Identifier	Average	Half Width	Minimum	Maximum	Observations
Entity 1.VATime	5.8106	(Insuf)	2.0123	9.9383	70
Entity 1.NVATime	.00000	(Insuf)	.00000	.00000	70
Entity 1.WaitTime	1.8148	(Insuf)	.00000	9.5649	70
Entity 1.TranTime	.00000	(Insuf)	.00000	.00000	70
Entity 1.OtherTime	.00000	(Insuf)	.00000	.00000	70
Entity 1.TotalTime	7.6255	(Insuf)	2.0123	17.313	70
Process 2.Queue.WaitingTime	2.1780	(Insuf)	.00000	9.5649	54
Process 1.Queue.WaitingTime	.58901	(Insuf)	.00000	3.0094	16

DISCRETE-CHANGE VARIABLES

Identifier	Average	Half Width	Minimum	Maximum	Final Value
Entity 1.WIP	1.1120	(Insuf)	.00000	5.0000	.00000
bank clerk.NumberBusy	.00000	(Insuf)	.00000	.00000	.00000
bank clerk.NumberScheduled	2.0000	(Insuf)	2.0000	2.0000	2.0000
bank clerk.Utilization	.00000	(Insuf)	.00000	.00000	.00000
bank clerk 1.NumberBusy	.17219	(Insuf)	.00000	1.0000	.00000
bank clerk 1.NumberScheduled	1.0000	(Insuf)	1.0000	1.0000	1.0000
bank clerk 1.Utilization	.17219	(Insuf)	.00000	1.0000	.00000
bank clerk 2.NumberBusy	.67520	(Insuf)	.00000	1.0000	.00000
bank clerk 2.NumberScheduled	1.0000	(Insuf)	1.0000	1.0000	1.0000
bank clerk 2.Utilization	.67520	(Insuf)	.00000	1.0000	.00000
Process 2.Queue.NumberInQueue	.24503	(Insuf)	.00000	2.0000	.00000
Process 1.Queue.NumberInQueue	.01963	(Insuf)	.00000	1.0000	.00000

OUTPUTS

Identifier	Value
Entity 1.NumberIn	70.000
Entity 1.NumberOut	70.000
bank clerk 1.NumberSeized	16.000
bank clerk 1.ScheduledUtilization	.17219

Figure 4.16: Results screen for Arena dual queue model.

We now provide animation facilities to the dual queue bank clerk simulation. Although we do not need to add animation features to the simulation to generate the results and undertake simulation experimentation, animation provides a useful validation tool to check model behavior and also provides a user-friendly demonstration tool for decision makers.

In order to animate entities (e.g., people, materials) in a model, Arena uses the concepts of stations and routes. Stations define the start and end points on the screen for movement and the routes define the path taken on the screen by entities when moving from one station to the next. Stations and routes are program modules found in the Advanced Transfer template. Load in the "Advanced Transfer" template panel in Arena by selecting the Template Panel Attach option from the menu and selecting "Advanced Transfer" from the list (Figure 4.17).

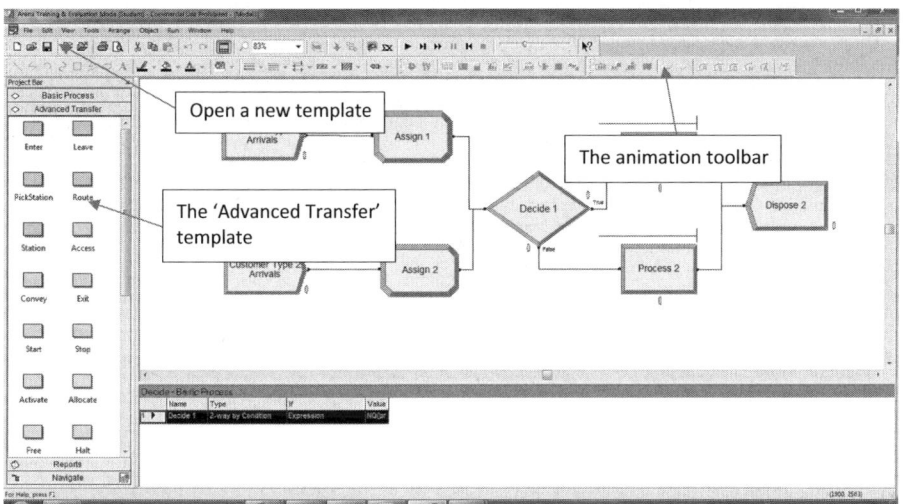

Figure 4.17: Adding the Advanced Transfer Template Panel.

Now we need to specify the stations that entities move through as they pass through the Arena model. To do this delete the connector line between the create module for customer type 1 entities and the assign 1 module. Do the same for the connector between the create module for the type 2 entities and the assign 2 module. Drag a station module from the Advanced Transfer panel between the create and assign module for type 1 customers. Drag another station module for type 2 customers. Connect the lines between the create, station and assign modules for both customer types. Double click on the station module for customer type 1 and define the station type as station and name as Station 1. Do the same for the remaining station naming it Station 2. Your model should look like as that shown in Figure 4.18.

The next stage is to move your entity from either station 1 or station 2, which is the entry point for the customer in the bank to the correct queue for the bank clerks. Delete the connector between the decide module connection and the Process 1. Add a route by dragging a route module from the Advanced Transfer template. Add a station module. Connect the decide module to the route module. Note that there are no connectors from the route module. Connect the station module to the process module for Process 1. Double click on the route module and enter a route time of 5, enter units as minutes, the destination type as station name and station as station 3. Do the same for the Process 2. Delete the else connector on the decide module.

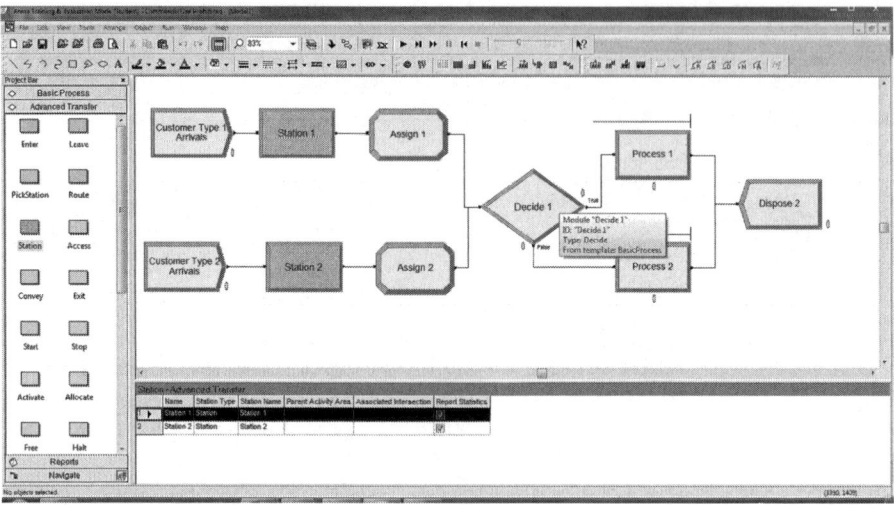

Figure 4.18: Adding the station modules to the simulation.

Add another route and station. This time the route should be to station 4 and the station name should be station 4. The simulation should look as in Figure 4.19.

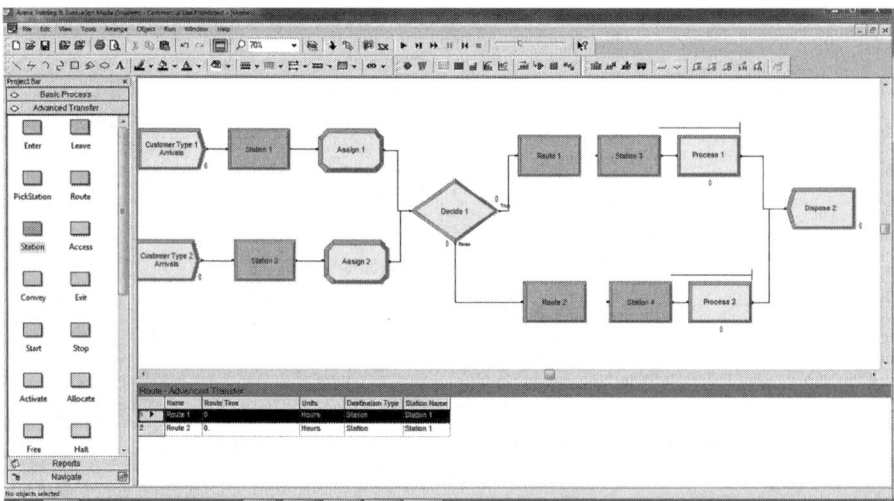

Figure 4.19: Simulation with station and route modules added.

The next stage is to define the entity and resource pictures you will use in your animation. Select the Entity Pictures option from the Edit menu on the toolbar. The pictures available for animation are shown on the left-hand scroll down bar. You can double click on any of these and create your own versions of these pictures.

You can also load in pictures from picture libraries (file extension .plb) using the open button on the right-hand side. Pictures can then be transferred from the library to the simulation using the ≪ button. Click on a picture of your choice from the icons on the right-hand side and click on the ≪ button to transfer it to your simulation. Then click on the picture in the left-hand list and enter the name picture.customer in the value box and enter a size factor of 3 (see Figure 4.20). You can now double click on the picture to enter the picture drawing facility to change the picture or you can select the OK button to proceed. Move to the Entity module in the Basic Process template and in the data spreadsheet window alter the initial picture name to picture.customer. (Pictures of entities can be changed at any time during a simulation run by changing the name of the Entity Picture type attribute.)

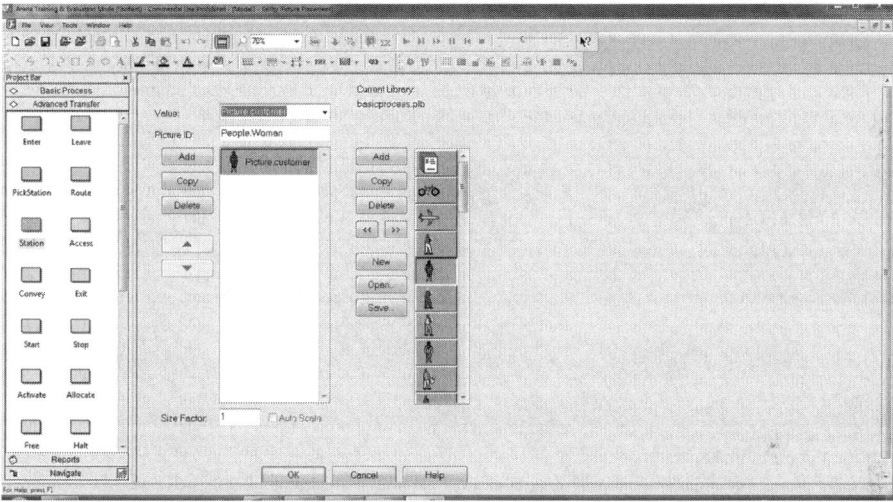

Figure 4.20: Adding an entity picture.

Next click on the resource button on the animate toolbar. Select any picture you like of a bank clerk. Click on the picture and repeatedly click on the ≪ button to transfer it to your simulation for an existing resource to overwrite the idle, busy, inactive and failed states. Enter the name bankclerk1 in the identifier box (Figure 4.21).

It is useful to see the status of the resource change when it is its busy mode. Double click on the busy version of the bank clerk 1 resource picture and you will enter the Arena edit picture screen. Change an aspect of the picture to a different color by clicking on it and choosing the fill option from the animate toolbar (Figure 4.22). Click on the close window button on the top right hand of the screen to close the edit picture screen.

Back in the resource screen change the size factor to 2.5 and tick the seize area box. Click on the close window button on the top right hand of the screen to close.

130 — Chapter 4 Build the Simulation

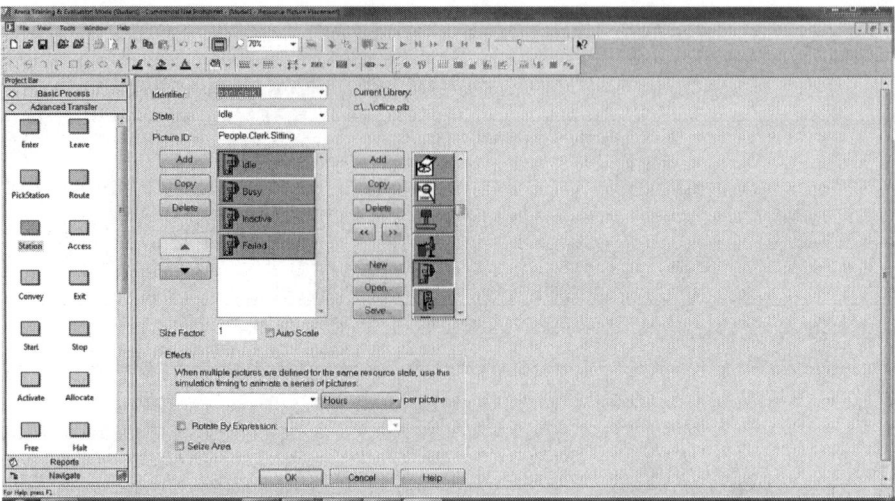

Figure 4.21: Adding a resource picture.

Figure 4.22: Editing the resource icon.

You will have a crosshair cursor on the simulation screen. Click the left button to place your resource on the view screen. Move the seize area to position the entity that is seizing your resource (i.e., the customer who is being served). Repeat the above operation to create another resource, but this time enter the name bankclerk2 in the identifier box.

You can now design your animation display. Move somewhere away from the Arena model on your screen and drag your bank clerk 1 and bank clerk 2 resource pictures to an appropriate location. You will now define the movement of the entities to the bank clerks. Select the station option from the animate transfer toolbar. Select identifier as station 1. Place the station at the entry point for customers. Repeat the same for station 2 (this will be next to station 1 as all customers enter the bank at the same location). Select the station option again and place the station 3 next to your bank clerk 1 resource picture. Repeat for station 4 next to bank clerk 2. Select the route icon from the animate transfer toolbar and click on station 1, then click as required to define the path, finally clicking on station 3. Repeat for the routes for station 1 to station 4, station 2 to station 3 and station 2 to station 4. This defines all possible routes that entities could take in the current simulation. The animation screen should look as shown in Figure 4.23.

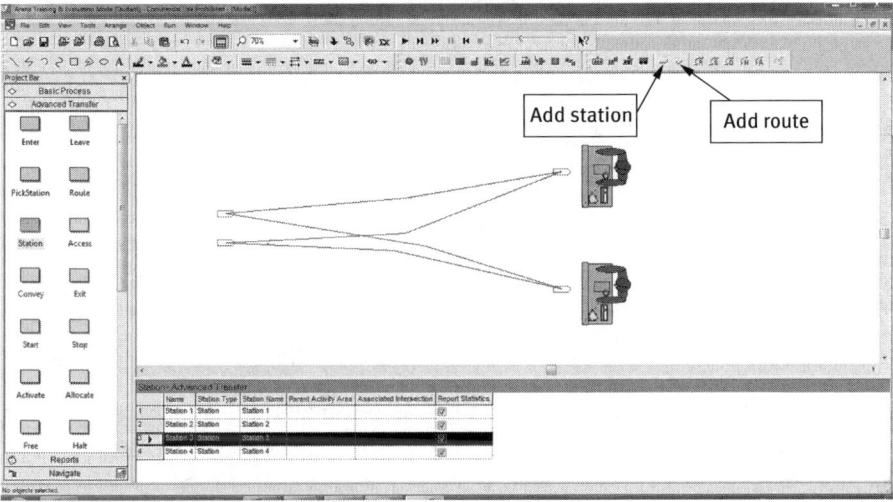

Figure 4.23: Animation display showing stations, routes and resources.

Now you can add other elements to the animation such as queues and counters. The queue displays will be on your flow version of your model above the process modules. If they are then drag each queue symbol adjacent to its resource, i.e. process 1 queue should be in front of bank clerk 1 resource. If you have no queues displayed at present, you can add queues using the queue option on the animate toolbar. You can add counters using the variables option on the animate toolbar. You can add counters next to each bank clerk for customers processed by selecting the "Process 1.NumberOut" expression from the list. It may also be useful to display the queue size next to each queue (the queue size may be too large to be displayed using the animation). Select the variables option from the animate toolbar and enter the expression NQ(Process 1.queue). Any other variables can be displayed using the variables option. You can display the simulation runtime using the clock option on the animate toolbar. Choose the digital display option and a start time of 9.00. Finally you can add background graphics (which are not animated) using the draw toolbar that lets you draw lines, boxes, shapes and text. You can add the background before the animated elements if you wish. Your display should now look as shown in Figure 4.24.

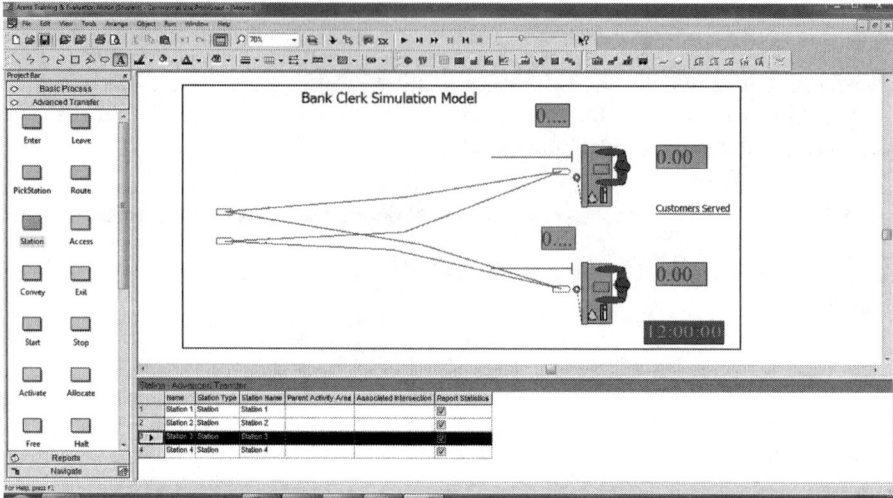

Figure 4.24: The animated bank clerk simulation.

Run the simulation and you should get an image as in Figure 4.25.

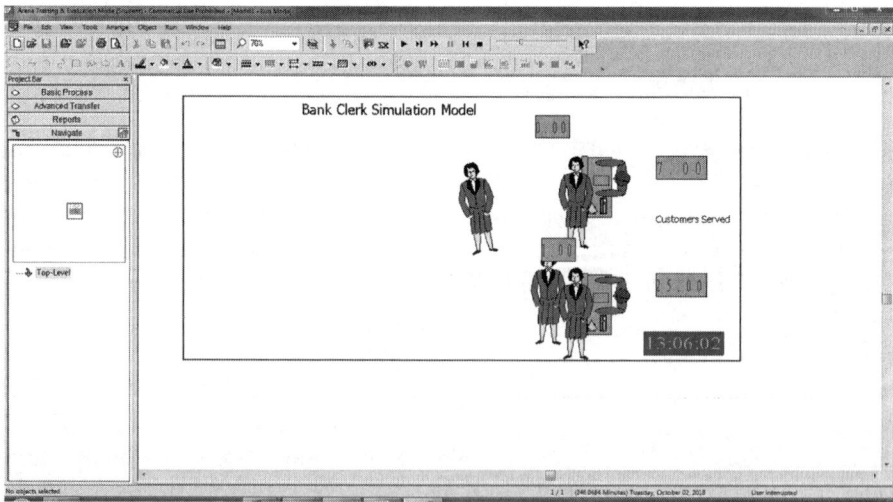

Figure 4.25: Running the animated bank clerk simulation.

Figure 4.25 is obviously a (very!) basic example of the kind of animation that is possible in Arena. The example does show how Arena separates the model flow version of the simulation (which is all that is needed to report results) from the animation display.

Building the Bank Clerk Model in Simio

When the Simio version 11 system is run, the screen display shown in Figure 4.26 should be displayed.

The ribbon across the top of the screen has a number of tabs that collect together commands into logical groups. Tabs are included for run commands and view options. Below the ribbon there is a further series of tabs called the Project Model tabs that are used to select options regarding the active model. If the Facility Tab is selected as in Figure 4.26, then to the left of the screen the object library is displayed. By default the screen will display the Standard Library and at the bottom of the screen the Project Library. The Properties Window is on the right-hand side of the screen and shows the characteristics of any object or item currently selected. The main area of screen (with grid) is named the Navigation Window. Objects are placed from an Object Library on to the Navigation Window and are defined/edited from the Navigation Window in the Properties Window. To move around the Navigation Window, hold down the left mouse button and move the mouse. To zoom in and out of the Navigation Window, hold down the right mouse button and move the mouse.

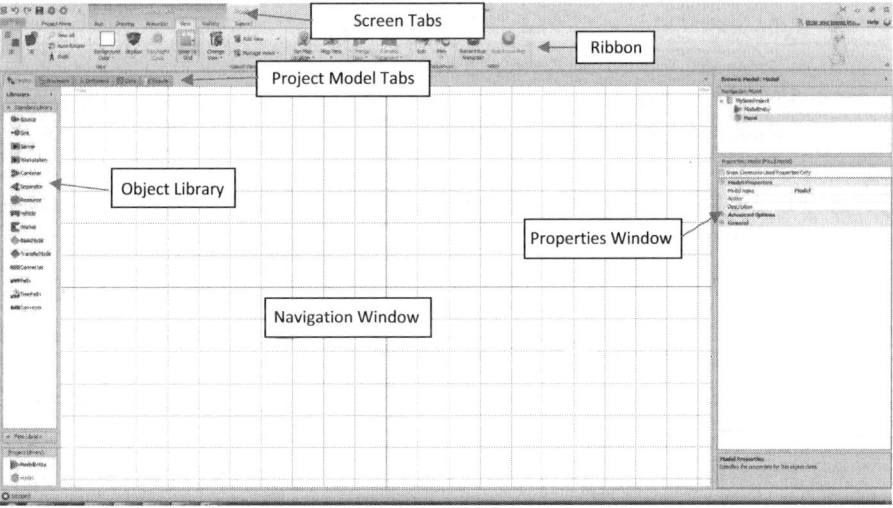

Figure 4.26: Simio simulation screen display.

Before we begin building the simulation to set the time units used in the software, click on the Run tab and select the Units Settings option. Select Minutes for Time Units. Make sure the Facility Tab is selected in the Project Model tabs. To begin the single queue bank clerk simulation drag two source objects, a server object and a sink object on to the Navigation Window. Also draw a model entity object on to the Navigation Screen (Figure 4.27).

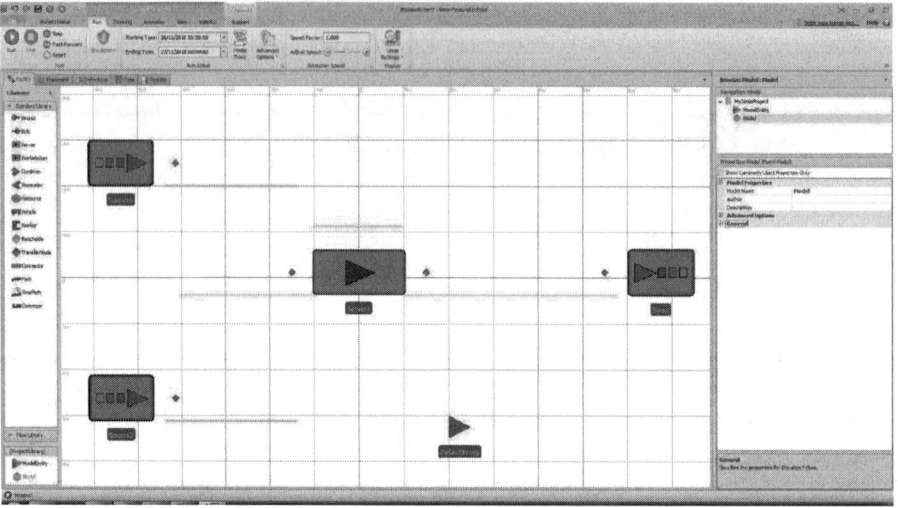

Figure 4.27: Placing the bank clerk simulation objects.

The next step is to connect the objects on the Navigation Screen. To do this, click on the Connector Object in the Standard Library. Then click on the Output Node of Source1 (shown as a blue diamond on the screen) and move the mouse to the input node (grey diamond) for the Server1. A left mouse click will define the connection. Repeat the operation to connect Source2 to Server1 and Server1 to the Sink (Figure 4.28).

Click on the Source1 object and enter Random.Exponential(15) for the Interarrival time in the Source1 Object Properties Window as shown in Figure 4.29. Make sure the Units entry immediately below the Interarrival Time entry is set to minutes.

We can now set the processtime attribute that will be used by the server to set the process time. In Simio in order to define a numeric or string value that we can vary during the simulation, we define a State variable. When a State is added to the main model object, it can be accessed by all the objects within the main model similar to a global variable in Arena. When a State is added to another object, such as the ModelEntity object it is part of that object's definition similar to an attribute variable in Arena. Thus in order to set the processtime variable at the Source1 and Source2 objects, we need to do the following.

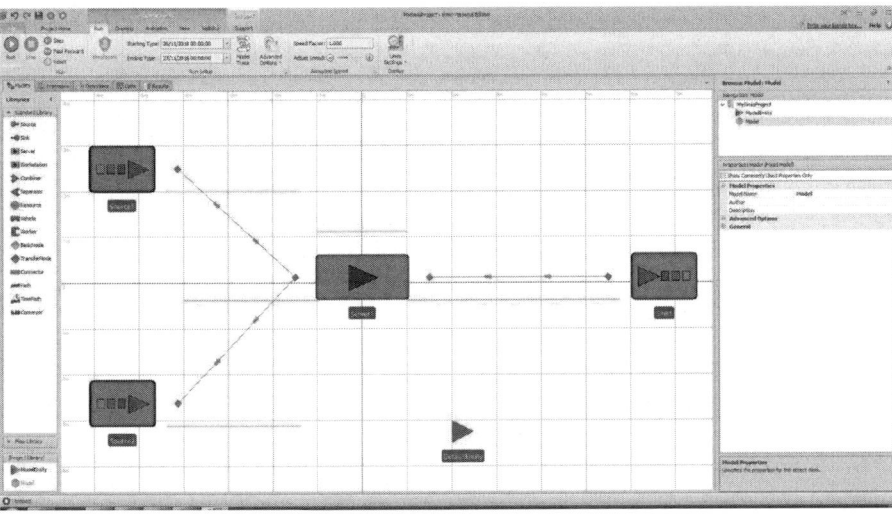

Figure 4.28: Connecting the bank clerk objects with connectors.

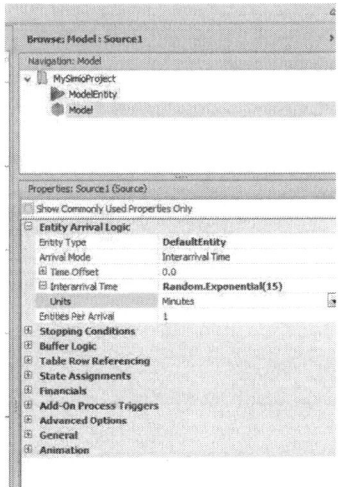

Figure 4.29: Entering the interarrival time property.

In the properties Window in the Navigation section, select the ModelEntity object. Click on the Definitions Tab and Select the States option. Click on the Real option in the Ribbon menu at the top of the screen. In the Properties Window enter ProcessTime for name (Figure 4.30).

Now having a State variable associated with the ModelEntity object (in effect an entity attribute), we can assign it a value. Click on the Model object in the Properties Window and then select the Facilitys tab and Select the Source1 object in the Navigation screen. Select the State Assignments option in the property Window and

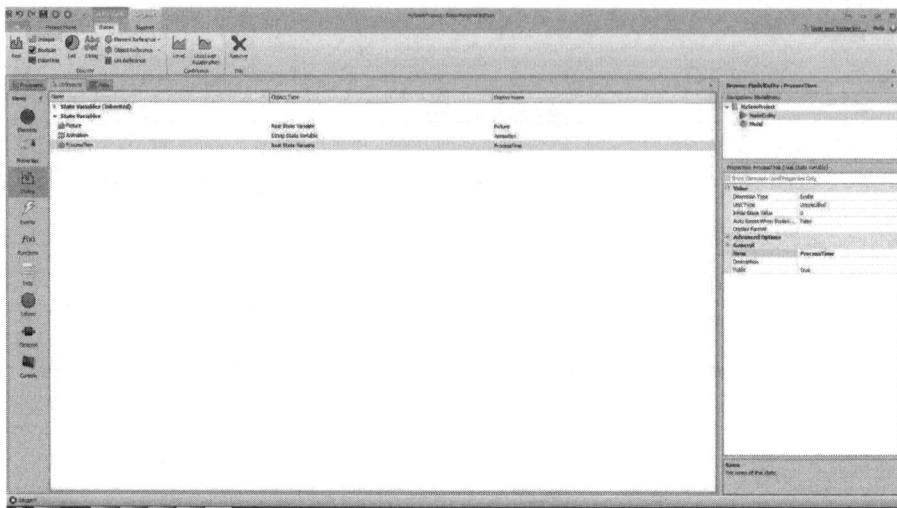

Figure 4.30: Defining the state variables.

Select the "Before Exiting" option and click on the dotted button. A menu will appear. Click on Add and enter ModelEntity.ProcessTime for the State Variable Name and Random.Uniform(2,6) for the New Value (Figure 4.31). Click on close. Now click on Source2 object and repeat, assigning a value of Random.Uniform(4,10).

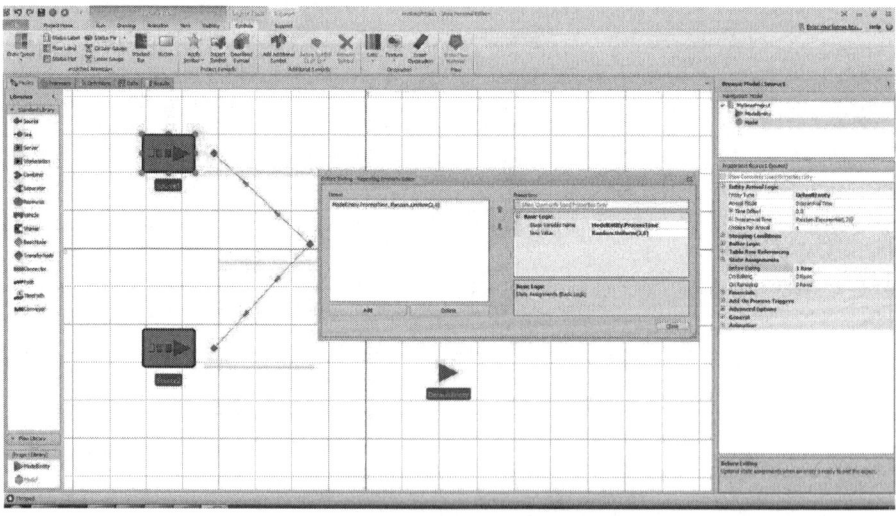

Figure 4.31: Entering the process durations.

Move to the Server1 in the Navigation Window. Enter ModelEntity.ProcessTime for the Processing Time entry in the Properties Window. Make sure the Units entry is set to minutes. Set the Initial Capacity entry in the Properties Window to 2.

We can now run the model. Click on the Run Tab in the Facility Ribbon and enter 480 minutes for the simulation end time. Set the speed factor to 100. Click in the Run button to the left of the tab. The simulation should now run through 480 minutes of simulated time. When the simulation run has finished, click on the Reports tab in the Project Model ribbon and the results will be displayed (Figure 4.32).

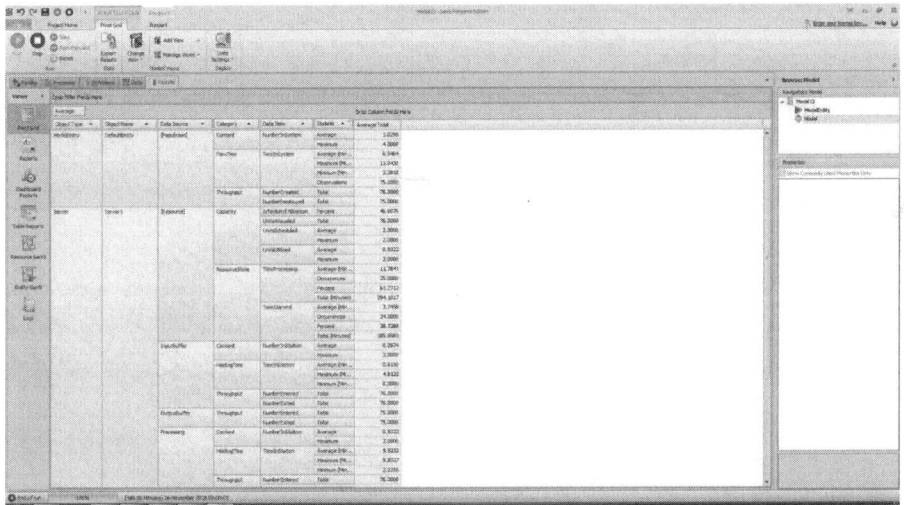

Figure 4.32: Single queue bank clerk simulation results.

The results show that the average time in the system for the customer is 6.55 minutes with a minimum time of 2.28 minutes and a maximum time of 11.04 minutes. The results should be similar (but not the same) as the results for the Arena version of the model shown in Figure 4.11

For the dual queue bank clerk model rather than using the single queue bank clerk model, it is more convenient to create a new model for the dual queue version. Select File and New to create a new model. Drag two Source objects, two Server objects, a sink object and a ModelEntity object to the Navigation Window. Now connect the objects, but unlike the single queue model that used connectors, use the path objects to do this. This allows us to direct the entities leaving the Source objects along different paths to the Server objects (i.e., allows implementation of the smallest queue rule). Source1 should be connected to both Server1 and Server2 as should Source2. Both Servers should be connected to the Sink. The model is shown in Figure 4.33.

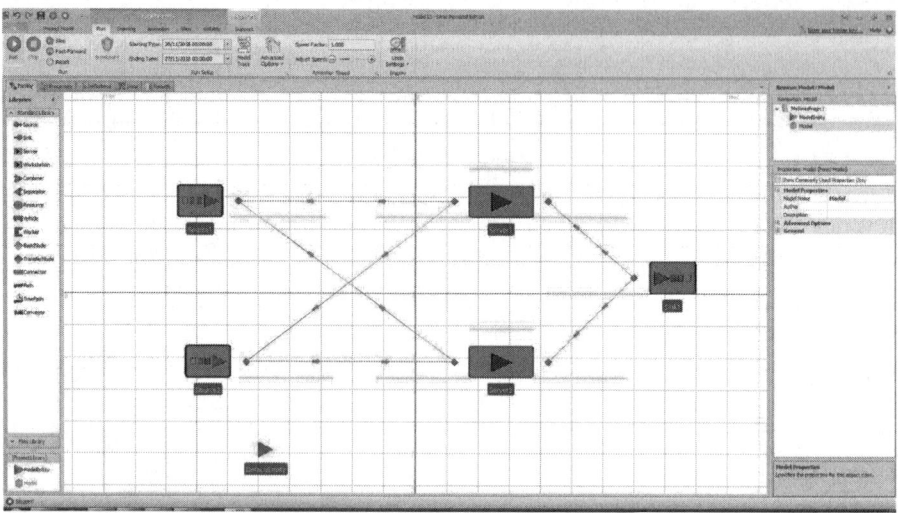

Figure 4.33: Connecting the bank clerk objects with paths.

Enter the interarrival rates as in the single queue model (Exponential (10) for Server1 and Exponential (15) for Server 2). Define processtime as a State Variable (in ModelEntity) and set the before Exiting State Assignment for processtime for Source1 and Source2. The value is Random.Uniform(2,6) for Source1 and Random.Uniform(4,10) for Source2.

We can now direct customers to the server with the smallest queue size for our dual queue model. We need to set up a list of destinations from which we can choose our destination. To do this select the Definitions tab and select the List option. Click on the Node option in the ribbon at the top of the screen. Give the node the name Servers in the Properties Window. Click on the Node grid and select from the pulldown menu the Input@Server1 option. Click on the Node grid again and select the Input@Server2 option. If further destinations are possible, they can be easily added here. For the two server bank clerk, the screen is as shown in Figure 4.34.

Click on the Facility Tab to see the model. Move to the Server1 in the Navigation Window. Enter ModelEntity.ProcessTime for the Processing Time entry in the Properties Window. Make sure the Units entry is set to minutes. The Initial Capacity entry in the Properties Window should be 1. Click on the output node for Server1 (named Output@Source1). In the properties Window, select Entity Destination and select the Select from List option. Select Node List Name and select the Servers option that should appear on the pulldown menu if it has been defined previously. For Selection Goal, select Smallest Value. For Selection expression enter Candidate.Node.AssociatedStationLoad. Note the default value is Candidate.Node.AssociatedStationOverload so that will need changing. The Properties Window should look as shown in Figure 4.35.

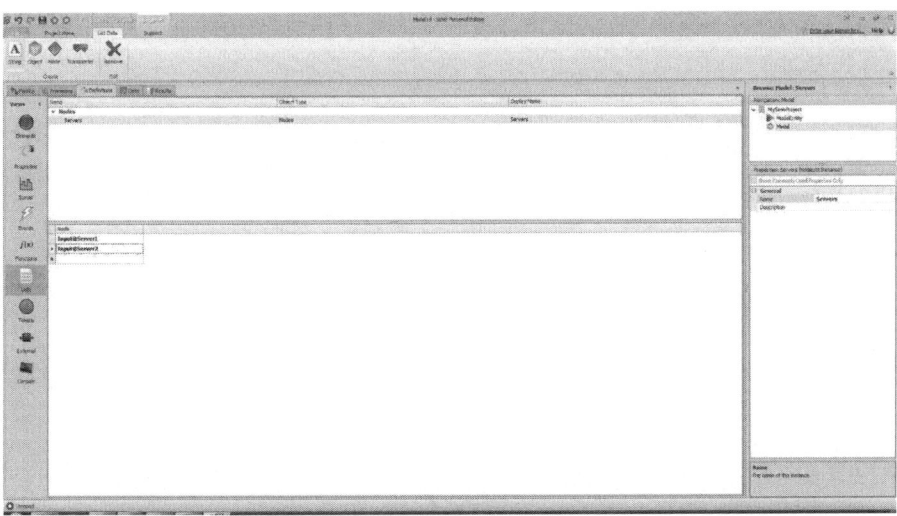

Figure 4.34: Defining the server list.

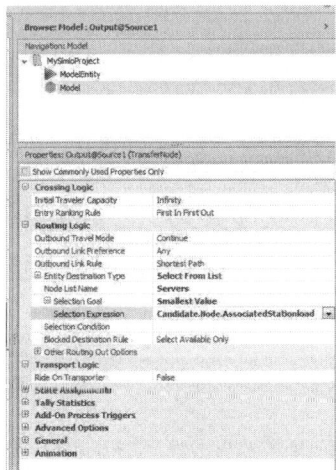

Figure 4.35: Entering the customer destination decision rule.

Repeat the above steps for Server2 to set the ProcessTime value and for the output node for Server 2 (Output@Source2). On the Run tab, set the ending time to 480 minutes and make sure the time units in the unit settings tab are set to minutes. Set the Speed Factor to 100. Run the model and the customers should be directed to the server with the smallest queue. At the end of the run select the Results tab for the results (Figure 4.36). The results should be similar to those shown for the ARENA model in Figure 4.16.

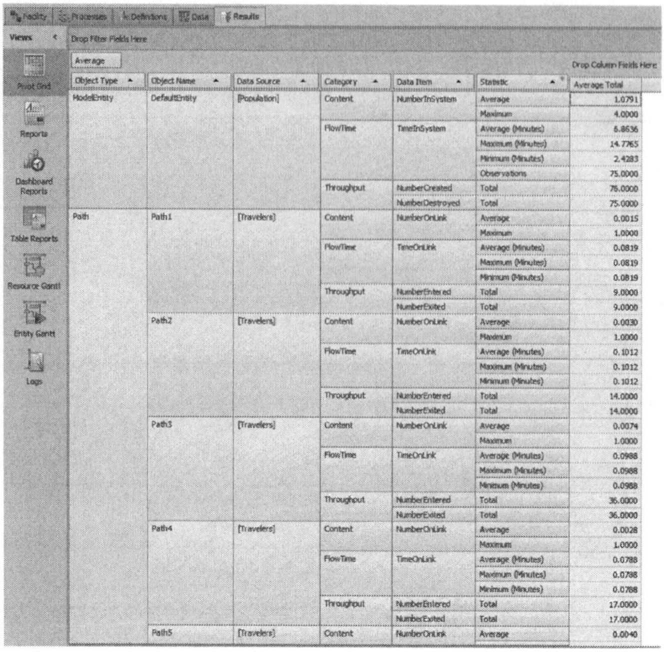

Object Type	Object Name	Data Source	Category	Data Item	Statistic	Average Total
ModelEntity	DefaultEntity	[Population]	Content	NumberInSystem	Average	1.0791
					Maximum	4.0000
			FlowTime	TimeInSystem	Average (Minutes)	6.8636
					Maximum (Minutes)	14.7765
					Minimum (Minutes)	2.4283
					Observations	75.0000
			Throughput	NumberCreated	Total	76.0000
				NumberDestroyed	Total	75.0000
Path	Path1	[Travelers]	Content	NumberOnLink	Average	0.0015
					Maximum	1.0000
			FlowTime	TimeOnLink	Average (Minutes)	0.0819
					Maximum (Minutes)	0.0819
					Minimum (Minutes)	0.0819
			Throughput	NumberEntered	Total	9.0000
				NumberExited	Total	9.0000
	Path2	[Travelers]	Content	NumberOnLink	Average	0.0030
					Maximum	1.0000
			FlowTime	TimeOnLink	Average (Minutes)	0.1012
					Maximum (Minutes)	0.1012
					Minimum (Minutes)	0.1012
			Throughput	NumberEntered	Total	14.0000
				NumberExited	Total	14.0000
	Path3	[Travelers]	Content	NumberOnLink	Average	0.0074
					Maximum	1.0000
			FlowTime	TimeOnLink	Average (Minutes)	0.0988
					Maximum (Minutes)	0.0988
					Minimum (Minutes)	0.0988
			Throughput	NumberEntered	Total	36.0000
				NumberExited	Total	36.0000
	Path4	[Travelers]	Content	NumberOnLink	Average	0.0028
					Maximum	1.0000
			FlowTime	TimeOnLink	Average (Minutes)	0.0788
					Maximum (Minutes)	0.0788
					Minimum (Minutes)	0.0788
			Throughput	NumberEntered	Total	17.0000
				NumberExited	Total	17.0000
	Path5	[Travelers]	Content	NumberOnLink	Average	0.0040

Figure 4.36: Dual queue bank clerk simulation results.

Simio provides facilities that allow 3D representations of a model to be developed quickly. For the bank clerk simulation with the Facilitys tab selected and the model visible, select the View Tab on the top ribbon and select the 3D option. The model will be redrawn in a 3D view (Figure 4.37). Hold down the right mouse

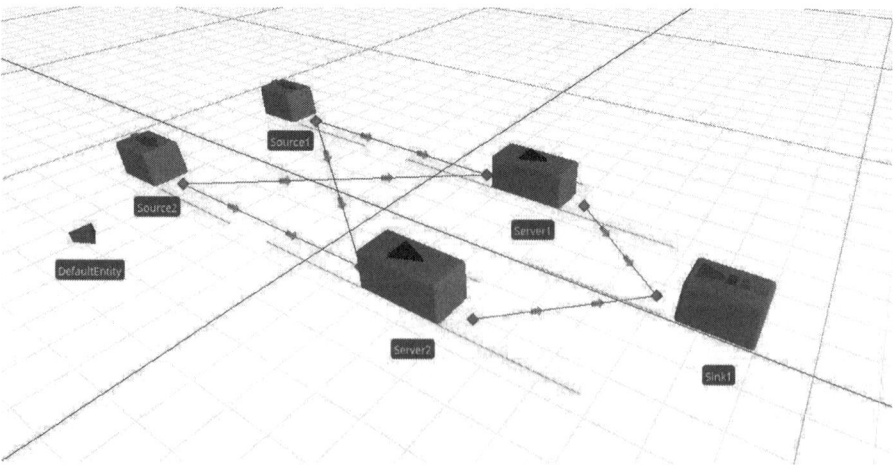

Figure 4.37: 3D view of bank clerk simulation.

button and move up and down to zoom and move left and right to rotate the image in the screen. Hold down the left button and move to move around the model landscape.

We can make changes to the image so that it more closely represents the system we are modeling. To replace the entity image from green triangles to people, select the Symbols Tab on the top ribbon and select the Apply Symbols option. A pull-down menu provides a selection of images to choose from. Select the people option in the Type selection box and the people images will be displayed. Scroll down and pick one of the images from the Library/People/Animated/Female category. Now click on Server1, and select an image from the same category for Server1 and from the Library/People/Animated/Male category for Server2. You can change the image display when the Servers are activated (move from idle to busy) by selecting the server image and selecting the Active Symbol option. Select the Processing option from the list and then apply a different symbol using the Apply Symbol option. When the simulation is run, the symbol image will change when the server is activated (Figure 4.38).

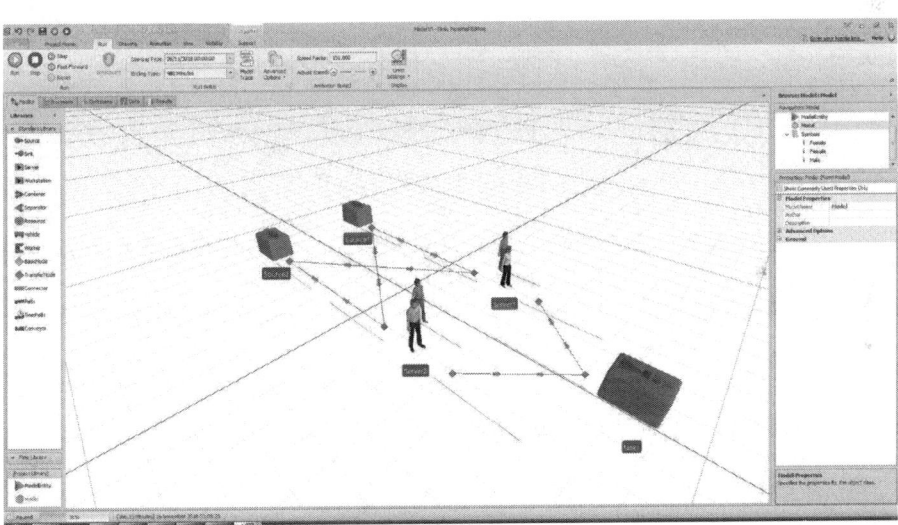

Figure 4.38: 3D animation of bank clerk simulation.

Verification and Validation

Before experimental analysis of the simulation model can begin, it is necessary to ensure that the model constructed provides a valid representation of the system we are studying. This process consists of verification and validation of the simulation model. Verification means ensuring that the computer model built using the simulation software is a correct representation of the conceptual model of the system under investigation. Validation concerns ensuring that the assumptions and simplifications made in the conceptual model about the real-world system are acceptable in the context of the simulation study objectives. Both topics will now be discussed in more detail.

> **A Simulation Model as a Theory**
>
> The simulation model we build can be seen as our theory for describing the structure and interrelationships of a system. We use our subjective beliefs in terms of our opinions and insights to gain knowledge about how the system works in order to build our model. Because this process is subjective, different people will develop different models given the same problem. The purpose of verification and validation is to make a largely objective assessment that the model is a suitable representation of the system we are studying.

Verification

Verification is analogous to the practice of "debugging" a computer program in order to check that the program does what has been planned. Thus, many of the following techniques will be familiar to programmers of general-purpose computer languages.

Model Design

The task of verification is likely to become greater with an increase in model size. This is because a large complex program is both more likely to contain errors and these errors are less likely to be found. Due to this behavior most practitioners advise on an approach of building a small simple model, ensuring that this works correctly, and then gradually adding embellishments over time. This approach is intended to help limit the area of search for errors at any one time. It is also important to ensure that unnecessary complexity is not incorporated in the model design. The design should incorporate only enough detail to ensure the study objectives and not attempt to be an exact replica of the real-life system.

Structured Walkthrough

This enables the modeler to incorporate the perspective of someone outside the immediate task of model construction. The walkthrough procedure involves talking through the program code with another individual or team. The process may bring fresh insight from others, but the act of explaining the coding can also help the person who has developed the code discover their own errors. In discrete event simulation code is executed nonsequentially and different coding blocks are executed simultaneously. This means that the walkthrough may best be conducted by following the "life-history" of an entity through the simulation coding, rather than a sequential examination of coding blocks.

Test Runs

Test runs of a simulation model can be made during program development to check model behavior. This is a useful way of checking model behavior as a defective model will usually report results (e.g., machine utilization, customer wait times) that do not conform to expectations, either based on the real system performance or common-sense deductions. It may be necessary to add performance measures to the model (e.g., costs) for verification purposed, even though they may not be required for reporting purposes. An approach is to use historical (fixed) data, so model behavior can be isolated from behavior caused by the use of random variates in the model. It is also important to test model behavior under a number of scenarios, particularly boundary conditions that are likely to uncover erratic behavior. Boundary conditions could include minimum and maximum arrival rates, minimum and maximum service times and minimum and maximum rate of infrequent events (e.g., machine breakdowns).

Trace Analysis

Due to the nature of discrete-event simulation, it may be difficult to locate the source of a coding error. Most simulation packages incorporate an entity trace facility that is useful in providing a detailed record of the life history of a particular entity. The trace facility can show the events occurring for a particular entity or all events occurring during a particular time frame. The trace analysis facility can produce a large amount of output, so it is most often used for detailed verification.

Animation Inspection

The animation facilities of simulation software packages provide a powerful tool in aiding understanding of model behavior. The animation enables the model developer to see many of the model components and their behavior simultaneously. A "rough-cut" animated drawing should be sufficient at the testing stage for verification purposes. To aid understanding model components can be animated, which may not appear in the final layout presented to a client. The usefulness of the animation technique will be maximized if the animation software facilities permit reliable and quick production of the animation effects. An animation inspection may be conducted by following the "life-history" of an entity through the animation displayed at a slow speed.

Documentation

It is important to document all elements in the simulation to aid verification by other personnel or at a later date. Any general-purpose or simulation coding should have comments attached to each line of code. Each object within a model produced on a simulation system requires comments regarding its purpose and details of parameters and other elements.

Verification with Arena

Arena provides a number of facilities for model verification. Animation facilities provide immediate feedback to the user from which the model logic can be checked by following the path of entities through the animated display. Errors can also be found by inspecting the measure of performance (e.g., machine utilization, queue length) within the system and comparing them to the estimated values made by using of rough-cut calculations. In testing both the model logic and performance, particular attention should be paid to any behavior at variance from the real system (taking into consideration simplifications and assumptions made) or expected behavior of a system that does not yet exist. As was stated earlier, verification is easiest with small simple models. With larger and more complex models, it may be necessary to temporarily simplify model behavior for verification purposes. This could be achieved by replacing distributions for arrival and process times with constant values or only routing one entity type through the model to check the entity path. If the model is not behaving in an appropriate manner, it is necessary to investigate the model design. This can be achieved through inspection of the model code and by analyzing the event calendar using the debugging facilities.

Arena converts the module specification you have placed in the model window into the simulation language SIMAN. This consists of a model file containing the simulation logic modules and an experimental file containing the data modules. To view these files for a simulation, estimate the Run/SIMAN/View option. The SIMAN files for the bank clerk simulation is shown in Figure 4.39 and Figure 4.40.

These files are of course most useful if you are familiar with the SIMAN simulation language. Also note that the coding in the model listing (Figure 4.39) does not necessarily follow the sequence of modules in the order of the model logic. Unfortunately, the edited code can not be converted back to an Arena program, so SIMAN code is restricted to an aid for verification. Also debugging from a code listing is more difficult than that for a general-purpose language, such as C, as many parts of the model can be executing simultaneously because many entities pass through the model at any given time.

To inspect the actions of each entity, an event debugger is required. The debugging facilities are available in the Arena run controller that provides a number of facilities for inspecting model behavior. The run controller is activated by the Run/ Run Control/Command menu option. When activated a window is opened and a prompt will appear. The SET TRACE command is used to provide a visual display of all the simulation events. Figure 4.41 shows the debugger used to provide a trace of the first lines of code executed as the simulation runs.

Figure 4.42 shows the trace cancel option (can trace) used to disable the trace display. The simulation is then run until time = 50 minutes (go until 50). The show command is used to find the number of customers in all the queues (show nq(*)). The view command then shows the attributes of the entities in the process 2.queue (view queue process 2.queue).

```
;
;
;       Model statements for module:   Arrive 1
;
42$             CREATE,         1:EXPO(15):MARK(arrivaltime);
43$             ASSIGN:         customertype=1:
                                   processtime=UNIFORM(2,6);
3$              STATION,        Arrive 1;
51$             TRACE,          -1,"-Arrived to system at station Arrive 1\n":;
6$              ASSIGN:         Picture=Default;
27$             DELAY:          0.;
56$             TRACE,          -1,"-Transferred to station Server 1\n":;
29$             ROUTE:          1,Server 1;
;
;
;       Model statements for module:   Arrive 2
;
121$            CREATE,         1:EXPO(10):MARK(arrivaltime);
122$            ASSIGN:         customertype=2:
                                   processtime=UNIFORM(4,10);
82$             STATION,        Arrive 2;
130$            TRACE,          -1,"-Arrived to system at station Arrive 2\n":;
85$             ASSIGN:         Picture=Default;
106$            DELAY:          0.;
135$            TRACE,          -1,"-Transferred to station Server 1\n":;
108$            ROUTE:          1,Server 1;
;
;
;       Model statements for module:   Server 1
;
0$              STATION,        Server 1;
237$            TRACE,          -1,"-Arrived to station Server 1\n":;
200$            DELAY:          0.;
244$            TRACE,          -1,"-Waiting for resource Server 1_R\n":;
161$            QUEUE,          Server 1_R_Q:MARK(QueueTime);
162$            SEIZE,          1:
                                Server 1_R,1;
271$            BRANCH,         1:
                                   If,RTYP(Server 1_R).eq.2,272$,Yes:
                                   If,RTYP(Server 1_R).eq.1,174$,Yes;
272$            MOVE:           Server 1_R,Server 1;
174$            TALLY:          Server 1_R_Q Queue Time,INT(QueueTime),1;
281$            DELAY:          0.0;
                TRACE,   -1,"-Delay for processing time processtime\n":;
163$            DELAY:          processtime;
245$            TRACE,          -1,"-Releasing resource\n":;
164$            RELEASE:        Server 1_R,1;
228$            DELAY:          0.;
250$            TRACE,          -1,"-Transferred to station Depart 1\n":;
168$            ROUTE:          1,Depart 1;
;
;
;       Model statements for module:   Depart 1
;
2$              STATION,        Depart 1;
312$            TRACE,          -1,"-Arrived to station Depart 1\n":;
282$            DELAY:          0.;
305$            COUNT:          counterset(customertype),1;
309$            TALLY:          service time,Interval(arrivaltime),1;
319$            TRACE,          -1,"-Disposing entity\n":;
311$            DISPOSE;
```

Figure 4.39: Arena model listing.

```
PROJECT,              ;
ATTRIBUTES:           arrivaltime:
                      customertype:
                      processtime:
                      QueueTime;
QUEUES:               Server 1_R_Q,FIFO;
PICTURES:             Default;
RESOURCES:            Server 1_R,Capacity(1,),-,Stationary;
STATIONS:             Arrive 1:
                      Arrive 2:
                      Depart 1:
                      Server 1;
COUNTERS:             customer type 1:
                      customer type 2;
TALLIES:              service time:
                      Server 1_R_Q Queue Time;
DSTATS:               NQ(Server 1_R_Q),# in Server 1_R_Q:
                      MR(Server 1_R),Server 1_R Available:
                      NR(Server 1_R),Server 1_R Busy;
REPLICATE,            1,0.0,1000,Yes,Yes;
SETS:                 counterset,customer type 1,customer type 2;
```

Figure 4.40: Arena experimental listing.

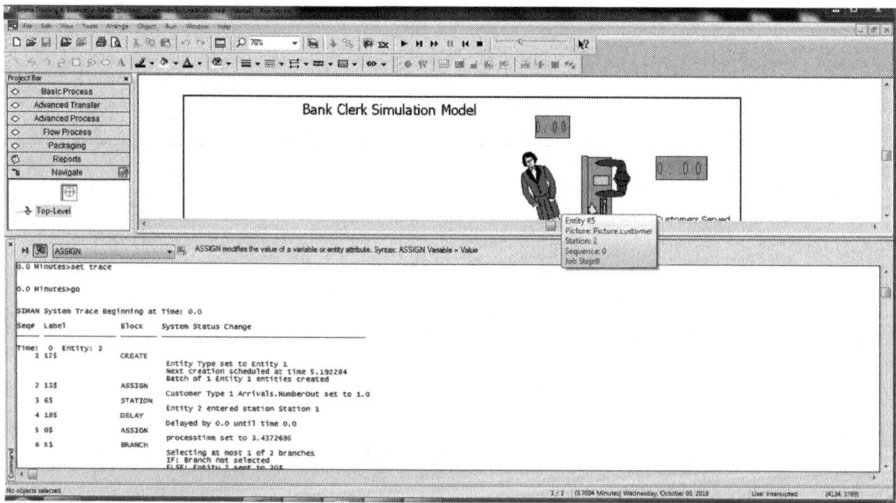

Figure 4.41: Arena trace listing.

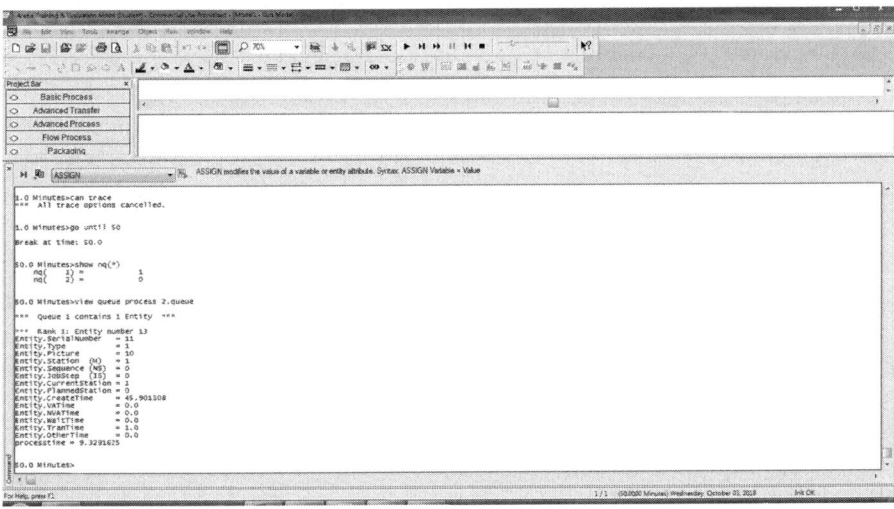

Figure 4.42 : Arena debugger display.

Verification with Simio

To assist with debugging Simio offers trace facilities similar to Arena. From the Run Tab select the Model Trace option. A window will appear at the bottom of the screen and will show trace information as the simulation runs (Figure 4.43).

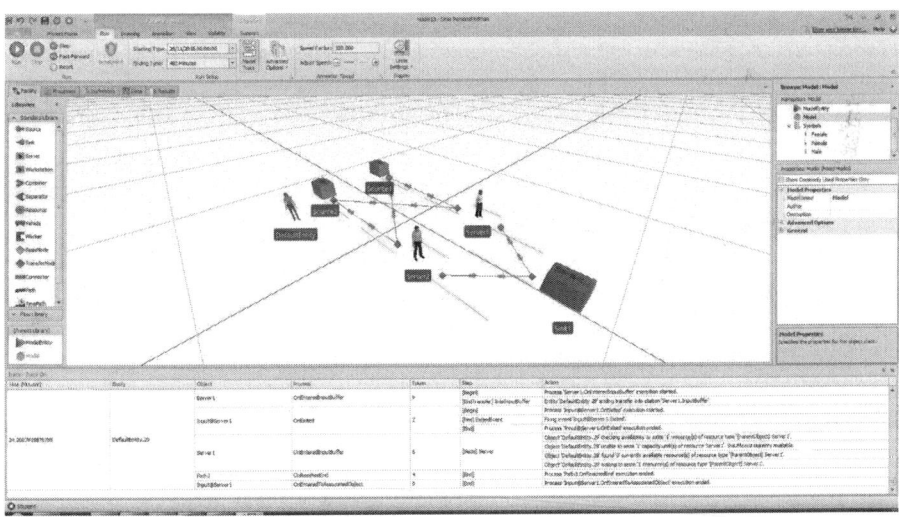

Figure 4.43: Simio trace display.

Validation

A verified model is a model that operates as intended by the modeler. However, this does not necessarily mean that it is a satisfactory representation of the real system for the purposes of the study. Validation is about ensuring that model behavior is close enough to the real-world system for the purposes of the simulation study.

Unlike verification, the question of validation is one of judgement. Ideally the model should provide enough accuracy for the measures required while limiting the amount of efforts required to achieve this. Validation is difficult to do well and insufficient time may be spent on this activity as there may be pressures to begin experimentation and analysis. There are a number of issues to consider such as the sensitivity of model results to initial run conditions and ensuring a correct understanding of real-system behavior to which the model can be compared. If the model fails the validation stage, then the conceptual modeling stage should be revisited and model revisions made. As a last resort and if no solution can be found to achieve model validation, then the modeling project should be cancelled.

For most systems of any complexity validation can be achieved in a number of ways and a key skill of the simulation developer is finding the most efficient way of achieving this goal. Pegden et al. (1995) outlines three aspects of validation:

- Conceptual Validity—Does the model adequately represent the real-world system?
- Operational Validity—Are the model generated behavioral data characteristic of the real-world system behavioral data?
- Believability—Does the simulation model's ultimate user have confidence in the model's results?

These three aspects reflect that model validation can be seen as proving that the assumptions and structure of the model have led to a truthful representation of the real system but also validation can be seen as being concerned with the accuracy of the predictions of the model. In this latter approach the underlying assumptions and structure of the model are irrelevant and this approach is often taken when validating data-driven analytics models. In reality most simulation model developers will take both of these perspectives into account when conducting model validation. The model results can be tested for reasonableness (operational validity) and the model assumptions and structure can be examined in terms of their representation of the real system (conceptual validity). Both the model developer and the model user (decision maker) will need to be convinced that these tests have been passed (believability).

Conceptual Validity

Conceptual validation involves ensuring that the model structure and elements are correctly chosen and configured in order to adequately represent the real-world system. This is primarily concerned with ensuring that appropriate assumptions and simplifications have been made when building the conceptual model. Thus there is a need for a consensus around the form of the conceptual model between the model builder and the user. To ensure that a conceptually valid model is produced, the model builder should discuss and obtain information from people familiar with the real-world system including operating personnel, industrial engineers, management, vendors and documentation. They should also observe system behavior over time and compare with model behavior and communicate with project sponsors throughout the model build to increase validity.

Operational Validity
This involves ensuring that the results obtained from the model are consistent with the real-world performance. Operational validity is primarily about ensuring that the amount and quality of the data used in the model is sufficient to represent the variability inherent in the real system. A common way of ensuring operational validity is to use the technique of sensitivity analysis to test the behavior of the model under various scenarios and compare results with real-world behavior. The technique of common random numbers can be used to isolate changes due to random variation. The techniques of experimental design can also be employed to conduct sensitivity analysis over two or more factors. Note that for validation purposes these tests compare simulation performance with real-world performance, while in the context of experimentation they are used to compare simulation behavior under different scenarios. Sensitivity analysis can be used to validate a model, but it is particularly appropriate if a model has been built of a system that does not exist as the data has been estimated and can not be validated against a real system. It should also be noted that an option may be to conduct sensitivity analysis on subsystems of the overall system being modeled that do exist. This emphasizes the point that the model should be robust enough to provide a prediction of what would happen in the real system under a range of possible input data. The construction and validation of the model should be for a particular range of input values defined in the simulation project objectives. If the simulation is then used outside of this predefined range, the model must be revalidated to ensure that additional aspects of the real system are incorporated to ensure valid results.

Sensitivity analysis should be undertaken by observing the output measure of interest with data set to levels above and below the initial set level for the data. A graph may be used to show model results for a range of data values if detailed analysis is required. (e.g., a nonlinear relationship between a data value and output measure is apparent). If the model output does not show a significant change in value in response to the sensitivity analysis, then we can judge that the accuracy of the estimated value will not have a significant effect on the result. If the model output is sensitive to the data value, then preferably we would want to increase the accuracy of the data value estimate. This may be undertaken by further interviews or data collection. In any event, the simulation analysis will need to show the effect of model output on a range of data values. Thus for an estimated value, we can observe the likely behavior of the system over a range of data values within which the true value should be located. Further sensitivity analysis may be required on each of these values to separate changes in output values from random variation. When it is found that more than one data value has an effect on an output measure, then the effects of the individual and combined data values should be assessed. This will require 3^k replications to measure the minimum, initial and maximum values for k variables. The use of fractional factorial designs may be used to reduce the number of replications required.

> **Using a Trace Simulation to Ensure Model Validity**
>
> One way to check both conceptual validity and operational validity is to use actual historical data (trace simulation) in the model rather than derived probability distributions. The data collected could be used for elements such as customer arrival times and service delays and by comparing output measures across identical time periods, it should be possible to validate the model. Thus the structure or flow of the model could be validated and then probability distributions entered for random elements. Thus, any error in system performance could be identified as either a logic error (conceptual validity) or from an inaccurate distribution (operational validity). The disadvantage of this method is that for a model of any size the amount of historical data needed will be substantial. It is also necessary to read this data, either from a file or an array, requiring additional coding effort. Also note that while it may be possible to estimate the amount of error in an input distribution the effect of missing or erroneous elements in the process map is more difficult to quantify. This implies the domain knowledge of the modeling team is crucial in understanding the relationship between the internal process logic of the model and the relationship between input and output parameters.

> **Sensitivity Analysis**
>
> We conduct sensitivity analysis to determine if the model behaves in a way in which we expect and to ensure that both the input data and model structure are appropriate for our needs. We should view sensitivity analysis in a broad way as not just a technical exercise but as an opportunity to obtain greater understanding of our abstraction of the real system and to indicate important processes and parameters that drive the cause and effect relationships we are interested in. This should be part of an iterative process and we may need to conduct additional data collection to improve the accuracy of our model if our conceptualization and/or understanding of the system is faulty. We should also not just look at sensitivity analysis in terms of input data, but as there are usually multiple ways in which a process can be represented in a model, it is important to evaluate how decisions about a model's structure affect its behavior.

Sensitivity Analysis Using Simio

Simio provides an inbuilt tool to undertake response sensitivity analysis. This first requires that input parameters such as those for interarrival times and service times are defined in the Input Parameters option found on the Data tab. From here select the Distribution option in the ribbon and enter the parameters for the distribution. Figure 4.44 shows the interarrival and customer service distributions entered for

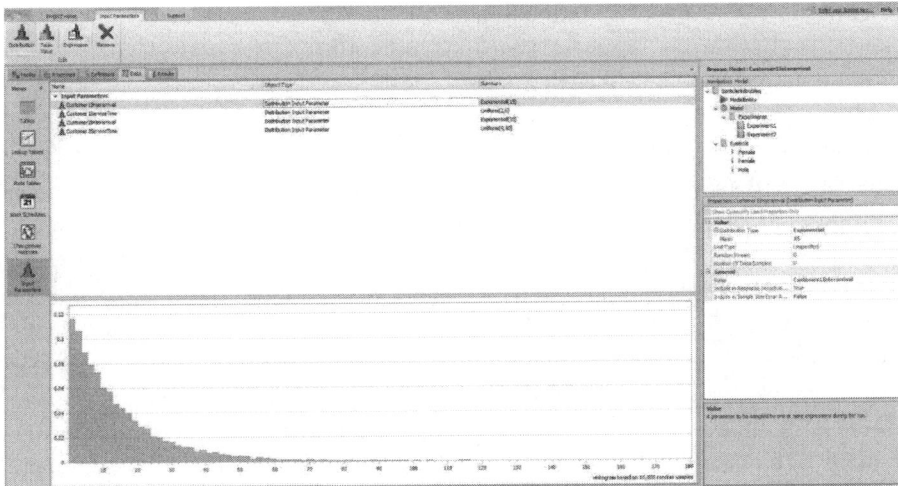

Figure 4.44: Input parameters definitions for the bank clerk simulation.

the Single Queue Bank Clerk Simulation model. Note for each input parameter, Simio displays a chart at the bottom of the screen showing the shape of the distribution for the modeler to check the range and shape are appropriate. This display is created by Simio based on 10,000 random draws from the defined distribution.

The name for each input parameter distribution should now be used in the bank clerk model instead of the original labels. Figure 4.45 shows the ModelEntity. ProcessTime being assigned to the Input Parameter Customer1ServiceTime and in the Properties window the interarrival time is assigned to the Customer1Interarrival input parameter.

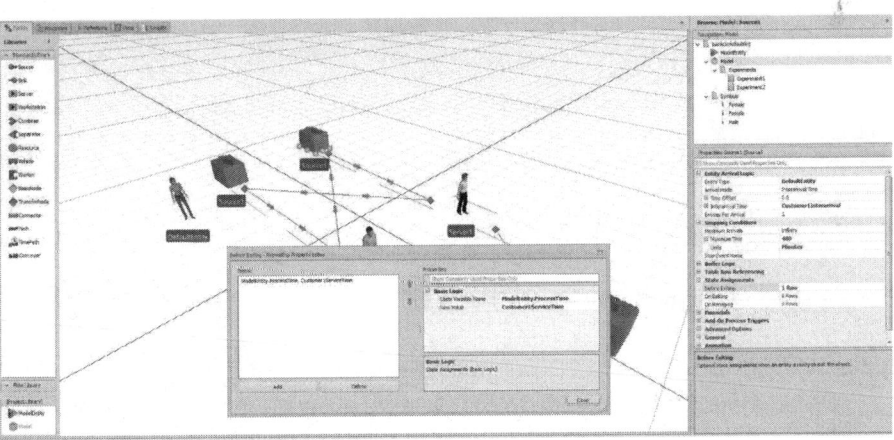

Figure 4.45: Assigning the input parameter labels in the bank clerk simulation.

After running the bank clerk simulation for 100 replications move to the input analysis tab and select the Response Sensitivity option to the left of the screen. Simio displays a Tornado chart of each input parameter sensitivity in terms of the target response (in this case defined as customer time in system). Figure 4.46 shows the chart with the parameters ordered by sensitivity from the top of the chart to the bottom. The chart shows the sensitivity of the response (time in system) to a change in the input parameter of 1 unit (in this case 1 minute) while holding all other input parameters constant. It is clear that the time in system metric is most sensitive to customer 2 service times and to a lesser extent customer 1 service times. The blue bar indicates a positive relationship between the service time and time in system; thus, increased service times will increase time in the system and will provide a useful validation check to see that these positive and negative relationships are as would be intuitively expected. This result of greater sensitivity to customer 2 than customer 1 service time distributions implies that if you wish to collect additional data to improve the input distributions and thus improve the accuracy of the model, then this effort should be focused around customer 2 services times as they effect the results the most in terms of time in the system.

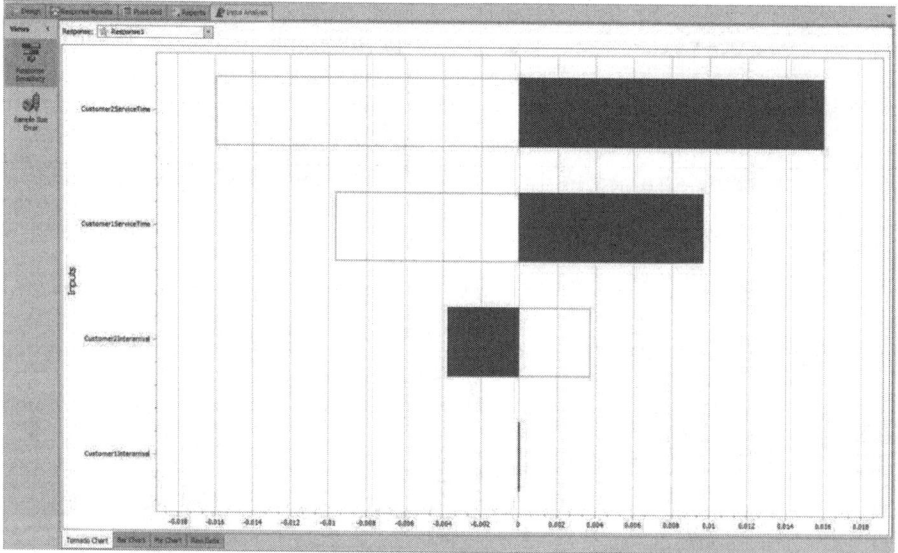

Figure 4.46: Simio response sensitivity analysis for bank clerk simulation model.

Believability

In order to ensure implementation of actions recommended as a result of simulation experiments requires that the model output is seen as credible from the simulation user's point of view. This credibility will be enhanced by close co-operation between model user and client throughout the simulation study. This involves agreeing clear project objectives explaining the capabilities of the technique to the client and agreeing assumptions made in the process map. Regular meetings of interested parties, using the simulation animation display to provide a discussion forum, can increase confidence in model results. Believability emphasizes how there is no one answer to achieving model validity and the perspective of both users and developers needs to be satisfied that a model is valid. This aspect emphasizes how simulation modeling is not just a technical exercise requiring model building and statistical skills but it also requires domain knowledge and social and political skills in order to interpret and ensure use of the simulation results.

Model Validation and Uncertainty

Simulation models are in essence an attempt to quantify uncertainty in real-world processes. This text covers the use of simulation for descriptive (understanding), predictive (scenarios) and prescriptive (recommendations) analysis of real-world systems. Models are abstractions of these real systems and the key concern of validation is how satisfactory this abstraction is. In one sense, because models are simplifications they are by definition wrong or false in that they deliberately omit real-world processes—if they didn't there wouldn't be much point in building the model! So models are never true, but we only need to make them useful for the purpose they were designed for. Thus validation may not be a major issue when the model is used as a tool for understanding and for generating interesting and testable hypotheses, but the issue of model validation and the "truth" of the model become more acute when it is used as a tool for prediction and prescription.

Chapter 5
Use Simulation for Descriptive, Predictive and Prescriptive Analytics

This chapter covers the use of the simulation model to generate descriptive, predictive and prescriptive analytics. As the final step in a simulation study and in order for the analysis to have served its purpose it is usually necessary to implement actions deriving from the simulation results.

When measuring performance using simulation one aspect deals with the variability inherent in the simulation model that leads it to generate different values for its performance metrics (such as queuing times) each time the simulation is executed over a time period. To address this issue, the main method employed in simulation is to perform multiple replications of the simulation and construct confidence intervals of the metrics of interest. Additional statistical tests, such as t-tests, may also be undertaken in which scenarios are compared. It should be noted that these procedures deal with the statistical uncertainty associated with the randomness and variability in the model. This does not necessarily mean that the model is representative of the real system. Our domain knowledge may also be uncertain. This kind of uncertainty is difficult to quantify as it may be about events that can not be considered random and repeatable. This issue relates to the topic of model validity and emphasizes that it is unlikely that a model will be wholly valid and certainly will not be a true representative of a system that does not yet exist. However, the model results should not be viewed in isolation but interpreted by people with the required knowledge of the model—its assumptions, simplifications and scope and knowledge of the real system that is being modeled.

There are two types of simulation system that need to be defined, each requiring different methods of data analysis.

Terminating systems run between predefined states or times where the end state matches the initial state of the simulation. Most service organizations tend to be terminating systems that close at the end of each day with no in-process inventory (i.e., people waiting for service) and thus return to the "empty" or "idle" state they had at the start of that day. For example, a simulation of a retail outlet from opening to closing time.

Non-terminating systems do not reach predefined states or times. Most manufacturing organizations are non-terminating with inventory in the system that is awaiting a process. Thus even if the facility shuts down temporarily, it will start again in a different state to the previous start state (i.e., the inventory levels define different starting conditions). Before a non-terminating system is analyzed, the bias introduced by the nonrepresentative starting conditions should be eliminated to obtain what are termed *steady-state conditions* from which a representative statistical analysis can be undertaken.

Terminating and Non-terminating Simulation in Transient and Steady-State Phases

Although terminating systems are associated with transient phase analysis and non-terminating systems are associated with steady-state phase analysis this relationship is not always true.

Terminating systems have an obvious end point such as a day's operation in a service operation or a production cycle in a manufacturing system. If we conduct output analysis over the complete terminating cycle (such as a day's operation in a retail shop) then the analysis may be considered transient. In this case average measures may not be an appropriate performance measure as they may be skewed by the transient phases. For example average customer queueing times over a day's operation may seem reasonable but may mask unacceptable queuing times at peak periods of customer demand during the day. Thus measures such as maximum queue times, maximum lead times and counters such as customers served may be appropriate performance measures. However terminating systems can also go through steady-state periods during the day where average queue times may be an appropriate measure.

Non-terminating systems have no obvious end point such as 24/7 service operations like hospitals and manufacturing systems with inventory. Non-terminating systems may be in a transient state such as the start-up period from an empty factory or when moving from one production cycle to another. Non-terminating systems may not reach a steady-state but if they do they can be measured in this phase using average and maximum performance of measures such as queues, lead times and throughput rates.

Steady-State Cycle and Concept Drift

Systems do not necessarily settle into transient or steady-state but may move between the two states.

Steady-state cycle systems move repeatedly between transient and steady-state phases. This can be caused by demand patterns that are defined by timeslots such as hour, shift, day, week and month. See Chapter 6 for an example of where emergency call demand is modeled for each call type by hour and shift for each day. Thus there is a transition when moving from each one hour slot to the next.

Another option is that there may be a shift from one steady-state to another due to external factors such as new product introduction or a change in staff levels. This reflects the fact that the system environment, although not part of the system, if modified can produce a change in the state of the system itself. Normally these external factors are held at a constant level for the duration of the simulation run or treated as scenario variables outside of the model. However when conducting real-time simulation with continuous data-streams it is important to distinguish between the natural random variation in data and external factors that change the context of the data. This has been recognized as an important aspect in process mining applications and is called concept drift.

An Example of Transient and Steady-State Behavior

Figure 5.1 shows a process in terms of transient and steady-state behavior. For this non-terminating simulation there is a warmup period represented by an initial transient phase were the system fills with products from empty. The system then quickly reaches a steady-state phase which fluctuates around a mean value. An outside event, in this case a breakdown event, causes the process to enter a transient phase. Shortly after the transient phase actions are taken to recover from the loss of output which involves running the system at a higher rate of output. This represents a new steady-state level that is caused by what can be termed concept drift as the system is operating in a different manner than before. Finally normal operating procedures are reinstated and thus the process returns to its long-run steady-state operation.

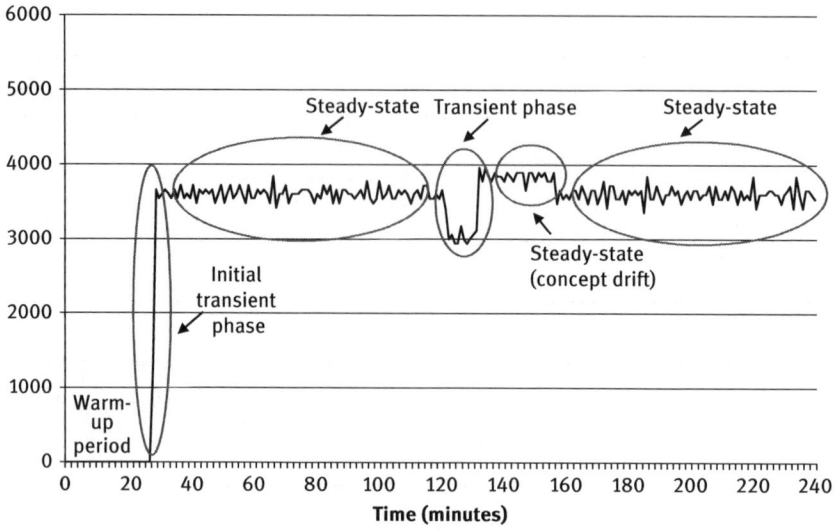

Figure 5.1: Steady-State and Transient Phases for a Non-Terminating System.

Statistical Analysis of Performance Measures for a Simulation

This section will provide statistical tools to analyze either terminating or non-terminating systems. For statistical analysis the output measure of a simulation model is a random variable and so we need to conduct multiple runs (replications) of the model to provide us with a sample of its value. When a number of replications have been undertaken, the sample mean can be calculated by averaging the measure of interest (e.g., time in queue) over the number of replications made. Each replication will use of a different set of random numbers and so this procedure is called the *method of independent replications*. We will conduct our statistical analysis of performance using confidence interval analysis for terminating systems before considering analysis of non-terminating systems.

Statistical Analysis of Terminating Systems

To assess the precision of our results, we can compute a confidence interval or range around the sample mean that will include, to a certain level of confidence, the true mean value of the variable we are measuring. Thus, confidence intervals provide a point estimate of the expected average (average over infinite number of replications) and an idea of how precise this estimate is. Thus, a 95% confidence interval means that if the experiment was repeated many times, then 95% of those confidence intervals would contain the true value of the parameter. The formula for the confidence interval involving the t-distribution is as follows:

$$\mu = \bar{x} \pm \frac{t^* s}{\sqrt{n}}$$

where
μ = half-width of the confidence interval
$\bar{x}$ = sample mean (from the replications)
t = t-distribution value $t_{df,\alpha/2}$ where df = degrees of freedom (n-1) and α = significance level
s = standard deviation (from the replications)
n = number of replications

Both the confidence interval analysis and the t-tests presented later for comparison analysis assume the data measured is normally distributed. This assumption is usually acceptable if measuring an average value for each replication as the output variable is made from many measurements and the central limit theorem applies. However the central limit theorem applies for a large sample size, and the definition of what constitutes a large sample depends partly on how close the actual distribution of the output variable is to the normal distribution. A histogram can be used to observe how close the actual distribution is to the normal distribution curve.

Confidence Interval Analysis Using Arena

Arena can be used to analyze the dual queue bank clerk simulation constructed in Chapter 4 (Figure 4.16). However, before the analysis can begin, an adjustment to the code must be made to ensure that the simulation is a true terminating system. At present, the simulation starts from empty and then customers arrive at the bank with a run time specified of 480 minutes. To be a true terminating system, the simulation must reach its starting condition (i.e., empty system) at the end of its run. To achieve this, the simulation must stop receiving new customers after a certain time period and then service any remaining customers in the system. A method of achieving this is to add an additional condition to the Arena decide module that directs all customers after closing time away from the bank. To update the Bank Clerk Simulation to a terminating system, load the dual queue bank clerk simulation into Arena. Double click on the Decide module and copy the current queue select expression onto the clipboard by dragging the mouse over it and selecting on the edit/copy menu option. Change the type field from 2-way by condition to *n*-way by condition. Click on the add button and enter the expression TNOW.GT.480 (Figure 5.2). TNOW is an Arena variable containing the current simulation time. This command will redirect customers to a dispose module if the current time is

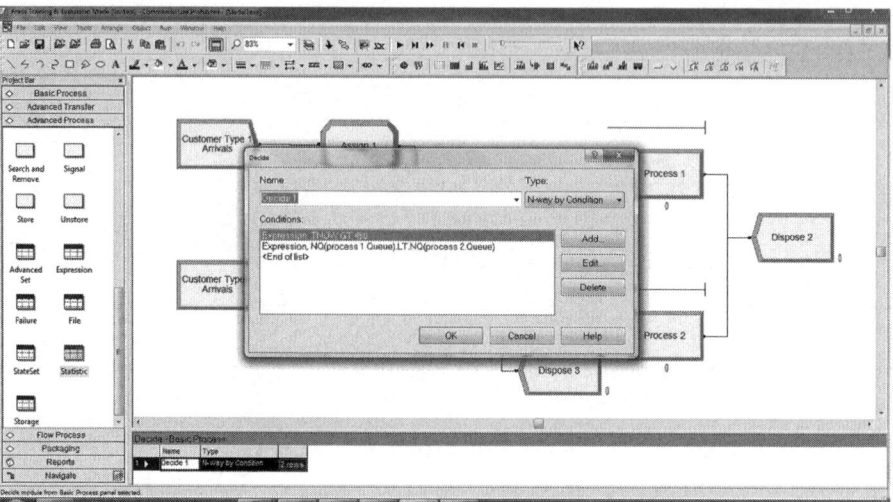

Figure 5.2: Entering the decide module parameters.

greater than 480 minutes (simulating that customers will be turned away after the bank has been opened for 480 minutes). Click on the add button again and select expression for the If field and paste the queue select expression to the value field by clicking on the field and selecting the menu/paste option.

Drag the dispose module (from the Basic Process panel) on to the model window. Use the connect button on the toolbar to connect the "GT.480" decision node on the decision module to the dispose module. Also use the connect button to connect the queue select option on the decision module to the route 1 module and the "else" decision node to the route 2 module. The simulation should be as shown in Figure 5.3.

Select the run/setup/replication parameters option from the menu. Enter 510 for the run length to provide 30 minutes for customers to leave the system after the closing at time 480 minutes. Enter 20 for the "Number of Replications" parameter and ensure the tick boxes in the initialize between replications area are checked for "System" and "Statistics" to achieve statistically independent replications. When running multiple replications, you may wish to use the run/run control/batch run (no animation) menu option, which will disable the animation display and run through the replications much quicker.

In order to save information to a data file for analysis, we use the Statistic module from the Advanced Process template. The Statistics module allows statistics to be saved to a data file, which can be analyzed by the Arena Output Analyzer. The Output Analyzer is a program that is supplied with the Arena system (you may need to search for the file Output.exe in Windows and run it separately from the main Arena system). To use the Advanced Process template, click on the template attach icon on the toolbar and select the Advanced Process.tpo template file from the list

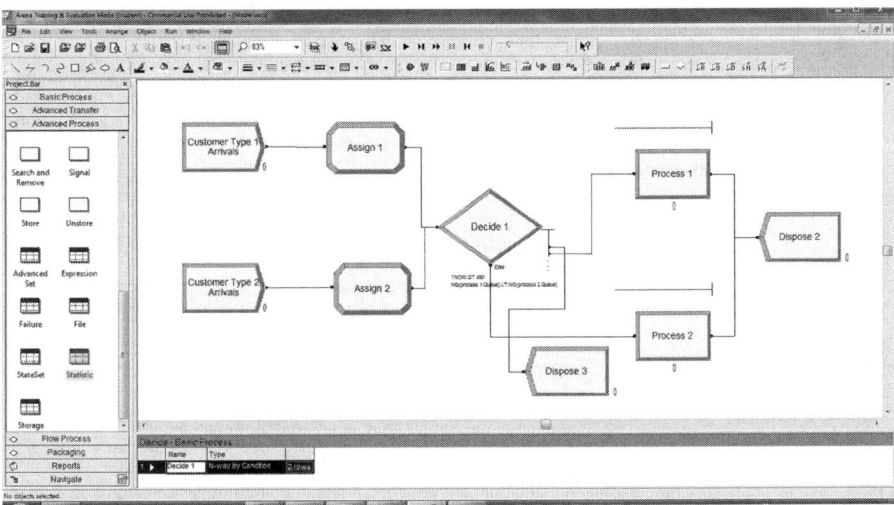

Figure 5.3: Bank Clerk Terminating System.

and select Open. If the file does not appear in the list, try the directory c:\program files\rockwell software\arena\template.

From the project bar with the Advanced Process panel selected, click on the Statistic module to obtain the spreadsheet view. Double click to add a new row. Click on the Type box and select Output from the drop-down menu.

To collect statistics on the average time it takes a customer to pass through the system enter TAVG(Entity 1.Totaltime) in the expression box. This will collect the average time of a tally variable over a simulation replication, in this case the variable Entity 1.Totaltime which represents the time it takes for a customer to pass through the system. Use the Arena simulation report to identify more variables to report and use the Arena help system to find other Arena expressions for data collection. For example, to collect statistics on the maximum time for customers in the bank clerk 1 queue, the following would be entered TMAX(process 1.queue.waitingtime).

Enter Average Time in System Dual Q in the Report Label cell and click in the Output File cell to define the save location of the report file. In this case, move to a directory to save your file and enter the file name BCD.dat (Figure 5.4). This creates a binary file with a .dat extension used by the Arena output analyzer.

Run the model for 20 replications and the file BCD.DAT holding the time in queue information will be created. The next step is to use the Output Analyzer to perform the statistical analysis. Run the Output Analyzer program and select the Analyze/Confidence Interval on Mean/Classical menu option. Add the file BCD.DAT and select "lumped" from the pull-down menu for the replications parameter. Leave the default confidence interval at 0.95 (95%). Click on OK. The analysis as shown in Figure 5.5 will appear.

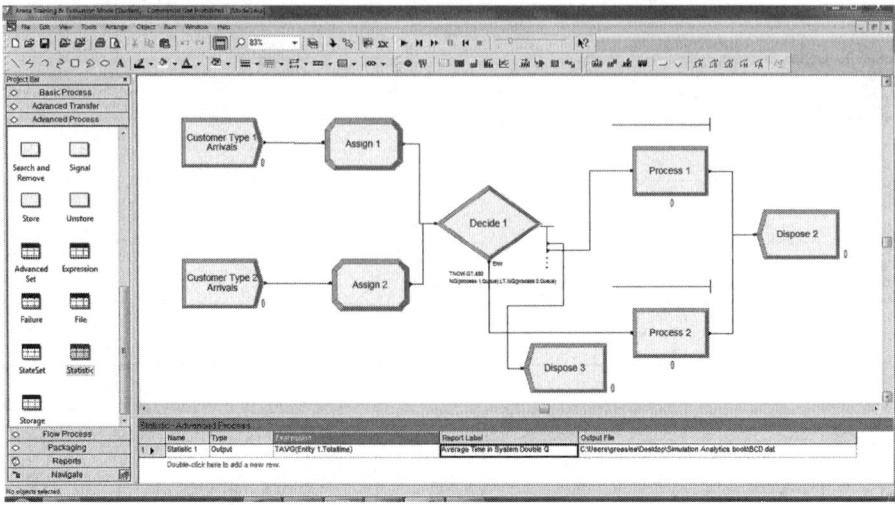

Figure 5.4: Entering the Statistics module parameters.

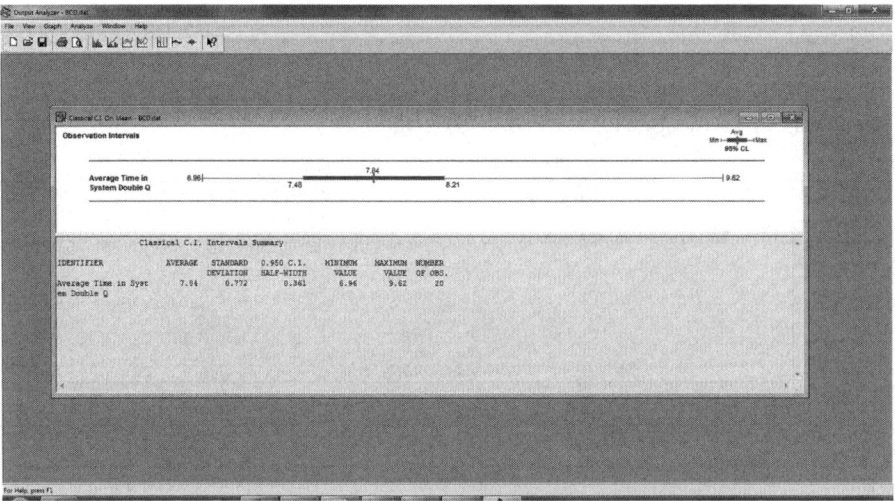

Figure 5.5: Arena confidence interval on mean analysis (20 replications).

Using the Arena output analyzer the results show the confidence intervals as the blue lines. The graphs show that 95% of confidence intervals would contain an average time in the system between 7.48 and 8.21 minutes.

In order to assess the effect of an increase in the number of replications, the analysis is repeated with 100 replications and the results are presented in Figure 5.6. Make sure the run/run control/batch run (no animation) menu option is selected to run this quickly.

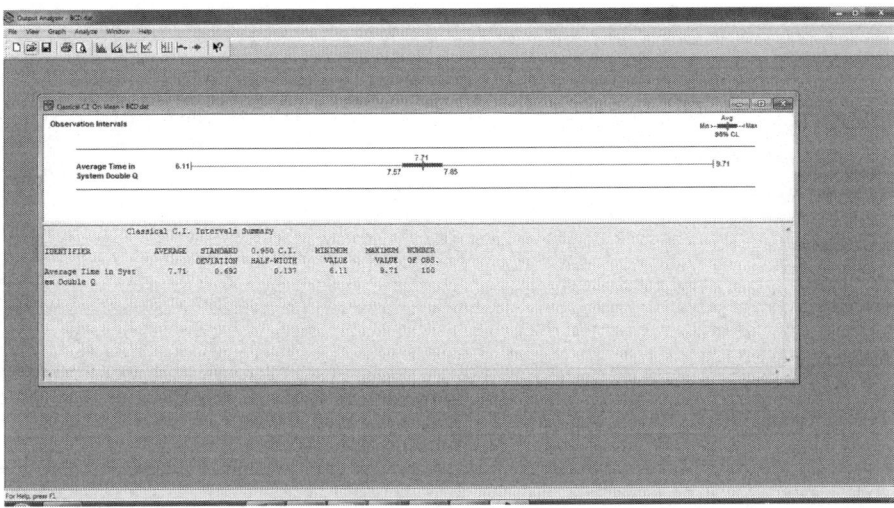

Figure 5.6: Arena confidence interval on mean analysis (100 replications).

The use of 100 rather than 20 replications has allowed us to produce a more statistically precise estimate of the average queue times. The half-width for dual queue average time in system has been reduced from 0.361 to 0.137. Thus, the results show that 95% of confidence intervals would contain an average time in system between 7.57 and 7.85 minutes.

Confidence Interval Analysis Using Simio

As with the Arena confidence interval analysis, this uses the dual queue bank clerk simulation created in Chapter 4 (Figure 4.36). For the Simio dual queue simulation model, the following steps are required to ensure that the simulation is terminating. The first step is to stop new customers entering the bank after 480 minutes. To do this, click on the Source1 object in the navigation window and in the properties window enter a maximum time of 480 for the stopping conditions. Enter minutes for the units (Figure 5.7).

Repeat this process for the Source2 object. Next Select the run tab and on the ribbon change the run time to 510 minutes. Click on the project home tab and select New Experiment from the Ribbon. Select the Design tab and click on the Add Response option on the Ribbon. Enter DefaultEntity.Population.TimeInSystem. Average as the expression in the Response1 properties menu. This will collect statistics on the average flow time for the customer in the bank clerk system. Set the Unit Type parameter to minutes (Figure 5.8).

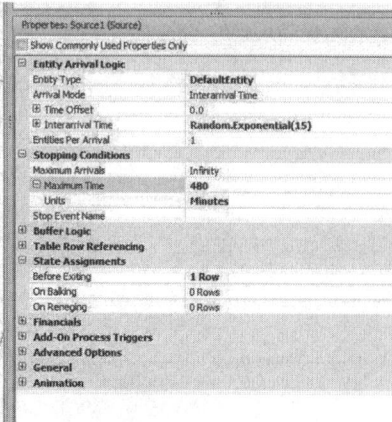

Figure 5.7: Setting the stop time for new customers.

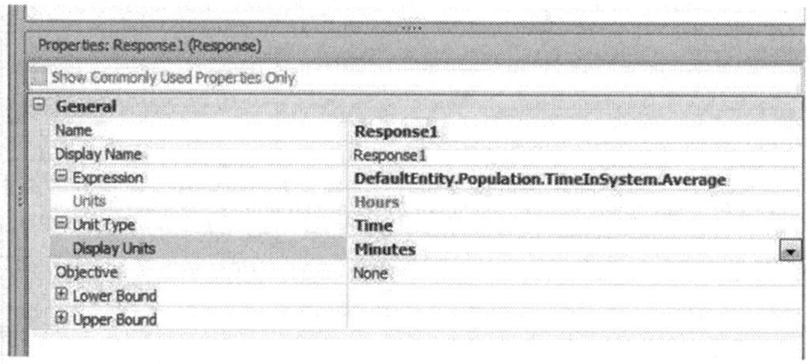

Figure 5.8: Setting the experiment statistics collection.

Set the Required Replications to 20 in the Design tab in the Navigation Window. Select Run in the Ribbon to run the simulation for 20 replications. Click on the Response Results tab in the Navigation window to show the box plot of the average time in the system for the bank clerk customers in the terminating simulation. Click on the Rotate Plot option in the Ribbon to provide a horizontal confidence interval and box plot display (Figure 5.9).

The confidence interval is shown as a brown block in the middle of the plot. The results show that 95% of confidence intervals would contain an average time in the system between 6.82 and 7.30 minutes. Running again for 100 replications gives a confidence interval between 6.96 and 7.22 minutes.

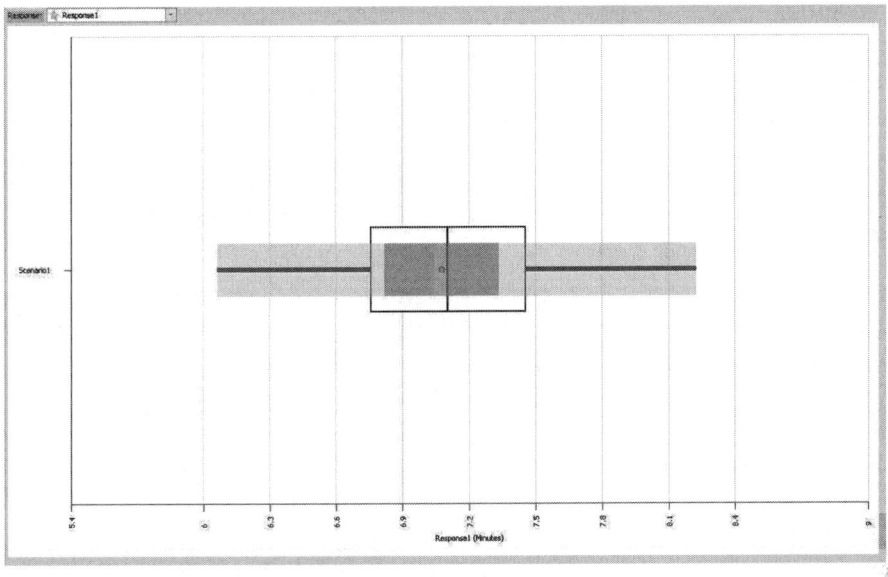

Figure 5.9: Simio confidence interval on mean analysis (20 replications).

Establishing Confidence Intervals at a Given Half-Width

There are instances when we wish to specify the half-width of the confidence intervals, thus providing a predetermined measure of the statistical precision of our results. In general, more replications conducted will lead to a narrower confidence interval, but the actual number to achieve a particular level of precision cannot be calculated in advance as it is a function of the sample size itself. An approximate value can be gained however by obtaining an initial sample standard deviation (say from five to ten replications) and solving for n as follows:

$$n = (z_{1-\alpha/2} * s_o/h_w)^2$$

where
$z_{1-\alpha/2}$ = value from normal distribution table at a significance α
s_o = sample standard deviation
h_w = required half-width of confidence interval

Note that $t_{1-\alpha/2,df}$ has been approximated to $z_{1-\alpha/2}$ because df depends on n which is the target value. When n replications have been completed the confidence intervals are calculated in the normal way. If the half-width is greater than required then the current value of s can be used to recalculate the number of replications, n, required.

Establishing Confidence Intervals at a Given Half-Width Using Arena

Normally a fixed number of iterations are made (say ten) without knowing the size of the confidence intervals of the values we are measuring. We can use Arena to check a particular confidence interval value after each simulation run and automatically stop running when this target value is reached. To do this we need some additional modules to control the simulation run behavior.

Load in the terminating dual queue bank clerk simulation file (Figure 5.3). Add a Create, Decide, Assign and Dispose module to the simulation screen away from the main model. Double click on the create module and enter 1 for max arrivals to create one entity at the beginning of each simulation replication. Double click on the decide module. Select the n-way by condition type. Add the expression NREP <= 2. NREP is an Arena variable holding the number of replications made. This condition ensures that at least two replications have been made and thus a confidence interval is formed. Add the expression ORUNHALF(1) > 0.2. ORUNHALF(1) is an Arena variable holding the value of the confidence interval 1 (defined in the number field of the outputs module). This condition runs the simulation until the defined half-width is less than the target value of 0.2. Double-click on the assign module. Click on the Add button. Select the other option. Enter MREP for other and NREP for new value. This sets the number of replications (MREP) to the current number of replications executed

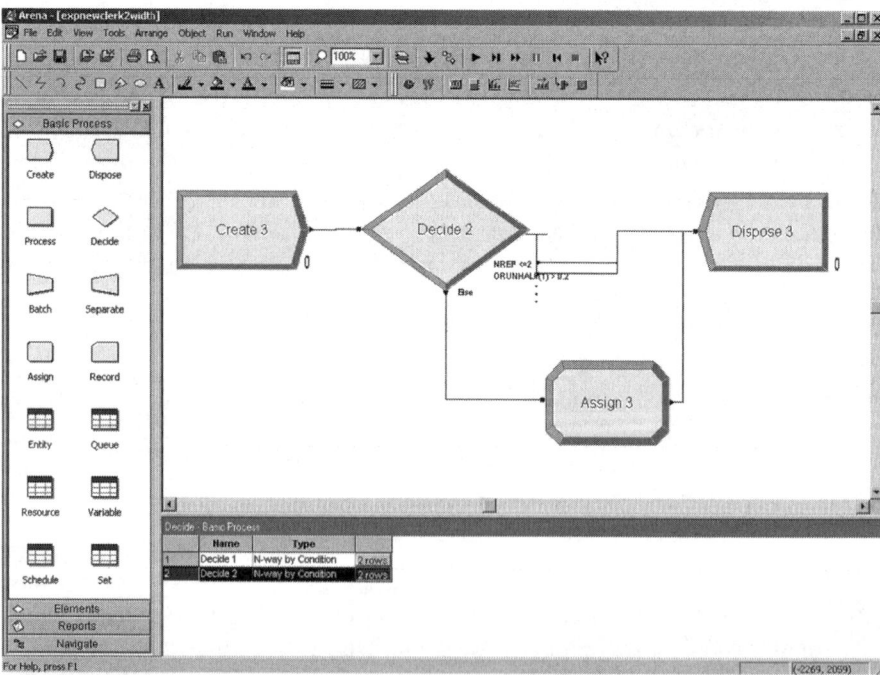

Figure 5.10: Logic for establishing confidence intervals at a given width.

(NREP) causing the simulation to stop at the end of the current replication. Select the run/setup/replication parameters option from the menu. Enter 99999 for the Number of Replications parameter. This is an arbitrarily high number, the replication number in this case being controlled by the confidence interval coding. Connect the modules using the connect button as in Figure 5.10. Run the model.

In this case the confidence interval for the dual queue average time in system is given as 0.198 (below the 0.2) target value. The number of replications required to reach this value should be around 42.

> **Simulation Replications and Hypothesis Testing**
>
> Simply increasing the number of model replications, with no changes to the model itself, will reduce the half-width of our confidence intervals and so increase the likelihood that out confidence intervals will not overlap when comparing model results. Thus a significant difference between results would be confirmed by the p-value reported from a hypothesis test. This behavior is associated with frequency based statistics in that sufficient replications can always yield a significant difference or effect because a p-value is simply a statement about whether you have enough data to detect an effect rather than about the size of the effect itself. Thus when comparing model results we need to think about the effect size–is the size of the difference important given the underlying variability of the model?

Statistical Analysis for Non-terminating Systems

The previous section considered statistical analysis for terminating systems. This section provides details of techniques for analyzing steady-state systems in which the start conditions of the model are not returned to. These techniques involve more complex analysis than for a terminating system and so consideration should be given to treating the model as a terminating system if at all possible.

A non-terminating system generally goes through an initial transient phase and then enters a steady-state phase when its condition is independent of the simulation starting conditions. This behavior could relate to a manufacturing system starting from an empty (no-inventory) state and then after a period of time moving to a stabilized behavior pattern. A simulation analysis will be directed toward measuring performance during the steady-state phase and avoiding measurements during the initial transient phase. The following methods of achieving this are discussed.

Setting Starting Conditions

This approach involves specifying start conditions for the simulation that will provide a quick transition to steady-state conditions. Most simulations are started in an empty state for convenience, but by using knowledge of steady-state conditions (e.g., stock levels), it is possible to reduce the initial bias phase substantially. The disadvantage with this approach is the effort in initializing simulation variables, of which there may be many, and when a suitable initial value may not be known. Also, it is unlikely that the initial transient phase will be eliminated entirely. For these reasons, the warmup period method is often used.

Using a Warmup Period

Instead of manually entering starting conditions, this approach uses the model to initialize the system and thus provide starting conditions automatically. This approach discards all measurements collected on a performance variable before a preset time in order to ensure that no data is collected during the initial phase. The point at which data is discarded must be set late enough to ensure that the simulation has entered the steady-state phase, but not so late that insufficient data points can be collected for a reasonably precise statistical analysis. A popular method of choosing the discard point is to visually inspect the simulation output behavior of the variable over time. It is important to ensure that the model is inspected over a time period, which allows infrequent events (e.g., machine breakdown) to occur a reasonable number of times.

In order to determine the behavior of the system over time and in particular to identify steady-state behavior, a performance measure must be chosen. A value such as work-in-progress (WIP) provides a useful measure of overall system behavior. In a manufacturing setting, this could relate to the amount of material within the system at any given time. In a service setting (as is the case with the bank clerk model) the WIP measure represents the number of customers in the system.

Using an Extended Run Length

This approach consists of running the simulation for an extended run length, thus reducing the bias introduced on output variables in the initial transient phase. This represents a simple solution to the problem and can be applied in combination with the other approaches.

Batch Means Analysis

To avoid repeatedly discarding data during the initial transient phase for each run, an alternative approach allows all data to be collected during one long run. The batch means method consists of making one very long run of the simulation and collecting data at intervals during the run. Each interval between data collection is termed a *batch*. Each batch is treated as a separate run of the simulation for analysis. The batch means method is suited to systems that have very long warmup periods and so avoidance of multiple replications is desirable. However, with the increase in computing power available, this advantage has diminished with run lengths needing to be extremely long in order to slow down analysis considerably. The batch means method also requires the use of statistical analysis methods, which are beyond the scope of this book.

Statistical Analysis of the Non-terminating Bank Clerk Simulation Using Arena
Load the non-terminating (original) version of the single queue bank clerk simulation in Arena developed in Chapter 4 (Figure 4.9). This version does not remove customers after the initial 480 minutes of operation. Select run/setup/project parameters from the menu bar. Enter 20 for the "Number of Replications" parameter and enter 10000 for the replication length. Ensure the tick boxes (in the Initialize between replications area) are checked for System and Statistics to achieve statistically independent replications. In the data spreadsheet view of the Statistics module, select Time Persistent for the type. Enter the expression DAVG(Entity 1.WIP); enter Average Time in System Single Q NonTerm for the report label and BCSNONTERM.DAT for the output file. Select the fast-forward button to run the model for 20 replications and run the Output Analyzer. Click on the PLOT button and add the filename BCSNONTERM.dat. Choose the replication all option. Click on OK. The plot will be displayed as shown in Figure 5.11.

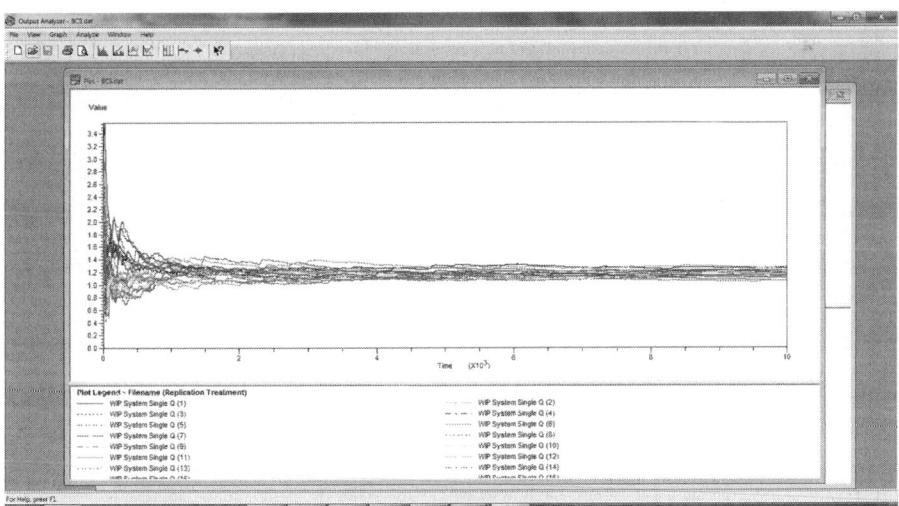

Figure 5.11: Plot of customers in system (WIP) (10,000 minutes).

From Figure 5.11 it is clear that a steady-state behavior is established quite quickly. This is not surprising for a simple system with only a single queuing point for customers. From the above-mentioned plot, a warmup period of 1000 minutes would seem sufficient. Once a warmup period has been selected, the value can be entered in the run/setup/project parameters dialog. The model when run will now simply discard statistical data during the first 1000 minutes of each replication. The model can then be analyzed in the same way as a terminating model simulation as outlined earlier in this chapter. Note that when comparing the results of different models, the warmup period and run length will need to be estimated separately for each alternative. Figure 5.12 shows a confidence interval on mean analysis for the non-terminating bank clerk simulation. The analysis should be treated in the same manner as that for the terminating analysis, but now the analysis is for the steady-state expected performance measures rather than for measures defined in relation to specific starting and ending conditions.

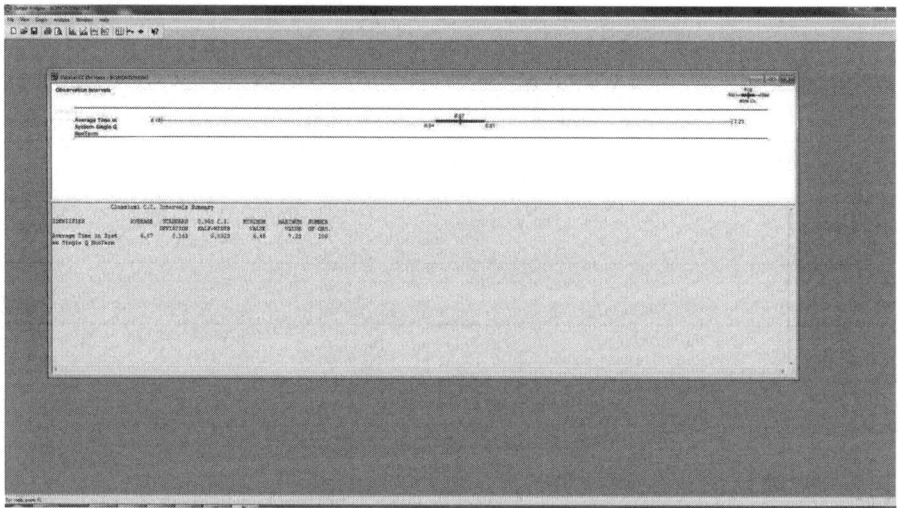

Figure 5.12: Confidence interval on means analysis for non-terminating bank clerk simulation.

Using the analysis shows that 95% of confidence intervals would contain an average service time between 6.79 and 6.95 minutes, with a mean of 6.87 minutes. Note that these values are higher than the terminating single queue simulation analysis where the 95% confidence interval is between 6.28 and 6.56 minutes, with a mean of 6.42 minutes. These higher values would be expected as the steady-state (non-terminating) analysis discards the initial recording from empty at the start of each replication and the model does not empty customers at the end of each replication. The confidence interval can be shortened by increasing the number of replications and thus the statistical sample size from which the confidence interval is derived.

An alternative way of shortening the confidence interval for steady-state analysis is to increase the run-length for each replication, which has the effect of decreasing the variability of each within run average.

Comparing the Performance of Alternative Simulation Models

When comparing between alternative configurations of a simulation model, we need to test whether differences in output measures are statistically significant or if differences could be within the bounds of random variation. Alternative configurations that require this analysis includes:
- changing input parameters (e.g., changing arrival rate)
- changing system rules (e.g., changing priority at a decision point)
- changing system configuration (comparing manual vs automated system)

Note that these changes imply that just a change to a single parameter value will create a new simulation model in terms of our statistical analysis of performance measures. Irrespective of the scale of the differences between alternative configurations, there is a need to undertake statistical tests. The tests will be considered for comparing between two alternatives, but can also be used to compare for more than two alternatives. The following assumptions are made when undertaking the tests:
- The data collected *within* a given alternative are independent observations of a random variable. This can be obtained by each replication using a different set of random numbers (method of independent replications).
- The data collected *between* alternatives are independent observations of a random variable. This can be obtained by using a separate number stream for each alternative. Note, however, that certain tests use the ability to use common random numbers for each simulation run in their analysis (see paired t-test using common random numbers).

The statistical tests are required so we can judge when comparing model results whether the means (over the replications) do actually suggest that a statistical change in performance has taken place. For instance, if the mean for the single queue scenario is 4.8 minutes and the mean for the dual queue scenario is 5.1 minutes, do these measures represent a statistically significant difference in performance or are they within the boundary of random variation? We now show three ways of doing this analysis.
1. Comparing Confidence Intervals
   The first is to compare the confidence intervals for the two means. If they do not overlap, we can say that the difference between the means is statistically significant. However, this is an informal test. In order to quantify how sure we are of this difference, we may need to conduct a hypothesis test, which will provide us with a decision based on a chosen level of confidence (e.g., 95% or 99%).

2. Hypothesis Testing

   A hypothesis test makes an assumption or a hypothesis (termed the *null hypothesis*, H_0) and tries to disprove it. Acceptance of the null hypothesis implies that there is insufficient evidence to reject it (it does not prove that it is true). Rejection of the null hypothesis, however, means that the alternative hypothesis (H_1) is accepted. The null hypothesis is tested using a test statistic (based on an appropriate sampling distribution) at a particular significance level α, which relates to the area called the *critical region* in the tail of the distribution being used. If the test statistic (which we calculate) lies in the critical region, the result is unlikely to have occurred by chance and so the null hypothesis would be rejected. The boundaries of the critical region, called the *critical values*, depend on whether the test is two-tailed (we have no reason to believe that a rejection of the null hypothesis implies that the test statistic is either greater or less than some assumed value) or one-tailed (we have reason to believe that a rejection of the null hypothesis implies that the test statistic is either greater or less than some assumed value). We must also consider the fact that the decision to reject or not reject the null hypothesis is based on a probability. Thus at a 5% significance level, there is a 5% chance that H_0 will be rejected when it is in fact true. In statistical terminology, this is called a *type I error*. The converse of this is accepting the null hypothesis when it is in fact false, called a *type II error*. Usually α values of 0.05 (5%) or 0.01 (1%) are used. An alternative to testing at a particular significance level is to calculate the *p*-value, which is the lowest level of significance at which the observed value of the test statistic is significant. Thus, a *p*-value of 0.045 (indicating a type I error occurring 45 times out of 1000) would show that the null hypothesis would be rejected at 0.05, but only by a small amount. Generally, the paired t-test is used to compare alternatives of real systems.

3. Analysis of Variance

   One-way analysis of variance (ANOVA) is used to compare the means of several alternative systems. Several replications are performed for each alternative and the test attempts to determine whether the variation in output performance is due to differences *between* the alternatives or due to inherent randomness *within* the alternatives themselves. This is undertaken by comparing the ratio of the two variations with a test statistic. The test makes the assumptions of independent data both within and between the data sets, observations from each alternative are drawn from a normal distribution and the normal distributions have the same variance. The first assumption implies the collection of data using independent runs or the batch means technique, but precludes the use of variance reduction techniques (e.g. common random numbers). The second assumption implies that each output measure is the mean of a large number of observations. This assumption is usually valid but can be tested with the chi-square or Kolmogorov-Smirnov test if required. The third assumption may require an increase in replication run-length to decrease the variances of mean performance. The F-test can be used to test this assumption if required. The test finds if a significant difference between means is apparent but does not indicate if all the means are different, or if the difference is between particular means. To identify where the differences occur tests such as Tukeys HSD test may be used. Alternatively confidence intervals between each combination can provide an indication.

To demonstrate the use of statistical tests for comparing between different types of models, a comparison will be made between the single queue and dual queue bank clerk models using confidence interval analysis, paired t-test and ANOVA.

Arena Comparison of Confidence Interval Analysis
Repeat the changes to the dual queue system for the single queue system presented earlier in this chapter in the Confidence Interval Analysis using Arena section. To do this load the single queue simulation into Arena. You will need to add a decide module before the process module in your model and direct all customers after 480 minutes to an additional dispose module. In this version of the simulation, save the time in system data to the file BCS.DAT.

Run both the dual queue and single queue simulations for 100 replications to create new BCD.dat and BCS.dat files for use by the Output Analyzer. Run the Output Analyzer and select the Analyze/Confidence Interval on Mean/Classical menu option. Add the file BCD.DAT and select lumped from the pull-down menu for the replications parameter. Data from the 100 replications are now presented together to compute the confidence interval. Click on OK. Add the file BCS.DAT. Select lumped from the pull-down menu for the replications parameter. Click on OK. Leave the default confidence interval at 0.95 (95%). Click on OK. The analysis as shown in Figure 5.13 will appear.

Using the Arena output processor, the results show the confidence intervals as the blue lines. The graphs show that we can be 95% confident when the average time in the system for the dual queue model is between 7.57 and 7.85 minutes and the average time in the system for the single queue system is between 6.28 and 6.56 minutes. We can use a visual inspection method of comparing to compare the confidence intervals and say that as the two confidence intervals (blue lines on the graph) do not overlap then there is a statistically significant difference between the time in the system for customers between the single queue and dual queue bank clerk models. If the confidence intervals overlap but the means do not overlap, we can say that there is probably a significant difference between the results, although some caution must be made in this assumption. Also note that multiple (more than two) confidence intervals may be compared on the same graph.

Arena Hypothesis Testing
The paired t-test calculates the difference between the two alternatives for each replication. It tests the hypothesis that if the data from both models is from the same

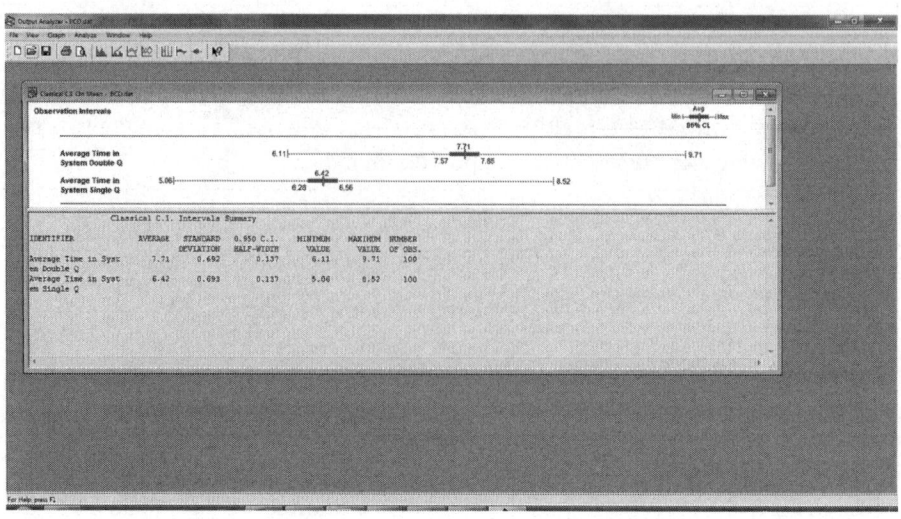

Figure 5.13: Arena comparison of confidence interval analysis.

distribution then the mean of the differences will be zero. The test contains the following steps:

1. Formulate the null hypothesis.

   Null Hypothesis: The means of both data sets are equal.

   Alternative Hypothesis: The means of both data sets are different.

2. Set a significance level.

   A significance level of α = 0.05 is usual.

3. Compute the t value.

$$t = \frac{\bar{x}_d - \mu_d}{\sigma_{\bar{d}}}$$

$\bar{x}_d$ = sample mean of the n differences

μ_d = population mean difference if the null hypothesis is correct

$\sigma_{\bar{d}}$ = standard error of the mean difference

Where

$$\sigma_{\bar{d}} = \frac{s_d}{\sqrt{n}}$$

where

s_d = standard deviation of the differences

n = number of differences

4. Interpret the results.

The critical value is now found from a t table for α significance level and n-1 degrees of freedom. If the calculated t value is greater than the lookup value then the hypothesis that the mean differences are zero is rejected.

In Arena undertake the paired t-test analysis by running the Output Analyzer program. Select the Analyze/Compare Means option from the menu. Select the Add File option and enter BCD.DAT for Data File A. Set replications to Lumped. Enter BCS. DAT for Data File B. Set replications to Lumped. Select OK. Select the "Paired t-test" radiobutton. Select OK. The Arena analysis is shown in Figure 5.14.

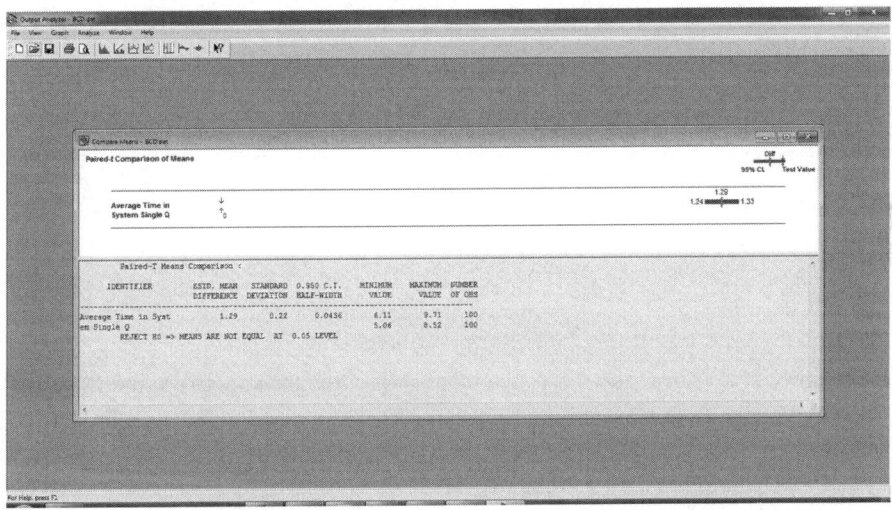

Figure 5.14: Paired t-test using Arena.

The results in Figure 5.14 show that the null hypothesis is rejected, so the means are different (with a mean difference of 1.29 minutes) at a 0.05 significance level. Thus, the change in average time in system is statistically significant between the single queue and dual queue bank clerk models.

Arena Analysis of Variance

In Arena to undertake the ANOVA analysis by running the Output Analyzer and selecting the Analyze/One-Way ANOVA option from the menu. Select the Add File option. Enter BCD.DAT for the Data File. Set replications to Lumped. Select the Add File option. Enter BCS.DAT for the Data File. Set replications to Lumped. Select Comparison Method to Tukey. The Arena analysis is shown in Figure 5.15.

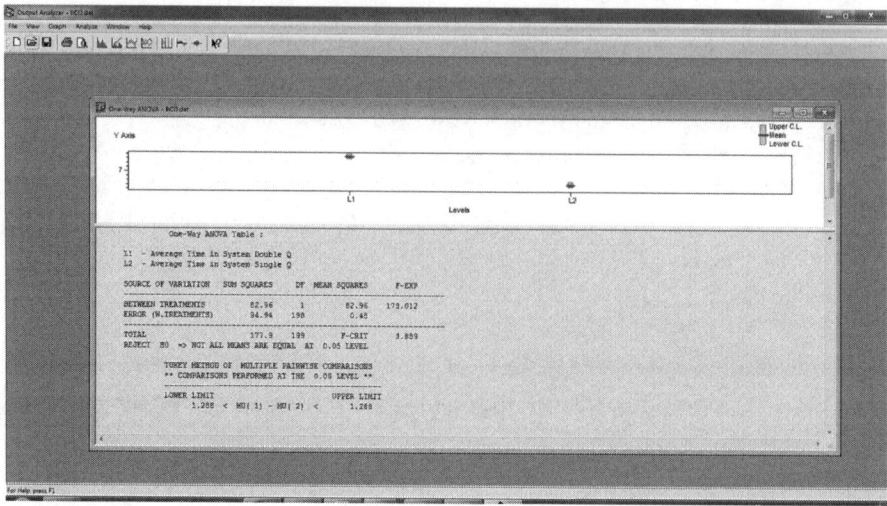

Figure 5.15: Arena One-Way ANOVA analysis.

From the results screen it can be seen that the null hypothesis has been rejected (the F-Test statistic of 173.012 is greater than the critical value of 3.889) and so the alternative hypothesis is accepted. Thus, the means are different at a 0.05 significance level. If we have more than two means, then the basic ANOVA analysis does not imply which means are different. In this case a comparison between the means has been made using the Tukey HSD (honestly significant differences) method. Arena also provides other methods of multiple comparisons. The Tukey method provides a comparison test between all the pairs of means in the analysis. In this case there is only one comparison ($1 \geq 2$) to be made. The analysis computes a difference between the means of 1.288.

Simio Comparison of Confidence Interval Analysis

In Simio to compare results between two alternative models create additional scenarios in the design table for each version of the model (Figure 5.16).

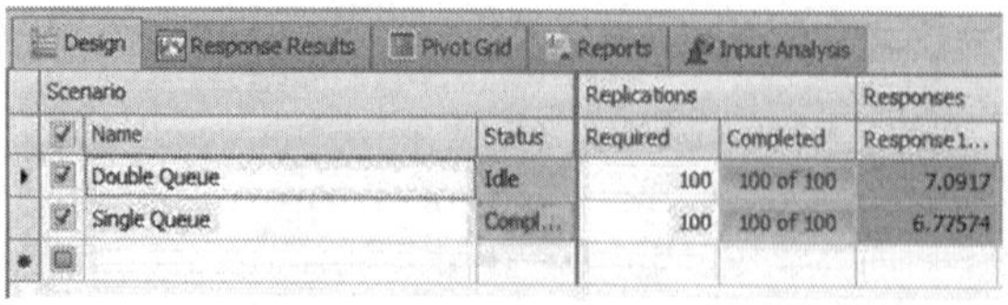

Scenario			Replications		Responses
	Name	Status	Required	Completed	Response 1...
✓	Double Queue	Idle	100	100 of 100	7.0917
✓	Single Queue	Compl...	100	100 of 100	6.77574

Figure 5.16: Simio create scenarios in experimental design.

Run the scenarios and the confidence intervals will be displayed on the Response Results tab (Figure 5.17).

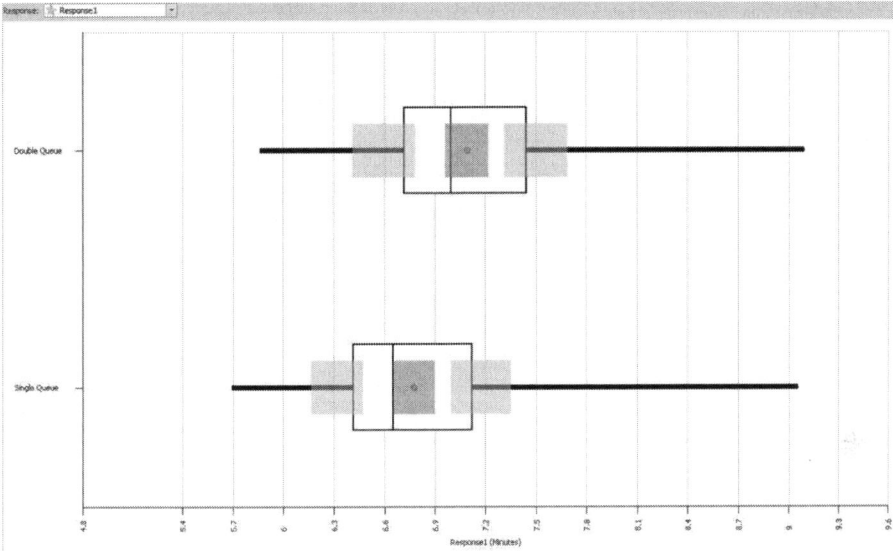

Figure 5.17: Simio confidence interval analysis comparing the single queue and dual queue models.

Further Statistical Analysis

Factorial Designs

In our simulation experimentation we may wish to analyze the effect of making changes to a variety of input variables and/or making a number of changes to a particular input variable and to see the effect on a number of output variables. In experimental design terminology experiments are conducted by changing a factor (input variable) in the model that has a level (value). A particular combination of levels is called a *treatment*. The output variable of interest is called the *response*. The standard way to investigate changes in a level of a factor would be to make a simulation run for each level and record the response. There are two issues with this approach:
- To investigate a number of factors requires a relatively high number of simulation runs.
- The effects of interaction (i.e., whether the effect of one factor depends on the levels of the other).

Thus, the objective of factorial design is to determine the impact of factors on a response.

Two-Level Full-Factorial Design

A two-level full-factorial design is when each factor is set at just two (high and low) levels. The levels could be different values of an input variable or different configurations of a model (e.g., different scheduling rules for a queuing system). No rules are provided as to what the levels of the factors should be, but levels need to be set that are different enough to show how the factor affects response, but within normal operating conditions for that factor. For a full-factorial design, each possible combination of factor levels is tested for response. This means for k factors there are 2^k combinations of low and high factor levels. These possible combinations are shown in an array called the *design matrix*. A design matrix for a 2^3 factorial design (i.e., 3 factors) is listed in Table 5.1.

Table 5.1: Two Factorial Design Matrix.

Factor Combination	Factor 1	Factor 2	Factor 3	Response
1	−	−	−	R_1
2	+	−	−	R_2
3	−	+	−	R_3
4	+	+	−	R_4
5	−	−	+	R_5
6	+	−	+	R_6
7	−	+	+	R_7
8	+	+	+	R_8

The advantage of following the factorial design approach over varying a single factor at a time is that the effect of interaction effects can be assessed. The ability to assess the impact of one factor change when the level of a second factor changes is important in finding the best system performance because the effect of two factors changing may not be the same as the addition of the effect of each factor change in isolation.

Optimization

Optimization involves choosing the "best" results rather than reporting the result for a particular scenario or comparing results between scenarios. Optimization thus provides a prescriptive analytics capability by recommending a choice of action. Many simulation software packages incorporate optimization software such as OptQuest (www.opttek.com) that use the machine-learning technique of genetic algorithms.

> **Optimization and Satisficing**
>
> Although optimization approaches can be useful, in practice decision makers are concerned with providing what they consider to be a satisfactory answer to a problem. This ensures analysis is not overly extended in search of the perfect answer, but they are also aware that the model does not take into account all aspects of the real system. The limitations of the model mean that the optimum solution provided is only optimal in comparison with the other solutions tried and there are likely to be other solutions that exist that have not been considered by the optimization. Also the decision maker is unlikely to make a decision solely on the basis of the model solution but is likely to consider other factors outside of the model scope to find a feasible and implementable solution. In Chapter 6 in a police call center a prescriptive analysis to find an optimum work schedule was undertaken by formulating a number of scenarios based on premises regarding ethical and moral concerns in terms of staff working conditions that would be difficult to codify as parameters in an optimization algorithm.

To show the use of OptQuest with Arena, a model of a petrol station is presented in Figure 5.18.

Customers arrive at the petrol station and 25% of customers head for the manual pumps (with payment at a separate till service). If no manual pumps are available, they drive away; otherwise, they refill their vehicle with petrol and then proceed to the payment till and continue with the payment process. About 75% of customers head for the pay at pumps. If no pay at pumps are available, they drive away; otherwise, they refill their vehicle with petrol and pay at the pump.

There current simulation parameters apply:
- The customer arrival rate is an exponential distribution with a mean of 3 minutes.
- The manual pump service time is a triangular distribution with a minimum of 4 minutes, mode of 6 minutes and maximum of 10 minutes.
- The pay at pump service time is a triangular distribution with a minimum of 6 minutes, mode of 8 minutes and maximum of 12 minutes.
- The payment at till service is a triangular distribution with a minimum of 1 minute, mode of 4 minutes and maximum of 6 minutes.
- Currently there are 2 manual petrol pumps, 2 pay at pumps and 1 payment till. There is enough space to increase this to 6 manual pumps, 6 pay at pumps and 4 payment tills.
- Management wishes to ensure that less than 12 cars drive away over an 8-hour period.
- Also there is a requirement that the customer average waiting time is no more than 5 minutes at the till.

The total cost per day of renting and operating the station is £50 per manual pump installed, £100 per pay pump installed and £200 per payment till.

There is an estimated income of £20 per customer served at the petrol station.

178 — Chapter 5 Use Simulation for Descriptive, Predictive and Prescriptive Analytics

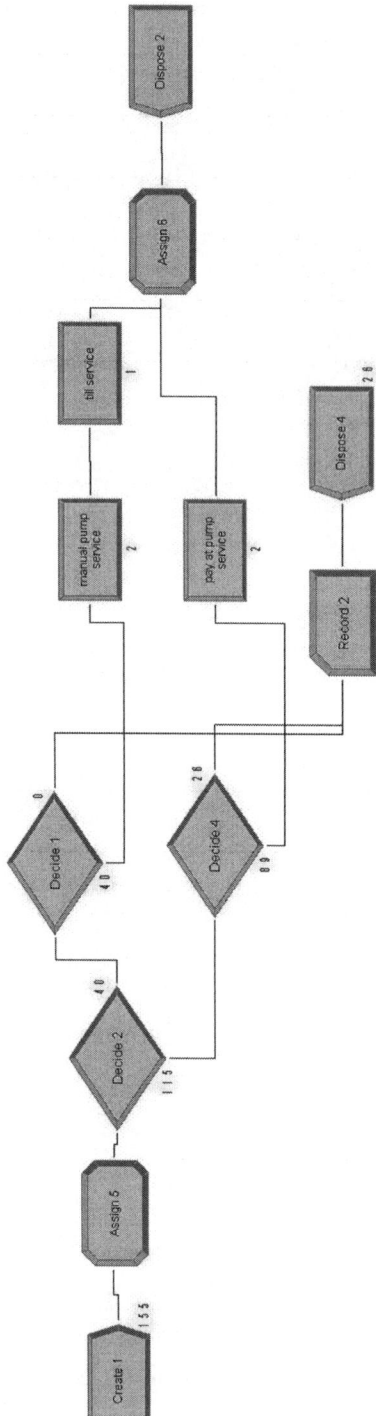

Figure 5.18: Petrol station simulation.

Management wish to know the best combination of pumps and tills to maximize profit per day and meet their performance targets on "drive aways" and till waiting time.

A method to tackle this problem is to take a trial-and-error approach and try combinations of pump and till values and observe the results. However, this is a time-consuming process and may miss the optimal solution. A quick way of undertaking the analysis is to use the OptQuest facility provided with Arena. From the model select the Tools/OptQuest for Arena option. Then from OptQuest select the File/New option and then select the OptQuest optimization icon from the screen. The screen will display all the variables you have defined as reported statistics in your Arena model under the Control summary (Figure 5.19).

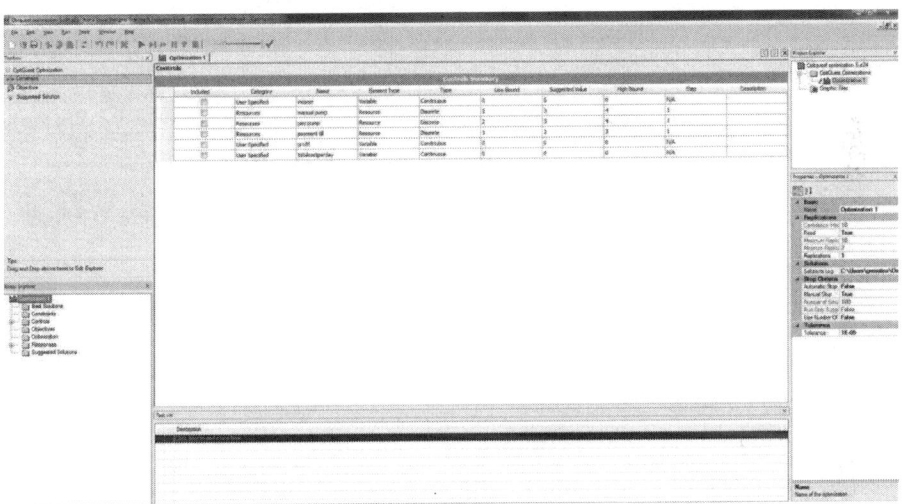

Figure 5.19: QptQuest control view for petrol station Arena model.

The optimization program requires four elements to be entered:
1. Controls (these are input parameters such as capacities of resources and Arena variables you have defined)
2. Responses (these are output parameters such as queuing statistics that either Arena or you have defined)
3. Constraints (these are minimum and maximum values that you can set for the controls and responses)
4. Objectives (these are the values you wish to optimize)

For the controls you need to select the resources of the pay pump, manual pump and payment till from the controls list by ticking the include box. Also adjust the upper bounds for the pumps to 6 and for the payment till to 4 as specified for the experiment.

For the responses click on the responses folder in the Editor Explorer to the bottom left of the screen. Select the till service.queue.waittime, the drive away and the profit variables from the list (Figure 5.20).

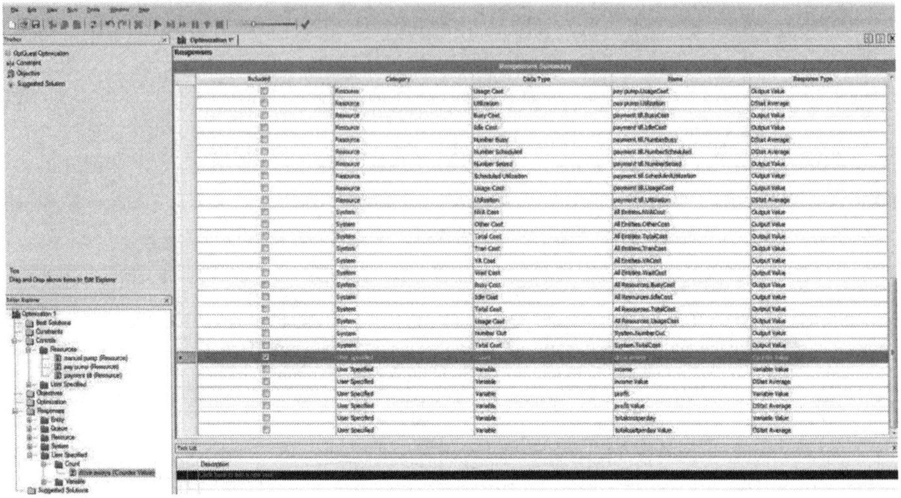

Figure 5.20: OptQuest responses selection.

Now right click on the Constraints folder in the Editor Explorer and select the Add option. From the table that appears double click on the Expression row and the expression menu will appear (Figure 5.21).

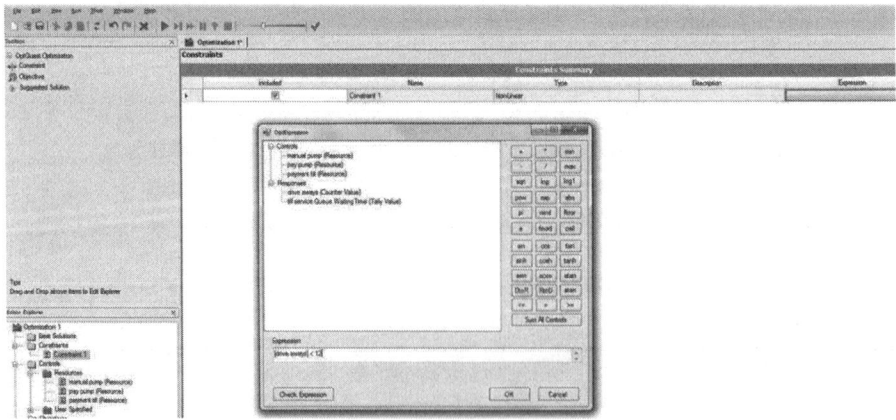

Figure 5.21: OptQuest add constraints.

Select the expressions you wish to add by clicking on them and they will appear in the expression box at the bottom of the menu. Add the constraint to the variable name. For example, amend the expression [drive aways] to [drive aways] < 12. This limits the number of drive aways to less than 12 for a single 8 hour run. Add a second constraint for the till waiting time of 5 minutes [till service.Queue.WaitingTime] < 5.

For the objective, right click on the Objectives folder and select the Add option. Double click on the Expression row and select the Profit variable in the Expressions menu. Make sure that the maximize option is selected for the profit objective. Run the optimization by selecting the go arrow on the top menu bar. The following analysis is displayed by clicking on the optimization folder (Figure 5.22).

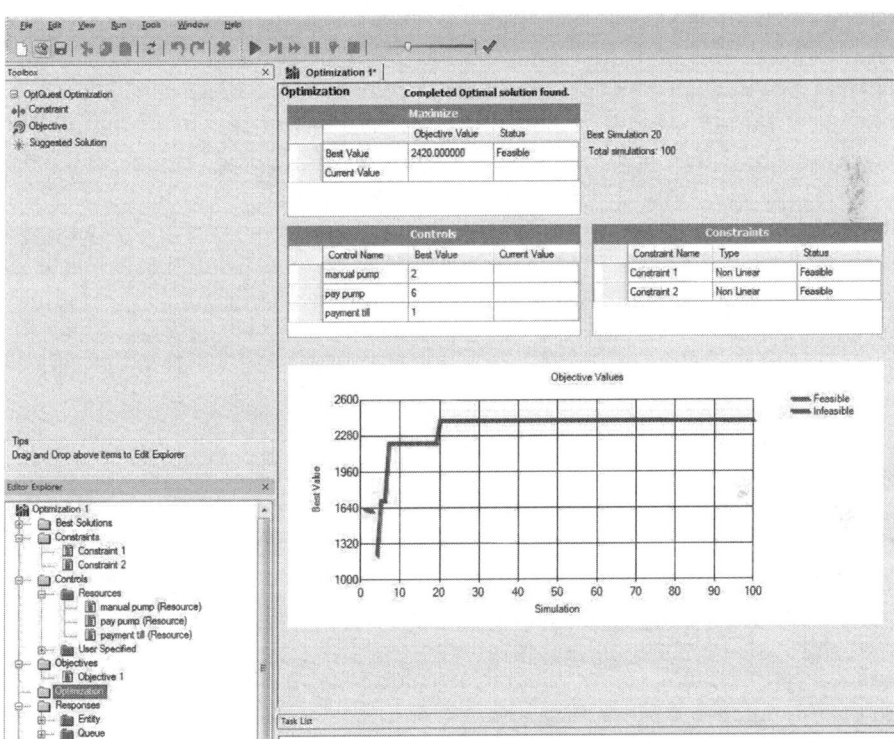

Figure 5.22: OptQuest optimization results.

The graph shows the best solution found as the optimization software worked through 100 scenarios. The optimum scenario that maximizes profit is found to be a mix of 2 manual pumps, 6 pay pumps and 1 payment till, giving a profit of £2420 for that day. This was achieved by meeting both constraints in terms of keeping "drive aways" below 12 on that day and the payment till queue size at less than 5 minutes. This example shows how optimization can enable the use of simulation for prescriptive analytics when a course of action is required.

Visual Analytics

For experimentation with systems that are complex we may have many input parameters that we can set to many different values. In order to analyze these systems, we need to execute simulation runs for different parameter combinations. Often in this situation, it is difficult to interpret the results of these experimental designs simply using statistics. Visualization or visual analytics simultaneously presents simulation results for a number of parameter combinations to the user. Thus, the technique uses the visual display of information and the domain knowledge of the user to observe the results of parameter combinations that may be selected for further investigation. Alternatively visual analytics may use analytics techniques such as a clustering algorithm that classifies the simulation experiments as a way of synthesizing large amounts of data and helping to reveal patterns and relationships between variables that might otherwise be hidden or difficult to find. Clustering methods can be used to explore simulation output data by treating each object in a cluster as a single simulation run allocated on selected parameter results. For example, in a two-dimensional analysis, the variables cycle time and throughput time may be used. Once the clusters are mapped out visually, analysts can investigate which input settings led to the corresponding systems performance measures that define this cluster. A limitation of visual analytics is that the identification of relationships using visual inspection may be less precise and more open to interpretation than traditional approaches to simulation output analysis. Furthermore, visual analytics may require the training in and use of new analytics software and analysis methods by simulation practitioners.

Various postprocessing software applications are available that supplement the experimentation and analysis facilities provided by the simulation software. For example, in Simio results can be exported as CSV files, which can be used by various statistical and analytics packages such as Excel, SPSS and R. An example of a dedicated visualization package is the Tableau software (https://www.tableau.com/products/desktop) that provides dashboard facilities that can be used for the presentation of simulation results (Figure 5.23).

Process-mining software can also be used to supplement the traditional reports generated by simulation software. The simulation can be developed to generate an event log, which is held in a CSV file. This file is then imported into the process-mining software package that provides extensive event-based graphical facilities for model validation and analysis of results. See Chapter 17 for generating simulation analytics with process-mining software.

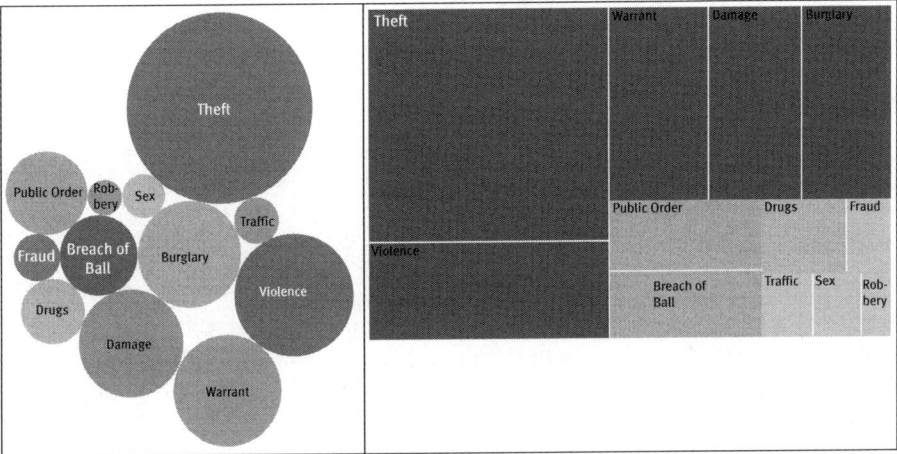

Figure 5.23: Tableau dashboard showing relative cost of simulated arrest types.

Implementation

This section covers the issue of ensuring implementation of changes recommended as a consequence of simulation study results. The need for a detailed project report is outlined in addition to a discussion of managerial and operational involvement in implementation.

Project Report

For each simulation study, the simulation model should be accompanied by a project report, outlining the project objectives and providing the results of experimentation. Discussion of results and recommendations for action should also be included. Finally a further work section will communicate to the client any possible developments and subsequent results that could be obtained from the model. For example, if there are a number of results to report, an appendix can be used to document detailed statistical work. This enables the main report to focus on the key business results derived from the simulation analysis. A separate technical document may also be prepared, which may incorporate a model and/or model details such as key variables and a documented coding listing. Screen shots of the model display can also be used to show model features. The report structure should contain the following elements:
- Introduction
- Description of the problem area
- Model specification

- Simulation experimentation
- Results
- Conclusions and recommendations
- Further studies
- Appendices: process logic, data files, model coding

Project Presentation

A good way of closing a simulation project is to organize a meeting of interested parties and present a summary of the project objectives and results. Project documentation can also be distributed at this point. This enables discussion of the outcomes of the project with the client and provides an opportunity to discuss further analysis. This could be in the form of further developments of the current model or a decision to prepare a specification for a new project.

Project Implementation Plan

It is useful to both the simulation developer and client if an implementation plan is formed to undertake recommendations from the simulation study. Implementation issues will usually be handled by the client, but the simulation developer may be needed to provide further interpretation of results or conduct further experimentation. Changes in the system studied may also necessitate model modification. The level of support at this time from the developer may range from a telephone hotline to further personal involvement specified in the project report. Results from a simulation project will only lead to implementation of changes if the credibility of the simulation method is assured. This is achieved by ensuring each stage of the simulation project is undertaken correctly.

Organizational Context of Implementation

A simulation modeling project can use extensive resources both in terms of time and money. Although the use of simulation in the analysis of a one-off decision, such as investment appraisal, can make these costs low in terms of making the correct decision, the benefits of simulation can often be maximized by extending the use of the model over a period of time. It is thus important that during the project proposal stage that elements are incorporated into the model and into the implementation plan that assist in enabling the model to provide on-going decision support. Aspects include the following:

- Ensure that simulation users are aware at the project proposal stage that the simulation is to be used for on-going decision support and will not be put to one side once the immediate objectives are met.
- Ensure technical skills are transferred from simulation analysts to simulation users. This ensures understanding of how the simulation arrives at results and its potential for further use in related applications.
- Ensure communication and knowledge transfer from simulation consultants and industrial engineers to business managers and operational personnel. The needs of managerial and operational personnel are now discussed in more detail.

Managerial Involvement

The cost associated with a simulation project means that the decision of when and where to use the technique will usually be taken by senior management. Thus, an understanding of the potential and limitations of the technique is required if correct implementation decisions are to be made.

Operational Involvement

Personnel involved in the day-to-day operation of the decision area need to be involved in the simulation project for a number of reasons. They usually have a close knowledge of the operation of the process and thus can provide information regarding process logic, decision points and activity durations. Their involvement in validating the model is crucial, where any deviations from operational activities seen from a managerial view to the actual situation can be indicated. Both the use of process maps and a computer-animated simulation display offer a means of providing a visual method of communication of how the whole process works (as opposed to the part certain personnel are involved in) and facilitate a team approach to problem solving by providing a forum for discussion.

Simulation can be used to develop involvement from the operational personnel in a number of areas. It can present an ideal opportunity to change from a top-down management culture and move to greater involvement from operational personnel in change projects. Simulation can also be a strong facilitator of communicating ideas up and down an organization. Engineers, for example, can use simulation to communicate reasons for taking certain decisions to operational personnel who might suggest improvements. The use of simulation as a tool for employee involvement in the improvement process can be a vital part of an overall change strategy. The process orientation of simulation provides a tool for analysis of processes from a cross-functional as opposed to a departmental perspective.

Finally it is important to remember that the use of a simulation model in a business context is to support decision makers in the organization by providing descriptive, predictive and prescriptive analysis. To be successful in this role the simulation model developer should ensure the steps in the simulation development such as data collection, model building and experimentation are undertaken well but should also remember that the end purpose of the study should lead to implementation of a decision. From the perspective of simulation used for decision-making:
- The decision-maker will need to recognize a problem and the ability of simulation to provide insight that can lead to a better decision.
- The decision-maker will be most interested in the usefulness of the model for decision making rather than the sophistication of the model itself.
- The simulation model should meet the needs of the decision maker in terms of providing them with confidence in its results and have been developed in a cost-effective manner.
- Confidence of the model from a decision-maker's perspective will be focused on comparing its behavior to the real-world system, more than on statistical tests of validity.
- The cost effectiveness of the simulation will be judged by comparing the cost of development of the model with the importance of the decision.
- The model developer must be able to explain the model results clearly and simply to the decision-maker avoiding excessive use of jargon and statistical references.
- The decision maker will use the model results in combination with their own experience and intuition when making the decision.

Simulation Case Studies

Based on industrial assignments conducted by the author, case studies 1–11 are presented to show some of the ways that simulation can be used for descriptive, predictive and prescriptive analytics (Table 5.2). A further three cases (cases 12–14) are used to demonstrate the use of simulation in combination with analytic techniques for analysis.

Case studies 1, 5 and 9 demonstrate the role of simulation to undertake descriptive analytics. Although not often associated with descriptive analytics, in some instances a dynamic model is required to enhance the understanding of the current process. An example of this is the estimation of cost. Most organizations are aware of costs in terms of a budget for a department including aspects such as staff costs. However, public sector organizations in particular may be required to reduce cost while maintaining performance in key areas. In order to do this, an understanding of how cost is being incurred is required. Simulation can be used to generate predicted

Table 5.2: Case Studies for Descriptive, Predictive and Prescriptive Analytics.

Case Study	Descriptive (Understanding)	Predictive (Scenarios)	Prescriptive (Recommendations)
1 Police Call Center	Estimate current staff costs	Shift patterns scenarios	Optimized shift pattern
2 Logistics System		Separate vs mixed delivery scenarios	
3 ERP System		Efficiency and flexibility for three ERP configurations	
4 Snacks Process		Conveyor breakdown scenario	Optimum case reintroduction rate
5 Police Arrest Process	Estimate current arrest costs	Late drinking scenario	
6 Food Retail Distribution		Secondary distribution route scenario	
7 Proposed Textile Plant		Capacity scenarios	
8 A Road Traffic Accident Process		Cost reduction scenarios	
9 A Rail Carriage Maintenance Depot	Show capability to operate under fixed constraints	Show planned schedule for maintenance	
10 A Rail Vehicle Bogie Production Facility		Line Balancing options	
11 Advanced Service Provision		Profit of Product-Service System (PSS) variants	

Case Study 12 Generating Simulation Analytics with Process Mining
This case shows how the facilities of process-mining software can be used for simulation output analysis.

Case Study 13 Using Simulation with Data Envelopment Analysis
The case shows the use of simulation with the analytics technique of Data Envelopment Analysis.

Case Study 14 Agent-Based Modeling in Discrete-Event Simulation
This case shows the implementation of an agent-based approach in simulation.

activity demand and provide an understanding of how cost can be reduced by reducing the cost of resources, the amount of resources needed to undertake an activity and the number of times that an activity is required over time. This analysis is presented in case studies 1 and 5. Case study 9 provides an example of the use of simulation to demonstrate the understanding of the operation of a system not just to the user of the simulation but also to the client of the proposed operation. Here the animation capabilities of simulation are used to provide a dynamic display of the operation of a system that does not yet exist.

Case studies 1–11 all demonstrate the main role of simulation to provide a prediction of future performance. Predictive analytics are normally presented in the form of scenarios that represent some change to the design or operation of the current system. Most scenario analysis will compare the current and new process designs to gauge the amount of change measured by a chosen performance metric.

Case studies 1 and 4 demonstrate the use of simulation for prescriptive analytics. Here specific design choices are recommended as "optimal" for implementation. Although it may be that scenarios presented in a predictive analysis are taken forward for implementation in prescriptive analytics, some attempt has been made to provide the best or optimal choice. In case study 1, a number of shift patterns were trialed using the simulation before one that met the requirements of the organization was taken forward. It was not feasible to find a solution using optimization software as many of the constraints around the schedule concerned contextual issues such as the well-being of staff that were difficult to codify in the model. In case 4 a specific aim of the study was to find the optimal reintroduction rate of material onto the conveyor system. This was found through repeated scenario analysis, although in this study optimization software could have been employed.

Case studies 12–14 show how the capability of simulation may be increased by combining its use with other analytics techniques. Case study 12 demonstrates the use of the analytics technique of process mining to present simulation output results. Case study 13 proposes how simulation can be used in conjunction with the analytics technique of data envelopment analysis (DEA). Case study 14 shows the implementation of a simple agent-based model in the Arena discrete-event simulation software.

A summary is now presented of each case study:

Case Study 1: "A simulation of a police call center" concerns the use of simulation to measure the performance of a UK police emergency call center. The simulation is used in a predictive analytics mode to identify the staffing cost of the current operation. Simulation is then used in a prescriptive mode to design a revised staffing rotation that enables the necessary speed of call response to be maintained while reducing staffing cost.

Case Study 2: "A simulation of a 'last mile' logistics system" concerns the use of simulation to measure the performance of a logistics service provider. Simulation is used in a predictive mode to investigate if delivery time windows can be met when moving from a policy of separate delivery runs for retail and nonretail customers to a mixed delivery policy for both retail and nonretail customers.

Case Study 3: "A simulation of an enterprise resource planning system" concerns the use of simulation to measure customer service performance when introducing an enterprise resource planning (ERP) system into a customer order processing activity. Simulation is used to measure performance of three scenarios, the original manual operation, the ERP operation and combined operations of an ERP and Enterprise Social System. Customer service quality is considered in terms of the trade-off between the flexibility provided in meeting individual customer needs and the cost of serving individual customers.

Case Study 4: "A simulation of a snacks process production system" concerns the use of simulation to measure the performance of a conveyor system in a continuous operation producing food items. When a breakdown occurred in the original manual system, flexibility was demonstrated in the downstream packing area to deal with the spike in demand when the breakdown is fixed. When implementing an automated packing facility, much of this flexibility was lost. The simulation was able to test polices for ensuring flexibility of operation of the automated system in response to conveyor breakdown events.

Case Study 5: "A simulation of a police arrest process" concerns the use of simulation to identify the costs of operating a police custody suite that processes arrested people for interview, detention or release. The simulation uses historical data in a descriptive mode to identify the costs of the operation from a process, resource and activity perspective. Simulation is used in a predictive mode to estimate the resource and thus cost implications of a change in the law, which leads to an increase in arrested persons.

Case Study 6: "A simulation of a food retail distribution system" concerns the use of simulation to model a food distribution network in order to assess its performance in terms of empty vehicle running. The model is then developed to encompass an extension to the distribution network that offers a pickup from tier 2 suppliers and a drop-off service to tier 1 suppliers as part of the return to depot route of the main distribution network design.

Case Study 7: "A simulation of a proposed textile plant" concerns the design of a proposed overseas textile production facility, which supplies garment manufacturers with rolls of material suitable for clothing manufacture. The simulation will assess the performance of the production system for two scenarios of production capacity. The case provides an example of the use of simulation for design purposes of a system that does not yet exist.

Case Study 8: "A simulation of a road traffic accident process" concerns predicting the cost savings made on front-line road traffic officer staff when changes are made to the road traffic accident reporting process. The changes were based around the use of mobile devices to record and map the location of traffic accidents at the location of the incident. Observation of performance measures provided by the simulation model helped to secure an acceptance of the need for change by demonstrating the increased performance of the proposed system. This case provides an example of how simulation can support public sector organizations in quantifying outcomes to support business cases for action.

Case Study 9: "A simulation of a rail carriage maintenance depot" concerns the use of the simulation technique to ensure that a service delivery system can undertake a number of service tasks to specified service levels. In this case, the requirement was to operate a rail carriage maintenance depot on existing infrastructure meant that capacity would be constrained by the number of existing stabling and refurbishment lines. Management needed to assess if sufficient capacity was available in order to carry out the refurbishment tasks in the time period between delivery to the depot and request for next service.

Case Study 10: "A simulation of a rail vehicle bogie production facility" provides an analysis of a line layout production facility and employs simulation to predict the effect of changes on the line cycle time and thus output. This case is used to explore how the value of simulation could be maximized in an organizational setting.

Case Study 11: "A simulation of advanced service provision" provides an analysis of three variants of service offering for a computer numerical controlled (CNC) machine manufacturer. The simulation reports on revenue and cost estimates and thus provides an estimate of profit for the three variants under base conditions. Variant C is also analyzed under two further scenarios involving changes to revenue payments and a decrease in equipment failure rate.

This case shows the use of simulation to estimate revenue and cost for future service provision under conditions of uncertainty. The information provided by the simulation can reduce risk when tendering advanced service offerings to clients.

Case Study 12: "Generating simulation analytics with process mining" concerns the use of the analytics technique of process mining, which provides automatic generation of detailed process models from event logs. As real-world systems have to evolve and adapt to be competitive the quantification of risk is often more important for day-to-day operations and decision making than long-run performance. Thus, more and more current and potential simulation users are interested in risk analysis, prediction and control, rather than system design. This case study demonstrates the use of process-mining software to provide an extended analysis of simulation output measures.

Case Study 13: "Using simulation with data envelopment analysis" concerns using simulation with the static model-driven analysis technique of DEA. This study suggests that simulation can be used in order to offer practical guidance to improving the performance of benchmark operating units identified in a DEA analysis by using sensitivity analysis of the benchmark unit to offer direct support as to the feasibility and efficiency of any variations in the operating practices to be tested. Simulation can also be used as a mechanism to transmit the practices of the benchmark unit to weaker performing units by building a simulation model of the weaker unit to the process design of the benchmark unit. The model can then compare performance of the current and benchmark process designs.

Case Study 14: "Agent-based modeling in discrete-event simulation" concerns the use of agent-based simulation as an alternative to the use of discrete-event simulation for dynamic modeling. There are differing views on whether an agent-based simulation offers capabilities that discrete event can not provide or whether all agent-based applications can at least in theory be undertaken using a discrete-event approach. This study presents a simple agent-based NetLogo model and corresponding discrete-event versions implemented in the Arena and Simio software.

Part 2: **Simulation Case Studies**

Chapter 6
Case Study: A Simulation of a Police Call Center

Andrew Greasley and Chris M. Smith

A sign of analytics maturity for an organization is the ability to use the output of descriptive and predictive models as input to prescriptive analytic models. This case study provides an example of the use of simulation for the combined use of descriptive, predictive and prescriptive analytics in a police communications center application. The first stage of the study provides a descriptive analysis using simulation in conjunction with activity-based costing (ABC) to understand how cost is generated in the process. This information then leads to a second-stage predictive and prescriptive analysis of design options for reducing cost.

The Case Study

There are 43 independent police forces in England and Wales with each force responsible for answering and responding to incoming calls for service through the use of communication centers. The police communications center examined in this case study has a total annual call volume of around 285,000 calls. Figure 6.1 shows the main processes involved in the communication center. 999 (emergency) calls are sent directly to call handlers with nonemergency calls sent via a switchboard. The switchboard operator will either resolve the caller query or direct the call to a call handler. Call handlers will take the relevant information from the caller and grade the call for an appropriate response. If attendance to an incident is necessary, call handlers pass the call information onto a team of controllers who manage the deployment of officers on the ground. It will be a specific controller who manages the incident. Controllers are responsible for a geographic area so if the incident occurs in their area they will have to manage it regardless of how busy they are. Thus, controllers control the resources in a geographical area unlike call handling where the call goes to the next available call handler. The simulation study boundary is indicated in Figure 6.1 and encompasses the incoming call and call handler process but with the controller process outside the remit of this study.

Step 1: Build the Conceptual Model

The first stage of the simulation study will use the framework provided by ABC to predict how cost is generated taking into account the variability of demand and

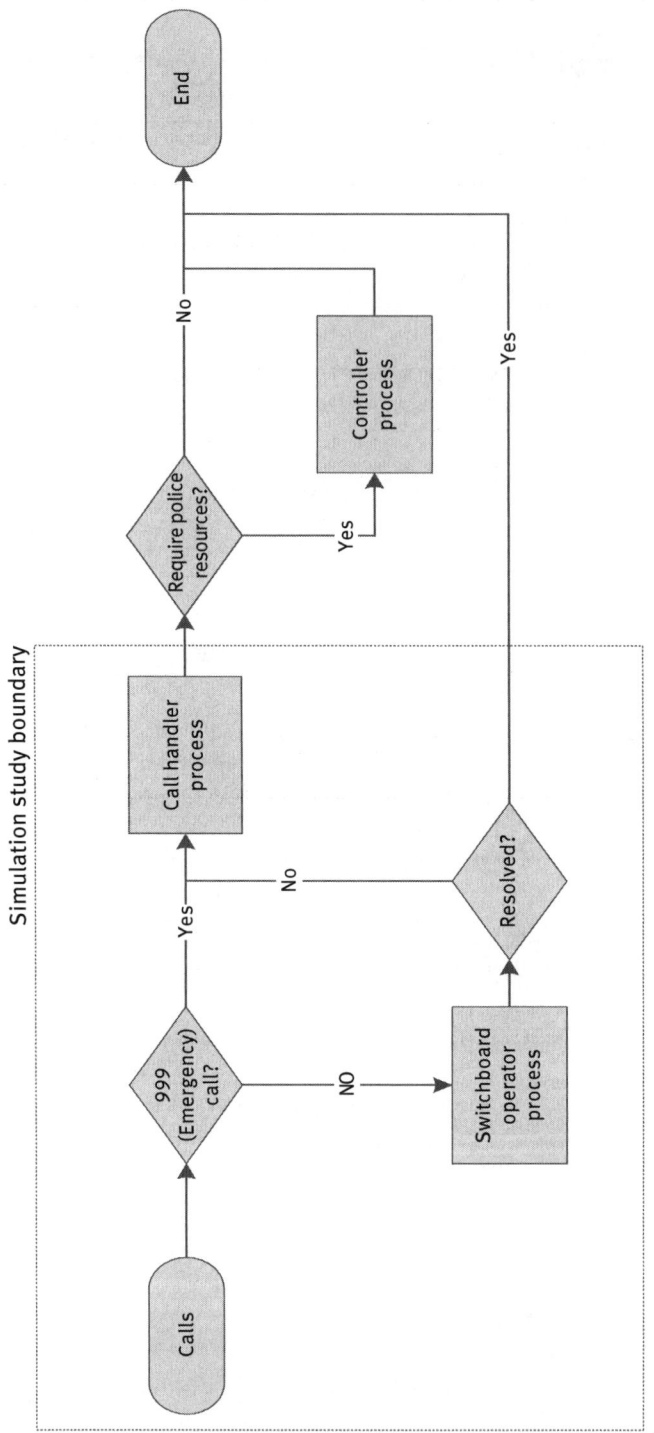

Figure 6.1: Police communications center process map.

variability in process durations that occur within the communications center. The second stage of the simulation study will then make an assessment of the relative reduction in cost and communications center performance between the current staff shift pattern and a proposed 9-hour, five-shift staffing scenario. The aim is to provide a prescription to managers which will enable them to improve the efficiency of the deployment of staff while maintaining target service levels.

For data collection, extensive use was made of the emergency services command and control application, which records call data and makes it available through a built-in MIS facility. The project involved the collection of data regarding the type of calls received, termed *skill sets*. Skill sets include 999 emergency calls, calls activated by house alarms, emergency calls from the fire service and calls from other police forces (Table 6.1). Information was collected on each skill set regarding its priority (emergency calls having highest priority and jump the queue for a response over lower priority skill sets) and the target response time to answer a call. The target maximum response time for 999 emergency calls from the public, which represent approximately 28% of all calls, is currently 10 seconds (for 90% of calls). For all other emergency and nonemergency calls, the target response time is 30 seconds (for 90% of calls). Calls from the public are routed via the national exchange and so can be distinguished from other emergency calls for performance monitoring purposes. Emergency calls from other services such as the fire brigade will typically be a request for police to attend an incident with them so speaking with an operator from the fire contact center.

Table 6.1: Skill Set Call Priority and Target Response Time.

Skill Set Name	Skill Set ID	Priority ID	Target Response Time (s) for 90% of Calls
999 Emergency	5682	10	10
999 Switchboard	5683	10	30
Other Force Emergency	5684	15	30
Other Force General	5685	25	30
Alarms	5686	10	30
Ambulance Emergency	5687	15	30
Ambulance General	5688	25	30
Fire Emergency	5689	15	30
Fire General	5690	25	30
Other Agency Emergency	5691	15	30
Other Agency General	5692	25	30
Switchboard Priority	5693	15	30
Switchboard Schedule	5694	20	30
Switchboard Info Line	5695	30	30
Coventry Airport	0	15	30

In order to model call demand, historical data was collected based on the number of calls for each skill set hour by hour over a 24-hour clock and on different days of the week. The demand for each skill set in terms of calls made during each hourly slot is assumed to be constant and so was modeled using an exponential distribution, which may be used to model the interarrival time of customers to a system that occurs at a constant rate. Data was also used to estimate statistical distributions for the talk time (time on the phone to a caller) for each skill set. For some skill set types such as Ambulance General, Other Agency Emergency and Coventry Airport, the number of calls over the sample period is very low and so was modeled using a triangular distribution which is recommended for activity times when there is little or no data. Other skill sets such as 999 Emergency were modeled using a log-normal distribution, reflecting a general tendency for the majority of calls to be short with a minority of much longer calls. This approach was seen as an improvement on the traditional approach of modeling call handling times using an exponential distribution based on average call handling times derived from the call center automated call distribution systems. In this instance, sample call handling times for each skill set were derived from skill set performance reports supplied by the force. Data was also collected and modeled on any required communication with controllers and paperwork subsequent to a call, termed the '*wrap-up*' *time*.

In addition, data was collected on calls that were not completed due to the caller "hanging up" the telephone. These are called abandoned calls. Abandoned calls within the target response time could be considered to be often made in error while abandoned calls outside the target response time could be said to be often due to slow response. Separate data was collected on abandoned calls both within and outside the target response time and separately for the skill set 999 emergency and these were modeled using an exponential distribution.

Step 2: Build the Simulation Model

The model is built using the Arena simulation software. A visual display of the Arena simulation is configured as a dashboard and is shown in Figure 6.2. The figure shows performance metrics for 16 skill sets. Further skill sets could be added to meet future requirements if necessary.

In order to explain the dashboard display, Figure 6.3 shows an enlarged view of the 999 emergency skill set.

The top of the skill set display shows the skill set number; in this case, 5682 and the skill set description. The top line metric is the average wait time for customer calls in seconds. The target response time for a call of that skill set is displayed on the left-hand side of the next row down (In this case, the target response time is 10 seconds). This row also displays the percentage of calls that have been

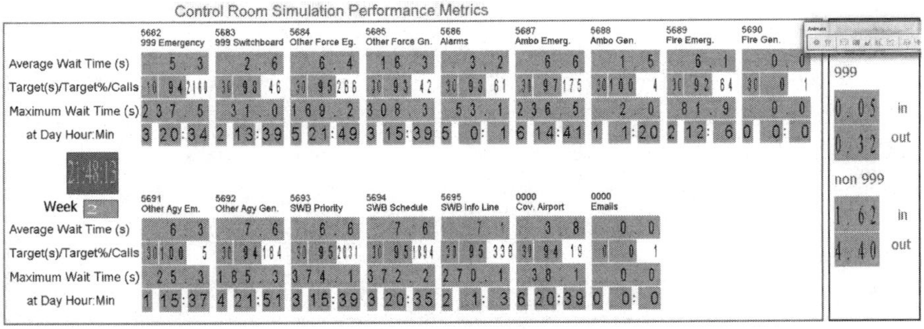

Figure 6.2: The police communications center simulation model dashboard display.

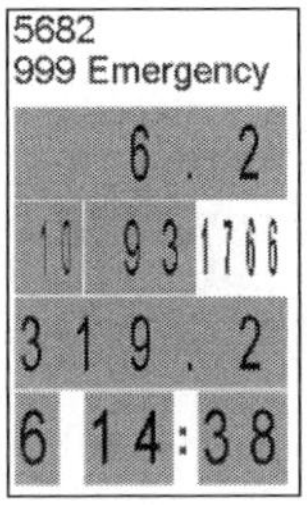

Figure 6.3: Skill set dashboard display.

answered within the target time (93%). This is the key indicator of performance and should be higher than 90% for all skillsets. The next value of this row is the number of calls made to this skill set during the simulation run period (1766). The next down row displays the maximum wait time for a customer call during the simulation run (319.2 seconds) and the final row indicates the day number (day 6) and the time of day that the maximum wait time occurred (14:38). This information was requested by the force as they were interested in being able to quickly identify lengthy calls in order to investigate the reasons behind them. The right-hand side of the dashboard display in Figure 6.2 shows the percentage of abandoned calls made both within the target response time and outside the target response time. The abandoned call metrics are displayed for both 999 emergency and other calls made.

The model was validated by simulating the current staffing profile and comparing the results to historical data on performance collected by the force. It became apparent at this stage that in order to provide an accurate assessment of the system, it was necessary to incorporate into the model a 2-second delay that was observed between the call entering into the Call Handler system (either from the switchboard or a direct 999 call) and then connecting to the call handler and alerting them that they are about to answer a call. This was implemented as a delay block in Arena with a fixed duration of 2 seconds.

Step 3: Use Simulation for Descriptive, Predictive and Prescriptive Analytics

A two-stage methodology is employed. In stage 1, the simulation is used to provide a descriptive analysis of the costs of the call center process from the three ABC perspectives of activity driver, cost driver and resource driver. Stage 2 of the analysis identifies how cost reduction can be achieved from the resource driver perspective by providing a predictive and prescriptive analysis of worker shift pattern scenarios.

Stage 1: Descriptive Analytics Using Simulation and Activity-Based Costing
In conjunction with the simulation approach, this study will incorporate the use of ABC. This allows the user to distinguish between resource usage and resource expenditure, the difference being unused capacity. Once identified, this capacity can either be eliminated, reducing costs or re-deployed, improving effectiveness. The ABC model incorporates three main drivers of cost: *resource drivers*, which determine the cost of resources; *activity drivers*, which determine the use of these resources; and *cost drivers*, which determine the effort needed to undertake the activity. Cost can be reduced by either reconfiguring the resources needed for an activity (resource driver), for example, by using different personnel on lower pay rates, or reducing the amount of resource required (activity driver), for example, by reducing the amount of demand for the service, or by reducing the resources needed to perform an activity (cost driver), for example, by incorporating information technology in the design. The study considers the communication center from the perspective of each of the three drivers of cost (Figure 6.4). The cost driver relates primarily to the design efficiency of the activities within the call handler process of the communications center. The resource driver relates primarily to staffing costs for personnel involved in the call handling process. The activity driver relates to the timing and frequency of the different call types made to the communications center.

In terms of activity driver analysis, Figure 6.5 shows the average total cost for each call type (skill set) to the call center over the simulated 4-week period. The graph shows the cost of the call handler staff determined by the nature of demand from members of the public seeking assistance. To decrease the overall cost requires a reduction in demand, and the cost information assists in showing where cost is being incurred. From an activity driver viewpoint showing costs by call type (skill set), the analysis prompted some discussion in terms of reducing the high volume of 999 emergency calls (many of which are not classified by police as actual emergencies) and discontinuing the information call line in favor of email and web-based facilities.

In terms of cost driver analysis, Figure 6.6 shows the average total cost of operation for a 4-week period, from breaking down the call handler task into its two

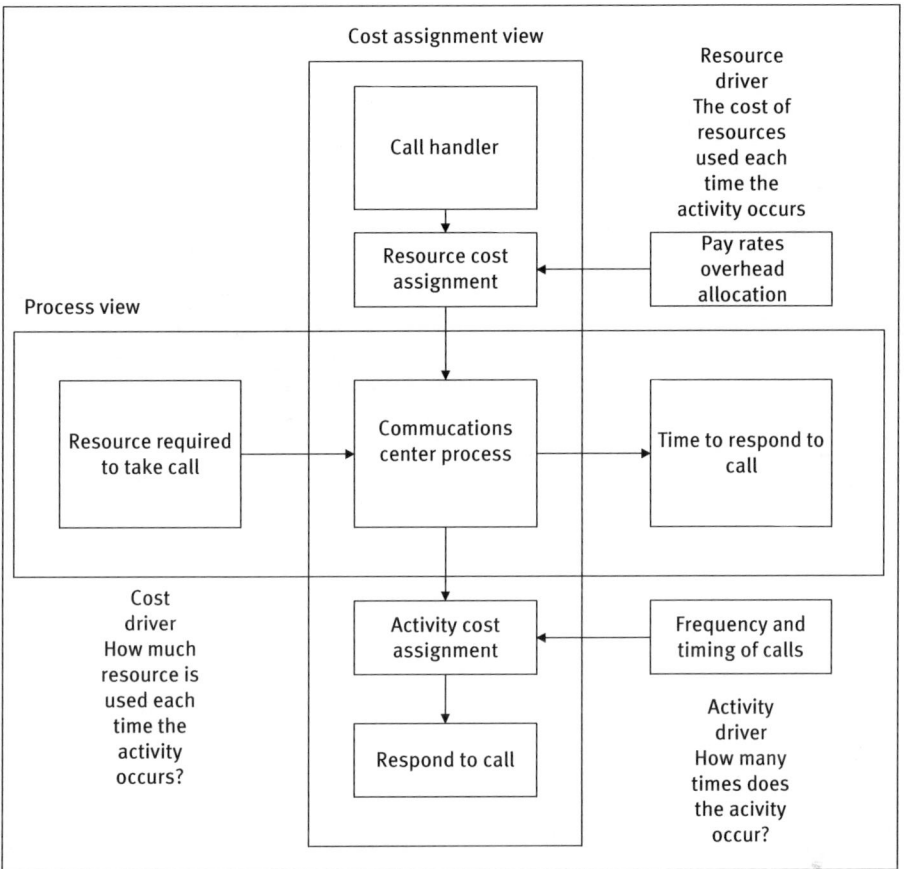

Figure 6.4: The ABC view of the police communications center.

main activities of direct talk time with a customer on the phone and a subsequent wrap-up time which includes any communication with the controllers and required paperwork. From a cost driver viewpoint, the analysis prompted discussion of the relatively high proportion of wrap-up time and the possibility of training to reduce this time.

In terms of resource driver analysis, Figure 6.7 shows the average total call handler cost over a 4-week period. It can be seen from the graph that a large proportion of call handler cost is taken up with idle cost when a call handler is not busy either taking a call or undertaking call wrap-up duties. Although there are a few administrative duties given to staff to complete during this idle time, they are not so onerous that they can not be achieved in less idle time than is currently available. Thus, there is a potential to improve efficiency by reducing this call handler idle time.

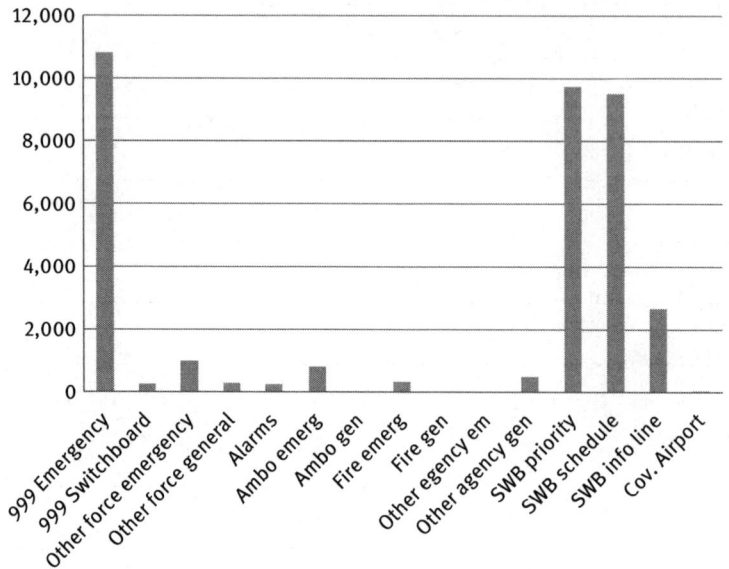

Figure 6.5: Average total cost by call type (activity driver).

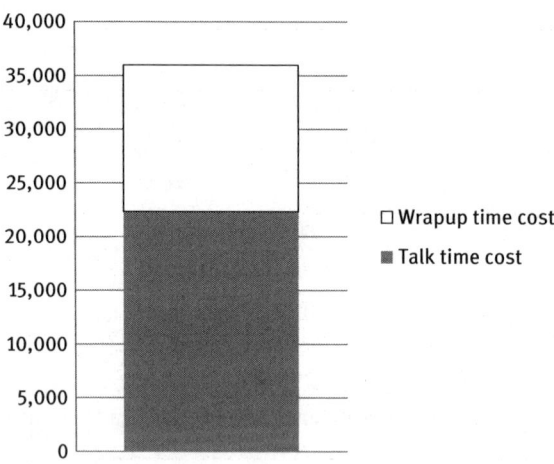

Figure 6.6: Average total cost by call handler task (cost driver).

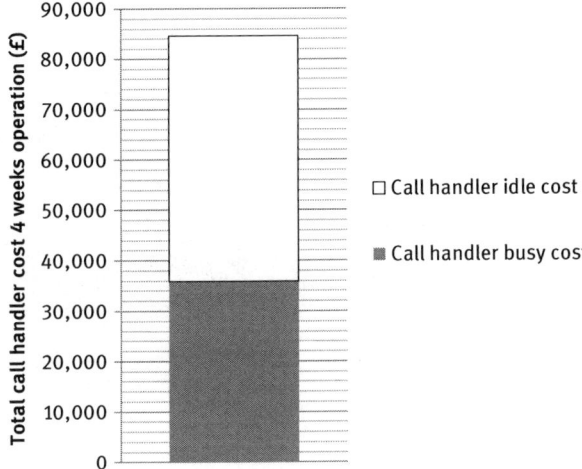

Figure 6.7: Average total cost by call handler allocation (resource driver).

Stage 2: Predictive and Prescriptive Analytics Using Simulation

The analysis in stage 1 showed potential improvements in operation from all three ABC perspectives. In this case, it was decided to investigate the call handling process from a resource driver viewpoint by considering if alternative workforce schedule scenarios could achieve a closer match between supply (call handler staff) and demand (calls) and thus reduce call handler idle time leading to a decrease in direct labor costs. As with any call center operation matching supply and demand represents a difficult task in that demand fluctuates over yearly, monthly and daily time horizons, and short-term demand spikes in customer calls may occur due to events such as a football match. The ability to buffer demand is very limited due to the short time span required to respond to calls. In addition, there is also a need to incorporate staff holidays and staff absences in the shift pattern, which may prevent the smooth running of the shift pattern.

Currently, the communications center staff are on an 8-hour shift working 7 days on then 2 days off covering a 24-hour period. Additional time owed to staff is made up with a floating rest day that is added either during a tour or added to the number of rest days owing. After extensive analysis involving the simulation of various shift pattern scenarios, it was decided that a shift pattern requiring a 9-hour shift working 6 days on then 4 days off would be proposed. The simulation model was used to investigate the ability of the new shift pattern to provide a closer match between staff levels and predicted call levels over time and thus improve efficiency by reducing staff idle time. The proposed shift pattern has been designed using workforce planning intervals of an hour in conjunction with overlapping shifts. This enables the number of employees to be scheduled to change from hour to hour with the aim of having just enough staff present to provide the desired level of service. The reduction in call handler idle cost estimated by the simulation is presented in Figure 6.8 and shows an average cost reduction of 9.4%.

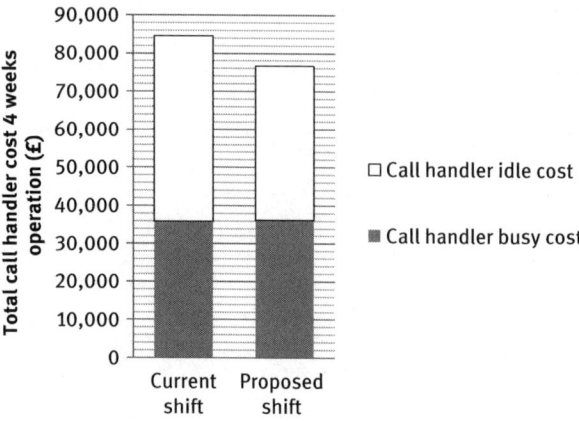

Figure 6.8: Comparison of average total cost by call handler allocation (resource driver).

Conclusion

Analytical models are employed to various degrees in organizations, and currently a large amount of data is collected and held by the communication center using its current command and control software application and is used for descriptive analytics of current performance. However, extracting strategic business value requires a move from a descriptive to a predictive and prescriptive use of analytics. A sign of analytics maturity for an organization is the ability to use the output of predictive models as input to prescriptive analytic models. The case study presents a methodology that uses data from predictive analytics to outline future options for change, which leads to prescriptive analytics that provides recommendations for action under the constraints of business rules. This is presented using a two-stage methodology, which uses ABC to identify how cost is generated using a descriptive analysis. Workforce options are then explored using a predictive analysis that evaluates design operating scenarios in terms of the performance metric of cost. The identification of a feasible schedule enables a prescriptive recommendation for action to be made.

From a practical perspective, the simulation analysis found that the new shift pattern design could lead to an overall reduction in direct labor staffing cost (by reducing staff idle time) of 9.4%. Further analysis of alternative workforce schedule scenarios could achieve a closer match between supply (call handler staff) and demand (calls) and thus reduce costs further. In addition, further exploration of costs incurred from the alternative perspectives of the ABC approach considered in the predictive analysis stage could be undertaken. For example, from a cost driver viewpoint the analysis showed the relatively high proportion of wrap-up time and the possibility of staff training to reduce this time. An improvement in response resolution could be incorporated into the model and used to predict the overall impact on cost.

A number of issues regarding the use of simulation as a tool for descriptive, predictive and prescriptive analysis of business processes were apparent from the case study analysis that can lead to further work. A key aspect of analytics is to respond to changing business needs in real time, and to achieve this, there needs to be automated linkages between real-time data and simulation modeling environments. The police center used a spreadsheet platform as an interface between the IT systems and the simulation software; thus, real-time data transfer was not possible. This implies that the generation of data for analytics techniques may require specific preparation in terms of infrastructure and data compatibility. Furthermore, real-time simulation applications may require the use of sensors to transmit the data to the simulation for immediate processing. A characteristic of simulation is that the solutions and inferences from a simulation study are usually not transferable to other problems because the model incorporates unique problem factors. An aspect of this is the difficulty for users to recalibrate the model as business rules change. This is because business rules are embedded within the simulation software model and although this is a high-level icon-based system (as opposed to program code) it still requires knowledge of simulation software development. This indicates a need for simulation methodology to emphasize the need for training of staff in order to ensure ongoing use of simulation as an analytics tool for analyzing business processes.

Chapter 7
Case Study: A Simulation of a "Last Mile" Logistics System

Andrew Greasley and Anand Assi

The importance of partners in the supply chain has led to a number of changes in the retail logistics sector in response to demands for time-sensitive distribution. Increased competition and eroding margins have created pressures on retailers to improve both inventory turnover and levels of customer service. In the past, retailers were once effectively the passive recipients of products allocated to stores by manufacturers in anticipation of demand, but as a result of increased use and integration of technology, retailers have moved into a strong position to control, organize and manage the supply chain from production to consumption. In fact retailers can set the pace in logistics systems by reacting to the pull of demand rather than the push of supply. The logistical transformation of the UK retailing sector was led by the development and adoption of IT, but was motivated by demand-driven customer needs and wants. This changed environment has exerted growing pressure and realization on retail headquarter functions to seek operational efficiencies and solutions for distribution services. This phenomenon presents a development opportunity for hub-and-spoke distribution systems and resultantly broadens the requirements for analysis to the "last mile" which spoke terminals handle.

This study investigates the "last mile" delivery link, which is the link between the distribution system at the spoke terminal and a customer who can be classified as nonretail (trade) or retail. Retail customers are defined as being directly linked to selling products to end customers and include high-street shops. The growth of these types of customers provides a number of significant challenges to the efficiency and effectiveness of distribution systems. Some of the distinguishing features of retail customers that led to these challenges relating to locational aspects of retail deliveries are provided in Table 7.1, and features relating to issues at the delivery point of retail deliveries are provided in Table 7.2.

One way of minimizing some of these issues from a retailer perspective is to require timed deliveries. These deliveries are specified at a particular time during the day and that can help the retailer with issues such as the allocation of personnel to assist with unloading. This policy also puts the responsibility to overcome the complexities of delivery onto the distributor. A major consideration for any retailer is the issue of fluctuating sales volume requiring timely delivery of inventory. Thus being at the end of the supply chain retail customers may have more short-term demand fluctuations, which are then passed onto the freight distribution system. Within the overall changes in volume, there may also be significant changes in

Table 7.1: Location Attributes of Retail Delivery.

Location Attributes of Retail Delivery
Road congestion due to city center location of retail outlet.
Parking restrictions, for example parking may be only available at certain times or not available directly outside the retailer.
Standard lorries may not be allowed in some city locations. Loads may have to be broken down and delivered by vans.

Table 7.2: Delivery Attributes of Retail Delivery.

Delivery Point Attributes of Retail Delivery
Retail customers may lack personnel and equipment for removing loads from lorries. Lorry drivers may need to unload and move delivery to a storage location. Nonretail customers may simply require curb-side delivery of an intact pallet.
Retail customers may have difficult unloading circumstances. For example, shared access yards with queues, internal stairs and corridors.
Retail customers may be delayed in providing assistance in unloading procedures as they have other duties. For example, the store manager may be required to sign off goods before they are unloaded (dedicated stores personnel are usually available for nonretail (business) customers).
Storage area may be small requiring frequent fast delivery of many items.
JIT policies may require frequent fast delivery of many items.

the product mix and retail customers tend to require delivery of low volumes of many products. This combination of shorter delivery windows, fluctuating volumes and higher product mix represents a significant challenge to suppliers if they are to maintain efficiency and continue to serve retail and nonretail customers well. From the distributor's point of view, timed deliveries require a move to excel at the performance objective of dependability. Thus, deliveries may not necessarily be required quickly but when a delivery slot has been defined then the delivery should be made at this time. This behavior should be maintained for multiple deliveries over time.

Hub-and-spoke distribution networks are widely used in a number of markets across the world. A number of logistic hub-and-spoke models exist, all of which aim to drive efficiencies into the supply chain through notions of collaboration. Hub-and-spoke arrangements are fundamentally highly organized mechanisms for collaboration. Generally, logistical hub-and-spoke systems exhibit a set of collaborative protocols that support the centralized distribution and consolidation activities performed.

In the United States, hub-and-spoke distribution networks are used to support the "less-than-truckload" (LTL) sector. Here, multiloads of freight are consolidated and trailer utilization is improved for the transit of shipments across the vast US land mass between the geographically widespread cities. Hub-and-spoke networks reduce the number of underutilized point-to-point direct loads so that trailer utilization is increased and total operating costs can be reduced. They also aim to reduce costs and achieve economies of scale via transporting large unit quantities to/from hubs in such a way that line haul trucks do not have to make long journeys with small loads. This LTL distribution phenomenon is also evident across mainland Europe and other markets of the world to varying degrees. Hub-and-spoke network design depends on a variety of factors such as the geography to be covered by the system, the number of spokes in the system and the necessary service-level requirements. LTL carriage is characterized as multiple shipments combined into a single truck for multiple deliveries within a multiuser network.

Spoke terminal operations concern the collection and delivery of freight over short distances by using smaller capacity vehicles. Spoke terminals cover specific geographical areas with defined collection and delivery points, and that each spoke terminal is connected by at least one hub. Outbound freight is collected by drivers during the day, is moved to the hub in the evening for trans-shipment and that the inbound freight arriving from other spoke terminals via the hub is delivered in the early morning. In summary, spoke terminals are the capillary networks of hub-and-spoke systems. They are coordinated by the hub in an effort to achieve the economy of scale freight movements necessary to drive hub-and-spoke efficiency. In principal, the hub acts as the heart of the system by pumping collections and deliveries to and from the extremities via the line haul arteries of the system.

Each spoke terminal has constraints and is therefore liable to congestion (e.g., due to limited space, resources and time). While spoke terminals within the hub-and-spoke systems are operated under the policies and the coordination of a center (hub), local decisions for delivery are handled by the spoke terminal and are under their local control and capability. For a number of years, hub-and-spoke networks have focused on volume-driven deliveries intent on supporting the volume-driven business model they have been built and thrived on. The current hub policies for spoke-terminal coordination have gravitated around manufacturing-type freight profiles and the policies have been formulated to handle the delivery of large volumes of freight. For example, historically, hub-and-spoke pallet networks have delivered intact pallets to curb-side delivery points, delivery yards and unloading bays. Deliveries of this type typically take 2–5 minutes at which point a proof of delivery is gained and the driver is back driving and proceeding to the next drop.

However, new retail customers have put traditional hub-and-spoke policies and operational practices under pressure. For example, generally these new types of deliveries require sophisticated added-value requirements (e.g., decanting of goods) as well as very stringent customer servicing needs (e.g., timely proof of delivery), which on the whole demand more time at the delivery point and often compete with core volume deliveries. Typically, spoke terminals employ experienced drivers and managers to make day-to-day routing decisions and uphold the policies set down by the hub. However, these policies are becoming outdated and inflexible to the changing network demands. As a result, there is a need to adapt these policies for different freight profiles.

The Case Study

Pall-Ex Group is a UK-based company that operates pallet distribution networks across mainland Europe. The company uses a hub-and-spoke distribution model where region-based member depots collect freight from customers and transport it to one of two Pall-Ex transshipment hubs. The hub operation sorts the freight by delivery area and transports the freight to the member responsible for the delivery zone. This member is then responsible for delivery of the freight to the end customer from their spoke terminal. The Pall-Ex network handles up to 10,000 times critical freight consignments daily (www.pallex.co.uk). This study investigates the operation of the Pall-Ex freight distribution network at the spoke terminal which is outlined in Figure 7.1.

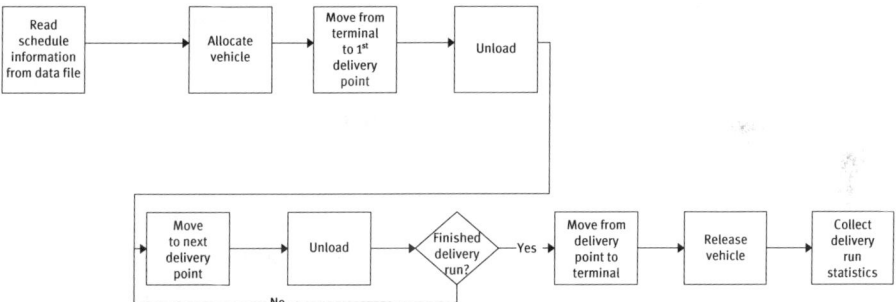

Figure 7.1: The vehicle scheduling process at the spoke terminal.

Line haul trucks typically arrive back from the hub in early morning. On arrival at the spoke terminal, the pallets to be delivered are off-loaded and a number of activities are undertaken, for example, discrepancy reporting and depot scanning. Deliveries typically commence from 7 to 8 am each day, and depending on volumes of freight, it can continue till afternoon and early evening. During the day delivery activity is combined with collection activity. Multiple collection and delivery tours are regularly undertaken in order to optimize the efficiency of resources.

The first step in the vehicle scheduling process is to allocate the daily demand for pallets for delivery (derived from the hub) to the vehicle fleet at the spoke terminal. The vehicle fleet is a mix of lorries and trucks of different capacities. Freight is allocated in such a way as to minimize the total travel distance as this along with the size of the vehicle determines the demand that can be met. In order to achieve this, pallets are allocated to vehicles using delivery zone areas defined by postcodes. Vehicle drivers are usually allocated to particular postcode areas so that they can build up knowledge of the traffic routes and conditions within that area. Once the routes have been planned, they are then assigned to drivers in the form of delivery run sheets. Run sheets provide the drivers with details such as delivery address, postcode and any special instructions. Drivers use the run sheets during their tours as a means to ensure that they are aware of their delivery requirements. However, delivery sequences are flexible and may be left at the discretion of an experienced driver. For retail customers, in particular, customers may require delivery at a certain time point within a daily route. Thus, the constraints of travel time, vehicle size and timed deliveries means that it may be necessary to assign customers to specific vehicle routes and decide the visiting sequence within those routes.

Step 1: Build the Conceptual Model

The aim of this investigation is to compare the performance of the current dynamic vehicle control policy of a mixed delivery run with the performance of separate delivery runs for retail and nonretail customers. Currently, the case study organization uses spreadsheets to analyze and present their vehicle routing schedules, which are developed by a traffic planning supervisor. A spreadsheet platform could also be used to investigate alternative policies such as separate retail and nonretail runs. However, it was decided that discrete-event simulation would be an appropriate tool for this investigation. In this case, variability in travel routes, travel times and unload times and the interactive nature of the vehicle routing policies meant simulation was an appropriate analysis tool. A particular reason to use simulation in this case was because one of the performance measures specified by the case study organization was the ability of the proposed schedule to meet customer service targets in terms of meeting timed delivery targets. This would mean that timed deliveries that were predicted to be met using the average times used on the spreadsheet planning tool would actually not be met due to variability in transport and unload times. The simulation was able to provide confidence interval predictions of delivery performance and so provide more useful information to management.

In order to provide information for the simulation model, data from a spreadsheet of the current schedule for a 10-driver delivery run from a spoke terminal was extracted. Each delivery run consisted between 3 and 10 delivery stops during the morning delivery period. In addition, sample data was collected on transportation times and unload times in order to derive distributions so that variability could be incorporated into the simulation model. Figure 7.2 shows a simplified process map

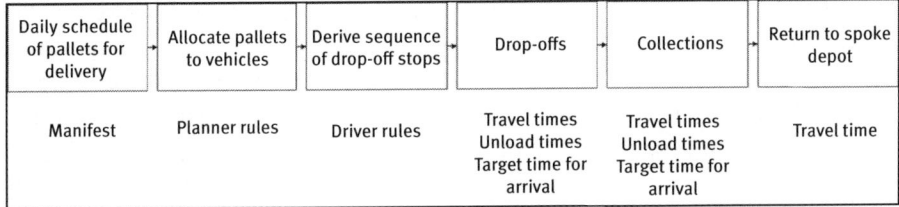

Figure 7.2: Process map of delivery run simulation.

for the model that provides the basic structure of the simulation. Schedule information including routing sequences and timings are held on spreadsheet files, which are loaded into array variables within the simulation. Vehicles are then routed along the delivery runs for each of the 10 driver/spokes defined. Performance information is collected at the end of each delivery run on total delivery run duration and number of missed delivery times.

Step 2: Build the Simulation Model
The simulation model was built using the Arena system. The software allows the modeling of complex transportation systems and allows the use of spreadsheets for data input. In this case, use was made of the ROUTE and STATION modules from the Advanced Transfer template to model the movement of the vehicles along the delivery route. Data validation was undertaken by comparing the results of the simulation, excluding variability factors, with the spreadsheet results for the current schedule. A visual trace could also be made of the movement of vehicles between delivery points using the animation facilities of the simulation.

Step 3: Use Simulation for Descriptive, Predictive and Prescriptive Analytics
The main objective of the simulation study was to compare performance of the current mixed delivery run policy with a separate delivery run policy with each run dedicated to either retail or nonretail customers. A separate delivery run was developed using the same resources currently used, that is, 10 delivery runs to the same delivery locations. The travel times between any new transportation routes between delivery points in this new scenario were estimated using the MapQuest website (www.mapquest.com). The main performance measures used to compare the policies were the successful completion of timed deliveries and the total transport time for the 10 delivery runs. The simulation was run for 50 replications and confidence intervals formed for both the return to depot time for each run and the arrival time at timed delivery locations.

Figure 7.3 shows the results of a single run of the simulation for a 10-spoke terminal with up to 10 timed delivery drop-off points for each spoke. Dependability performance is shown by a negative number representing the number of minutes of an early delivery occurrence before the target delivery time, and a positive number indicates the number of minutes that late deliveries occurred after the target delivery time.

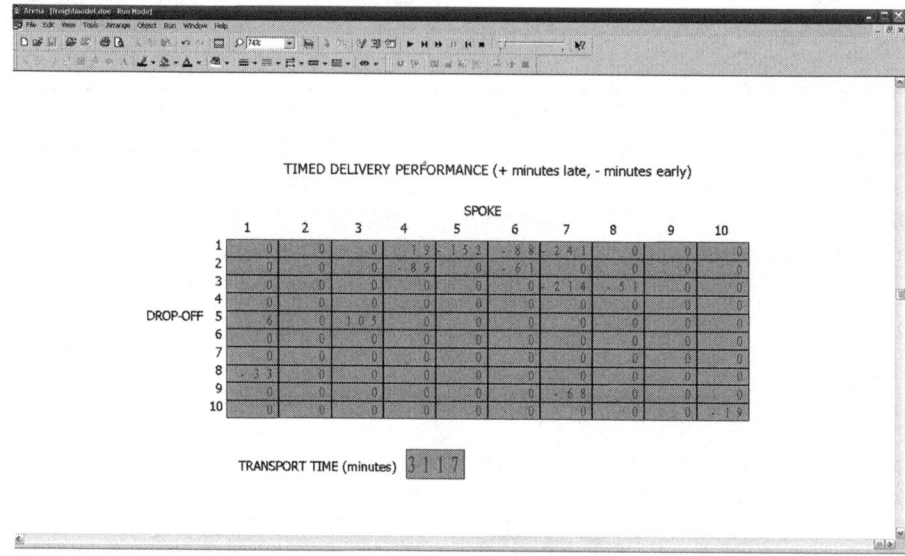

Figure 7.3: Simulation display showing timed delivery performance.

Running the simulation for 50 replications indicates that for the current mixed delivery schedule the average total transport time for the 10 delivery runs is 52 hours and 59 minutes and of 13 timed deliveries, two are not met. The separate delivery run scenario undertakes the same deliveries but drivers are allocated either retail deliveries only or nonretail deliveries only. Here the total transport time for the 10 delivery runs is an average of 54 hours and 50 minutes and of 13 timed deliveries all are met. The confidence interval analysis shown in Figure 7.4 indicates that there is a statistically significant difference between the speed of delivery performance of the two systems.

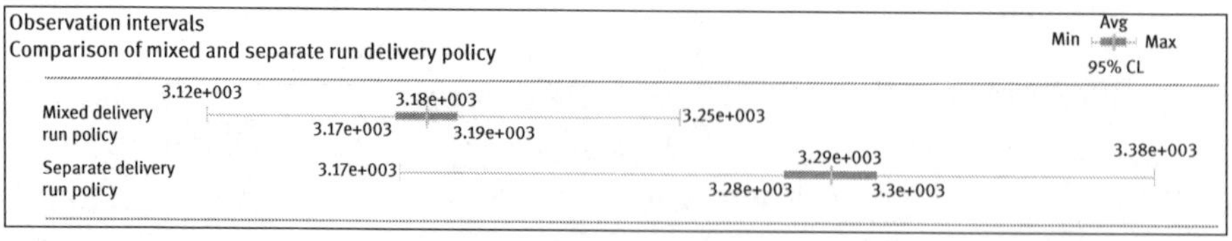

Figure 7.4: Confidence interval analysis comparing separate and mixed delivery run performance.

Thus, the simulation results show that separating retail and nonretail delivery runs can lead to an increased transport time which implies higher driver and fuel costs. This may be caused by the decrease in scheduling flexibility when separating retail and nonretail delivery runs. However, the simulation results do show a decrease in the number of missed timed deliveries, with their elimination from the separate delivery run schedule.

Conclusion

A simulation study has indicated the potential increase in performance in meeting timed deliveries (dependability) that could be made by separating out retail and nonretail deliveries. Separating these delivery types has the significant operational advantage of providing the opportunity to utilize specialist staff and equipment to meet the specific challenges of retail deliveries outlined in the study. However, the improved retail delivery performance should be assessed in the context of an overall increase in transportation time for both delivery types, which implies overall higher driver and fuel costs. As stated earlier, the simulation model is not intended to replace current methods of vehicle routing but to test a change in overall delivery policy in response to a changing delivery profile of increased retail deliveries. The simulation is able to provide a more realistic prediction, then the current spreadsheet-based tools due to its ability to incorporate the variability in transportation and unload times.

Chapter 8
Case Study: A Simulation of an Enterprise Resource Planning System

Andrew Greasley and Yucan Wang

When an enterprise resource planning (ERP) system is applied in the service industry, particularly in front-office operations, there is a particular challenge in undertaking processes not just efficiently but also with sufficient flexibility to address issues that arise during interactions with customers. This capability to both run current business processes efficiently and be able to adjust to a changing competitive environment is sometimes referred to as *organizational ambidexterity*. Thus, while trying to be as efficient as possible to reduce costs, organizations must also ensure sufficient service quality is provided to maximize revenues. A key consideration while implementing an ERP system is its compatibility with current business processes and its effect on the strategic capability of the firm. This chapter considers three different implementations of a customer order process and their performance in terms of ensuring the minimization of cost and the delivery of sufficient levels of customer service quality. To demonstrate the approach we have presented a case study of a customer order processing operation at a service firm based in China. The case study traces the development of the customer order process through its initial manual operation to the implementation of an off-the-shelf ERP installation and then to a modified system consisting of the ERP system linked to an *enterprise social software* (ESS) platform. Discrete-event simulation is used to assess the performance of these three configurations over time in terms of efficiency and flexibility.

The Case Study

This empirical study was conducted in a middle-sized Chinese organization, called the *Jinsheng Group*, which own 11 furniture shopping centers/malls in the east of China, with approximately 1,500 employees. The main service provided by the company is to let out individual retail shops within the centers to customers (tenants) in the form of furniture retailers. The company derives income from both the shop rents and receives a proportion of sales income taken by each retail shop. Thus, there is a dual aim of increasing profits from individual shop rents and in marketing the shopping center in order to increase sales income from end consumers. Tenant demand for shop units varies due to changes in market demand from customers. However, when market demand falls, tenant demand is buffered to some extent due to the 1-year period of tenant leases, although some tenants may break their lease and leave immediately. Government intervention may also affect demand, for example, a government policy of encouraging better treatment of smaller retailers may need to be considered when dealing with tenants. The focus of this chapter is based on two areas that support customer service operations of tenant management and contract management and the process design for the three implementations of a manual process, an ERP process and a hybrid (ERP and ESS) process.

The Manual System Process

The processing of tenants was originally undertaken using a manual system (Figure 8.1). The tenant management process allocates the tenants to individual shops within the store layout. The shopping center consists of six floors with each floor containing shops in three sizes (small, medium and large). The identification of a tenant and their leasing contract is linked to the unique identification of each shop. The policy of allocating shop space is based on the available shop space and the floor (different floors are allocated to different types of furniture retailers) and the size of the space that the tenant requires. If a shop space is available that fits the requirements of the tenant, then a space will be allocated. If no suitable space is available, staff in the leasing department will check whether the tenant has a "good relationship" (GR) with the company. GR tenants are defined by experienced staff on the basis of having a good reputation, are large furniture retailers or have had a previous GR with the company. For these GR tenants, experienced staff will allocate a shop space based on a policy that matches for either the floor or the size of the shop units that the tenant requested. This is a manual process based on the experience of frontline staff to flexibly allocate space to tenants in order to improve service to their valuable customers. If no space can be found for either normal tenants or GR tenants after checking each day for a month, then the application for space for the tenant is rejected. If the tenant still wishes to be allocated a space in the mall, they must submit a new application.

The contract management process supports three contract services of creating a new contract, renew a contract and ending a contract. Once a store space has been allocated to a customer, the next stage is for the Contract Department and Marketing Department to sign a new contract for the tenant. The Finance Department receives rents and sets up an account for the tenant. Each contract is stored with the standard terms, including the period of the lease, the size of property to be let out, the renewal of the lease, and the frequency and method of adjustment of rent. Usually the contract duration is for 12 months but GR tenants may have a longer contract of up to 2 years to maintain a longer-term relationship. All the contracts for non-GR tenants need to be approved by a branch manager and the fixed contract duration is 1 year. If the tenant chooses to renew the contract, the contract department and marketing department will prepare a renewed contract document for the tenant with the GR tenant having priority to sign the contract without checks. For non-GR tenants, the Finance

216 — Chapter 8 Case Study: A Simulation of an Enterprise Resource Planning System

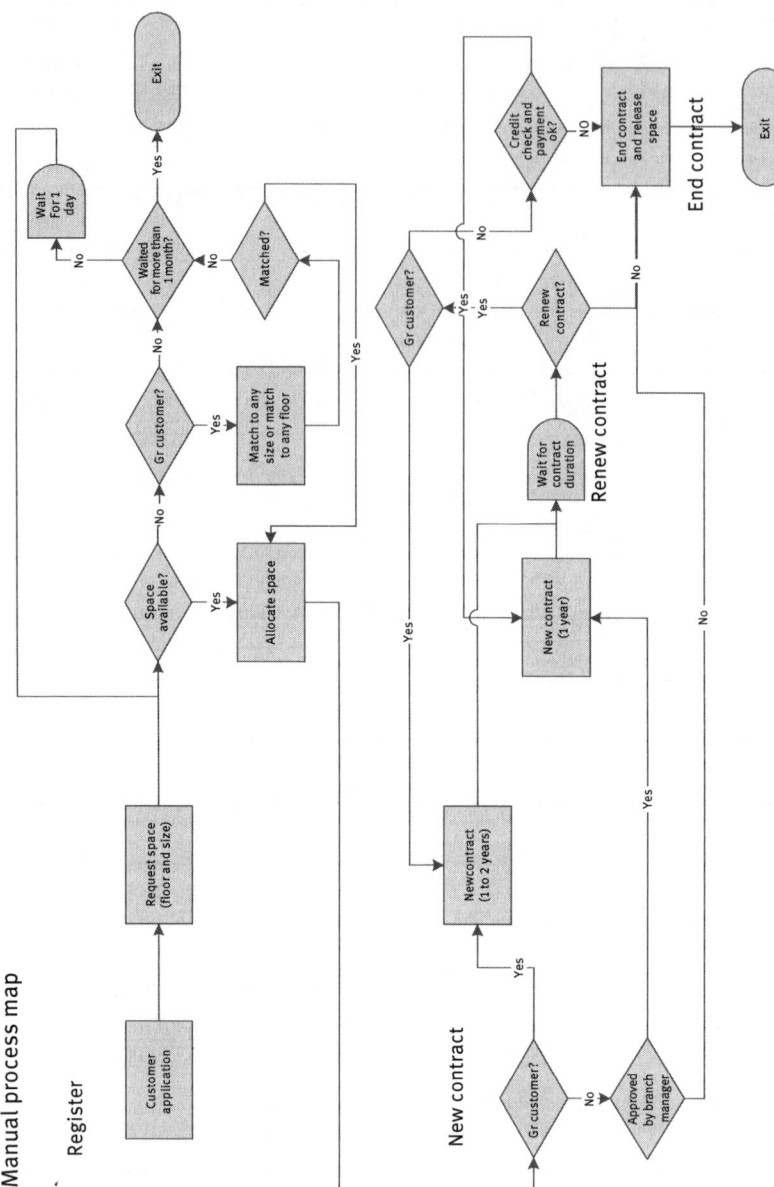

Figure 8.1: The manual system process map.

Department will undertake a credit check to ensure that the tenant that used a store unit in the shopping center has made appropriate payments to date, before renewal of the contract. For an end contract process information on the shop space released will be communicated to the leasing department, which will then attempt to allocate a suitable tenant to this space when possible.

The ERP System Process

This original version of the ERP system was an off-the-shelf package supplied by a Chinese enterprise software company Digital China and implemented by Jinsheng HQ. The system covers the core business processes around marketing, operations and finance with a Business Intelligence functionality, which compares organizational performance across the shopping malls. The main aim of implementing the ERP was to integrate information across the group and so provide an efficient standardized service across all of the malls, thus reducing costs and increasing profitability. The ERP process is shown in Figure 8.2. Here the decision making regarding the allocate of shop spaces is formalized within the ERP system and so all the tenants will be treated with the same procedures to allocate space that is based on the policy of first come first served. All tenants will wait in a queue until an available space is released and if no space is found for a tenant within a month then the tenant is removed from the queue and is required to make a new application for a space within the store. The ERP system also contains the contract-related procedures, and the fixed contract duration is 1 year. If a tenant chooses to renew the contract, all the tenants have to go through a credit check before contract renewal and contracts are renewed using the ERP procedures.

The ERP and ESS System Process

When the ERP system was adopted the project team came to realize that the predetermined procedures in the ERP implementation could not support their day-to-day operation. As a service company, the firm had frequent interactions to flexibly fulfill tenant requests with varied services. In particular, it was found difficult to work with the off-the-shelf ERP system in the following areas:
- It was found infeasible to incorporate into the ERP system, the flexibility in terms of store configuration and overall negotiation in order to quickly secure the signing of a contract.
- Various customized agreements are sought with GR tenants to provide some insurance against falls in sales due to market recessions. Both the identification of GR tenants based on factors such as market influence and the nature of the terms to be offered were difficult to codify in the ERP.

218 — Chapter 8 Case Study: A Simulation of an Enterprise Resource Planning System

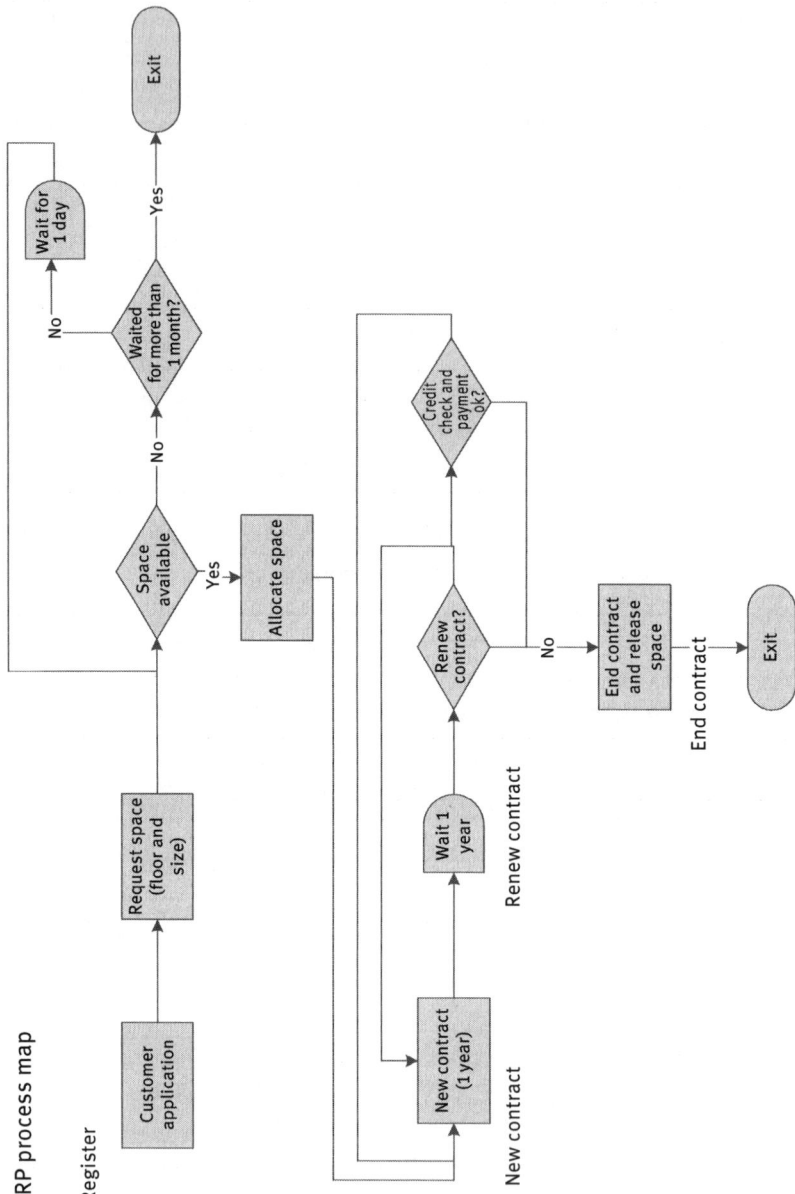

Figure 8.2: ERP process map.

– The use of what are called *market insights* at Jinsheng, enabled by repeated employee engagement with tenants to understand their relationship with their customers and to provide early prediction of any fluctuations in sales. Due to the formalized nature of the ERP, these interactions and thus understanding had been reduced.

The ERP and ESS Architecture

A recent development has been the support of manual knowledge practices by an ESS system, also known as Enterprise 2.0. ESS allows individual-level interactions by which people can question and obtain a response from others using Web 2.0 technologies such as discussion forums and blogs. Due to the limitations of the off-the-shelf ERP system, the firm implemented what is termed in this study a hybrid system supporting both ERP and manual processes (Figure 8.3). In this case, the manual processes are supported by an ESS in the form of the Office Assistant (OA) application, which is used in parallel with the ERP system.

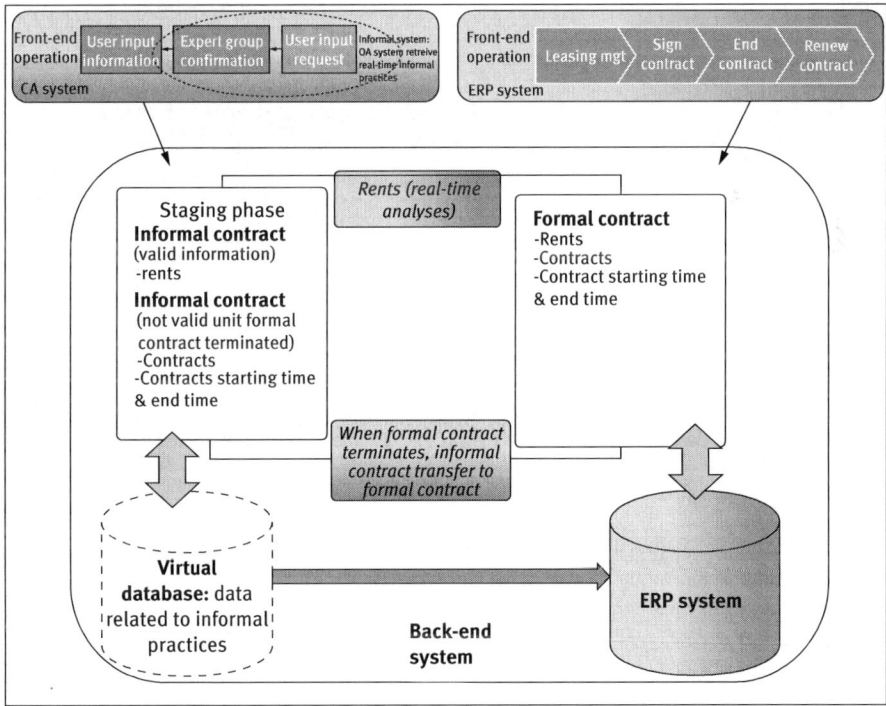

Figure 8.3: The ERP and ESS system.

The front-end operation of the OA system includes "user input requests" and "expert group confirmation" to enable the information transparency of the manual practices. Changes such as adjusting a contract duration or reallocating shops will be implemented once experts authorize the changes. All of these will be documented in a virtual contract. In the back-end system, formal contracts and virtual contracts are held in separate databases. The formal contract contains contract information of shop location, rental fees and contract starting time and end time, which is stored in the ERP system. However, the virtual contract information is stored in a separate database to be recoded into the ERP system as soon as a formal contract is signed. At that point, the finance department is able to analyze income/profits with real-time information. However, the contract contents and contract duration of a virtual contract are not valid until the formal contract of the previous shop is expired, ensuring that one shop can not be rented twice.

The ERP and ESS Process

When the company uses the hybrid system process (Figure 8.4), it is able to provide preferential treatment to the GR tenants, as in the manual system, but the decisions must be approved by an expert group in the regional management center supported by the ERP/ESS architecture. Decisions are supported in the areas of shop allocation, the awarding of a new contract and contract renewal.

Thus, the company had come to realize that a more creative solution to the installation of an off-the-shelf ERP system was required in order to ensure effectiveness in customer processing as well as efficiency in operation. However, in order to avoid a suboptimal implementation of the proposed hybrid ERP/ESS system, there was recognized a need to evaluate the performance of the system under the dynamic operating environment of the mall. The subsequent simulation study is outlined in the next section.

Step 1: Build the Conceptual Model

The study objective is to measure the relative performance of the three scenarios of a manual process, an ERP process and an ERP + ESS process for the shopping center customer processing operation. In this study, objective measures of operations capabilities are used with cost estimated by allocation of staff payroll costs to order processing activities and the response time to customer requests used as a proxy measure of flexibility. The scope of the model is defined around the main customer processes of register customer, new contract, end contract and renew contract. Staff within the model are categorized by role and allocated as per the number of people actually available to service customers. The simulation study assumes that each tenant requests only one shop unit in the mall at a time. A further assumption of the model is that staff are

The Case Study — 221

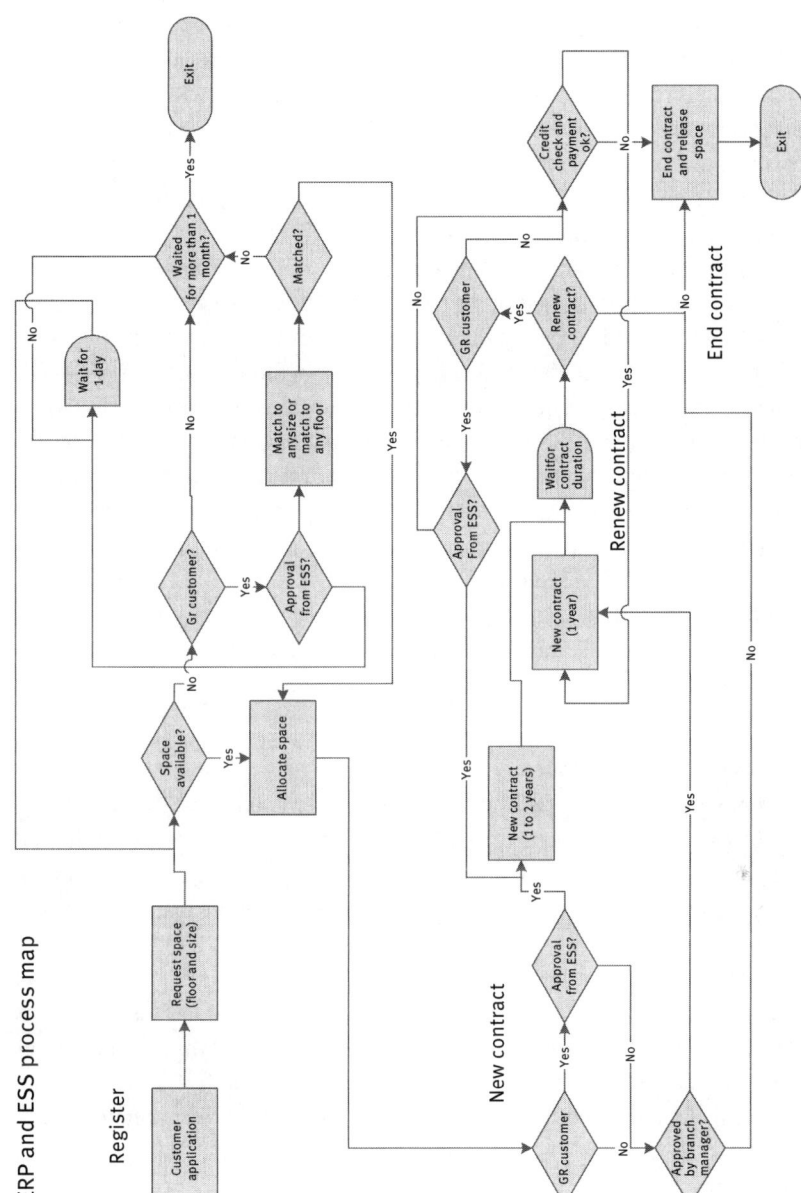

Figure 8.4: ERP and ESS process map.

available continuously with no breaks or absence. These assumptions are constant across the three model scenarios and have been made to simplify the model.

The collected data included process durations, task allocations, the resources involved, demand patterns and process layout. In addition, the process logic of each of the three systems was observed in order to define process maps for the simulation. The field study was conducted in Jiangdongmen Road Mall of Jinsheng, which was the first mall in the company to use all three systems.

The main areas of input data modeling concern the demand for tenant space received by the mall over time, process durations for tasks undertaken when processing tenants, staff availability and coding of the process flow of customers through the process. Process durations were modeled as triangular distributions, which have the advantage of being able to capture processes with small or large degrees of variability, have parameters (minimum, most likely, maximum) that are a natural way to estimate activity time and allow nonsymmetric distribution of values around the most likely, which is common in real processes. The overall customer demand rate for tenant space is modeled using an exponential distribution which is often used for independent interarrival times in service applications. Customer demand for a department floor (six floors are defined into furniture market sectors) and shop size (three basic shops sizes are offered of small, medium and large) is modeled as based on historical data shown in Table 8.1.

Step 2: Build the Simulation Model

The model is implemented using the Arena discrete-event simulation software package (Figure 8.5). In the ERP system scenario, the simulation only represents the formal documented procedures in the ERP system as outlined in the conceptual model. In the hybrid and manual system scenarios, it is necessary to represent manual practices within the simulation. Another element of the simulation model is the flexible allocation of shop space undertaken in the manual and hybrid ERP scenarios. The model incorporates Arena code that will instigate a daily search for available shop space that matches for either floor or size specifications for GR tenants waiting in the tenant queue. The ERP-based system simply operates on a first in first out (FIFO) priority rule.

Verification/code debugging was undertaken by using the Arena animation display to observe the behavior of components within the system. Validation was undertaken by comparing simulation performance to actual performance of the system in operation. To ensure a valid experiment requires removing initialization bias, identifying run length and analyzing replications. An issue that arose in model validation was the need to address initialization bias in the results due to the mall operating from empty at the beginning of the simulation run. It was found that steady-state behavior, with the mall operating at a normal capacity level, takes place after 6 weeks of operation. In order to minimize this initial bias, an extended run of 10 years of operations was chosen for 100 simulation replications.

Table 8.1: Tenant Request Shop Unit Profile.

Floor	Tenant Requests (%)	Shop Size	Tenant Requests (%)
1	18	S	44
		M	33
		L	23
2	10.5	S	45
		M	40
		L	15
3	11.2	S	53
		M	26
		L	21
4	20.3	S	73
		M	16
		L	11
5	19.5	S	53
		M	27
		L	20
6	20.5	S	12
		M	66
		L	22

Step 3: Use Simulation for Descriptive, Predictive and Prescriptive Analytics

The simulation study was able to compare the three implementation scenarios by operating under the same demand pattern and assessing performance using the measures of efficiency (process cost) and flexibility (speed of response to changing customer requirements).

Efficiency Analysis

For the efficiency analysis, cost was allocated to processes based on staff on-cost pay rates that were aggregated by department. The study compares the total cost for the four customer processing activities for each model with a 95% confidence

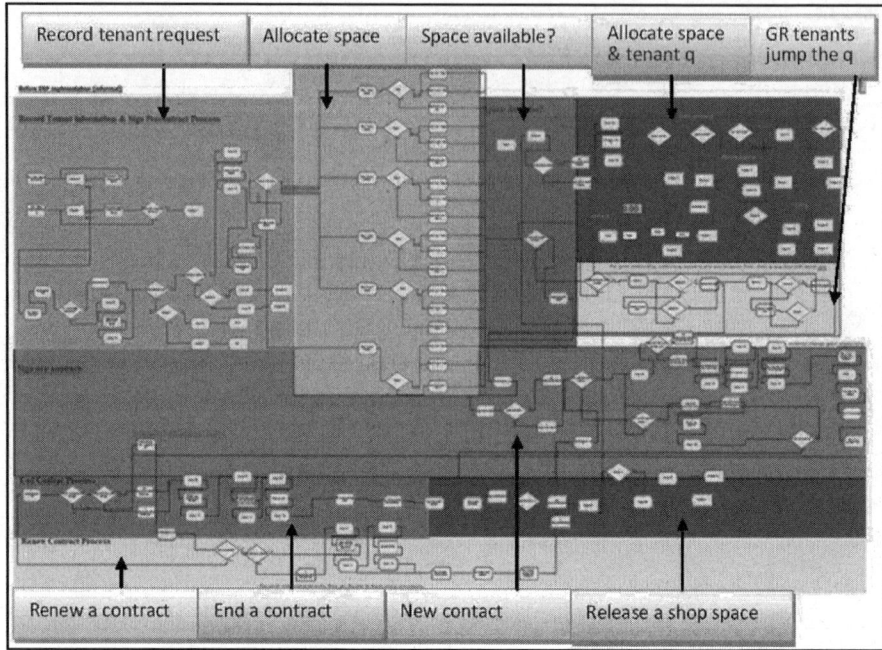

Figure 8.5: Arena simulation model.

interval analysis over 100 replications. Figure 8.6 shows that the ERP system is the most efficient, with total costs at 44% of those of the manual model and 68% of those of the ERP + ESS system. Cost is expressed in the Chinese currency the Renminbi (RMB).

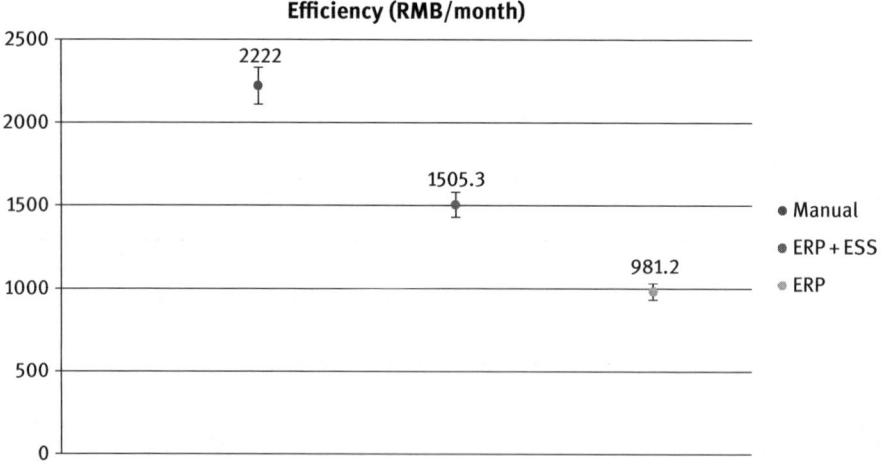

Figure 8.6: Efficiency (RMB/month).

These results can be explained by referring to the activity-based costing (ABC) analysis presented in Figure 8.7. In terms of *cost driver* analysis, one point of interest is that the costs of renew contract for the hybrid model are much higher than the other two models. This is because when the firm uses a hybrid system model, all the manual processes need to be approved in the renew contract services, such as approval procedures on confirming GR tenants' discount and providing a new contract to GR tenants when the old contract expires. In terms of *resource driver* analysis it can be seen that there is a redefinition of the roles of the staff involved in the order processing process after the introduction of the ERP and ERP/ESS systems. For example, it was found that certain activities undertaken in the marketing department and contract department were being duplicated in the new and renew contract processes. This was due to the lack of clearly defined responsibilities in the original manual system operation. Thus, marketing costs were eliminated on implementation of the ERP. It can also be seen how the expert group decisions in the hybrid system impact its overall cost performance in comparison with the off-the-shelf ERP system. In terms of *activity driver* analysis due to the personal service offered to all tenants under the manual system, costs are highest here. Costs for non-GR customers represent total customer costs for the ERP system as the category of GR tenants is not recognized in this process. The relatively high cost of serving GR tenants through the use of the expert group support can be seen in the activity costs for GR tenants in the hybrid (ERP + ESS) system.

Flexibility Analysis

Regarding flexibility analysis, the study considers how quickly the mall reacts to a variety of demands in terms of time to react to a tenant's demands for a shop unit (Figure 8.8). The graph shows the response speed to customer requests which is related inversely to the flexibility of the process. The differences in performance shown in Figure 8.8 are due to the manual model being more flexible than the other two models, with GR tenants being allocated to a shop unit in the mall based on the experience of frontline employees. The hybrid model shows a delay in providing a space for a GR tenant as the hybrid process requires approval by an expert group. The model for the ERP system does not have a policy to react flexibly to the needs of the GR tenant, and the model shows the lowest performance in terms of response speed. Figure 8.8 shows that the manual process has the fastest response speed, which is 27% of the speed of the ERP process and 64% of the speed of the ERP + ESS system.

In order to define the nature of the relationship between the measures of efficiency and flexibility for the tenant process, a performance curve graph is presented (Figure 8.9).

226 — Chapter 8 Case Study: A Simulation of an Enterprise Resource Planning System

Cost by process (cost driver)

	Manual	ERP+ESS	ERP
register	726.4	165.9	168.7
new contract	1078.2	865.2	540.5
renew contract	193.8	409.8	166.2
end contract	223.7	64.3	105.8
	2222.1	1505.2	981.2

Cost by staff (department) (Resource driver)

	Manual	ERP+ESS	ERP
finance	908.4	101.3	500.8
marketing	298.8	0.0	0.0
Contract dept.	501.6	49.3	236.5
expert group	0.0	771.0	0.0
management	354.9	559.6	214.2
leasing dept.	158.4	23.9	29.7
	2222.1	1505.1	981.2

Cost by staff Tenant (Activity driver)

	Manual	ERP+ESS	ERP
normal	1790.8	434.6	981.2
GR	431.3	1070.7	0.0
	2222.1	1505.3	981.2

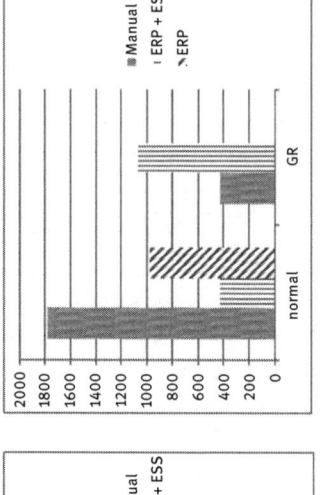

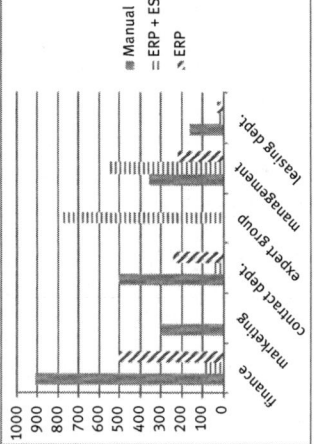

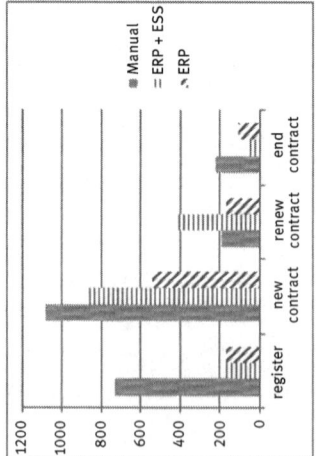

Figure 8.7: Activity-based costing analysis (RMB/per month).

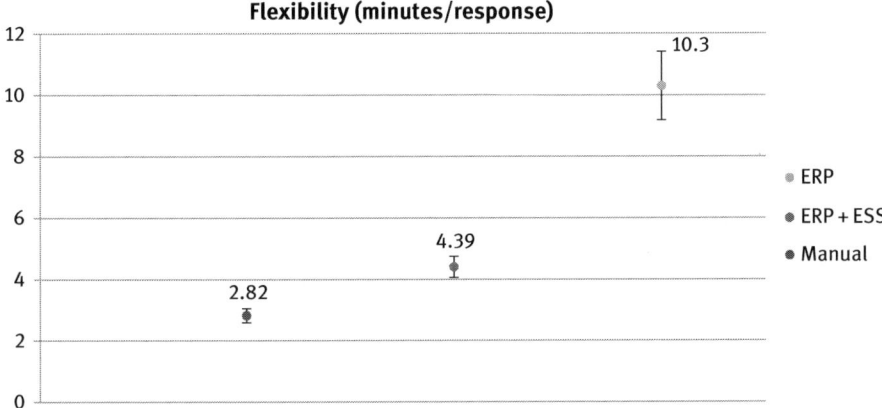

Figure 8.8: Flexibility (response/minute).

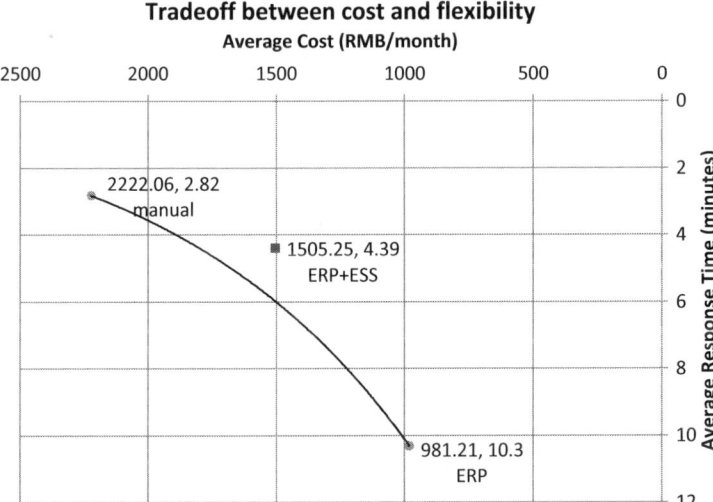

Figure 8.9: The performance curve for the trade-off between cost and flexibility.

The convex curve represents the theoretical limit of performance that the company can achieve when managing the balance between performance measures; in this case, cost (efficiency) and flexibility (speed of response to customer needs). The performance of the hybrid system, above the curve, implies that the hybrid system has not just found an alternative balance between cost and flexibility but is showing increased capability of the process itself.

Conclusion

The company found that the original change from a manual to a traditional ERP system did provide a more efficient (lower cost) solution for tenant processing by using a high degree of automation, which streamlines the entire business transaction. It achieves this performance by enterprise-wide resource allocation that mitigates costs and eliminates duplicated work activity. However, in this case it was found that the gap between the best practices of the ERP software and existing organizational practices was quite large, and a loss of flexibility was experienced in dealing with customer orders. In terms of the design of the hybrid systems, two options are available of either customizing the ERP software or through the use of work-arounds, which is when end-users continue to conduct their practices outside of the ERP system. Here a hybrid ERP and ESS system was employed, which enabled work-around policies concerning GR tenants, implemented by front-line staff but then authorized by experts through the ESS platform. From an organizational perspective, implementations can be considered in terms of their level of decentralization, with the manual system providing decentralized decision making, the ERP system imposing a centralized structure and the hybrid system providing a solution between the other two.

In order to assist the company in judging the suitability of ERP implementation options, a simulation methodology was then undertaken to make explicit the positioning of the three design options in terms of the balance of efficiency and flexibility. The simulation tool provides the following capabilities:
- Quantifies the relative performance of the three options in terms of process efficiency and flexibility in order to ensure customer service quality.
- Provides an ABC analysis which assists in indicating the cause of the costs incurred and thus efficiency of each option.
- Provides the ability to report efficiency and flexibility performance with alternative customer demand scenarios.
- Provides the ability to report efficiency and flexibility performance with alternative customer order processing design options.

The ABC analysis also permits the company to drilldown into the detailed figures to assess the operation of the process. For example, the activity cost analysis presented in Figure 8.7 indicates the heavy workload for employees when implementing the combined ERP + ESS system with the proportion of cost incurred on GR tenants rising from 19% in the manual system to 71% in the ERP + ESS system. This is due to the additional workload when operating both the ERP and ESS systems and with the need to consult senior management when making decisions. Thus, it might be that these costs could be reduced by the simplification of the operation of the ERP + ESS system. In terms of demand scenarios, further experiments by the company confirmed the impact of the policy of segmenting GR tenants. This is particularly important at high demand periods when store availability is limited and so greater discretion is required in allocating stores to clients to ensure a fast response time and thus flexibility. Finally, the simulation method provides the capability to assess the performance of further developments of the three options presented or to assess additional design options for the order processing activity.

Chapter 9
Case Study: A Simulation of a Snacks Process Production System

Andrew Greasley

This chapter presents a simulation study of a major investment in automation, specifically the design of an automated sorting and packing facility at a large-scale snacks process production facility. One of the reasons why simulation modeling is arguably more widely applied to manufacturing systems in general than any other application area is the competitive environment in many industries, resulting in a greater emphasis on automation to improve productivity and quality. Since automated systems are complex, they typically can only be analyzed by simulation. Another factor is that the cost of equipment and facilities can be quite large, thus a relatively small expenditure on simulation can reduce the risk of failed implementation. Thus, the process industries with their generally high level of automation and capital investment would be an ideal opportunity to utilize the simulation technique. In this study the main focus of the simulation investigation was on the effect of conveyor breakdowns on system performance.

The Case Study

This case study concerns a large-scale chips and snacks production facility with a potential annual output of approximately 30 million cases of product, in a market worth £2 billion per annum in the UK alone. The company processes the raw material, potatoes, through a preparation stage and then a cooking process. The product is then packaged in bags and stored in cardboard boxes, termed *cases*, for transportation. Cases are of various sizes, depending on customer requirements and may hold over 100 bags of chips or snacks. The cases are moved using a conveyor system to a packing point and are stacked manually on wooden pallets for transportation by lorry to customers. Inventory management is a major issue due to the high volume and continuous nature of the product flow. The size of the boxed products means that any stoppage in the conveyor or packing system will lead to a build-up of inventory which can quickly consume a large amount of storage space.

It is proposed that the conveyors will feed into two automated sorter conveyors from which cases would be removed by a number of robotic arms. The robots would then stack the cases on a pallet, and on completion of the pallet, it would be shrink-wrapped by machine. Currently, cases are manually taken from the conveyor systems by work teams, placed on pallets and shrink-wrapped, ready for delivery by lorry.

Although it was envisaged that the replacement of the current manual system by the automated system would improve efficiency, it was important to arrive at the correct specification to ensure smooth operation, but without overinvestment. Of particular interest was the volume of inventory produced in a high-volume, continuous output system when a breakdown occurs. Currently the manual system provided flexibility in enabling the fast re-deployment of personnel to deal with the inventory produced as the result of a breakdown. The study would assist in developing procedures that enabled the automated system to continue to operate efficiently during and after these breakdown events.

Step 1: Build the Conceptual Model
The main aim of the study was to quantify the effect of breakdowns in the feeding conveyor system, which could potentially generate a large volume (in terms of number and space) of inventory, causing a blockage in a downstream proposed automated sorting facility.

A series of up to 23 production schedules can be created each feeding the conveyor system with a series of product batches. Each batch is given a *stock keeping unit* (SKU) number, and this represents a product type (chip or snack). Also specified is the case size. Cases are designed for particular customers in terms of size, thus chips for supermarket outlets are packaged in different case types compared to the same product packaged for local convenience stores. The schedule specifies the number of cases to be produced for each batch, the rate of output of cases from the production facilities on to the conveyor system and the conveyor the batch has been allocated to. All this information is read by the simulation from a spreadsheet, which can be prepared to represent a production scenario. If the simulation reads an empty line on the spreadsheet, this represents the end of that particular schedule (each schedule consists of a number of lines, each with information on each batch). The model then resets the schedule to the start and repeats the schedule. Before a new batch arrives a delay occurs to represent the changeover time on the production lines between products. After this delay the schedule details (case size, conveyor number, etc.) are transferred to the case object and it is directed to the assigned conveyor for transportation. Another case object is also created which is delayed by the case inter-arrival time from the production system (this is calculated from the production output rate provided in the production schedule). After the delay a check is made to examine if a shift change is occurring (the production facility operates a 24-hour three shift system). When the shift change period has ended a check is made to see if the production batch size for this SKU has been exceeded. If the batch has not been exceeded the case object is allocated to a conveyor and another case is generated. Otherwise the next line of the schedule spreadsheet is read containing the next SKU details. A separate spreadsheet, containing information on conveyor efficiencies and shift changeover patterns, is also used by the model.

Existing documentation was used to provide the details of the SKU batches and the conveyor specifications. A number of production scenarios were created on spreadsheets and used to drive the model. In particular, a "worst case" scenario was constructed, which attempted to demonstrate the maximum rate of cases flowing on the conveyor system and thus feeding the proposed upstream automated sorter and robot facility.

Step 2: Build the Simulation Model

The simulation model was built using the Arena system which has specific facilities for the modeling of conveyor-based systems, which were utilized in this study (Figure 9.1). The model was verified or debugged by tracing the route of the cases generated by a simple schedule through the model. Calculations were made to check that the number and rate of output of cases from the conveyor system were correct. Validation was undertaken by driving the model with a typical production schedule and by comparing the model with real-world results.

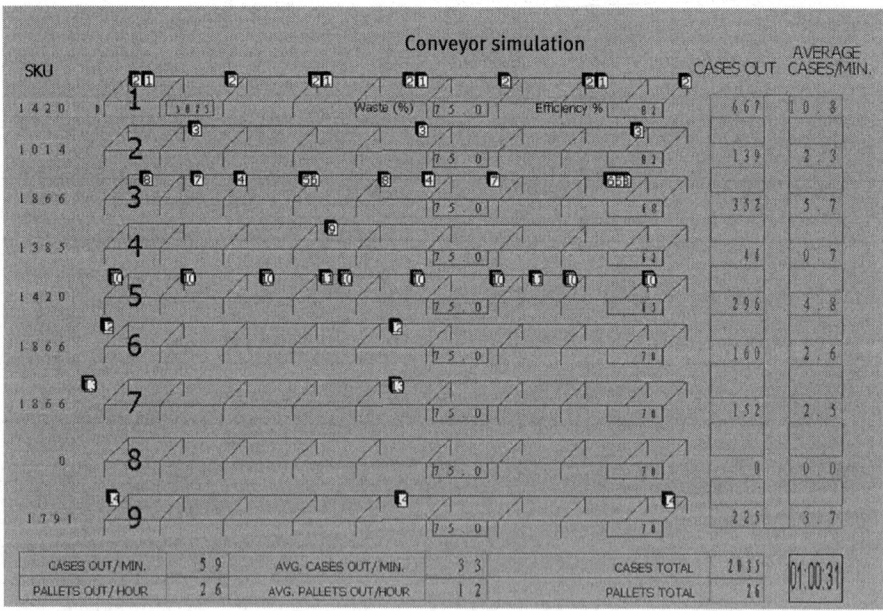

Figure 9.1: The Arena snacks simulation model.

In Arena the full Visual Basic for Applications™ (VBA™) programming environment is provided to enable Visual Basic code to be written directly in Arena and automatically saved with the simulation model. Arena has a number of built-in

VBA events including four routines that are called when the simulation is running. The ModelLogic_RunBeginReplicaton and the ModelLogic_RunEndReplication routines are activated at the start and end of each model replication. The ModelLogic_RunBeginSimulation and ModelLogicRunEndSimulation are activated once at the start and end of the whole simulation experiment. The code to record the cases per hour measure in an Excel spreadsheet is shown in Figure 9.2.

Option Explicit is a Visual Basic command to ensure all variables in the code are defined. Global variables, defined outside a routine, are available to all routines in the coding. Their use is indicated in the coding listing. The ModelLogic_RunBeginSimulation routine first sets the oSIMAN data object which provides access to the values in the running simulation. The oSIMAN.SymbolNumber function converts a model element (in this instance the cases per hour variable) into an index number. This is used later in the ModelLogic_RunEndReplication routine. The remaining code creates and opens an EXCEL spreadsheet into which the simulation results can be written. The ModelLogic_RunBeginReplication routine records the current replication number and uses this to set the spreadsheet column into which the results are placed. The row counter is also reset. The ModelLogic_RunEndReplication and the ModelLogic_RunEndSimulation routines contain no coding in this example. The VBA_Block_1_Fire routine is called by an element placed in the simulation model. A number of elements can be placed in the model, each one activating user coding. In this case it is called every 5 minutes to record the cases per hour measure which is retrieved from the model and placed in the variable ncasesperhour. The current simulation time is placed in the variable ncurrenttime. The values are then written to the spreadsheet in adjacent columns and the spreadsheet row counter is incremented.

Step 3: Use Simulation for Descriptive, Predictive and Prescriptive Analytics
The first stage of using the model was to estimate the maximum rate of output from the conveyor system on to the proposed automated sorting and packing facility. For this a "worst case" schedule was constructed. In addition the robustness of the system was checked by simulating conveyor breakdown events. Although initially these cause a drop in output, product is still being fed to the conveyor point from the production system (the system cannot be stopped because it is fed by large ovens which operate continuously to avoid excessive warmup times). When the conveyor problem has been rectified, output rises above normal levels as the inventory created during the downtime is re-introduced on to the conveyor system along with the normal output.

Figure 9.3 shows the EXCEL graph of the total cases per hour for a historical production schedule over a period of 2 weeks. This was modeled for validation purposes to compare with real-world performance. The vertical lines on the output graph represent a short loss of output during the shift change periods at the plant.

```vba
Option Explicit                    ' all variables must be declared
'Global Variables
Dim oSIMAN As Arena.SIMAN          ' obtain values from simulation
Dim nNextRow As Long, ncolumn As Long   ' spreadsheet row/column values
Dim ncasesperhourindex As Long     ' index value of case per hour attribute
'Global Excel variables
Dim oExcelApp As Excel.Application ' gain access to Excel spreadsheet
Dim oWorkbook As Excel.workbook
Dim oworksheet As Excel.worksheet


Private Sub ModelLogic_RunBeginSimulation()' run this code at start of simulation


Set oSIMAN = ThisDocument.Model.SIMAN   ' provide access to simulation variables
ncasesperhourindex = oSIMAN.SymbolNumber("casesperhourattr") ' set cases index
Set oExcelApp = CreateObject("Excel.Application") ' provide access to excel
oExcelApp.Visible = True                ' setup excel spreadsheet
oExcelApp.SheetsInNewWorkbook = 1
Set oWorkbook = oExcelApp.Workbooks.Add
Set oworksheet = oWorkbook.ActiveSheet
oworksheet.Name = "simulation results"


End Sub


Private Sub ModelLogic_RunBeginReplication()   ' run at start of each replication


Dim nReplicationNum As Long             ' current replication
nReplicationNum = oSIMAN.RunCurrentReplication ' get replication value from sim.
ncolumn = (nReplicationNum * 2) - 1     ' set spreadsheet column
nNextRow = 2                            ' set spreadsheet top row


End Sub


Private Sub ModelLogic_RunEndReplication()   ' run at end of replication

End Sub


Private Sub ModelLogic_RunEndSimulation()   ' run at end of simulation

End Sub
```

Figure 9.2: Visual Basic for Applications Coding for Writing Results to Excel.

```
Private Sub VBA_Block_1_Fire()        ' run when requested by simulation
Dim ncasesperhour As Double           ' case per hour value
Dim ncurrenttime As Double            ' current time value


' get cases per hour and current time from simulation
ncasesperhour = oSIMAN.EntityAttribute(oSIMAN.ActiveEntity, ncasesperhourindex)
ncurrenttime = oSIMAN.RunCurrentTime
' write values to spreadsheet
oworksheet.Cells(nNextRow, ncolumn).value = ncurrenttime
oworksheet.Cells(nNextRow, ncolumn + 1).value = ncasesperhour
nNextRow = nNextRow + 1               ' increment spreadsheet row counter


End Sub
```

Figure 9.2 (continued)

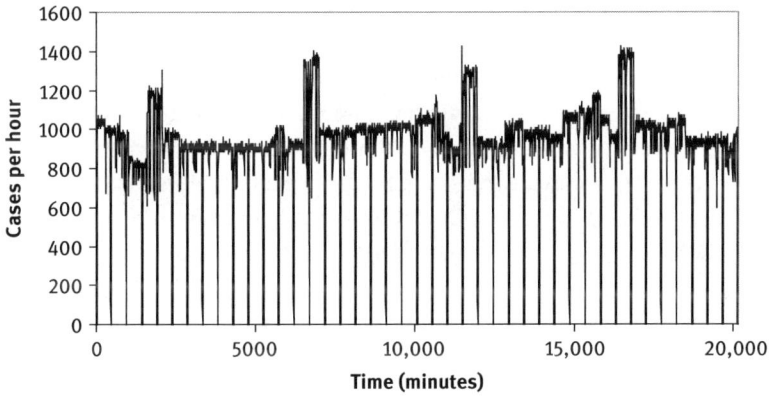

Figure 9.3: Cases per hour for "historical" production schedule.

The graph shows a steady output of around 1000 cases per hour interrupted by output peaks of around 1400 cases per hour. This is due to the uneven loading on the system presented by this particular schedule. A more balanced pattern of output could be achieved by re-scheduling certain high output case types.

Figure 9.4 shows the total cases per hour output for a theoretical "worst-case" scenario created for the simulation study. In this scenario a steady output of 3600 cases per hour is recorded. This represents an output of approximately 0.6 million cases per week and provides an estimate of the maximum capacity required for the proposed automated sorting and packing facility. In this scenario a steady output level is maintained because the schedule is based on the peak throughput expected for each of the nine conveyor systems. In reality the output will fluctuate below this level.

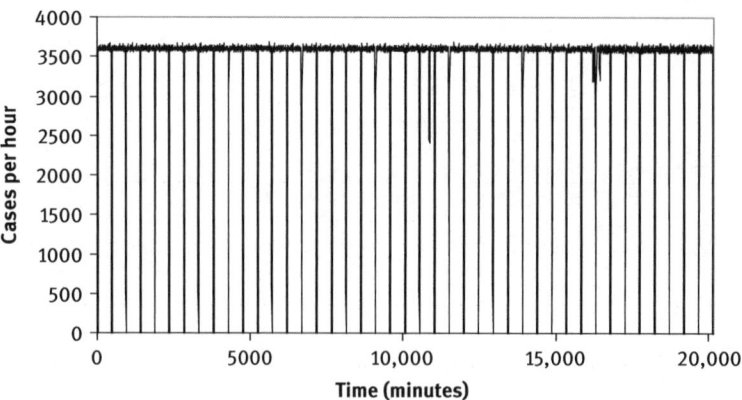

Figure 9.4: Cases per hour for "worst case" production schedule.

Once the first stage of the simulation study had been addressed, it was decided to use the model to study the effect of conveyor breakdown events. The continuity of operations is very important in such plants both for economic reasons and technical reasons; specifically, shutdowns interrupt the continuous flow of production and can cause expensive and time-consuming shut-down and start-up situations. Because of the expense of shutting down the output from the ovens feeding the conveyor system, inventory generated during a breakdown event is stored and then reintroduced to the conveyor system after the problem has been fixed. The simulation was used to investigate a breakdown event and any potential implications for the proposed automated system.

Figure 9.5 shows the initial loss of output due to a failure on one of the nine conveyor systems. The output of each of the nine conveyor systems differs according to the current production schedule. In this case approximately 15% of total output is lost due to the breakdown on the conveyor line chosen for this experiment. After the breakdown event has ended (after approximately 10 minutes) there is an increase in output to approximately 5500 cases per hour before returning to the steady state value. This increase is due to the inventory created during the downtime being reintroduced to the conveyor system immediately on its restart. The model reintroduces the inventory at an estimated rate of 2 seconds to manually load the cases on to the conveyor. However, although the increase in cases per hour is only a transient occurrence this, increase over a limit of 4000 cases per hour could cause a blockage to the proposed automated sorting system.

One solution to this potential problem is to reintroduce the excess inventory at a rate slow enough not to cause an excessive output rate from the conveyor to the sorter. The simulation was used to determine an optimum rate of reintroduction keeping the cases per hour rate to the sorter below 4000, but minimizing the time taken to reintroduce the cases to the conveyor. It was found through scenario

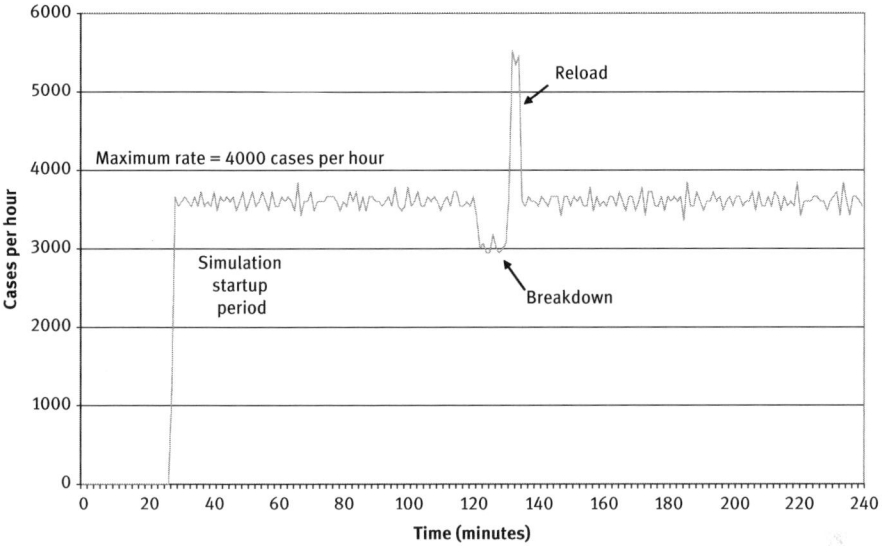

Figure 9.5: Cases per hour for 2 second case conveyor reload time.

analysis that a reintroduction rate of 15 seconds between cases would meet this target and take approximately 25 minutes to complete the operation (see Figure 9.6). In order to put this policy into practice either a stopwatch could be used to time the case reintroduction rate or the timing could be converted into a distance between cases reintroduced on to the conveyor. For example, for a conveyor moving at a speed of 1 meter/second, a 15-second reintroduction rate would translate into cases placed at 15-meter intervals on the conveyor.

Conclusion

The case study represents an example of the use of the simulation technique in providing information for the design specification of a major investment in automated machinery. Although simulation is often seen as a tool for analysis at an operational level, when major investment decisions are made, the success of these strategic decisions is dependent on the subsequent operational effectiveness of the investment. In this case the success of the strategic decision to invest in a multimillion pound automated system was dependent on its smooth operation over time. The usefulness of the simulation technique is demonstrated in its ability to model transient events, which can have major effects on automated machinery in process industries exhibiting high volume and continuous operations. By observing the graphical output of inventory levels over time, it became apparent that the rate of reintroduction of inventory generated during the breakdown event would need to be regulated in order

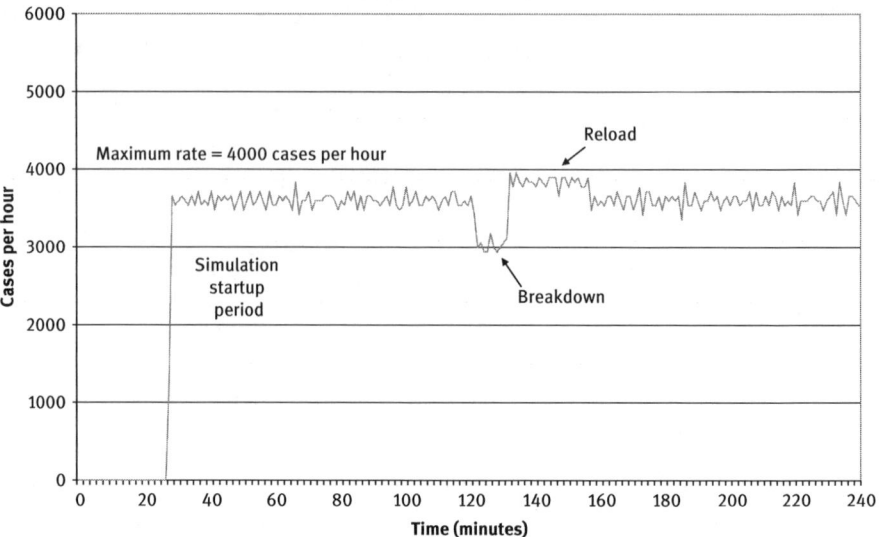

Figure 9.6: Cases per hour for 15-second case conveyor reload time.

to prevent overloading of the proposed automated system. Flexibility was, in a sense, built in to the manual system as people could observe an appropriate rate to introduce inventory with no overloading. Flexibility was lost when moving to the automated system, and hence the simulation was required to assist in quantifying suitable rules for inventory reintroduction.

Chapter 10
Case Study: A Simulation of a Police Arrest Process

Andrew Greasley

The following case study describes the use of a simulation study, in conjunction with the activity-based costing (ABC) approach, to improve process performance at a UK Police Force. The process under investigation is the arrest process, from actual apprehension of a suspect, to processing through a custody suite, to possible interview and court appearance. This process was chosen because it incorporated a reengineering effort in the custody suite and the model could be used to assist analysis in this area. Police management also requested a planning tool for their major human resource, the police constable (PC). The police service is characterized by having a large part of its resource as labor. The wide range of activities that a people-based organization undertakes often leads to a situation of management of resources by inputs (i.e., budgets) because of the difficulty of classifying the wide range of outputs that police personnel can perform. The amount of resources (people) deployed are based on historical departmental budgets with a large proportion classified as overhead and fixed with an annual addition for inflation. Departments are then managed by tracking variances in expenditure from budgeted amounts. However, resource allocation decisions in the police service could also be informed by moving from costs defined in a general organizational budget to an output-oriented budget. The ABC approach allows the user to distinguish between resource usage and resource expenditure, the difference being unused capacity. Once identified, this capacity can either be eliminated, reducing costs or redeployed, improving effectiveness. This study will outline the use of ABC as a framework for identifying how cost is generated and will utilize discrete-event simulation to enable the variability of demand and process duration to be incorporated into the cost analysis.

The Case Study

The first step in the study was to estimate the costs associated with the 12 main arrest types of a police force. Up to this point, because of the use of budget accounting, the actual cost for each arrest type had not been estimated. The purpose of the next stage of the study was to estimate the effect of a change in demand caused by a proposed change in government legislation on resource usage. Their study relies on deterministic cost relationships built within the activity structure of the cost model. This study implements a cost management system utilizing a discrete-event simulation approach that takes into account the variability of process duration and decision rules over time.

In ABC resources such as buildings, equipment and energy are termed committed resources when resource expenditure is independent of the actual amount of usage of the resource in any period. This will also cover employees whose costs are constant, independent of the quantity of work performed by them. In service sector examples, this capacity is actually acquired before the actual demands for the service are realized. Thus the independence in the short-run supply and expense of these resources has led them to be treated as fixed costs. Flexible resources are those that can be matched in the short term to meet demand. These can include materials, energy, temporary workers hired on a daily basis and the use of overtime that is authorized as needed. ABC estimates the cost of both committed and flexible resources used by activities and recognizes that almost all organizational costs (other than those of flexible resources) are not in practice variable in response to short-term demand fluctuations. Rather committed costs become variable costs over longer time periods by a two-step procedure.

1. The demand for resources supplied changes because of shifts in activity levels (through the demand mix changing, for example).
2. The organization changes the supply of committed resources (up or down) to meet the new level in demand for activities performed by resources.

For committed costs to increase, demand exceeds capacity leading to delays, and service levels will drop unless more capacity is added. For committed costs to become variable in a downward direction, the organization must not only recognize the unused costs, but either redeploy resources elsewhere or reduce the level of resources thus reducing cost.

Step 1: Build the Conceptual Model

The arrest process is shown in Figure 10.1 within the ABC matrix.

From the process view, the cost driver is the resource required to undertake each activity. From a cost assignment view, the resource driver relates primarily to pay rates for personnel involved in the arrest process. The activity driver relates to the timing and frequency of arrests and provides the focus of this study. The activity driver is dependent on environmental factors such as the crime rate and government policy on crime as well as factors under the control of the police. This study estimates the personnel cost of each arrest type and then investigates the effect of proposed legislation to extend the opening times of public houses (bars) from 23.00 to midnight, termed the "late drinking" scenario. This change represents a change to the activity driver represented in the ABC model.

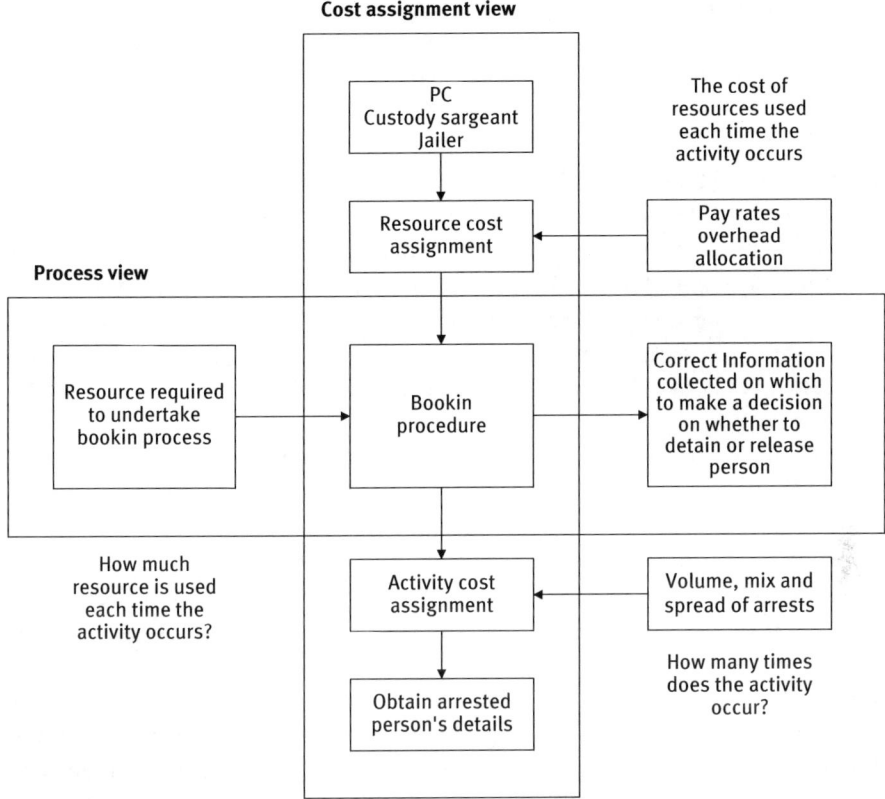

Figure 10.1: The arrest process within the ABC matrix.

Thus the study was to consider the custody process from the perspective of each of the three drivers of cost.
- The "cost driver" relates primarily to the design efficiency of the activities within the custody/arrest process. Costs were computed for each activity (e.g., booking-in, interview) by the simulation by multiplying the activity duration by the appropriate staffing pay rate.
- The "resource driver" relates primarily to staffing costs for personnel involved in the arrest process. Pay rates (including "on-costs") were collected for each staff rank (e.g., PC, Jailer) involved in the custody process. Staffing costs were computed by staff rank by the simulation as staff were allocated to activities within the custody process.
- The "activity driver" relates to the timing and frequency of arrests. Costs were computed by the simulation for each arrest type (e.g., theft, warrant) for the

activities engaged by the arrested person within the custody process. The overall level of the activity driver is dependent on environmental factors such as the crime rate and government policy on crime as well as factors under the control of the police.

The study considers the arrest process, from the initial arrest of a suspect by a PC, through the booking-in process at a custody suite to possible detention and interview. The requirement, if necessary, of a court appearance by the PC is also considered. The administration resulting from each arrest is considered both for the PC and the appropriate administration section. The boundary is determined by the need to estimate the main cost of an arrest and particularly the utilization and cost of PC time. The main activities in the arrest process are shown in Figure 10.2.

The first decision point in the arrest process is whether to conduct a search of the location of the arrest. For all decisions during the arrest process, a probability distribution is used for each type of arrest at each decision point. The human resource rank required for each process is indicated above the process box. Personnel involved in the arrest process include the PC, custody officer (COF), jailer and inspector. The role of each rank is indicated on the conceptual model for each process.

In terms of data collection, the probability of a location search, transportation from arrest location to the custody suite, interview, detention, charge and not guilty plea are estimated for each arrest type. A demand pattern was determined for each of the arrest type for each of the three shifts worked at the custody suite. This approach was taken due to the need to estimate resource usage for each of the three shifts on duty. It also enabled the change in demand over each day to be modeled more accurately than with a single daily distribution. The user is able to enter the number of arrests (for each arrest type) and the estimate will occur in each shift which is translated in the model into an exponential distribution during the shift. The actual arrivals modeled can be compared to the estimates by viewing the simulation display. Finally, to estimate the process duration a number of distributions were estimated using a curve-fitting program from data collected on activity durations.

Step 2: Build the Simulation Model

The model was built using the Arena modeling system (Figure 10.3). Verification or "de-bugging" was carried out making extensive use of the animation facilities to observe the behavior of components in the system. The model was validated by comparing its performance to the real-world system.

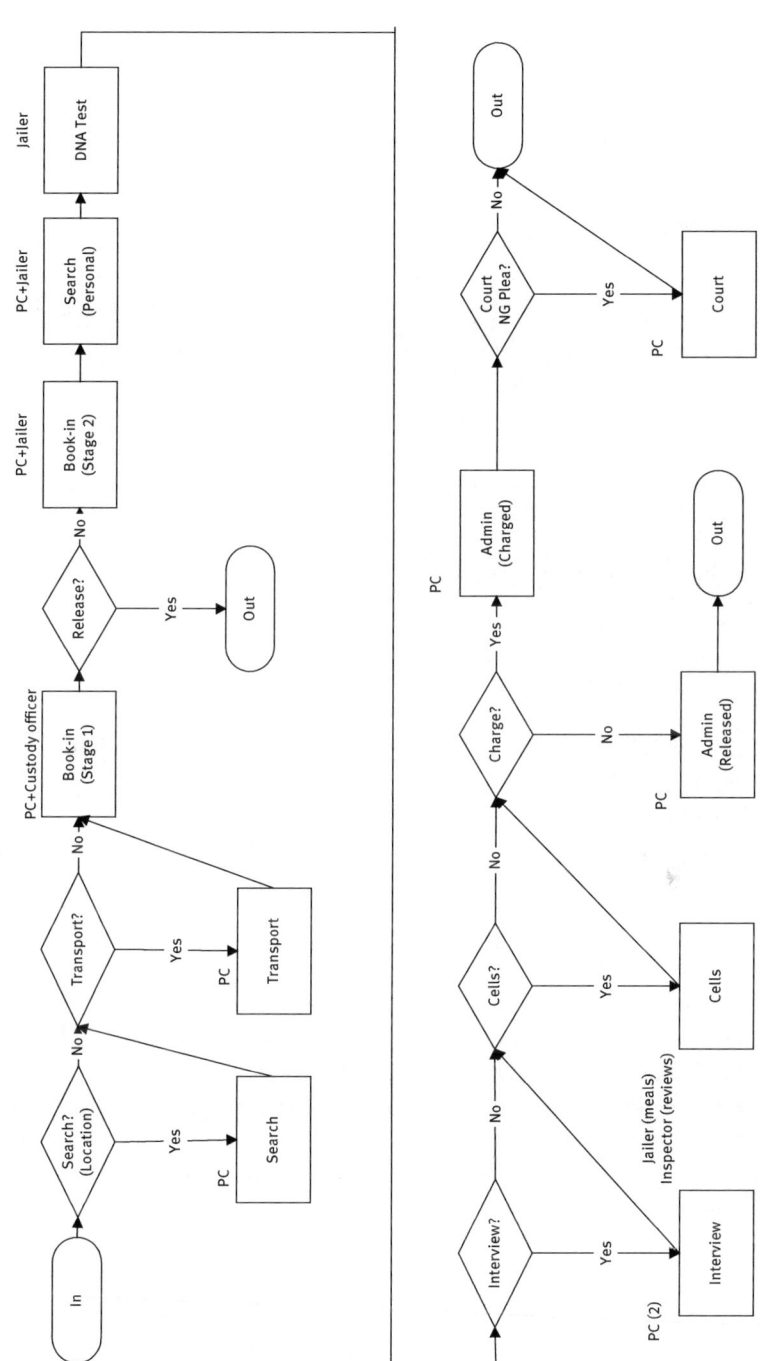

Figure 10.2: Conceptual model for arrest process.

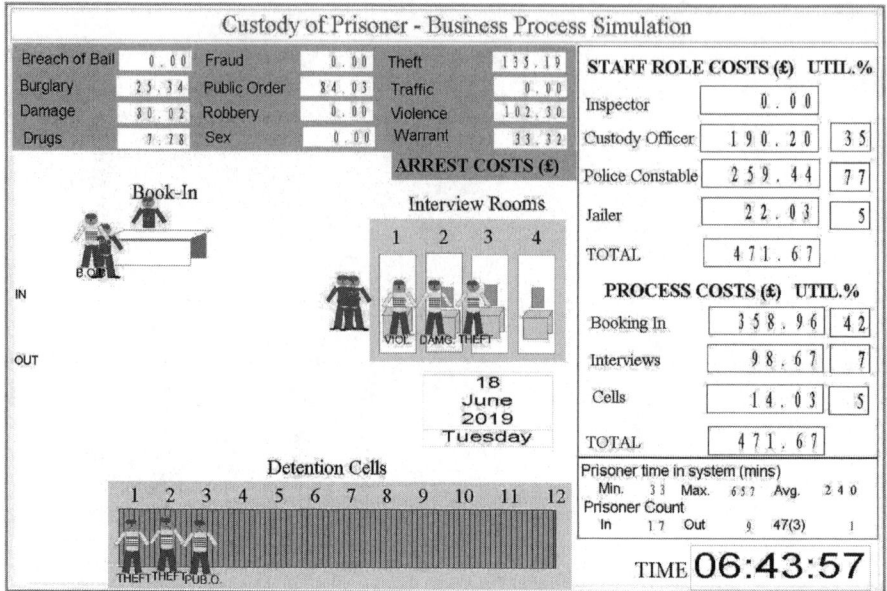

Figure 10.3: Arena police arrest simulation model.

Step 3: Use Simulation for Descriptive, Predictive and Prescriptive Analytics

Descriptive Analytics

The main aim of this part of the simulation experimentation was to provide an estimate of the costs incurred in the custody process from the perspective of the three drivers of cost.

Activity Driver

To estimate the arrest cost for each arrest type, the simulation was run for a period of 50 days. The results are shown in Table 10.1.

Please note at this time that costs include PC, COF and jailer pay costs for activities included in the conceptual model only. There will be other costs such as inspector reviews, meal costs and PC costs for escorting suspects to court. Other overhead costs are also not included. The figures in Table 10.1 do, however, provide an indication of the proportion of costs incurred for different arrest types. Of particular interest is the high proportion (33%) of costs incurred from theft offences and the difference between the proportion of arrests on warrant (20%) with the proportion of the cost of these arrests (9%). Thus, the overall cost figure provides an indication of the amount of resource allocation for each arrest type both from its frequency and cost per arrest.

Table 10.1: Costs by Arrest Type (Activity Driver).

Arrest Type	Average Number	Average Cost (£)	Average Cost per Arrest (£)	% of costs	% of arrests
THEFT	266	18600	70	33%	28%
BURGLARY	85	7172	84	13%	9%
VIOLENCE	104	6755	65	12%	11%
DAMAGE	91	5522	61	10%	9%
WARRANT	189	5349	28	9%	20%
DRUGS	43	3522	82	6%	4%
PUBLIC ORDER	63	3083	49	5%	7%
BREACH OF BAIL	49	2695	55	5%	5%
SEX	15	1362	91	2%	2%
TRAFFIC	20	983	49	2%	2%
FRAUD	19	972	51	2%	2%
ROBBERY	12	822	67	1%	1%
	958	56837			

Resource Driver

Table 10.2 shows the staffing costs for the PC, jailer and COF derived from the multiplication of pay rate by the total activity duration. Further development of the model will also incorporate inspector costs for reviews of detention periods, for example. By estimating resource costs, in this case staff wages, it was possible to estimate the effects and feasibility of proposals to reallocate and civilianize staffing duties within the custody process. The legal requirements surrounding the custody process constrained the amount of discretion available to personnel in the area and so facilitated the model building process. More loosely based activities would require the use of further experimentation to judge the effect on performance measures. It was envisaged that tasks within the custody area would evolve over time.

Cost Driver

Table 10.3 shows the costs assigned to each process element within the custody process. The detention process shows a zero cost as the model does not currently include staffing costs for this item. It is envisaged that the model will be developed to

Table 10.2: Cost per Staffing Grade (Resource Driver).

	Average Cost (£)	% of Total Cost
Cost PC	45,171	79.5%
Cost jailer	8564	15.1%
Cost COF	3102	5.5%
	56,837	

Table 10.3: Cost by Process (Cost Driver).

Process	Average Cost (£)
Search (location)	5770
Transport	4192
Book-in stage 1	5690
Book-in stage 2	5036
Search (personal)	3180
DNA	4351
Interview	11,826
Detention	0
Admin. if released	3409
Admin. if charged	13,384
Court	0
	56,838

include detention costs such as the costs of delivery of meals or release from cells by the jailer. Data is also required on the expected duration of PC time in court to compute court attendance staffing costs. The cost driver relates to the design efficiency of the process elements within the custody operation. At a higher level of analysis, a program of centralization of custody suites to smooth demand and focus resources is being implemented, in conjunction with an increase in the level of facilities (e.g., number of cells) to meet predicted peak demand levels. This requires a model providing aggregated costs of custody suites located within a geographical area.

Predictive Analytics

In order to estimate changes in resource allocation for the late drinking scenario, estimates of the increase in demand for each relevant arrest type are required. The following increases in arrest occurrences in the appropriate shift (22.00 until 6.00) were estimated by the police personnel: damage 5%, public order 7%, violence 7%, traffic 20% and sex 25%. In order to assess the effect on resources of the late drinking scenario, the number of PC hours was estimated from the simulation over a period of 50 days. The simulation was run five times, and the mean of the PC hours was estimated for each shift.

Table 10.4: Mean Number of PC Hours.

	PC Hours	Shift 1 6–14	Shift 2 14–22	Shift 3 22–6
Existing drinking hours	Mean	557.0	859.4	962.0
	Std. dev.	24.3	43.7	36.3
Late drinking scenario	Mean	628.0	851.0	975.6
	Std. dev.	23.2	41.8	35.7
t-Value		23.05*	1.22	2.17*

The critical t-value for the significance test at 5% level is $t_{8, 0.05} = 1.86$
*Significant at 5% level.

Table 10.4 shows the effect on the mean number of PC hours required of the policy to extend drinking hours from 23.00 to midnight. A one-sided two-sample t-test shows that there is a statistically significant difference in PC hours for shift 1 and shift 3 only. The results show that although the increase in arrests occurs in shift 3 (22.00 until 6.00), most of the additional resources required in response to the predicted increase in arrests will occur in shift 1 (6.00 until 14.00). This is because of delayed activities such as interviews and administration required for court appearances.

Conclusion

At present, the custody suite is considered as an essentially fixed cost with an annual budget and there has been no attempt to correlate demand on the facility with costs.

The first stage in the study estimates the arrest costs for each arrest type. This is a function not only of the number of arrests but the likelihood of an arrest leading to interview, detention and court procedures. A Pareto analysis can identify the few activities causing a large proportion of costs. In this case, relatively trivial theft offences (usually involving children shoplifting) are causing a heavy workload. This could lead to policies to decrease this workload through crime prevention activities, for example.

This study also describes the use of the model as a resource planning tool for management. Various scenarios can be modeled and the consequences for resource usage (and thus cost) estimated. Here the effect on the implementation of a law regarding late drinking was assessed. These costs will be difficult to model accurately without the use of a simulation model because of the stochastic nature of the system and the interaction between activities within the arrest process. The model can help in providing organizations such as the police with information on which to provide a case to supplying agencies, such as the government, for an increase in resources. Without this information there can be a tendency to assume that service providers can "absorb" the consequences of policy decisions. This can lead to inefficient allocation of resource and poor service quality if the resources available are insufficient.

The model can also assist police management in planning future allocation of staff. With the wide discretion available in how management utilizes its main staffing rank (i.e., the PC), it is important that management is aware of the resource implications of their decisions and so the simulation study has analyzed the performance of the custody process from the perspective of the three drivers of cost. From the activity driver perspective, the simulation can provide information on the source of cost by arrest type. Arrest types, such as theft offences, accounting for a high proportion of costs can be targeted to reduce overall costs. From the resource driver perspective, in professional service organizations such as the police, staffing costs account for a high proportion of total costs. In this case, staffing costs could be reduced by reallocating tasks from the COF to a jailer and investigating the civilianization of the jailer role. From the cost driver perspective, the effect of increased process efficiency achieved through the redesign of activities can be estimated using the simulation. In this case, the introduction of a computerized custody booking-in system was able to decrease the time and cost of the custody operation.

Whichever perspective is used it should be recognized that a reduction in staffing cost obtained will be offset by an equivalent increase in the cost of unused capacity. For example, the reduction in cost of COF time obtained through reallocation of tasks and computerization of the booking-in process will not lead to an overall spending decrease unless the committed cost of this staffing rank becomes variable. This is achieved by the management decision to either redeploy or eliminate the unused capacity created.

Chapter 11
Case Study: A Simulation of a Food Retail Distribution Network

Andrew Greasley and Melissa Venegas Vallejos

In order to maximize transport efficiency, many retail companies are using more precise and sophisticated planning methods that connect and synchronize the transport flows that work separately. In the case of "supplier collection" practice, the shop delivery vehicles instead of returning to a distribution center (DC) empty can be routed to the supplier's sites to collect orders and deliver them to the retailer's DC. Whereas in an onward delivery practice, the supplier's vehicle off-load products at the retailer's DC and backload with goods to the retailer's shops. In general, the suppliers deliver the goods to shop premises that are on the way back to the factory to minimize the time and kilometer deviation. In this study, ways to improve the transport efficiency are explored by focusing on the collaboration among retailers, tier 1 suppliers and tier 2 suppliers.

The Case Study

The case study presented in this research is about an international multichannel retailer given the name "Retailer Alpha." An analysis of the current performance of the distribution network is presented to identify the improvement opportunities related to the transport operations. The operation consists of a food supply chain network delivering to retail stores. Both primary distribution and secondary distribution processes are illustrated in Figure 11.1. In the case of primary distribution, the Long Life Ambient and Beer/Wines/Spirits food types are consolidated into National Distribution Centers and then sent either to the Regional Distribution Centers (RDCs) or directly to the stores, whereas the chilled, short-life, frozen foods are collected from supplier sites, sent to a consolidation center and then delivered to an RDC. The second part of the food retailer supply chain network involves the secondary distribution where the products stored in the RDC are delivered to the Retailer Alpha stores 7 days a week.

A key aspect of the current operation is that a number of Retailer Alpha suppliers of primary products such as meat, fish, poultry and bread also supply raw materials to other Retailer Alpha suppliers for use in Retailer Alpha processed chilled foods. However, Retailer Alpha suppliers manage the supply independently with suppliers' vehicles and/or other haulage companies. Moreover, it was identified that Retailer Alpha's distribution network has hundreds of vehicles moving between sites across

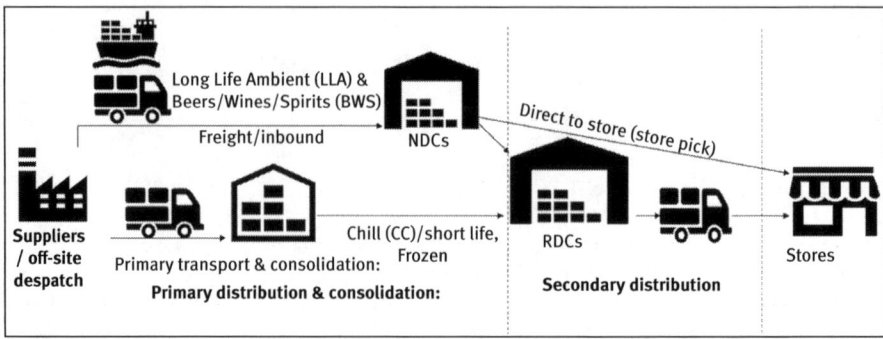

Figure 11.1: Food retailer supply chain network.

the country on a daily basis. It was thus decided to identify and assess the existing opportunity to extend the transportation network to integrate raw material sourcing to suppliers. The reason for this selection was the following. First, the secondary distribution network, where the store delivery trucks operate, has high empty running levels and so there is an opportunity to use the existing spare capacity. Second, as currently the sourcing from Retailer Alpha tier 2 suppliers and tier 1 suppliers is managed independently, these trips may be done by the store delivery trucks of Retailer Alpha that move in the area to use the spare capacity and as a consequence increase the distribution network efficiency. The efficiency of the transportation is critically dependent on the degree to which the vehicle's capacity can be maximized and used in both directions. The key performance indicators (KPIs) used to measure transport performance include empty running, fuel efficiency and capacity utilization of road freight transport vehicles. The most common indicator of vehicle underutilization is empty running. Empty running commonly happens when transport operators are not able to find a return load. In reality it is almost impossible to eliminate completely empty running journeys and raise load factors to 100% levels due to the complexity of the variety of operation conditions, geographical differences or scheduling constraints, but there are still many improvement opportunities. Reducing empty running will increase the transport efficiency by reducing the operational costs and at the same time provide environmental benefits.

Step 1: Build the Conceptual Model

The simulation study will model the current food distribution network in order to assess its performance in terms of empty running. The model will then be developed to encompass an extension to the distribution network that offers a pickup from tier 2 suppliers and a drop-off service to tier 1 suppliers as part of the return to depot route of the main distribution network design.

To understand the current situation of the secondary distribution network of Retailer Alpha, data was collected corresponded to 176 journeys from an RDC to 66 Retailer Alpha stores located in the surrounding areas to the RDC. Data collected included journey summary reports that include vehicle routes, arrival/departure time and distance from/to RDC or stores, type of journey, loading and unloading information including postcode locations. The vehicle routes, arrival/departure time, loading/unloading time were used to measure the total time of the journey and identify the time spent in each part of the journey. The journey schedule for 1 week is shown in Figure 11.2. The table shows the number of truck routes taken for each day, the depot departure time for each route and the number of unload stops taken for each route.

In order to begin building the model of the current secondary distribution network, it is important to create a process map that represents the sequence of steps in the process to be analyzed. Figure 11.3 shows the main activities and steps that take place along a truck journey from the departure from the depot, including store deliveries and the way back to the initial depot. It is important to mention that the process map shown in Figure 11.3 shows a simplified map that does not include any disruption in the trip such as breaks or any other occasional stops that are not part of the main process to be analyzed.

Step 2: Build the Simulation Model
Having finished with the initial data collection, analysis and process mapping the simulation model that represents the current situation of the secondary distribution network was built. The model was built using Arena software with each entity in the model representing a truck, which is directed along a distribution route using Arena modules STATION and ROUTE. The schedule information, including routing sequences and timings, were uploaded to the simulation model from an Excel spreadsheet. When the entity arrives to the destination station the time spent in the unloading process is represented using a theoretical distribution derived from sample data collected and analyzed using the Arena Input Analyzer software. When the entity finishes with the first store delivery it reads its next destination. This last sequence repeats until the entity reaches its last station. When the entity reaches its last point, it goes back to the initial depot where it departed from. An animation that has been designed in order to monitor the flow of entities and sequences can be seen in Figure 11.4. Figure 11.4 only includes the visual representation of one of the 176 routes simulated with four unload locations.

Figure 11.5 shows the results for 7 days operation of the distribution network. The simulation records 176 observations relating to the 176 routes defined in the weekly schedule. The average traveling time on the road is recorded as 275 minutes (4 hours 35 minutes). The entity.totaltime variable does not take into account the

ROUTES	SUNDAY Dep. Time	Stops	MONDAY Dep. Time	Stops	TUESDAY Dep. Time	Stops	WEDNESDAY Dep. Time	Stops	THURSDAY Dep. Time	Stops	FRIDAY Dep. Time	Stops	SATURDAY Dep. Time	Stops
1	2:22 AM	2	4:20 AM	2	3:46 AM	4	2:15 AM	1	2:23 AM	1	3:46 AM	3	4:33 AM	1
2	3:40 AM	2	4:01 AM	2	3:56 AM	2	3:04 AM	3	7:32 AM	6	5:17 AM	2	4:14 AM	1
3	3:48 AM	3	2:36 AM	2	3:03 AM	2	3:52 AM	1	3:54 AM	2	2:09 AM	1	2:16 AM	1
4	4:23 AM	4	5:46 AM	3	2:14 AM	2	2:31 AM	3	2:33 AM	3	3:34 AM	3	4:20 AM	2
5	4:47 AM	4	3:19 AM	2	3:56 AM	2	3:15 AM	2	4:33 AM	1	3:38 AM	1	4:29 AM	1
6	4:47 AM	3	4:37 AM	1	4:10 AM	1	3:46 AM	2	10:23 AM	1	3:59 AM	2	4:59 AM	2
7	5:05 AM	3	4:02 AM	3	2:10 AM	2	4:09 AM	1	3:51 AM	3	3:59 AM	1	4:52 AM	1
8	5:10 AM	3	4:53 AM	3	3:34 AM	3	3:58 AM	1	4:29 AM	2	4:12 AM	1	12:22 AM	1
9	5:14 AM	2	3:42 AM	4	4:06 AM	2	4:05 AM	3	3:46 AM	2	8:43 AM	6	3:14 AM	1
10	5:30 AM	2	2:35 AM	1	3:16 AM	1	4:36 AM	3	3:52 AM	1	4:19 AM	1	2:31 AM	3
11	5:31 AM	4	2:48 AM	1	10:56 AM	1	3:42 AM	2	3:09 AM	3	4:42 AM	3	4:20 AM	2
12	5:34 AM	4	3:31 AM	3	4:41 AM	3	4:47 AM	4	9:34 AM	6	4:16 AM	2	3:21 AM	1
13	5:53 AM	4	2:28 AM	2	4:36 AM	3	3:41 AM	1	8:33 AM	5	3:36 AM	2	3:51 AM	2
14	6:15 AM	3	4:45 AM	3	4:36 AM	3	2:09 AM	1	4:36 AM	3	3:41 AM	1	4:05 AM	4
15	6:16 AM	2	4:18 AM	2	4:38 AM	2	2:56 AM	1	3:48 AM	1	2:25 AM	1	4:46 AM	3
16	6:24 AM	3	3:29 AM	4	4:31 AM	1	4:34 AM	1	3:31 AM	1	4:55 AM	1	3:44 AM	3
17			3:12 AM	4	4:21 AM	2	4:34 AM	2	2:16 AM	2	4:03 AM	2	4:39 AM	4
18			3:11 AM	3	5:37 AM	3	4:02 AM	2	2:49 AM	1	3:26 AM	1	3:31 AM	1
19			5:36 AM	2	4:38 AM	2	4:20 AM	3	4:38 AM	2	2:51 AM	2	3:27 AM	3
20			4:13 AM	3	3:50 AM	1	4:37 AM	3	3:59 AM	2	3:17 AM	2	4:33 AM	1
21					4:07 AM	3	3:08 AM	4	4:21 AM	4	2:54 AM	4	3:47 AM	2
22					2:18 AM	3	4:25 AM	1	2:26 AM	1	4:49 AM	1	4:00 AM	1
23					3:21 AM	3	3:12 AM	1	4:00 AM	2			2:29 AM	2
24					3:48 AM	2	4:02 AM	2	4:43 AM	1			4:22 AM	1
25					2:16 AM	1	2:17 AM	3	2:33 AM	1			3:16 AM	1
26					3:24 AM	2	4:40 AM	2	4:12 AM	3			4:06 AM	3
27					1:49 AM	1	2:57 AM	1	9:41 PM	1			5:01 AM	3
28					2:13 AM	1	2:36 AM	2	3:51 AM	3			5:22 AM	1
29					4:43 AM	1	3:10 AM	4						
30					3:32 AM	3	5:27 AM	2						
31							5:04 AM	1						
32							3:28 AM	3						

Figure 11.2: Example weekly schedule for secondary distribution.

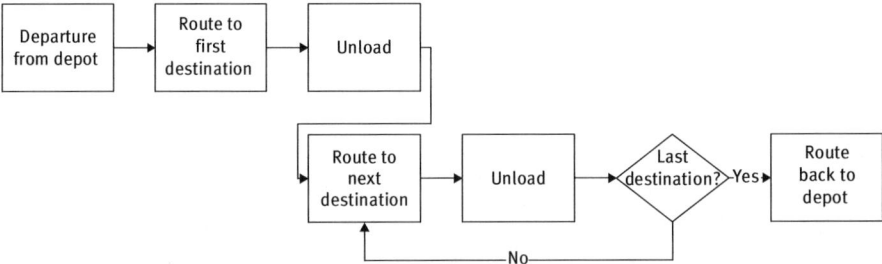

Figure 11.3: Process map of secondary distribution network.

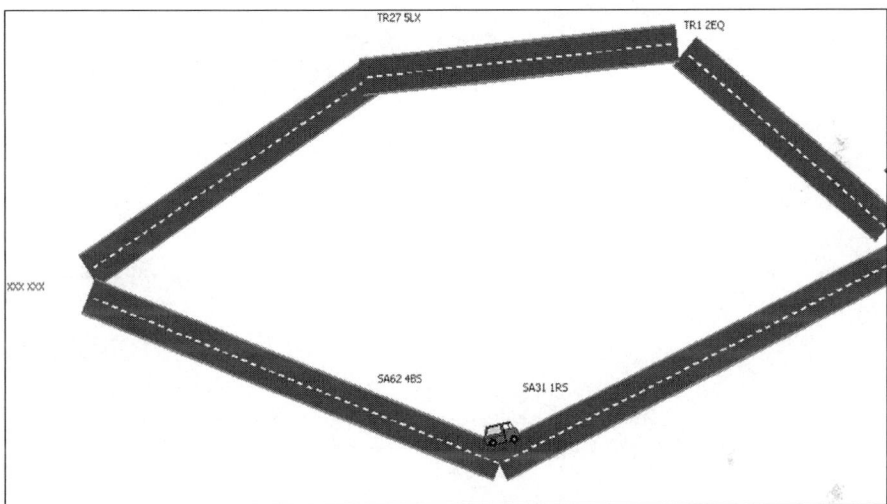

Figure 11.4: Simulation animation of one route on secondary distribution network.

depot leave time, so overall travel time including unloading time is reported as 434 minutes (7 hours 13 minutes). This gives an average unload time for all the stops on the journey of 159 minutes (2 hours 39 minutes).

In order to further validate the model, event data was saved to an event log and process mining software (Minit Process Mining Software) was used to analyze the data. Figure 11.6 shows the discovered process map confirming all 176 routes are simulated with leave depot and return depot events.

Figure 11.7 displays the active events (truck journeys) for 1 week's operations. Each peak in the graph shows 1 day's operation with trucks leaving, being on route and then returning to the depot. The process mining software also provides metrics of leave and return to depot times that can be cross-checked to ensure validation.

```
                              Summary for Replication 1 of 1
Project: Unnamed Project                              Run execution date :10/30/2018
Analyst: ISA                                          Model revision date:10/30/2018

Replication ended at time    : 10140.0 Minutes (Sunday, August 26, 2018, 01:00:00)
Base Time Units: Minutes

                                  TALLY VARIABLES

Identifier                        Average    Half Width  Minimum    Maximum    Observations

Empty Running Percentage           25.525     (Insuf)     2.8900     69.251     176
Entity 1.VATime                    .00000     (Insuf)     .00000     .00000     176
Entity 1.NVATime                   .00000     (Insuf)     .00000     .00000     176
Entity 1.WaitTime                  .00000     (Insuf)     .00000     .00000     176
Entity 1.TranTime                  275.08     (Insuf)     36.389     590.89     176
Entity 1.OtherTime                 438.51     (Insuf)     56.478     2095.8     176
Entity 1.TotalTime                 713.59     (Insuf)     119.52     2409.1     176

                              DISCRETE-CHANGE VARIABLES

Identifier                        Average    Half Width  Minimum    Maximum    Final Value

traveltime Value                   434.83     (Insuf)     .00000     826.63     768.11
Entity 1.WIP                       12.527     (Insuf)     .00000     33.000     .00000

                                      OUTPUTS

Identifier                        Value

Entity 1.NumberIn                  178.00
Entity 1.NumberOut                 178.00
System.NumberOut                   176.00


Simulation run time: 0.03 minutes.
Simulation run complete.
```

Figure 11.5: Arena results.

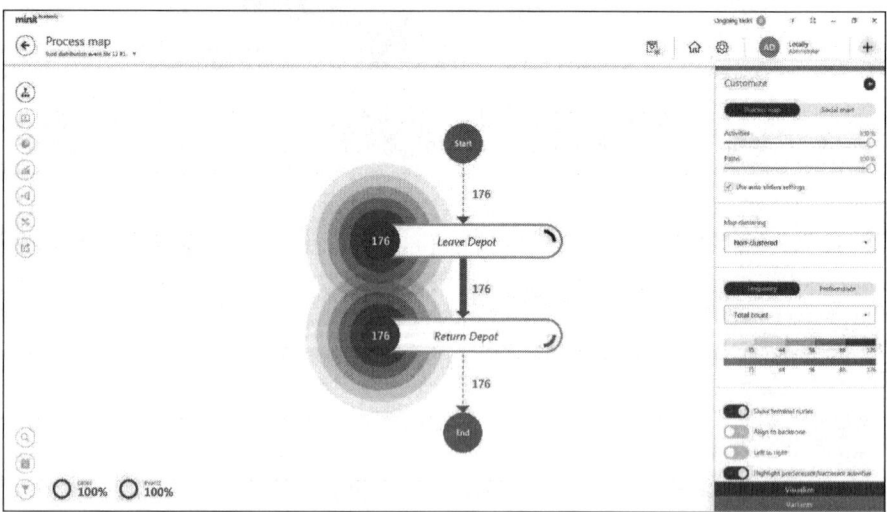

Figure 11.6: Process map generated using process mining software (www.minit.io).

Figure 11.7: Truck journeys over 1 week (www.minit.io).

Step 3: Use Simulation for Descriptive, Predictive and Prescriptive Analytics

After running the simulation for 10 replications, the results are shown in Figure 11.8. The results suggest that the average empty running time is 25.5%.

The analysis of the data suggests that there is a relatively high level of empty running of approximately 25% in the secondary distribution network that is affecting its efficiency. Hence, it is proposed to schedule additional deliveries for trucks when they have entered their empty running phase on their way back to the depot. These additional deliveries added to the secondary distribution network correspond to sourcing from Retailer Alpha tier 2 suppliers and delivering to tier 1 suppliers. These activities are currently managed separately by the suppliers. The simulation is presented using a manual method for extended delivery selection using Google Maps for location analysis.

Manual Selection of Additional Pickups and Drop-Offs in the Extended Distribution

Figure 11.9 shows the process map for the extended distribution network. After the completion of the secondary distribution route, it is necessary to select a suitable tier 2 supplier for each route. However, as there are less tier 2 pickups than secondary routes then some secondary routes will return directly to the depot. With the initial version of the simulation, the Arena model incorporates information for each extended route on the time to route from the last location to the pickup point, the time from pickup to drop-off, the time from drop-off to base, pickup load time and drop-off unload time. A mapping analysis using Google Maps was used to identify

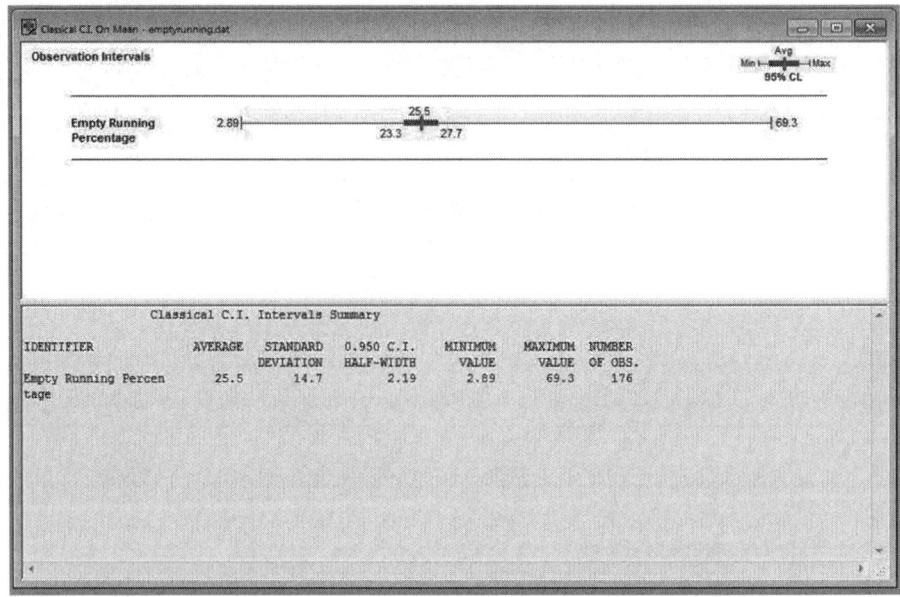

Figure 11.8: Empty running percentage for secondary distribution network.

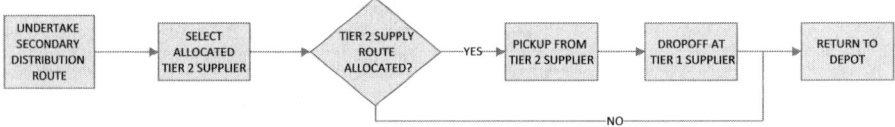

Figure 11.9: The extended distribution supply network with manual tier 2 pickup selection.

the locations of tier 1 and tier 2 suppliers and verify if their locations were close to the end point of the secondary distribution route. The extended distribution route was selected based on a pickup point as close to the end point of the secondary distribution route as possible and a return to depot time that was within the allocated shift allowance for the driver.

The new version of the simulation model of the extended secondary distribution network incorporates both deliveries from the RDC to Retailer Alpha stores and predefined deliveries from tier 2 suppliers to tier 1 suppliers. The animation of the potentially improved scenario can also be seen in Figure 11.10.

Figure 11.11 presents the results of the analysis of the secondary distribution networks and its potential extension that includes the sourcing from Retailer Alpha tier 2 suppliers to tier 1 suppliers. The figure shows that the average empty running percentage is 19.9% in the extended distribution scenario. This represents

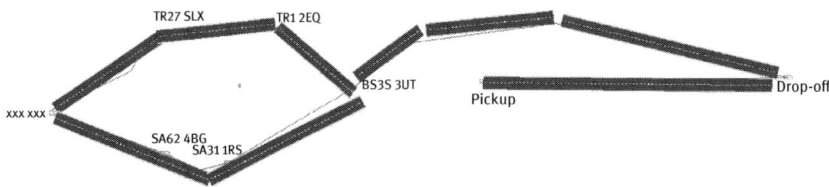

Figure 11.10: Simulation of one route of the extended secondary distribution network.

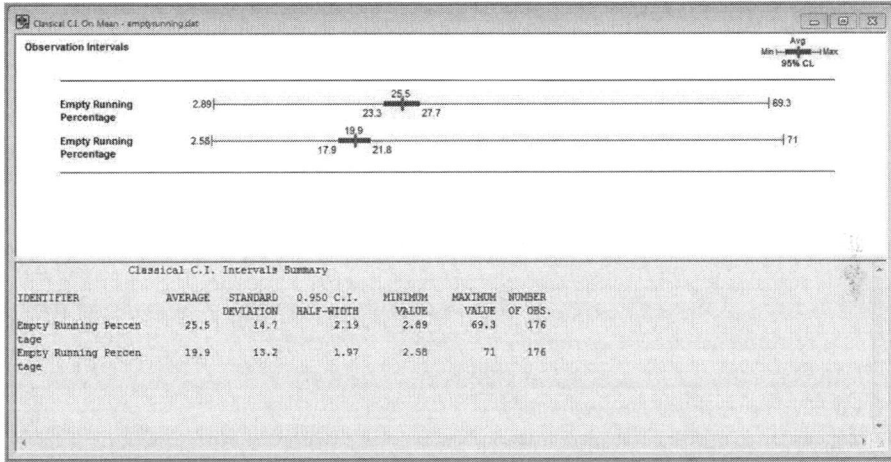

Figure 11.11: Comparison of empty running percentage for secondary and extended secondary distribution network.

a reduction of empty running from the current scenario of 25.5–19.9 = 5.6%. The confidence intervals do not overlap so there is a statistically significant difference between the results of the two scenarios.

Conclusion

A simulation model was built to represent the current secondary distribution network operations and assess the efficiency impact of the network's expansion (including the sourcing between Retailer Alpha tier 2 and tier 1 suppliers). The results suggested that the integration of the raw material sourcing to suppliers into the secondary distribution network of Retailer Alpha decreases the empty running levels and as a consequence increases the efficiency of the distribution network. An initial model represents the store delivery journeys from the RDC to the assigned Retailer Alpha stores and the way back to the initial RDC. It was shown that the current secondary distribution network has relatively low efficiency levels represented by the percentage time of empty running. Therefore, there was an opportunity to include additional deliveries to the store delivery journeys in their way back to the depot in order to decrease the empty running levels and as a consequence increase the efficiency of the distribution network. According to the analysis performed, the additional deliveries chosen to be added to the secondary distribution network were the deliveries that correspond to the sourcing from Retailer alpha tier 2 suppliers and tier 1 suppliers which are currently managed separately by the suppliers. A simulation model was built to represent this new scenario and the simulation results confirmed that the proposed integration of raw material sourcing to suppliers in the secondary distribution network increases the transport efficiency of the network. The simulation model can be easily adapted in terms of routes, stations (e.g., stores and supplier sites), entities (e.g., trucks) to represent a retailer's distribution network. Future areas of investigation include:

- The human factor effect in transport efficiency could be explored. The driving habits of the truck drivers could be explored to identify how driving style, for example excessive speed, affects fuel efficiency. As it was identified in this research, the main transport cost was the fuel cost; therefore, any improvement that reduces the fuel cost such as the change in drivers' habits may generate significant savings in the retailer's distribution network.
- The evaluation of other transport efficiency indicators such as vehicle load factor and space utilization to complement the efficiency analysis. By using other indicators, it would be possible to have a more accurate estimation of the variation of the efficiency levels and savings achieved through a distribution network expansion.
- The integration of suppliers' sourcing to the secondary distribution network could be further extended to include integration of the primary distribution network. As it was identified in the analysis section, the primary and secondary distribution networks of the retailer are managed by two different companies that work separately and do not share resources. Therefore, it may be argued that there are still missed efficiency opportunities that can be achieved by using the spare capacity of the primary distribution network.
- A detailed analysis using simulation of potential spare capacity in the primary distribution network and an assessment on efficiency of further supply chain integration.

Chapter 12
Case Study: A Simulation of a Proposed Textile Plant

Andrew Greasley

Due to global competitive pressures, many garment manufacturers have scaled down or closed their operations in the UK and moved overseas. Due to lower labor costs, in what is a labor-intensive industry, production has increased in such areas as Asia. This study involves the design of a proposed overseas textile production facility which supplies garment manufacturers with rolls of material suitable for clothing manufacture.

The Case Study

The case study organization produces a range of cotton and lycra textile mixes, which are used for garments such as t-shirts and women's tights. In response to the relocation of garment manufacturers overseas and the need to reduce transportation costs of a bulky product, the organization has decided to supplement its UK operations and locate a textile production facility in Sri Lanka. The move will also lower costs due to lower labor rates and permit the design of a more efficient layout in a purpose-built factory, as opposed to the current facilities that are placed across a number of locations and buildings within the UK. The main stages in the production process are shown in Figure 12.1. Each stage is staffed by a locally managed team and all materials pass through the knit, preparation, dye, finish and dispatch processes.

Each process is now described in more detail.

Knit
The knit process, also termed ring spinning, takes yarn from the warehouse and knits into 25 kg rolls of cloth. A product mix is created by allocating a number of knit machines to a product type in proportion to the mix percentage. Table 12.1 gives a product mix of seven main product types of different materials and weights for the plant configuration to be modeled.

After knitting, the 25 kg roll is placed in a doff box (rectangular container), and quality is examined at one of three knit examination tables. After the quality examination the output from each knit machine is grouped separately to form a batch. This ensures that material within a batch is consistent as it is from the same knit machine

Figure 12.1: Main stages in textile plant production process.

Table 12.1: Product Mix.

Product Type	Product Mix (%)
1	6
2	18
3	18
4	6
5	18
6	28
7	6

and source yarn. With the current configuration, this requires 48 batch areas (one for each knit machine). The batch quantity is determined by the dye machine type that this product type has been allocated.

Preparation

The yarn has now been knitted into sheets of material in 25 kg rolls. The preparation stage sews these individual rolls together into a batch termed *a lane for dying*. At this stage, certain material types are set to shape using a heated conveyor termed *a stenter*. The process flow for the seven product types are shown in Figure 12.2.

Product types 1 and 5 are processed through the Prep (TF) flapper that sews the individual 25 kg rolls from the knit process together. Product 2 requires setting on the preset stenter after sewing. Product 3 is sewn on the Prep (UF), preset on the stenter and then its edges are sewn into a tube on the monti-tuber machine. Product types 4 and 6 are sewn on the Prep (UF) and preset on the stenter. Product 7 is reversed on the sperotto before sewing on the Prep (TF). Materials awaiting the sperotto, prep (TF) and prep (UF) processes are stored in the preparation storage area. Materials awaiting the preset stenter and monti-tuber processes are stored in the greige (i.e., undyed cloth) storage area. After completion of the preparation process, batches are stored in the dry storage area awaiting the dye process.

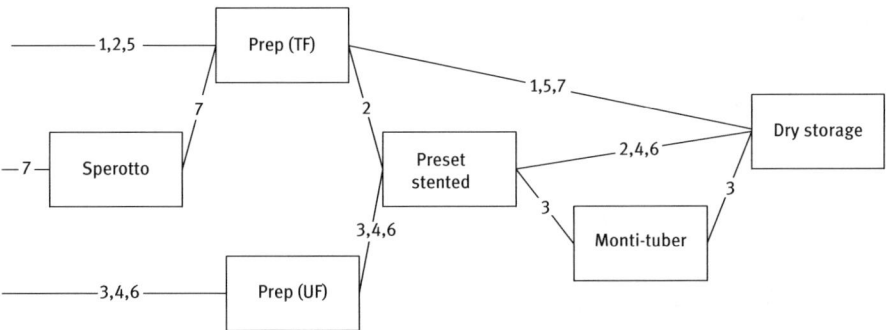

Figure 12.2: Preparation stage process flow.

Dye

The cloth is dyed in one of three shades (dark, medium, light) in a dye machine, which resembles a large domestic washing machine. There are four types of dye machine (1 lane, 2 lane, 3 lane and TRD), which have different load capacities. A lane relates to the capacity of one drum within the dye machine. The batch size is derived by multiplying the lane capacity with the number of lanes for each machine. The batch and lane size for each dye machine is given in Table 12.2. For example, materials allocated for a 3-lane dye machine will consist of three lengths (lanes) of 9 × 25 kg rolls stitched together to form a batch. The lanes are transported between production stages as a batch to ensure that materials from the same source are kept together.

Table 12.2: Batch Size by Dye Machine.

Dye Machine Type	Lane Size	Batch Size	Weight (kg)
1 lane	9	9	225
2 lane	9	18	450
3 lane	9	27	675
TRD (2 lane)	8	16	400

The allocation of batches to a dye machine type is undertaken before the knit process and is determined by the product type (see Table 12.3). For example, batches of product type 1 will only be allocated to the 1-, 2- or 3-lane dye machine types. The specific mix of machine types allocated to each batch from this selection is determined by the production schedule to ensure that a balanced load is achieved through all dye machine types. The reason this allocation is determined by the

Table 12.3: Dye Machine Allocation by Product Type.

Product Type	Dye Machine Type Allocation
1	1, 2, 3 lanes
2	1, 2, 3 lanes
3	1, 2, 3 lanes
4	1, 2, 3 lanes
5	80% 1, 2, 3 lanes/20% TRD
6	50% 1, 2, 3 lanes/50% TRD
7	TRD

schedule before the knit stage is that batches must contain materials from the same knit machine and so can not be split or combined and the batch size for each dye machine is different.

The batches arrive at the dry storage area ready for dying by one of the dye machine types. Each batch must now be allocated to a particular dye machine of the correct type. For example, there may be five 2-lane dye machines available. Dye machines must undertake a lengthy setup process when changing from one dye shade to a different dye shade and so rules have been developed for allocating a batch to a particular dye machine which aims to minimize the number of setups undertaken. Thus, each batch must be allocated to the correct machine type for that product type and if possible, a machine that has previously been used for the same dye shade. The rules for allocating a batch in the dry storage area to a dye machine are as follows:

1. If a dye machine of the allocated dye machine type is available, process the batch on this machine (idle machine).

Otherwise

2. If the shade of the last batch on any dye machine of the allocated dye machine type matches the shade of the batch, wait in dry storage until this machine is available and process the batch on this machine (match shade).

Otherwise

3. Wait in dry storage for the dye machine of the allocated dye machine type with the smallest queue (shortest queue).

The dye process time is dependent on the dye shade and is adjusted for batch weight. Note that a 3-lane (675 kg) batch on a 3-lane dye machine has a process time equal to a 1-lane (225 kg) batch on a 1-lane dye machine. After the dye process, the wet material is unloaded into wheeled tubs (1 lane to a tub) and stored in the "tubs and wet storage" area awaiting the finishing process.

Finishing
The finishing process dries and, if necessary, sets the shape of the material. The process map for finishing for the seven product types is shown in Figure 12.3.

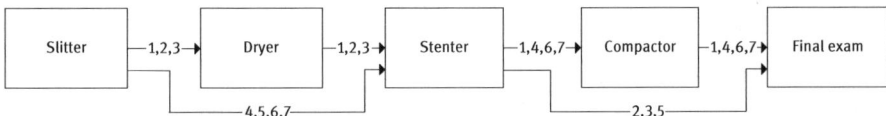

Figure 12.3: Process route for finishing process.

Note that the material is now held in a tub and consists of a lane (eight or nine 25 kg rolls) stitched together in a tube. The slitters slit open the tube to form a material length that is flapped to aid drying. Products 1, 2, 3 are passed through a further drying process. All products pass through the stenter machine that sets the material in its final width and weight and provides any chemical finishes that are required. Products 1, 4, 6, 7 are shaped by the compactor. All products are visually inspected individually as lanes and then batched and moved to the finished goods warehouse.

Dispatch
Batches of material are held in the finished goods warehouse ready for dispatch. Material is held for local, air or sea dispatch in the proportion of 50%, 25% and 25%, respectively. Local dispatches are undertaken daily. Air dispatches wait for five batches in storage, then send all in storage 24 hours later. Sea dispatches wait for 10 batches in storage, then send all in storage 7 days later. There may be more than 5 or 10 batches sent by air or sea at a time if further batches arrive in the warehouse after the trigger levels have been reached and before actual dispatch.

Step 1: Build the Conceptual Model
The aim of the simulation study is to assist the layout planning activity by estimating the quantity of work-in-progress (WIP) inventory within the proposed facility to be situated in Sri Lanka. The estimation of inventory levels is critical because the relative bulk of inventory means the amount of floorspace required could be

considerable. The need to sink drainage channels for effluent from the knit and dye machines and the size and weight of the machinery means that it would be expensive and time consuming to change the factory layout after construction.

The study collected data on the main stages within the production process and modeled seven product types through the factory using data from current experience of operations in the UK and from machine vendor estimates. The plant runs on a continuous (7 days a week, 24 hours a day) production cycle with an efficiency rating used to compensate for lost resource availability due to machine setup and other downtime factors.

Step 2: Build the Simulation Model

The simulation model was built using the Arena system. Figure 12.4 is a view of the animated model showing the proposed textile production facility. Entities flow through the system as product batches, shown as colored circles on the animation display, with a color representing each of the seven product types. A letter L, M or D within the circles represents light, medium and dark dye shades, respectively. The animation display shows the batches waiting simulation resources such as in the preparation area, the dye area and examination areas.

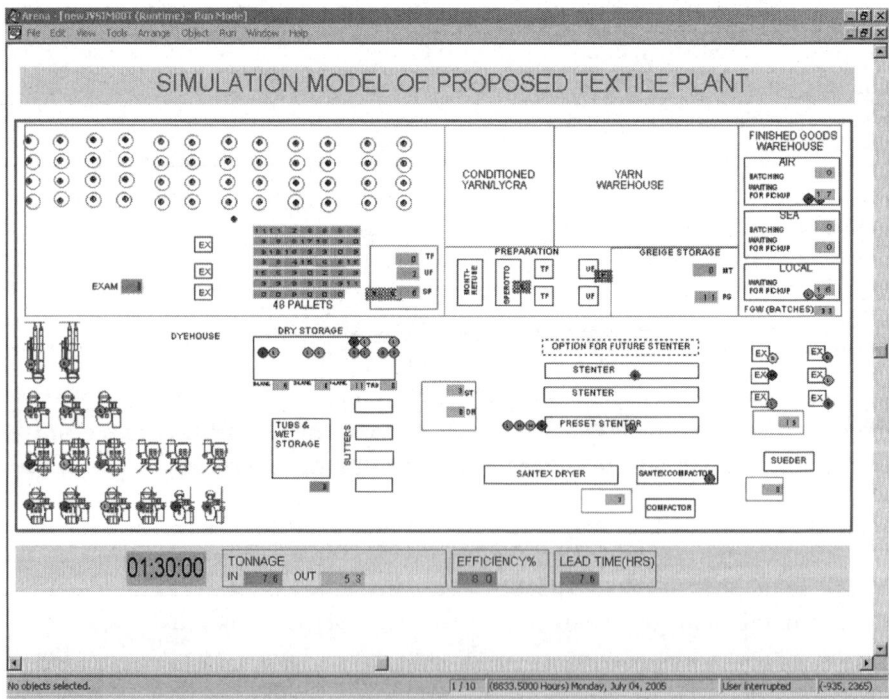

Figure 12.4: Simulation of proposed textile plant.

The simulation coding is extensive with over 100 elements, but Figure 12.5 shows the main logic within the Arena model itself. Here the seven product types are generated and flow through the simulation and use resources within the textile plant. The routing and process duration of each product type on each resource is defined in an Excel spreadsheet to allow the client to easily change parameters without the need to make changes to the simulation model itself. The logic for the allocation of entities/product batches to dye machines is also shown in Figure 12.5. Here the logic of matching the product batch to dye machine is implemented.

Model validation was undertaken by comparing output levels and lead-time measurements with projected figures from the scenarios defined. Detailed walk-throughs of the model were then undertaken with production personnel to validate the behavior of each production stage in the simulation.

Step 3: Use Simulation for Descriptive, Predictive and Prescriptive Analytics
The main objective of the simulation study was to predict the amount of WIP in the proposed layout under two scenarios of dye capacity, which has been identified as the bottleneck constraining overall plant capacity. The experimentation assessed the performance of the production system for two scenarios of a 28-lane dye facility and a 39-lane dye facility, representing target output capacity levels of 60 tons per week and 100 tons per week, respectively. The dye capacity details for each scenario are given in Table 12.4.

The production system is operated using the technique of line balancing and must therefore be balanced before results can be collected from the model. A balanced system will match the output level with input level and maintain a steady level of WIP. The dye machines are the production bottleneck or constraint on capacity and so it is necessary to balance the system through this production stage. Because each batch of the material is allocated with a dye machine type at the knit stage, it is necessary to balance the workflow through each dye machine type (i.e., the 1-lane, 2-lane, 3-lane and TRD) separately rather than the dye process as a whole. Thus to balance the system, two factors are adjusted: the rate of input into the system (i.e., the output from the knit machines) and the mix of dye machine type by product type.

The simulation results report on the WIP amount, derived from the resource queue lengths, and thus provide a measure of storage area required for all major WIP areas. The simulation was run 100 times over a 5-week run period. The 100 runs are necessary because the variability in the system (derived from process time variability and independence of product flows) means that the output measure of interest, the storage area requirement, is a random variable and must be adequately characterized in order to make statistically valid conclusions. A run duration of 5 weeks for each replication was chosen in order to achieve steady-state operation of the model for data collection. To calculate the maximum floorspace required for

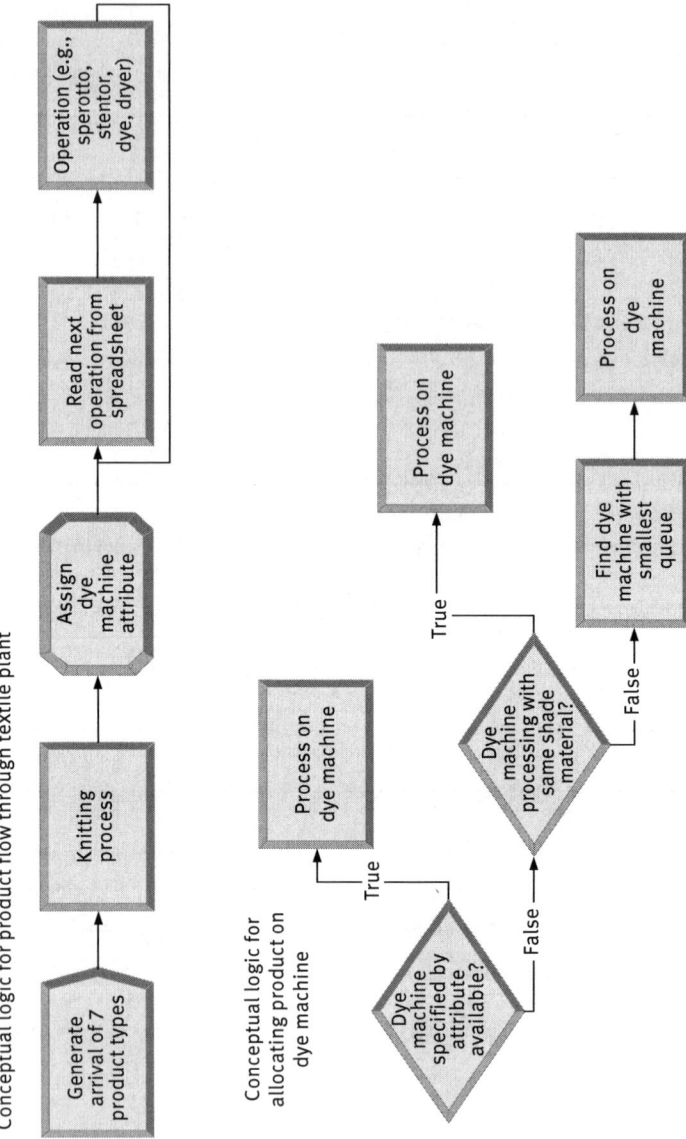

Figure 12.5: Conceptual logic for Arena simulation model.

Table 12.4: Dye capacity for simulation scenarios.

Dye Machine	28-Lane Scenario		39-Lane Scenario	
	Machines	Lanes	Machines	Lanes
1-Lane dye	3	3	2	2
2-Lane dye	5	10	6	12
3-Lane dye	3	9	7	21
TRD (2 lane)	3	6	2	4
Total	14	28	17	39

each storage area, the maximum WIP amount at that location for each simulation replication is recorded on a spreadsheet. The 95th percentile of the sample of 100 measurements taken from the simulation replications is derived by selecting the 95th value from the sorted list of 100. This measurement is used in conjunction with the floorspace area for the relevant storage type to derive a maximum floorspace area required for each storage location for each of the 28-lane and 39-lane scenarios (Tables 12.5 and 12.6).

Table 12.5: Floorspace Required by the Storage Area (28-Lane Scenario).

Storage Area Name	Maximum WIP (95th percentile)	Storage Area Type (Dimension)	Maximum Area (m^2)
Knit exam	21 rolls	Doff box (1 m^2)	21
Knit batchup	48 batches	Pallet (2.5 m^2)	120
Preparation	37 lanes	Wheeler (2.5 m^2)	92.5
Greige	34 lanes	Wheeler/stillage (2.5 m^2 / 2.5 m^2)	85
Dry storage	153 lanes	Stillage (2.5 m^2)	382.5
Tubs and wet storage	13 lanes	Tub (2 m^2)	26
Stenter	25 lanes	Wheeler (2.5 m^2)	62.5
Compactor	11 lanes	Wheeler (2.5 m^2)	27.5
Final exam	20 lanes	Wheeler/A-frame (2.5 m^2 / 2.5 m^2)	50
Finished goods	32 batches	Pallet (2.5 m^2)	80

Table 12.6: Floorspace Required by the Storage Area (39-Lane Scenario).

Storage Area Name	Maximum WIP (95th Percentile)	Storage Area Type (Dimension)	Maximum Area (m^2)
Knit exam	62 rolls	Doff box (1 m^2)	62
Knit batchup	48 batches	Pallet (2.5 m^2)	120
Preparation	47 lanes	Wheeler (2.5 m^2)	117.5
Greige	52 lanes	Wheeler/stillage (2.5 m^2 / 2.5 m^2)	130
Dry storage	160 lanes	Stillage (2.5 m^2)	400
Tubs and wet storage	18 lanes	Tub (2 m^2)	36
Stenter	34 lanes	Wheeler (2.5 m^2)	85
Compactor	13 lanes	Wheeler (2.5 m^2)	32.5
Final exam	27 lanes	Wheeler/A-frame (2.5 m^2 / 2.5 m^2)	67.5
Finished goods	42 batches	Pallet (2.5 m^2)	105

In summary, the simulation was able to estimate the amount of factory WIP, and thus floorspace area is required under two scenarios: a "28-lane" and a "39-lane" dye configuration. These relate to two investment proposals, providing two capacity capabilities of 60 and 100 tons, respectively. The dye stage was identified as the system bottleneck and so in order to balance the system, enough work must be provided to the dye facility to ensure the machines are fully utilized, but not too fast a rate that queue build-up occurs. In order to achieve a balanced system, the overall rate of work entering the dye facility was controlled by adjusting the rate of output from the knit process. However, each product type that is preallocated is a dye machine type at the knit stage, which means that the volume through each dye machine type (i.e., 1 lane, 2 lane, 3 lane, TRD) must be balanced separately. This was achieved by adjusting the volume mix on the four dye machine types. Because of this relatively complex procedure, a number of trial simulation runs were necessary to adjust both the overall product volume and the mix of products allocated to each dye machine type in order to balance the system. This process is complex because of the variability of the time lag between the decision taken at the knit stage and the effect of that decision when the batch reaches the dye area. This variability is due to each product batch taking an independent route through the intermediate preparation process and the variability of queue lengths at these intermediate processes.

Conclusion

In the case study described, a simple spreadsheet model could have been used to calculate maximum loading and thus inventory levels in a standard line facility layout. A discrete event simulation has the ability to carry information about each entity (by setting an attribute of the entity to a value) which was needed in this instance because the allocation of a dye machine type for each batch of material is made before the knit stage of the process in order to ensure consistency of the material. Thus, when a batch arrives at the dye stage a machine is allocated based on an attribute set at the beginning of the process. Also the ability of the simulation to show queuing behavior was essential because the overall objective of the study is to show the maximum inventory level, and thus floorspace requirement, necessary for the proposed facility layout. Thus, discrete-event simulation was chosen because of its ability to both store attribute values and to show queuing levels at an individual product level.

In terms of assessing the outcomes of the simulation study what became clear from the case study analysis was that discrete-event simulation provided more than a quantitative analysis of floorspace, but generated qualitative data for decision making. First, the simulation demonstrated the relationship between decisions made at the knit stage and the effect of these decisions on the downstream dye stage. This issue was important because each production stage (e.g., knit, preparation, dye) had a separate manager responsible for their area of operations. Thus, the simulation study underlined the importance of communication and collaboration between these areas in establishing a balanced production cycle and it was proposed to use the visual representation provided by the model as a training tool for the production stage managers in understanding the dynamics and relationships between operations. Second, at an operational level the need to codify decisions made by personnel in the production process caused their assumptions to be questioned. Specifically, as part of the model data collection process, the rules regarding allocation of work to dye machines were classified and formalized after the discussion with the personnel.

The case study also demonstrated that one of the important factors in achieving client confidence in the model was the intuitive way in which the discrete-event method represents elements such as machines, people and products as recognizable objects. The ability to observe the animation display, which incorporated the CAD drawings of the proposed facility layout, was seen as an essential check of accuracy from the client's perspective. In retrospect, it was clear that the study was undertaken on the basis of assumptions about how the process worked that were incorrect. The consequence of this was that additional time was required to form an understanding of the process requiring the project completion date to be extended. These qualitative outcomes are generated because simulation modeling is not just about analyzing results from a model, but is a process that takes place over time. What the process of designing and building a model did offer was a way of initiating discussion among decision makers about the system in question through such actions as data collection, process mapping and visual inspection of the simulation animation display. Indeed it is not a requirement of a simulation modeling exercise that a model is actually built, but qualitative outcomes from the process mapping stage, for example, could generate useful knowledge.

In this case study, a line balancing approach to production planning was preferred by the client and the main objective of the simulation study was to predict WIP levels under steady-state or balanced conditions. Line balancing is a common method used to maximize output from a serial line layout, where the output of the line is traditionally thought to be determined by the stage with the least capacity. A further use of the simulation model would be for it to be developed so it could provide a comparison between these operating policies before implementation of the plant.

Chapter 13
Case Study: A Simulation of a Road Traffic Accident Process

Andrew Greasley

A study is presented based on a process-based redesign of a road traffic accident (RTA) reporting system based within a UK Police Force. The study will examine a process-based approach to change in the context of a public sector organization using the supporting tools of process mapping and business process simulation. The technique of process mapping involves interviewing personnel and observation of the relevant process, which provides information that is used to draw a process map. The analysis shows the interrelationships between activities and identifies the elements and roles involved in process execution.

The Case Study

A case study is presented of a proposed process change initiative to a police RTA reporting system. Two aspects of performance of the RTA system require particular attention. The need to speed process execution is seen as essential to provide a faster and more efficient service to vehicle drivers. In particular, there is a need to provide the UK government agencies, such as the Department for Transport, with accident statistics within a 4-week time period. The second aspect of performance which requires improvement is the need to reduce the relatively high staffing cost associated with the process. The total cost of traffic police staff is relatively high as their on-costs need to include the purchase and maintenance of a police patrol vehicle. There is also a need for extensive administrative support at locations across the area covered by the police force. The current and proposed process designs for actions leading from an RTA will now be discussed.

The Current Road Traffic Accident Reporting System

The current process at the selected constabulary for the reporting and recording of accidents involves a police officer completing a number of paper-based forms following the report of an incident by the public. These forms are distributed to the traffic administration and data headquarters (HQ) departments for processing. The traffic administration section oversees the submission of witness evidence, either by post or in person and the collation of an abstract containing officer and witness statements for use by interested parties such as insurance companies and court proceedings. The data HQ section oversees mapping of the geographical location of the accident that is used for road transport initiatives such as traffic calming and speed cameras. The main stages of the RTA process are now described.

Following the notification of a road traffic incident to the police by the public, a decision is made to attend the scene of the incident. It may be that for a minor incident the parties involved are instructed to pursue proceedings with their insurance companies and the police have no further involvement. If it is necessary to attend the RTA scene the officer travels to the location of the incident. After an assessment is made of the incident the officer returns to the station to complete and submit the appropriate paperwork. Three forms are used by a police officer attending an RTA. Form "54" is used for injury accidents and is triplicated on yellow, pink and white forms. The yellow and pink forms are forwarded by the officer to the witness proforma process and the white form is forwarded to the data HQ section for location mapping. A single form "55" is used for noninjury incidents, which is filed unless further action is to be taken as a result of a dispute or claim, when it is then passed to the witness proforma process. In addition, pocket book entries are taken when no official record is required but provide data that could be retrieved at a later date and transferred to the appropriate form. Amendment of forms may take place at a later date. Form "54" amendment forms contain yellow, pink and white sections for distribution. Form "54" (yellow and pink) and Form "55" amendments are scrutinized to see if changes require further action such as new witness statements. Form "54" (white) amendments are communicated to data HQ.

A location mapping process collates information and passes it to a local council which provides a location grid reference from sketches and location information provided by the officer who attended the accident scene. The data is collated, sorted and then forms are mapped in batches by entering location codes on new forms. If all the necessary information is not available, a memo is sent to the officer for further information and the process is repeated. The information is then sent electronically to the local council who return the required geographical location details.

The witness proforma process obtains accident witness and driver information and places it on a proforma sheet. If a witness is identified, their details are taken and a proforma is sent to them. If a fatal accident has occurred, then the officer obtains further details in person at a later date. If the proforma has not been returned after 3 weeks, a reminder letter is sent to the witness. If there is still no response from the witness and the information requested is required for further proceedings, then an officer will obtain the statement in person.

The abstract preparation process collates and checks documents associated with the RTA process to ensure all the data needed has been received. A decision is made at this stage if further action is required after reviewing the evidence collected. If further action is required a number of forms are collated. If at this stage no prosecution is to take place, a letter informing the driver of this decision is sent. If a prosecution is to take place the officer will write an abstract, summarizing the details of the case. If a court case is scheduled and a not guilty plea has been entered, then the officer will be required to attend the court proceedings in person. Otherwise, this is the end of the involvement of the officer.

The Proposed Road Traffic Accident Reporting System

In the proposed computerized RTA reporting system, the attending officer completes paper-based forms as before but this information is promptly converted to a digital form using a document image processing system. This is achieved by a combination of image capture and data recognition through a facsimile link. Data recognition systems, such as optical character recognition (OCR) are used to process information that is entered in a structured format, such as options selected using a ticked box format. Image capture is used in the following ways. Documents are stored as images to enable input bureau staff to validate the OCR scanned data. Images that can not be interpreted by data recognition software, such as hand-drawn sketches of the RTA scene, are stored for later retrieval. Images of text such as officer written notes can be entered by the input bureau staff, saving officer time. Once in digital format, the documents can be delivered electronically preventing data duplication and enabling faster distribution. Physical documents are held in a central repository for reference if needed.

Location details are currently based on a written description of the RTA by an officer, which leads to inconsistent results. The current location description by the officer is usually acceptable for city incidents where nearby street intersections and other features can be used to pinpoint a location. However, on long stretches of road it is often difficult to pinpoint an exact spot. This is important because of the need to accurately pinpoint areas with high accident rates for road safety measures (e.g., road humps) and speed camera placement. Further inaccuracies can also occur when the officer description is converted by the local council using an Ordnance Survey map grid reference which is only accurate to 200 yards. In this proposal, each officer is issued with a portable digital map on which to indicate the RTA location. This information is transmitted by a mobile link to a geographical information system (GIS), which provides accurate location analysis of both injury and noninjury incidents using the geocode system. The geocode system is a network of grids covering the UK, which allows a location to be assigned within a 10 m^2 area. The GIS system will combine the accident location analysis with data relating to the location of pelican crossings, traffic lights, street parking and anything else that might contribute to accidents or affect schemes being proposed. Along with data on details on road conditions at the time of the accident this information will help determine a prioritized list of road safety improvement measures.

Step 1: Build the Conceptual Model

Data is required in order to construct a process map, which describes the logic of the model (i.e., how the process elements are connected) and decision points within the process. Decision points can be modeled by a conditional rule-based method or by a probability distribution. Probability distributions for decision points, such as the proportion of injury and noninjury events are derived from the sample data and take the form of a percentage. A process map of the proposed RTA reporting system using Microsoft VISIO software is shown in Figure 13.1.

The second area of data required for the simulation model is for additional elements such as process durations, resource availability schedules and the timing of RTA occurrences. In this case, probability distributions for process durations are derived from the sample data. In general, a triangular distribution has been used for process durations, which requires minimum, mode and maximum parameter values. Resource availability, in terms of a police officer attending the RTA, is assumed to be infinite as an RTA incident is treated as an "emergency situation" and if the designated officer is unavailable an alternative officer is found. Over a period of 6 years there had not been an incident when no officer could be found, when required, to attend an RTA scene. In terms of the timing of RTA occurrences, a 3-month sample of RTA incidences was collected for the study. Although seasonal variations will occur in RTA patterns, the model is used to compare before and after redesign scenarios and not for forecasting purposes.

Step 2: Build the Simulation Model

The business process simulation was built using the Arena simulation system. Before experimental analysis of the model can begin, it is necessary to ensure that the simulation provides a valid representation of the system. This process consists of verification and validation of the simulation model. Verification is analogous to the practice of "debugging" a computer program. In this case, the first check was to run the simulation model animation at a slow speed and observe the progress of the entities through the system to check for any logic errors. Then a number of test runs were undertaken and the results of the simulation noted and checked against real system performance and common-sense deductions. A verified model is a model that operates as intended by the modeler. However, this does not necessarily mean that it is a satisfactory representation of the real system for the purposes of the study. This is the purpose of validation. In this case, the results from the current RTA reporting system model could be compared against historical data of the actual system. A decision is made if model behavior is close enough to the real system to meet the objectives of the study. Unlike verification, validation is a matter of judgment which involves a trade-off between the accuracy of measurement required and the amount of modeling effort required to achieve this.

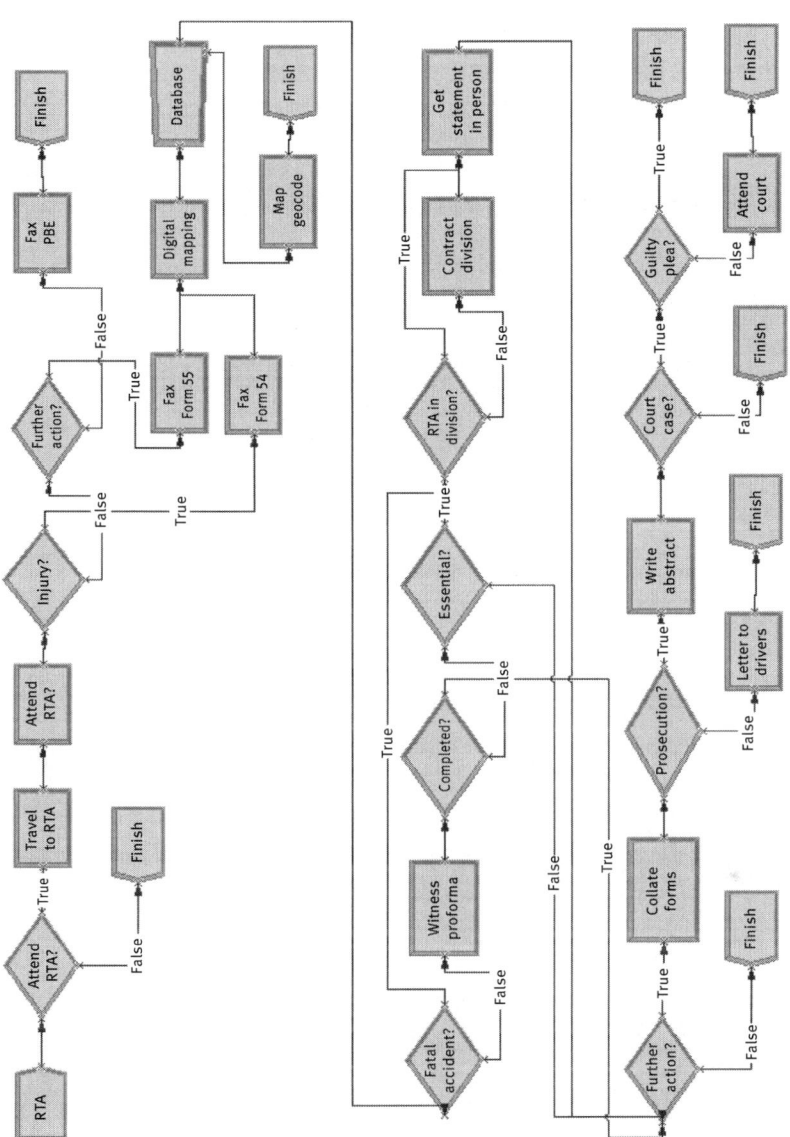

Figure 13.1: Process map of the proposed road traffic accident reporting system.

Step 3: Use Simulation for Descriptive, Predictive and Prescriptive Analytics

Because of the probability distributions used for RTA events, process times and decision points, the output measures of the simulation vary each time the simulation is run. Therefore, it is necessary to run the simulation multiple times and form a confidence interval within which the average of the measure should lie. In this case, the simulation was run 10 times for a simulated 28 days for the current and redesigned systems. The amount of road traffic officer time in hours was noted for each run for each scenario and a confidence interval calculated at a 95% level (Figure 13.2).

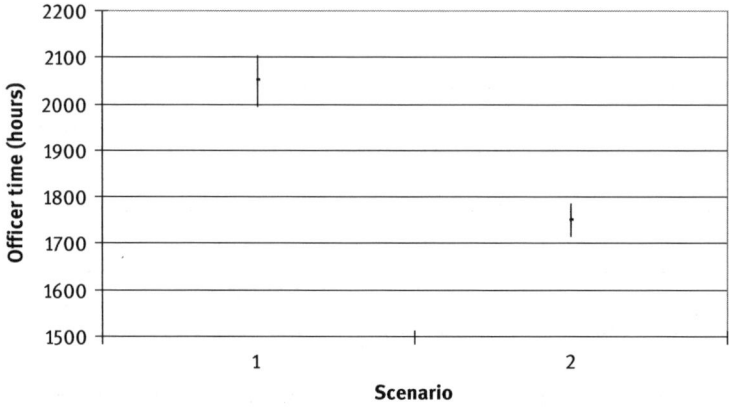

Figure 13.2: Road traffic accident confidence interval analysis.
Scenario 1: Current Process Design. Scenario 2: Redesigned System.

In this case, the confidence intervals do not overlap and so there is a significant difference in the results. In other words, the difference in the result for the current and computerized systems is not due to random variation alone but due to an actual difference in performance. The results show that the mean officer hours required to undertake all the tasks associated with the RTA process is 2049 hours under the current system and 1750 hours under the new process design. These savings are dependent on a number of changes in process design. The need for officer time for transcribing and updating notes will be minimized by the use of OCR transcription of officer notes by the data center personnel. A centralized data store will also save officer time by quicker storage and retrieval of information for the proforma and abstract preparation process. In addition, the location mapping exercise will be simplified by the use of portable digital maps from which officers can indicate the RTA location. Process time will be speeded by workflow automation software, which will prompt for timely response to requests for information in the witness proforma and abstract preparation processes. The use of a single point of contact for all data submissions and information requests will also reduce process execution time by eliminating search and delivery delays associated with paper records. The IS system will also have the benefit of improved data accuracy with a single database of all information and location analysis through the use of geocodes.

The simulation study focused on savings made on the frontline road traffic officer staff but substantial savings can also be made by the centralization of the traffic administration units. These units are currently located at a divisional level, which is a geographical subdivision of the police force area. This is necessary so that paperwork can be processed from officers returning to their local stations. However, with the use of digital transmission of RTA information the geographical location of the administrative support can be centralized at a force level. This can lead to less staff needs due to a centralized automation of processes through workflow and database technologies. The demand on separate divisions would also be aggregated at a corporate level leading to more efficient staff utilization.

Conclusion

The study has demonstrated the use of a process-based approach to change regarding the implementation of a process for RTA reporting. The new process design offers a number of potential benefits including faster delivery of RTA information to government agencies through the use of digital mapping technology replacing location analysis by a third party. Faster process execution of document flows through workflow technology rather than the movement of paper records is also envisaged. Cost savings in terms of road traffic officer time are gained by eliminating the need to return to the police station to undertake administration duties. Savings are also predicted though a centralized administration facility, enabled through the digitization of data, rather than paper records kept at a divisional level. The quality of the process is improved by the greater accuracy of RTA location analysis through the use of digital mapping and geocodes. Improved accuracy of RTA information will be gained through the use of a centralized database store replacing paper documentation. A discussion of the approach taken in the context of public sector organizations now follows.

A traditional view of a public sector organization is that of an unchanging organization structure, where the principal linkages between parts are expressed in the form of reporting relationships. A process-based approach attempts to move to a situation where the focus is on concerning the flow of work, interactions of staff and the involvement of stakeholders such as customers, suppliers and government. For example, there is a tendency for staff in different occupational groups, such as frontline police officers and administrative support staff, to concentrate on activities within the boundaries of that group. This tendency for each occupational group within a government agency to focus on only their particular area of operation is also apparent across different organizational types such as hospitals and universities. It could be argued that public sector organizations focus redesign efforts on frontline staff where failure to deliver service to the customer is highly visible (e.g., failure to attend an RTA). There is less focus on "back-office" staff whose failure to complete a task may not be so visible in terms of their effect on performance measures. The process-based approach utilized in this study offered the opportunity for these groups to assess their role in the delivery of service in a number of ways. For example, the actual procedure of building a process map helped people define roles and see who else does what. The simulation tool was also able to investigate how local performance affected overall performance across organizational boundaries. For example, the overall process speed is determined by the addition of multiple task durations and the sensitivity of the overall process speed to a change in the duration of a particular task can thus be determined by the simulation. In this case, although the need to improve the efficiency and effectiveness of frontline officers provided the impetus for change, it became apparent during the process mapping stage that the support staff would play a vital role in delivering the objectives of the study. In fact the major organizational change in terms of human resources initiated by the study was the centralization of the support staffing structure.

In this case, the approach was able to link the changes made at an operational level to strategic targets set by the organization. By definition, strategic targets are determined by performance over time which can make it difficult to predict if they will be met when inputs such as service demand and staff availability can change. With suitable data, the simulation is able to show the performance of the proposed internal process design in terms of financial and nonfinancial (e.g., officer utilization) measures over an extended period and thus determine if strategic targets could be met.

A feature of public sector agencies is the need to react to changing strategic objectives defined by external stakeholders such as the government. It is proposed that the use of process mapping and simulation is able to quickly test the ability of the organization to meet these challenges and thus increase its flexibility to do so.

When undertaking process management studies, public sector organizations also need to take into consideration the need to meet regulatory or minimum service-level requirements, the standardization of processes across operating units (e.g., the definition of the role of a police officer is extensively documented and standardized across forces) and constraints imposed by external stakeholders who may not necessarily have an interest in the outcome of the process (e.g., most people do not expect to be arrested but may try to influence police arrest procedures). This suggests a "blank sheet" approach to process redesign is not realistic and in this case mapping the current process design was a valuable exercise in understanding actual and assumed constraints on the process design. It is proposed that the simulation tool is then able to facilitate a more creative approach to redesign, within the constraints placed on public sector organizations, by allowing experimentation without risk.

A major issue in this organization was a lack of confidence in the introduction of information systems due to the fact that previous IS projects had often been delayed or of over-budget. The publication of performance data by the government in order to provide information to consumers can make failures more visible than in a commercial organization and so increase the risk of failure further. What the simulation was able to do was to both demonstrate how the new process would execute and quantify savings in officer time. Demonstration of the operation of the new design using the simulation animation display reduced uncertainty in how the new system would operate. Observation of performance measures provided by the model helped to secure an acceptance of the need for change by demonstrating the increased performance of the proposed system. In particular, information provided by the model of staff cost savings quantified the benefits of change in terms of traffic officer on-costs. In general, the need for public sector organizations to quantify outcomes to support business cases for action is likely to become prevalent.

There are, however, limitations to the approach that must be considered. The process mapping stage permits understanding of the structure of current and proposed process designs, but only provides a static view and thus behavior over time in response to fluctuating demand and resource availability can not be predicted. A limitation of simulation is that each scenario modeled only represents one possible outcome, and over long periods of time, these outcomes could greatly differ from actual performance. It is therefore essential to undertake a series of experiments and judge the sensitivity of model results to changes in input factors. This will provide some indication of how useful the simulation results are likely to be. Personnel involved in the process change need to be aware of the organizational context within which the simulation is based. For instance, the real constraints to change must be known, not just constraints determined by culture and working practices, or else the redesign will be excessively conservative. The process mapping stage of the study provides a medium where new design ideas can be communicated between the redesign team, and the animation facilities of the simulation can also be used to communicate new ideas.

The redesign of the RTA system required a number of complex organizational issues to be addressed, such as the management of a reduction of staffing levels and the movement of staff from divisional to a centralized traffic administration unit. Finally, there follows suggestions for areas of development of support from modeling tools for a process-based approach to change. In order for the project to be successful, it was necessary to integrate new technology systems with legacy systems (e.g., the integration of database systems). Further studies could extend the process design analysis with a study of the information infrastructure required. A model of the information infrastructure would also have the advantage of assessing the feasibility of the project in terms of determining a specification for hardware such as communication devices and database systems.

Chapter 14
Case Study: A Simulation of a Rail Carriage Maintenance Depot

Andrew Greasley

This case study describes the use of the simulation technique to ensure that a service delivery system can undertake a number of service tasks to specified service levels. The study concerns a major UK-based manufacturer of railway rolling stock and equipment. The company was preparing a bid for a major order to construct a number of rail carriages for an underground transportation system. The bid included a service contract to maintain the carriages over their lifetime. This would entail operating a maintenance depot on the existing track and rail infrastructure. Although the company had extensive knowledge in rail vehicle design and construction, it had less experience of maintenance operations. However to secure the contract, it would be necessary to show capability in meeting service quality levels for the depot. These quality indicators were contained in a service-level agreement and focused on ensuring the reliability of service supply, i.e., the client had to demonstrate that refurbished trains would be available, at a time specified by the train timetable, every time. Penalty fines would be imposed if service levels did not match the targets set in the agreement. In this case, the requirement to operate the depot on the existing infrastructure meant that capacity would be constrained by the number of existing stabling and refurbishment lines. Demand was also fixed in terms of the quantity of trains requiring refurbishment and the arrival time at the depot that was derived from the local train timetable. Thus, management needed to assess if sufficient capacity was available in order to carry out the refurbishment tasks in the time period between delivery to the depot and request for next service. After a feasibility study, it was decided to use a simulation model to address both the operational issues involved in running the depot and to use as a tool to assist in proving capability of operating the depot to the client.

The Case Study

The depot is located on a current site with a fixed number of lines and facilities available. Carriages are delivered from the main underground line to a changeover point to the left of the depot site. The entry and leave time for carriages to the depot are determined by the local train timetable and so is not under the control of the client. A single shunter is utilized to transfer carriages both to and from the depot and for movement within the depot site. On entry, carriages move along the sidings and progress to the stabling points, workshop, cleaning shed or lift shop facilities as appropriate. The depot consists of 14 stabling points for carriages that are either waiting for service or maintenance. In addition, there is a covered workshop consisting of four available lines, a cleaning shed of two lines and a lift shop that can accommodate a further carriage.

The demand on the depot consists of scheduled trains that arrive for stabling and refurbishment and "casualties," which are trains that have developed a fault while in operation and return to the depot for repair.

Scheduled Trains

The existing timetable operates with 23 carriages entering the depot a day at a time predefined from the train service timetable. The carriages are then submitted for one of three operations. A 14-day clean lasts on average 2 hours and occurs once a fortnight. A more extensive heavy clean lasts on average 4 hours and takes place in the cleaning shed. Carriages not due for cleaning are stored at stabling points until needed. Three lines are available in the workshop for the 14-day clean operation and two lines are available in the cleaning shed for a heavy clean. The trains are rotated between the maintenance depot and other depots on the underground system to ensure all trains in the sector are cleaned as appropriate.

Casualties

In addition to processing scheduled trains, the depot must have the capability of repairing trains that develop a fault during an operation, with the minimum of disruption to service delivery. It is assumed that a train that develops a fault (called a *casualty*) can be returned to the depot. Thus, casualties arrive at a predefined rate to the depot and are replaced by a train ready for service. If no trains are ready for service, the casualty is replaced as soon as one becomes available. The casualties enter the depot and can make up to five visits to the workshop (lines 1–4) for assessment and repairs. Each visit is separated by a wait at a stabling point for a predefined duration to simulate an interruption to the repair process caused by factors such as a wait for parts. Once the train has been repaired, it is now ready for service.

Step 1: Build the Conceptual Model

The study was structured in two stages. Stage one involved building a model of the depot without casualty arrivals. This allowed the project team to concentrate on the task of forming rules that govern the movement of the carriages within the depot by the single shunter. Because of the limited line capacity available and the need to ensure a clear path for movements, a clear set of operational rules for train movement was seen as critical in maximizing performance. Once a feasible model was operational, then the second stage of the project involved inserting randomly generated casualty arrivals into the model and observing the effect on service-level performance.

As a first step, a project team was formed consisting of the author as consultant to construct the simulation, an industrial engineer based at the company with experience of simulation, the project manager for the proposal and a project engineer who would be responsible for depot operations. A variety of data were collected including a local train timetable from which depot arrival and departure times could be estimated, timings for depot operations and a depot layout plan.

In order to provide an initial analysis of the problem, the author suggested using a Gantt chart to map out the train arrivals and departures. Following meetings of the project team, a chart was produced that showed the arrival and departure of trains during the day, and from this a subsequent capacity loading profile could be derived for the stabling, workshop and cleaning shed resources (Figure 14.1). It was clear from the loading graphs that the focus of the study would involve ensuring that a service would be maintained despite the changes in demand caused by the peak morning and afternoon service. As trains begin leaving the depot at peak service time, the depot is near capacity and so too many casualties entering the depot at this time could overload the facilities. Also, when no trains are on depot and all are out to service, casualties arriving can not be replaced immediately, causing loss of service.

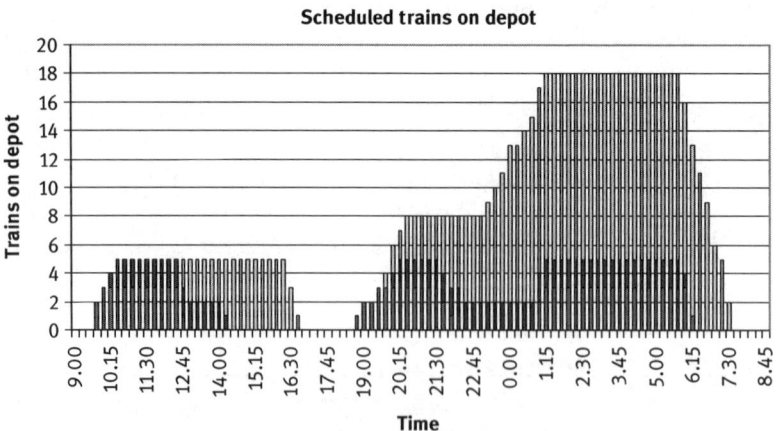

Figure 14.1: Loading graph for scheduled trains at the depot.

The next step was to formulate rules for the movement of carriages within the depot. This was achieved by mapping out the positions of carriages in the depot after each carriage movement on an enlarged schematic of the depot. After a number of walkthroughs, a series of rules were generated. A conceptual model was developed that outlines the main movements of carriages within the depot to provide a guide for the model translation stage (Figure 14.2).

Step 2: Build the Simulation Model
A model was generated using the SIMAN/CINEMA simulation system. This contains a number of constructs relevant for transportation problems and provides excellent animation facilities. SIMAN is a computer software language designed for constructing simulation models, which can be run and generate results independent of the CINEMA facility. CINEMA is a computer draw package that allows background and animated objects to be specified. The SIMAN/CINEMA system is now replaced by the Arena simulation software package. A screen display of the depot simulation is shown in Figure 14.3.

The display is in the form of an overview schematic that shows the logic governing the movement of carriages within the depot.

Verification is the process of checking that the simulation coding provides a current logical representation of the model. This process includes aspects such as ensuring clarity of coding design, extensive debugging and adequate documentation. Validation is the process of checking that the model provides an adequate representation of the real-world system. An important aspect of validation is that the client of the model has confidence in the model results. In this case, a major objective of the simulation was to model the movement of carriages within the depot. This was achieved by using the animation facilities of the simulation software. This proved critical in enabling the operation of the facility to become readily observable and describable, thus increasing the level of confidence regarding how closely the simulation represented the problem itself. A number of walkthroughs were conducted with the project team, which led to a number of refinements to the rules governing carriage movements in order to generate more realistic behavior. For example, carriages processed shortly before peak service time would remain in the workshop or cleaning shed as appropriate, thus eliminating unnecessary shunting movements to the stabling lines.

When a satisfactory operation was achieved, the fixed process durations could be replaced by probability distributions. The arrival time between casualties was modeled using an exponential distribution with a mean derived from the casualty rate per day. Data was also supplied on the process duration of visits required to the workshop to repair faults and these were modeled in Table 14.1.

Once the behavior of the casualty trains was validated, experimentation on the full model could begin.

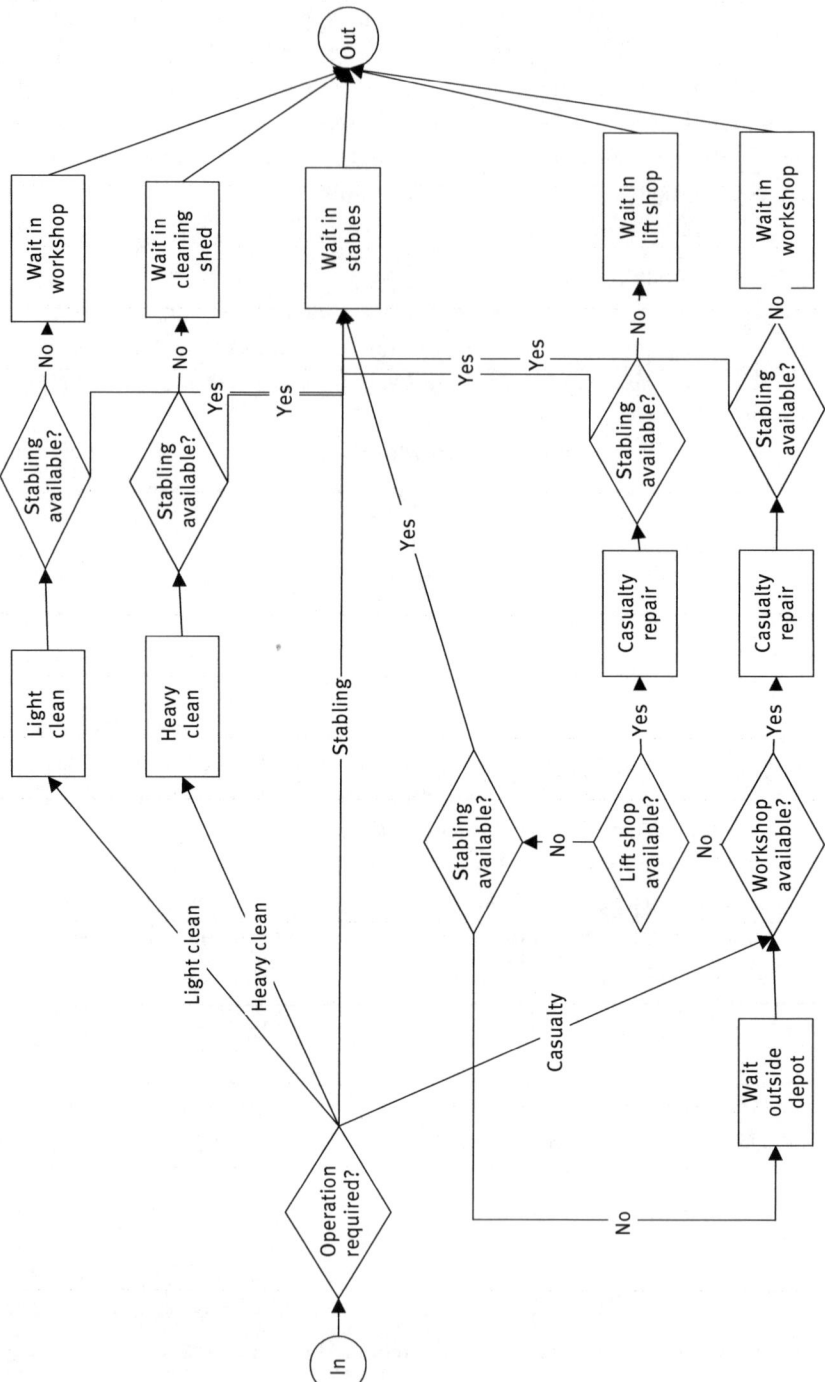

Figure 14.2: The maintenance depot conceptual model.

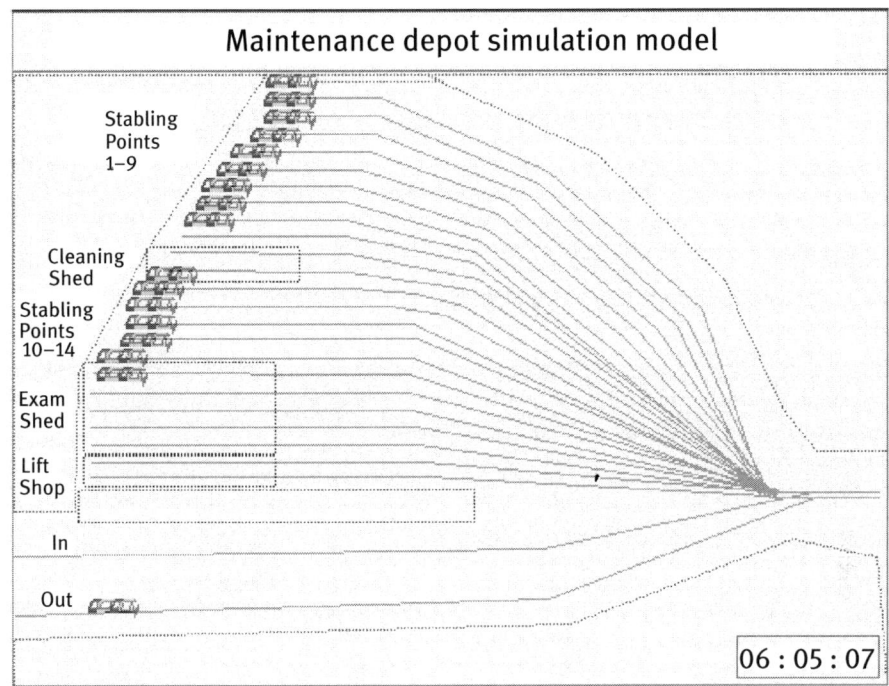

Figure 14.3: Depot simulation model display.

Table 14.1: Fault Repair Time.

Percentage of Casualty Arrivals	Mean Process Duration (Minutes)
66	120
23	180
5	300
6	420

Step 3: Use Simulation for Descriptive, Predictive and Prescriptive Analytics

Due to the random nature of the distributions used in the model, the animation facilities were used to observe the performance of the model over a number of simulation runs. It became clear that service levels could not be maintained with the casualty rate envisaged and that new operating procedures had to be devised. The performance of the depot was observed using different operating procedures over a number of runs until satisfactory operation was ensured. There are two main approaches to capacity management in services. One approach is the "level capacity" strategy in which capacity levels are seen as fixed. In this case, an attempt is made to influence demand to meet capacity. The alternative approach is the "capacity following demand" strategy when capacity levels are altered to meet demand levels by adjusting resource levels. In this study, the model incorporated a mix of the two approaches in order to ensure reliable service delivery. In order to avoid overloading the depot at peak demand, it was decided to only allow repairs to casualty trains at off-peak times, represented in the model by a workshop "window." This allowed the user of the model to specify time slots in which casualty trains could not enter the workshop but would remain at a stabling point. Thus at peak time, only the workshop line 4 is available for casualties, while at off-peak times lines 1–4 are available.

The assessment of the capacity of the depot to service scheduled and casualty trains was used to assess resource requirements for a preventative maintenance program. If depot capacity is full, a queue of trains will form at the depot entrance. The simulation is able to provide statistics on queue length and time in queue for trains under a number of scenarios. Another problem was the absence of trains on depot after they had departed for peak service and before any had returned. To ensure any casualty trains could be replaced immediately at this time, two "spare" trains, over and above those required to meet service levels, were placed on depot to replace casualties. A line in the Lift Shop is available to casualties for emergency use only (i.e., if there is no other space for the casualty to be repaired or stored). Again, this strategy is designed to ensure that service levels are met.

The simulation experimentation was designed to both prove that the depot could operate without "missed service" events (a missed service is a request for a train from the timetable that is not met immediately) during normal service with no casualty events occurring. The second phase of the experimentation was to assess the performance of the depot with a range of casualty arrival rates. The effect of placing one or two spare trains on depot on performance was also investigated. The results of the simulation experimentation are listed in Table 14.2.

The simulation was run for a time period of 28 days for each of 10 scenarios. The time period of the simulation run was chosen to provide sufficient time for a number of missed service events to occur, while not requiring excessive computer time to record. Results were collected for missed service events for five simulation runs. The mean value of these observations was computed to provide a measure of the average number of missed service events that could be expected over the 4-week time period of the simulation run. The simulation was configured with starting conditions to minimize initial bias and the method of independent replications was used to analyze the results of the simulation model. Thus, a different random number stream was used for each simulation run. Five runs were performed to ensure that the effect of random variation (in casualty arrival times and maintenance process times) could be assessed. The accuracy of the results could be improved with additional simulation runs.

Table 14.2: Missed Service Events by Casualty Rate and Spare Trains.

Casualty Rate Per Day	Spare Trains on Depot	Mean Missed Service Events in 4-Week Period
0	0	0
1	0	1.4
	1	0.4
	2	0
2	0	2.6
	1	1.6
	2	0.6
3	0	2.8
	1	1.8
	2	0.8

The results show that with no casualty arrivals and no spare trains, no missed service events are likely to occur. With a casualty rate of one per day and two per day, two spare trains are required to ensure no missed service events. With a casualty rate of three casualties per day, even two spare trains will give an 80% chance of a missed service event during a 4-week operating period. This performance could be improved by reducing the failure rate of trains, through preventative maintenance for example, or increasing depot capacity by decreasing maintenance and repair process times or increasing the number of spare trains available.

Conclusion

The simulation was successful in showing how the depot could operate to the service levels specified through the collection of data on the number of missed service events. A number of changes to the basic depot design were assessed and the ability to meet "normal" service demand proved.

The simulation was then able to assess the performance of the depot with a randomly distributed arrival of casualty trains that represented an extra demand over the normal maintenance cycle. It would be difficult to assess the performance of the depot by other means because of the variation in maintenance process and repair times and casualty arrival rates. The timing of casualty arrivals may also lead to varying performance as the demand on the depot is not constant during the day.

The simulation model was able to assess the effect of introducing spare trains on depot to buffer the system from these demand variations.

A further development occurred when the project engineer became concerned that future changes in timetable requirements would significantly alter the demand requirements on the depot. Thus, the project manager requested that the model be adapted to allow to carry out further investigations alone. This was achieved by using a menu system that allows the user to change the arrival and leave times for the trains.

Chapter 15
Case Study: A Simulation of a Rail Vehicle Bogie Production Facility

Andrew Greasley

The study in this chapter concerns an autonomous division of a major UK based manufacturer of railway rolling stock and equipment. The plant manufactures a range of bogies which are the supporting frame and wheel sets for rail vehicles. The company has a history of supplying the passenger train market in the UK, but over a period of time with low demand and increased competition, it entered new markets including European inner-city transport and the supply of freight bogies to Far East countries. The need to compete on a global basis led the company to re-evaluate its manufacturing facility with particular emphasis on the need to increase output, reduce lead times and increase flexibility. To meet these demands management had identified areas where substantial investment was required.

The Case Study

The rail vehicle bogie production facility is designed on a line layout basis with the manufacturing process consisting of six main stages: fabrication, welding, frame machining, painting, fitting and quality audit. Each stage must be completed in order for the next stage to begin. The stages are now briefly described:

Fabrication

The fabrication stage prepares the bogie frame sections from sheet steel and third party castings. A custom template is designed from which the parts required are cut from sheet steel to standard batch sizes. Parts not needed immediately are held in storage. Processed parts and castings are brought together to form a bogie 'kit' which is assembled on a jig and taken to the subsequent welding stage.

Welding

A bogie sub-assembly is manually welded on a jig at a work station to form a main bogie frame.

Frame Machining

The main bogie frame is then transferred to a CNC center for the machining of any holes or bores needed for the fixing of sub-assemblies such as the braking and suspension systems. Bogies are affixed to a slave table and the machine processes the frame according to a preset operation sequence.

Painting

The frame is then manually painted while being suspended from an overhead moving circular track.

Fitting

Manufactured sub-assemblies and third party components such as motors are then assembled on the bogie frame. The frames are placed on supports and are moved along a line at different stages of assembly with overhead cranes.

Quality Audit

Final inspection is carried out to ensure all bogies meet the required specification. It was usual that a certain amount of paint touch-up work is required at this stage due to damage caused to the paint finish during the fitting stage.

Step 1: Build the Conceptual Model

The focus of the study was on line layout design with the main objective being to ensure that the performance of the whole manufacturing system would meet required output levels. The output level was converted into a target cycle time (i.e. time between manufacture of products or output rate). As stated, the line layout consists of six main stages with the product passing through each stage in turn. This means that the effective cycle time for the whole system is determined by the stage with the longest cycle time. Thus, the simulation study was undertaken to ensure that any investment in a particular production stage would not be nullified by a longer cycle time elsewhere. The simulation would provide an analysis tool to signal any process improvement activities needed before installation took place. The objective was to obtain a balanced line (i.e. all cycle timings are equal) which would enable a smooth parts flow through the production stages. The project team for the study included the production manager, an industrial engineer, an internal consultant (from another site) with some experience in simulation and the author acting as an external consultant. When objectives had been agreed upon, most contact was made between the author and the industrial engineer based at the facility. Information was supplied by the industrial engineer on components flows, setup times, process times and other relevant information. Most of the data was gathered from the manufacturing resource planning (MRP II) control system in use.

Step 2: Build the Simulation Model
The model was built using the SIMAN/CINEMA system now superseded by the Arena Simulation software. The software provided extensive manufacturing modeling facilities as well as a high resolution (pixel-based rather than vector-based) graphical display. A plan view of the manufacturing facility was constructed overlaid with an animation of parts moving through the system. Figure 15.1 shows a 'zoomed' portion of the simulation model display.

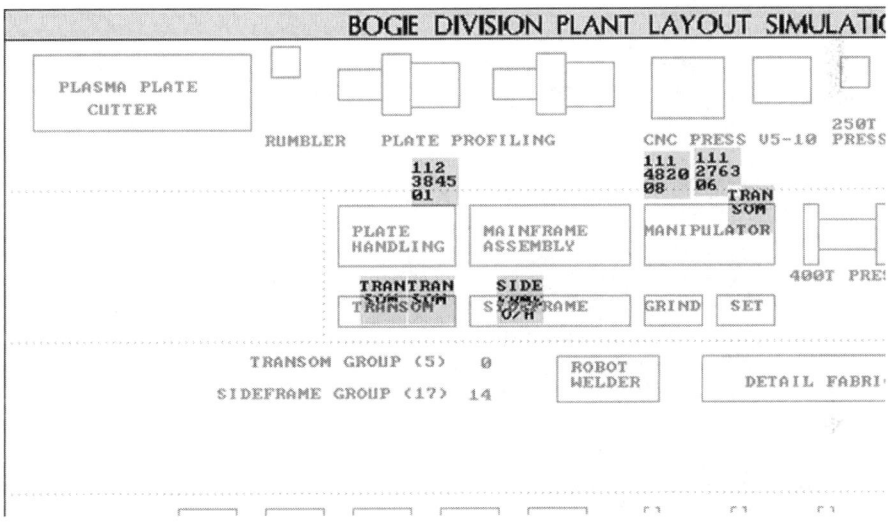

Figure 15.1: Bogie manufacturing simulation model (partial zoomed view).

The debugging and animation facilities of SIMAN/CINEMA were used to ensure that the model was free from any errors. The model was validated by simulating the present system and discussing the results with management to identify any anomalies.

Step 3: Use Simulation for Descriptive, Predictive and Prescriptive Analytics
The first stage of the simulation analysis was driven by the need to reduce cycle time (i.e. maximize production output) below a target level. Any stage above the target was investigated by the project team and changes were made to machinery

or working practices changes were suggested. The results of these changes were entered into the model and the simulation was re-run to observe the effect on whole system performance. One aim was to achieve a synchronized pull system in which the fabrication process would only produce material when needed. This meant operating with a batch size of one bogie. At the time, cutting templates were individually designed to produce batches of parts when needed. They were replaced with a standard template which produced only the parts for one bogie and proceeded through the fabrication stage as before. From welding times provided for the bogie assemblies, a welding line configuration was constructed. Manual welding was used and welding times were considered fixed so to meet demand additional welding lines were allocated. Figure 15.2 shows the observed average cycle times from the simulation for each production stage and the major fabrication processes. The graph shows the quality audit and machine stages where management effort was needed to achieve the target cycle time.

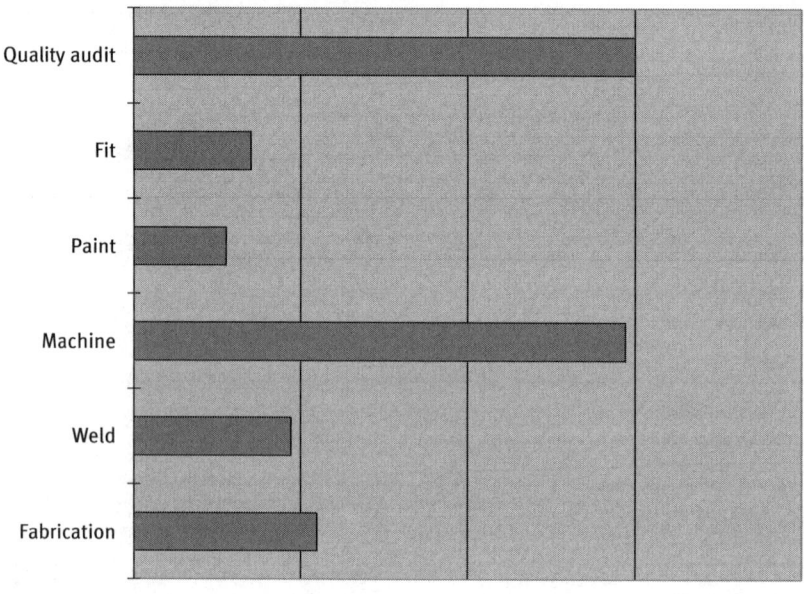

Figure 15.2: Present system average cycle time performance.

In terms of the quality audit stage cycle time, this was set at a nominal amount by management. Significant problems had occurred at this stage with the spray finish on the bogie frames being damaged during the sub-assembly fitting stage. This had to be rectified by a manual touch-up process which could take longer than the original spray time. The paint area would also need to be re-configured due to new environmental controls. The problems had been recognized by management and an investment in an epoxy paint plant producing a hard-wearing finish was planned.

The bogie frame machining center had previously been recognized by management as a bottleneck process. The bogie frame went through a number of pre-programmed steps on the machine and the cycle time was dependent on the capability of the machining center itself. Consequently, a major part of the planned investment was a new machining center with a quoted cycle time below the target. An investigation of the fabrication processes revealed that although the cycle times were above target, the majority of this time was used for machine setup. Figure 15.3 shows the effect on cycle time of a reduction in setup time of 10% to 90%.

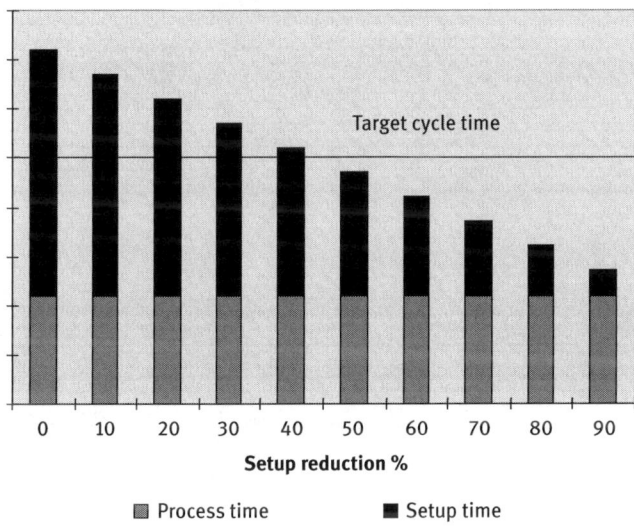

Figure 15.3: Setup reduction for fabrication stage.

From Figure 15.3 it is clear that to achieve the target cycle time a setup reduction of 50% is required. A team was assembled to achieve this target and it was met by the use of magnetic tables to hold parts ready for processing. The simulation was run with the target demand cycle time to assess system performance. Surprisingly a queue of parts was observed in front of the edge bevel machines indicating a bottleneck process which could not achieve the target cycle. Further investigation revealed that the sequence of parts introduced to the two machines led to an uneven distribution of loading on one machine, thus taking it over the target cycle time limit. Consequently a fixed process sequence was devised to ensure an even loading distribution across the machines. The simulation was re-run and the results (Figure 15.4) show the system achieving the required performance. It can be seen that a further reduction in fabrication setup times and a re-configuration of the welding line would reduce the overall cycle time, producing a more balanced line and increasing capacity utilization.

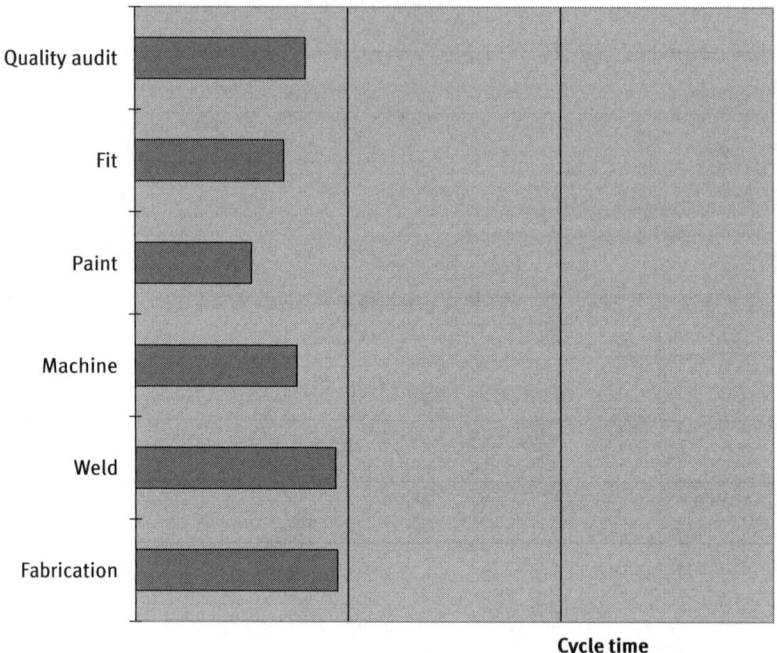

Figure 15.4: Proposed system average cycle time performance.

By implementing the changes outlined above, the simulation was able to predict the following improvements in performance (Table 15.1). These are substantial improvements in performance and meet the output targets set by management.

The second stage of the simulation study involved assessing the effect of disturbances on the system once the required performance had been met. Management was interested in simulating breakdown events on the edge beveling machines which had no backup and had a history of intermittent breakdown. The experiment was based on an average machine failure of three times a working week with an average repair time of 40 minutes. It was assumed breakdown events were dependent on time, not the number of pieces processed on the machine. The high utilization (over 90%)

Table 15.1: Results Table.

Performance Measure	Change (%)
Cycle Time	−65
Lead Time	−19
Output per Week	+220
Cycle efficiency*	+29

*Cycle Efficiency = 100%- % Idle Time where %Idle Time = Idle time per cycle / total cycle time

made these two approaches essentially the same. An exponential distribution for time between breakdowns and a 2-Erlang distribution for breakdown length was used. These distributions were chosen using a combination of observation of graphs of historical data and reference to theoretically appropriate distributions. It was found that random breakdowns represented a 3% loss of capacity and so the system was still able to meet the target cycle time.

The final stage of the study involved the use of simulation to investigate various facility layouts within the factory. The simulation was able to show a clear picture of the flow of parts over time, although as no routing times were changed, the simulation results were identical for different runs. Adjustment to the layout is a time-consuming process and requires in-depth knowledge of the simulation package used. Consequently, its usefulness is limited in allowing management to experiment with various layouts.

Conclusion

It is clear from the case that the simulation model achieved its aim in terms of providing a tool for management in improving system operation before the introduction of the proposed machinery. This highlights the main advantage of the simulation method: the reduction of risk. However, within the case company there was a lack of awareness of the potential benefits of simulation which are now discussed.

Use as a 'One-Off' Technique

The research found that there was still a perception within the industrial engineers and management involved in the project that the simulation study was a 'one-off' project. Once the simulation was used and the decision made regarding the introduction of machinery, the simulation model was put to one side. On questioning whether there would be any further use for the model, one manager said that 'the simulation had done its job and paid for itself'. There was no attempt by any of the project group to see if the simulation model could be extended and used in another area, or as part of the training and education process. It was seen as a decision making tool and once the decision was made, then it was redundant.

Expertise Transfer

The above lack of awareness of the scope of the technique was found to be connected to other findings within the case study. In particular, the lack of technical skills and understanding in applying and interpreting the results of simulation. The author acted as a consultant on the model building stage of the project and was surprised at the lack of understanding of the technique. Only the internal consultant had some knowledge, but he was situated on a different site. The project group seemed unwilling to try and learn how simulations worked and instead of training and educating their own staff with the necessary skills, which could be drawn upon at any time, they preferred the use of consultants. This has a number of effects in not only achieving a superficial understanding of the simulation process, but a lack of appreciation for the potential for simulation in other areas. Without understanding it, they will not be able to adopt it, for example in the training area of the change process. This is combined with the observation that those who do know how to use simulation, become "experts" within a technically oriented environment. This means that those running the business do not fully understand the technique which could impact on their decision to use it or go with the decisions. Thus, the point of using simulation as a decision-making tool for managers is becoming lost within the technical computerized sphere of a small number of individuals. Although within the case study there were no "experts", the use of the simulation was still restricted to a small number of people.

Communication Tool

A further finding from the case study was the lack of involvement from the shop floor in the development of the simulation model and the subsequent decision. The company was going through a period of organizational change, not only in the way they manufactured the product, but also in their approach toward human resources. They were attempting to move away from adversarial labor relations with a multi-union site to a single union agreement, and a reorganization of the management hierarchy to a much flatter system with managers reporting directly to the managing director. Within this context of change, the company could have used the simulation project to develop involvement from the shop floor in a number of areas. When requiring information on the current configuration of machinery the industrial engineers and management were not inclined to ask the shop floor. If they were unsure, a guess was made between the group, rather than approach those on the shop floor. Although this probably reflects the traditional nature of the organization, it was an ideal opportunity in the current climate of change to break away the traditional mold and move to shop floor input on the project. Simulation can be a strong facilitator of communicating ideas up and down an organization. Engineers for example, could have used the simulation to communicate the reasons for taking certain decisions to shop-floor personnel who might suggest improvements. The use of simulation as a tool for employee involvement in the improvement process could be a vital part of the overall change strategy.

Chapter 16
Case Study: A Simulation of Advanced Service Provision

Andrew Greasley and Emmanuel Musa

In general manufacturers offer services to some extent (a maintenance contract offered with equipment for example) but often compete on a strategy based around their products in terms of product innovation and product cost reduction. Servitization represents a process that enables manufacturing companies to move to a service-led competitive strategy. This entails viewing the manufacturer as a service provider and enhancing traditional manufacturing strategy built around product-based innovation with one that aims to improve their customer processes. Advanced services are a special case of servitization when the manufacturer offers contracts to customers that encompass payment based on the performance of a product over an extended period of time. Advanced services are delivered by product-service systems (PSS) in which the manufacturer provides a capability to undertake a process for the customer. This capability can entail choosing suitable equipment and consumables, monitoring performance and undertaking maintenance and disposal. The manufacturer receives payment for the capability that is used by the customer. To increase revenue and competitive advantage, original equipment manufacturers (OEM) have increased the level and sophistication of service components in their offering to be delivered as product-service systems (PSS). Although PSS promises immense benefits for OEMs, managers in servitizing firms are faced with the challenge of determining the cost of achieving outcomes or performance and what to charge. This study presents discrete event simulation models comparing three variants of product-service systems for a precision machine manufacturer.

There are three types of services that OEMs can provide. These include *basic services* which comprise the supply of spares and telephone support; these services are aimed at asset provision. The second class of service is *intermediate services* which consist of the installation services, maintenance services, upgrade services, repair services, and training services and re-use. The third class of service is *advanced services* which is a result-oriented service, where the service provider delivers outcomes, functions or capabilities that are essential to the core of the customer's business. As the nature and class of services shift from basic to advanced services, the service provider gets deeply involved in the customer's operations and assumes more risks. The focus shifts from the product plus services to all activities required to achieve outcomes. Thus advanced services focus on the delivery of outcomes and results and require a much closer relationship and collaboration between the supplier and customer. The outcome is the provision of capabilities to accomplish operational performance. The term advanced services is sometimes used interchangeably with the definition of a product-service offering. Generally though, the product-service combination can be defined as what the service provider offers or proposes to the customer, while the advanced service can be defined as the value created which represents the benefit or outcome the customer gains from utilizing the equipment or the service provision.

When PSS are presented based on the orientation of the PSS offering, the options are of a product-oriented PSS, use-oriented PSS and result-oriented PSS. Since these types of contracts run over a long period (with some contracts running up to 50 years), the service provider is confronted with the challenge of estimating the cost of delivering on mutually agreed outcomes inherent in the contract. In some environments, these types of contracts are sold at a pre-agreed price, while cost depends on the long-term performance of the system or on the achievement of outcomes requires a coordination of all activities and processes within and outside the firm in ways that result in the achievement of the agreed upon performance. This involves an assessment of the service delivery system, capabilities of the service provider, human resource requirements, relationships with suppliers, maintenance services required, dealing with uncertainty of future events, estimating and forecasting cost estimates and pricing the offering. Underestimating the costs of service delivery can lead to financial loss and poor service, while over-estimation of costs can result in a loss of the contract and customer goodwill. Therefore, a good understanding of the operational criteria required to fulfill contractual outcomes along with associated costs is essential to deciding whether to bid for a contract or offer a specific type of PSS variant or not.

The Case Study

For all PSS contractual arrangements the payment criterion should be based on tasks and activities carried out by the service provider. For example, for basic services such as the sale of spares or advisory and consulting services, the service provider should earn extra income. In some maintenance contracts, a fixed price is charged monthly, quarterly or periodically. For advanced services where the focus is on result and performance, payment is based is on the achievement of results. For example, results could be in terms of number of hours the asset is available (pay-on-availability). This approach constitutes the basic payment model of advanced services in many manufacturing industries and in this payment model, the focus is exclusively on asset availability and independent of the actual utilization of the machinery or equipment.

Another payment model could tie compensation to actual performance such as a per unit approach. Here actual output from asset utilization is the basis of compensation. This model is also known as pay-on-production. Other payment models include pay-per-use, where the customer pays for how many units are consumed (intensity) or how long it is used (frequency and duration). Choosing a payment model is at the discretion of the terms of the contracts. An example of this is the practice in the defense and transport sectors, where the supply of engine availability is charged on a per-flight basis and the leasing of trucks is charged on a per-mile basis. Another payment model is where payment is based on the customer's economic results as a consequence of using the equipment. Failure to achieve agreed cost savings attract a penalty in the form of a discount on the payment made for the period the target cost saving was not achieved. Regardless of what indicator is used to represent achievement of outcome or performance, a service provider must ensure that the value proposition is appropriately priced on a basis that delivers profitability.

Advanced services that are delivered through a PSS comprise multiple cost objects. The PSS delivering the outcomes is a service delivery system (as opposed to an individual product, service or process) which aims to meet service demand. Thus, the object of costing is the service delivery system with the underlying system comprising spares, consumables, staffing and intangible items such as customer support, knowledge and training. In advanced services delivered through a PSS where the outcome is the availability of an asset, typical metrics include time-related non-monetary metrics such as mean time between failure (MTBF), mean time to repair (MTTR), fast response time and availability of parts. The objective of this study is to examine the profitability of three variants of PSS based on their costs and payment model. The PSS delivery system is considered as a gamut of processes that interact to deliver outcomes. Data regarding the operational environment, the range of support services offered by the firm and suppliers as well as revenue models were explored. The service delivery system was divided into processes and activities, showing the relationship between components within each process and between processes.

Step 1: Build the Conceptual Model

The company in this case is a manufacturer of computer numerically controlled (CNC) machines. These machines are used for cutting, turning, grinding and milling. The service provider deals with clients from both defense and oil and gas industries. The manufacturer has adopted the use of sensors for remote monitoring of its machines to optimize the delivery of services. Parts can suffer wear, obsolescence and damage over time because of short lifespan and from the intensity and frequency of usage. The service provider is moving into increasing services as part of its competitive strategy and has decided to offer heavy and expensive CNC machines as part of an integrated solution offering utilizing availability contracts. Variants of its service offerings are described below and summarized in Table 16.1.

Table 16.1: A Description of Processes for a PSS Service Provider.

Process	Component Variables	Variant A	Variant B	Variant C
Payment Method		Customer bears cost of MRO (maintenance, repair and operations)	Fixed monthly price	Customer pays for availability of asset over contracted hours
Maintenance	Resources, spares, maintenance schedules, travel costs, labor costs, MTBF (mean time between failure), MTTR (mean time to repair)	Corrective maintenance Demand for maintenance	Preventative maintenance at fixed interval	Conditional Maintenance based on age of equipment, remaining useful life, operational conditions
Remote Monitoring	Labor cost	No	Yes/No	Yes
Inventory Management	Starting inventory, stock holding costs, re-order inventory	Customer pays for spares	Service provider	Service provider
Administration	Contract processing, Asset delivery, Payment processes	Yes	Yes	Yes

Variant A: Traditional Product Sale + Supply of Spares, Repair and Replacement Services

In this variant, the service provider sells new, used and refurbished spares. It has dedicated customer service lines that attend to customer queries and requests. Requests for after-sale repair and replacement service is done either at the service center of the service provider or at the site of the customer depending on the magnitude of the fault, damage or degradation. The service provider incurs travel costs when repair and maintenance services are carried out at the customer site. Providing after-sales repair and maintenance service at the cost of the customer provides an opportunity for the service provider to earn more revenue. However, the sale of new and used machines have declined over the years, therefore the after-sales service is seen as an opportunity to increase profit. A disadvantage of this service offering variant is that there are several competitors within the after-sales market offering the same services as the company of interest among whom are non-manufacturers and dealers upstream in the supply chain.

Variant B: Sale Plus Maintenance Contract
Under this bundle, the customer purchases the machine plus a maintenance contract comprising a host of services (for example repair, replacement and overhaul) in the form of a fixed interval preventive maintenance schedule. The focus here is to prevent an unexpected breakdown of the equipment and to keep the machine in good health. For this service, the customer is charged a fixed monthly payment. As part of the contract terms, the fixed monthly payment is subject to usage intensity and operational condition limits. In case of unexpected failures, the service provider bears the costs, provided there is no breach on the terms of usage of the machine.

Variant C: Lease and Guarantee Availability
Here, the focus is on providing a machine that is in an operable state. Therefore, the service provider is responsible for all the activities that are necessary to ensure the machine is in an operable condition. The use of advanced technologies is essential for the monitoring of asset condition and health. The customer pays for the availability only and in case of downtime within the contracted hours, the service provider pays a downtime fee in the form of a discount applied to the payment for the following month. Failure and downtime outside the contracted hours for asset availability does not attract any penalty. Conditional monitoring allows the service provider to proactively leverage the data collected to design appropriate service strategies in terms of maintenance, repair and overhaul.

For this study the following assumptions and simplifications were made as relevant for each of the three variants of the service offerings described above.
- The usage intensity for all variants is assumed to be the same.
- The machine has a mean time between failure (MTBF) of 180 days following an exponential distribution. Repair time is 1 to 2 days depending on the severity of the repair/replacement. Charges for repair work and replacement also vary depending on the part repaired/replaced and severity of damage or fault.
- Staff cost is £10/hour for each of the maintenance staff.
- Travel cost to customer location is triangularly distributed.
- Monthly payment for the preventive maintenance (variant B) is £500.

For all variants, the input variables were set at base levels at the time of initial instance for each of the variants to observe the delivery and profitability over a ten-year period. The service provider provides all services in-house by bringing in-house all previously out-sourced services. In addition, the number of locations were reduced from three to one to drive effectiveness and efficiency of communication and service delivery. The service provider operates a 24-hour operation hence a non-terminating model was constructed. A conceptual model is shown in Figure 16.1.

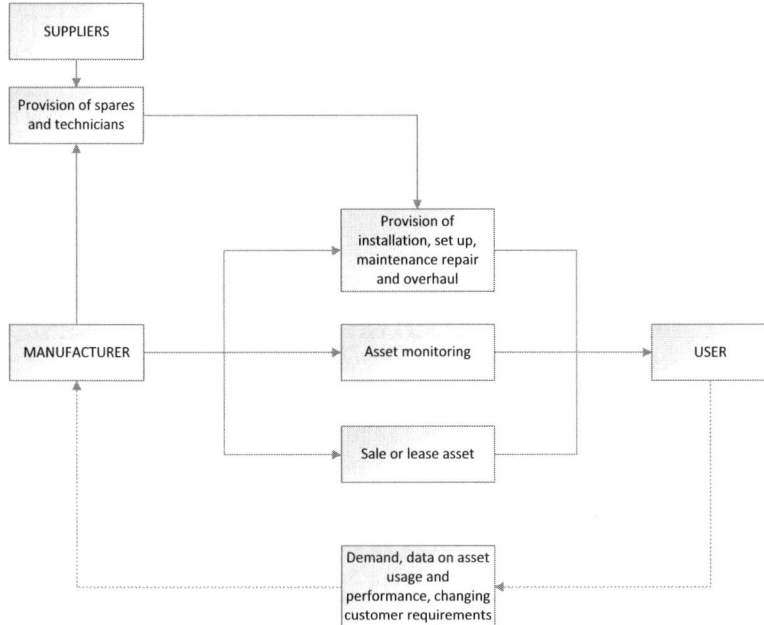

Figure 16.1: A conceptual model of the service provider operation.

Step 2: Build the Simulation Model

The model was developed using Arena simulation software. A part of the model is shown in Figure 16.2.

Step 3: Use Simulation for Descriptive, Predictive and Prescriptive Analytics

Tables 16.2 to 16.4 outline some of the analytic data that can be extracted from the simulation regarding the performance of the three variants of PSS investigated in the case study. First, revenue and cost are estimated for the three variants under base conditions shown in the tables.

An example of the use of simulation to project PSS contract costs is to decrease the mean time between failure (MTBF) rate which will increase the replacement, repair and staff costs (Table 16.5). An alternative experiment was to increase the quarterly payment rates for variant C PSS (Table 16.5).

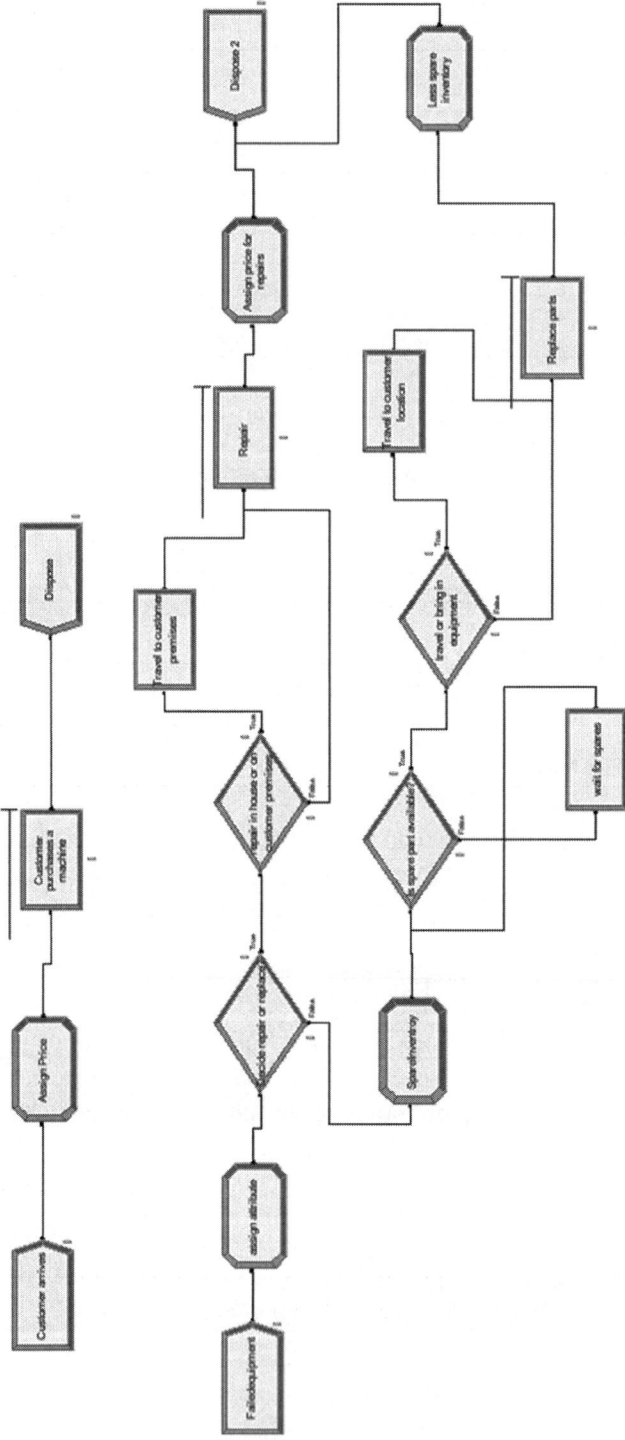

Figure 16.2: A simulation model for advanced service provision.

Table 16.2: Revenue and Cost for Variant A under Base Conditions.

Variant A		
Revenue	Price of Equipment	69943
	Revenue on Replacement	330000
	Revenue on Spare Side	18993
	Revenue from Repair	290000
	Total Revenue	**708936**
Cost	Staff Costs	3951
	Travel Costs	16
	Stockholding Costs	1614
	Total Costs	**5581**
Profit (Total)		**703355**

Table 16.3: Revenue and Cost for Variant B under Base Conditions.

Variant B		
Revenue	Purchase of Asset	7000
	Monthly Payment	20500
	Total Revenue	**27500**
Cost	Cost on Replacement	936
	Cost on Spare Supply	1857
	Cost of Repair	848
	Staff Costs	7916
	Travel Costs	22
	Stockholding Costs	1618
	Total Costs	**13197**
Profit (Month)		**14303**

Table 16.4: Revenue and Cost for Variant C under Base Conditions.

Variant C		
Revenue	Quarterly Payment	20000
	Total Revenue	**20000**
Cost	Cost on Replacement	436
	Cost on Spare Supply	4635
	Cost of Repair	2404
	Staff Costs	6804
	Travel Costs	16
	Stockholding Costs	1640
	Installation + Setup + Training + Consulting	7870
	Total Costs	**23805**
Profit (Quarter)		**−3805**

Table 16.5: Simulation Experiments for Variant C PSS.

Experiment 1: Decrease the MTBF for variant C PSS		
Revenue	Quarterly Payment	20000
	Total Revenue	**20000**
Cost	Cost on Replacement	545
	Cost on Spare Supply	4635
	Cost of Repair	3289
	Staff Costs	8089
	Travel Costs	21
	Stockholding Costs	1640
	Installation + Setup + Training + Consulting	7870
	Total Costs	**26089**
Profit (Quarter)		**−6089**
Experiment 2: Increase payment for variant C PSS		
Revenue	Quarterly Payment	40000
	Total Revenue	**40000**
Cost	Cost on Replacement	436
	Cost on Spare Supply	4635
	Cost of Repair	2404
	Staff Costs	6804
	Travel Costs	16
	Stockholding Costs	1640
	Installation + Setup + Training + Consulting	7870
	Total Costs	**23805**
Profit (Quarter)		**16195**

Conclusion

When using simulation, a PSS is viewed as an open system comprising processes and activities which consist of inputs (such as resources, information, manpower, materials) and outputs (availability, speed of service delivery, maintainer utilization). Simulation allows the modeling of complexity (due to the interconnectedness) inherent within PSS systems with the intrinsic complexity of a PSS increasing as the relationship between customer and service provider shifts from transactional to relational and collaboration spreads across a large number of stakeholders. Furthermore, when considering customer involvement in the value co-creation process, many elements within the system assume stochastic and variable status, hence resulting in a stochastic output. Simulation software also provides a range of probability distribution types that facilitate the modeling of randomness of any input variable or parameters such as failure times, mean time between failure and mean time to repair. The prediction of life cycle costing for the supply of services through a PSS can range from simple to complex cost models depending on the complexity involved in the service provision and the PSS business model. For these models, performance measures such as operational availability and operational capability to meet contract outcomes are of high priority. Simulation provides the information that links through life cycle service support costs to system results/ performance or availability.

Simulation is well suited to estimating operations and maintenance costs that traverse a long-time frame. Maintenance constitutes a major activity for all PSS business models and usually occurs over the in-service phase. The main purpose of maintenance is to restore product condition (product-oriented), function (use-oriented PSS) and capability (result-oriented PSS). The term "maintenance" is a broad term used to represent a range of tasks and actions such as inspection, upgrade, spare management, replacement of spares, and deployment of resource maintainer(s). In some studies, service cost is used as a proxy for all range of maintenance activities undertaken over the in-service phase of the product life cycle. Maintenance in the context of PSS can be made up of several policies such as reactive maintenance (corrective), preventive and condition-based maintenance. Preventive maintenance is specifically aimed at preventing failures by undertaking a range of activities such as inspections, tests, measurements, adjustments or part replacements at predetermined intervals based upon a time interval such as hours or days, or the number of operations. In corrective maintenance, the focus is on replacing a failed system. It follows the principle of "run to failure" where the effect is not necessarily serious or disruptive to the mission. Corrective maintenance also covers unplanned failure or downtime, which can be disruptive to the operations of the customer. Condition based maintenance is based on monitoring the performance, state and condition of components and based on certain criteria, they may be replaced. Conditioned-based maintenance can be used to support preventive maintenance. This ensures that design defects or safety and reliability issues (that were not detected or anticipated in the original design) are tackled or resolved. It also helps to prevent machine failures and downtime which impact reliability and availability respectively. All three types of maintenance strategies are utilized across the three PSS business models. In traditional product-oriented PSS (fixed when broke), corrective maintenance is common. However, preventive maintenance is being used in after-sale maintenance contracts. With advances in monitoring technologies, the use sensors and monitoring devices in condition-based maintenance is designed to enable service providers to plan and optimize their maintenance strategies and management. Comparing cost models under multiple scenarios provide service providers with a decision support tool for the sale, delivery and support of service contracts supplied through a PSS. However, for the provider of advanced services, uncertainty lies in the linkages across economic actors involved in the service delivery process and the focus of cost modeling should reflect the socio-technical status of a PSS delivering advanced services.

Chapter 17
Case Study: Generating Simulation Analytics with Process Mining

Andrew Greasley

The main advantage of process mining is that it provides automatic generation of detailed process models from event logs. If the event logs are of sufficient size and data quality, then the full complexity of the process flow can be discovered including many variations in flow that may occur due to factors such as human behavior. The process models discovered by process mining are thus particularly useful in predicting conformance of current process execution with best practice. Model-driven approaches to simulation used for process analysis have been used for a number of years. They use methods of abstraction based around the domain knowledge of the model builder to ensure a valid process model from the perspective of the modeler and the client of the model. In general, discrete-event simulation is a widely used modeling tool and in general simulation process models are particularly useful in testing system designs of current systems or systems that may not exist in different scenarios.

Reflecting a tradition of use for system design purposes, simulation performance measures tend to average everything across time, masking time-dependent, dynamic effects, and create high-level summaries, making it difficult to evaluate risk or predict actual system behavior. However as real-world systems have to evolve and adapt to be competitive, the quantification of risk is often more important for day-to-day operations and decision making than long-run performance. Thus, more and more current and potential simulation users are interested in risk analysis, prediction and control, rather than system design.

This case study will assess the use of process mining software to provide an extended analysis of simulation output measures. This will be achieved by adapting a simulation model to generate an event log, which can then be used as a data source for the process mining software. The analysis provided by the process mining software will be evaluated and compared to that provided by the discrete-event simulation. Using data generated by a simulation offers a number of new possibilities for performance analysis using process mining software.

Some of the features that distinguish the generation of data by the use of simulation and the use of real-world data in big data analytics are presented and their implications for the use of process mining as a performance reporting tool are listed in Table 17.1.

Thus, there is the potential for a combined use of simulation and process mining to be used in a complementary fashion to report process performance for real and planned systems at an instance and aggregate level.

The methodology used will follow a three-step process as shown in Figure 17.1.

Table 17.1: The Implications for Process Mining of the Use of Simulated Data.

Characteristic of Data Generated by Simulation	Implication for Process Mining Analysis
Simulation data are clean and complete.	The process discovery algorithm does not have to contend with noise and data incompleteness.
The quantity of data is determined by the simulation.	Large data sets can be generated in minutes, rather than weeks or months.
The probability models that describe the underlying stochastic inputs are known and under our control.	We understand the cause of variability in the model that generates the data.
The logical structures that cause state transitions are known and can be manipulated.	We understand the underlying structure of the system that generates the data.
Alternative scenarios are simulated, which may or may not yet exist.	We are not constrained to historical data, but can analyze any system that exists or not.
Simulations generate sample paths (as opposed to transaction instances) for each replication.	The discovered process map can replicate the entity flow of customer, materials or information through the system.

Figure 17.1: A combined simulation and process mining methodology for performance analysis.

Build and Run Simulation

The simulation development is now outlined.

Collection of data such as process durations, task allocations and process relationships for the study was undertaken by the authors and employees of the organization in order to construct the process maps and simulation used in the analysis of the process designs. These tools thus provided a way of achieving an understanding about the current and future potential design of organizational processes without the risk of disruption to the real system itself. The conceptual model is shown in Figure 17.2.

In order to build the simulation model, a number of data collection activities are required. The probability of interview and detention in the cells are estimated from sample data collected for each arrest type. A demand pattern was determined

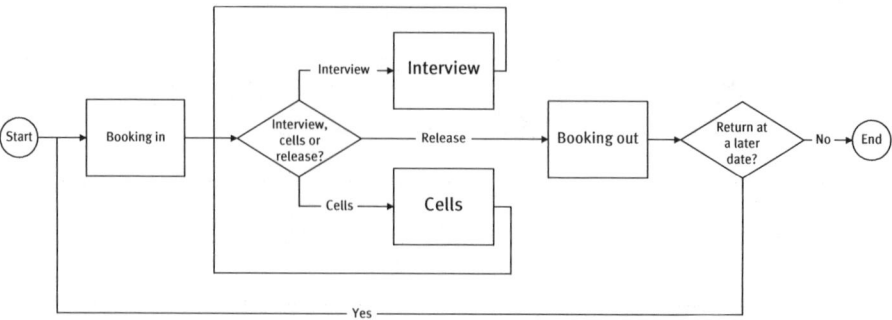

Figure 17.2: Process map for custody process.

for each of the arrest type for each of the three shifts worked at the custody suite. This approach was taken due to the need to estimate resource usage for each of the three shifts on duty. For the estimation of the process durations for the booking in, interview, cell detention and booking out activities, theoretical distributions were estimated based on data collected.

The model was built using the Arena modeling system. See Chapter 10 for more details of the simulation model.

The main issues in obtaining accurate simulation model results are to remove any initial bias from the results from the starting state of the simulation and to ensure that enough output data is generated by the simulation to obtain an accurate estimate of performance. For a terminating system, we would normally undertake a number of simulation replications to generate multiple samples and record a mean value over these. Because the custody process is in continuous operation, the simulation is a nonterminating type that allows us to use one long-run simulation, generating one large sample from which performance is estimated. This method is preferred as it generates a single event log file for the process mining performance analysis. To select the extended run length, the method shown in Robinson (2014) is used in which cumulative means of output data are compared over three replications of the model. If the cumulative means converge to a target value of less than 5%, then this can be considered acceptable. In this case, a run length of 500 days operation provides a convergence of 1.32%. This extended run length is also considered to minimize the effect of any initial bias from the start-up period. The results of a single run of the simulation over a time period of 500 days is shown in Figure 17.3 and are presented in three sections.

Tally variables are those that result from taking the average, minimum and maximum of a list of numbers, in this case the time in system or flowtime for each of the 12 arrest types and a value for all arrest types termed *overall flowtime*. This section also contains the number of observations of each person arrested for each arrest type. Discrete-change variables are those that result from taking the average,

```
                Arena Simulation Results
Replication ended at time    : 720000.0 Minutes
Base Time Units: Minutes
                                         TALLY VARIABLES
Identifier                    Average   Half Width  Minimum    Maximum      Obs

Breach of Bail Flowtime        80.674     3.4213     16.430     445.87      544
Burglary Flowtime             110.17      2.2243     53.513     349.77      790
Damage Flowtime                92.199     1.5093     48.293     233.43     1018
Drugs Flowtime                 92.491     4.2431     43.203     231.73      370
Fraud Flowtime                 81.507    (Insuf)     64.380     190.30      224
Public Order Flowtime          77.040     3.6366     44.560     739.53      641
Robbery Flowtime               81.582    (Insuf)     66.883     168.54      123
Sex Flowtime                  104.16     (Insuf)     77.197     217.32      140
Theft Flowtime                 96.887    (Corr)      18.199     573.67     2708
Traffic Flowtime               68.060    (Insuf)     16.949     192.75      231
Violence Flowtime             106.29      2.3547     48.472     473.55     1077
Warrant Flowtime               39.138    (Corr)      19.660     142.25     1907
Overall Flowtime               83.748     .89914     16.430     739.53     9773

                          DISCRETE-CHANGE VARIABLES
Identifier                    Average   Half Width  Minimum    Maximum    Final

Breach of Bail Cost           8485.4    (Corr)      .00000      16784.    16784.
Burglary Cost                14341.     (Corr)      .00000      29399.    29399.
Damage Cost                  14901.     (Corr)      .00000      30189.    30189.
Drugs Cost                    5848.6    (Corr)      .00000      11138.    11138.
Fraud Cost                    2753.1    (Corr)      .00000       5677.9    5677.9
Public Order Cost             9056.8    (Corr)      .00000      18179.    18179.
Robbery Cost                  1629.8    (Corr)      .00000       3254.8    3254.8
Sex Cost                      2291.7    (Corr)      .00000       4976.2    4976.2
Theft Cost                   46752.     (Corr)      .00000      94475.    94475.
Traffic Cost                  2593.3    (Corr)      .00000       5334.9    5334.9
Violence Cost                20024.     (Corr)      .00000      39077.    39077.
Warrant Cost                 16124.     (Corr)      .00000      32237.    32237.
COF_Busy                       41.440    1.2903     .00000        600.00    .00000
PC_Busy                        68.580    1.8344     .00000        800.00   100.00
jailer_Busy                    31.571     .66688    .00000        500.00    .00000
costPC                       68020.     (Corr)      .00000 1.3655E+05 1.3655E+05
costCOF                      49731.     (Corr)      .00000      99860.    99860.
costJAILER                   27052.     (Corr)      .00000      54319.    54319.
costBOOKIN                   71940.     (Corr)      .00000 1.4447E+05 1.4447E+05
costINTERVIEW                36546.     (Corr)      .00000      73338.    73338.
costCELLS                    27052.     (Corr)      .00000      54319.    54319.
costBOOKOUT                   9264.8    (Corr)      .00000      18594.    18594.
booking                          6.8580   .10437    .00000         30.000   .00000
interviewq                        .95969  .01808    .00000          8.0000  .00000
cellsq                           2.3137   .05309    .00000         24.000   .00000
bookoutq                         2.1919   .06085    .00000         24.000   .00000
waittime                        21.134    .21652    .00000         80.000  24.000

                              COUNTERS
Identifier                     Count    Limit

count_in                       10287    Infinite
count_out                       9773    Infinite
count booking_in               10287    Infinite
count_interview                 7024    Infinite
count_cells                     8246    Infinite
count_bookout                    513    Infinite
Simulation run time: 0.03 minutes.
Simulation run complete.
```

Figure 17.3: Arena simulation results report.

minimum or maximum of a plot of something during the simulation where the *x*-axis is continuous time. In this case, the maximum (total accumulated) cost is calculated by arrest type, resource type and process. Information is also provided on the utilization of resources and queue times at the custody processes. Counters are simply accumulated sums of a variable. The report shows the number of arrested persons (cases) entering the booking in and further processes. In addition to the results as shown in textual form, there are limited graphical facilities integrated into the Arena software, and confidence interval analysis can be undertaken by the Arena output analyzer software.

Once completed, the next stage of the study is to adapt the simulation model to produce an event log and then use process mining software to perform process performance analysis based on the event log data.

2 Generate Event Logs

The data required to make an event log can be obtained from a variety of sources including collected data in spreadsheets, databases and data warehouses or directly from data streams. An event log consists of a number of entries termed *events*. For each event, the minimum data required to construct an event log consists of a list of process instances (i.e., events), which are related to a case identification number and for each event a link to an activity label such as "check ticket." Activities may reoccur in the event log, but each event is unique and events within a case need to be presented in order of execution in the event log so that casual dependencies can be derived in the process model. It is also usual for there to be a timestamp associated with each event in the event log. Additional attributes associated with each event may also be included such as the association of a resource required to undertake the event and the estimated cost of the event. Event logs can be held in spreadsheet format or within the de facto exchange format for process mining termed *XES*. The construction of the event log covers ensuring that not only the data held is of the correct format but also making choices regarding what data is to be contained in the event log and which is to be omitted. This issue of scoping should be driven by the need to only include data that is required to meet the objectives of the process mining project. Thus, different event logs may be extracted from the same data set for different purposes.

To compare the performance metrics provided by the simulation and process mining software, the simulation is used for data farming to create the data needed for the event log, which is to be subsequently analyzed by the process mining software. To achieve this, extra coding is added to the Arena simulation model to write event data to a spreadsheet file as they occur during a simulation run. The generic coding needed to write the event log is shown in Figure 17.4.

An ASSIGN block is used to save the current simulation time (called TNOW in Arena) before the allocation of resource is made to undertake the process. This enables start timestamp data to be written on completion of the process using the READWRITE command. The required resource (in this case PC, COF or Jailer) is then requested by the simulation. If the required resource is not available immediately, this will register as a waiting time in the event log data. The PROCESS block

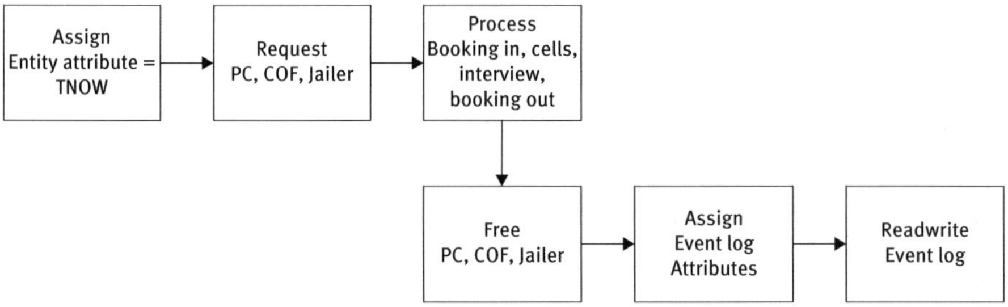

Figure 17.4: Generic Arena code for event log.

in Arena undertakes the process and on completion the resource is made free (available) for other processes. An ASSIGN block then sets the required attributes for the subsequent event log entry including incrementing the event ID counter, setting the process ID name, resource name and cost value. The Arena READWRITE command writes an event row to the CSV spreadsheet containing the information as shown in Figure 17.5. This code is required for each of the processes within the model (booking in, booking out, interview and cells). Each row in the spreadsheet represents an event and the file contains 35,843 events (9774 cases) generated by the simulation when run for 500 simulated days with an execution time of 0.03 minutes.

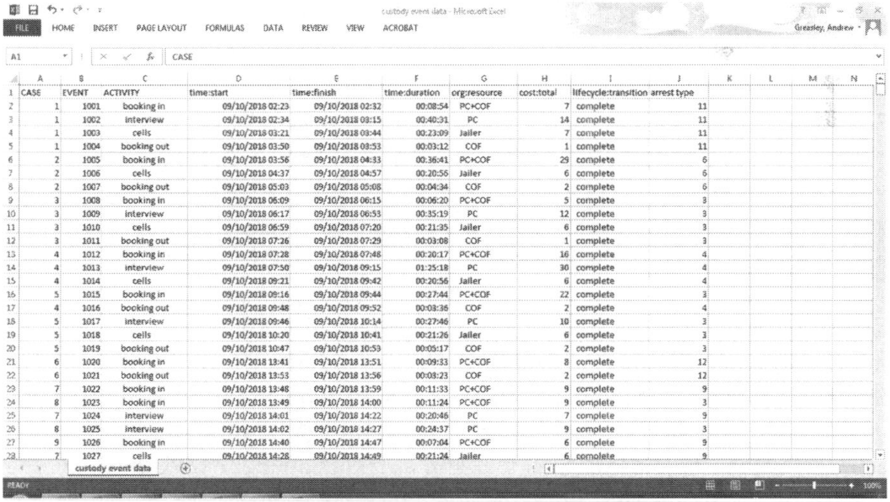

CASE	EVENT	ACTIVITY	time:start	time:finish	time:duration	org:resource	cost:total	lifecycle:transition	arrest type
1	1001	booking in	09/10/2018 02:23	09/10/2018 02:32	00:08:54	PC+COF	7	complete	11
1	1002	interview	09/10/2018 02:34	09/10/2018 03:15	00:40:31	PC	14	complete	11
1	1003	cells	09/10/2018 03:21	09/10/2018 03:44	00:23:09	Jailer	7	complete	11
1	1004	booking out	09/10/2018 03:50	09/10/2018 03:53	00:03:12	COF	1	complete	11
2	1005	booking in	09/10/2018 03:56	09/10/2018 04:33	00:36:41	PC+COF	29	complete	6
2	1006	cells	09/10/2018 04:37	09/10/2018 04:57	00:20:56	Jailer	6	complete	6
2	1007	booking out	09/10/2018 05:03	09/10/2018 05:08	00:04:34	COF	2	complete	6
3	1008	booking in	09/10/2018 06:09	09/10/2018 06:15	00:06:20	PC+COF	5	complete	3
3	1009	interview	09/10/2018 06:17	09/10/2018 06:53	00:35:19	PC	12	complete	3
3	1010	cells	09/10/2018 06:59	09/10/2018 07:20	00:21:35	Jailer	6	complete	3
3	1011	booking out	09/10/2018 07:26	09/10/2018 07:29	00:03:08	COF	1	complete	3
4	1012	booking in	09/10/2018 07:28	09/10/2018 07:48	00:20:17	PC+COF	16	complete	4
4	1013	interview	09/10/2018 07:50	09/10/2018 09:15	01:25:18	PC	30	complete	4
4	1014	cells	09/10/2018 09:21	09/10/2018 09:42	00:20:56	Jailer	6	complete	4
5	1015	booking in	09/10/2018 09:16	09/10/2018 09:44	00:27:44	PC+COF	22	complete	3
4	1016	booking out	09/10/2018 09:48	09/10/2018 09:52	00:03:36	COF	2	complete	4
5	1017	interview	09/10/2018 09:46	09/10/2018 10:14	00:27:46	PC	10	complete	3
5	1018	cells	09/10/2018 10:20	09/10/2018 10:41	00:21:26	Jailer	6	complete	3
5	1019	booking out	09/10/2018 10:47	09/10/2018 10:53	00:05:17	COF	2	complete	3
6	1020	booking in	09/10/2018 13:41	09/10/2018 13:51	00:09:33	PC+COF	8	complete	12
6	1021	booking out	09/10/2018 13:53	09/10/2018 13:56	00:03:23	COF	2	complete	12
7	1022	booking in	09/10/2018 13:48	09/10/2018 13:59	00:11:33	PC+COF	9	complete	9
8	1023	booking in	09/10/2018 13:49	09/10/2018 14:00	00:11:24	PC+COF	9	complete	3
7	1024	interview	09/10/2018 14:01	09/10/2018 14:22	00:20:46	PC	7	complete	9
8	1025	interview	09/10/2018 14:02	09/10/2018 14:27	00:24:37	PC	9	complete	3
9	1026	booking in	09/10/2018 14:40	09/10/2018 14:47	00:07:04	PC+COF	6	complete	9
7	1027	cells	09/10/2018 14:28	09/10/2018 14:49	00:21:24	Jailer	6	complete	9

Figure 17.5: Extract from the event log generated by the simulation.

The event log file illustrates the main requirements for process mining. A case number identifies each unique customer (or material or information) flow through the model. In this example, each case is related to each arrested person defined as an entity in the simulation. Each separate entry on the spreadsheet is given a unique event number (optional). Each activity is classified using the simulation process names of booking in, interview, cells or booking out. The start and finish time for each event is recorded and also the duration (optional). The resource undertaking the activity is then recorded. Multiple resources can not be allocated to an event, so a resource name PC + COF is used to indicate that both of these resources are allocated to the booking in process. The lifecycle transition is defined as "complete" for each event (optional). Additional attributes can be saved for the analysis. In this study the type of arrest (numbered 1–12) is recorded for each event as well as the staffing cost.

3 Use Process Mining for Performance Analysis

In terms of transforming the event log into a process model, there are a variety of process mining tools available including the open-source tool ProM (www.prom tools.org), which has a range of process discovery algorithms available as plug-ins that can be used and assessed. However, this study is focused on the use of process mining as a performance reporting tool rather than the method of process discovery. The tool that was chosen for this analysis is Minit 3.2 (www.minit.io), which has a focus on performance analysis. In terms of data entry, the software will accept event log files in a variety of formats such as CSV spreadsheet files and the process mining standard file format XES (www.xes.standard.org). Files can be downloaded as individual files, from an SQL server or from an ODBC driver. In terms of process discovery, the software uses a discovery algorithm similar to ProM's Fuzzy Miner. Although different simulation and process mining packages will have different capabilities and features, the assessment is intended to provide a general overview of the approach taken by process mining software to provide metrics for process performance. Figure 17.6 shows the process map created by the Minit 3.2 process mining software from the simulation generated event log. Please note that the software will provide warning messages regarding the event log timings generated by the simulation as they are in the future but will still process the log! It can be seen from the display that the map generated by the process mining software aligns with the simulation process map in Figure 17.6. The process mining also displays additional useful information in terms of a count of the number of flows between each of the activities within the process. This is useful as a validation tool. For example, the number of arrested persons returning at a later date is shown as 513 from 10,286, confirming the proportion defined in the simulation at a 5% chance on average. There is also evidence of a stray(!) arrested person who has left the custody suite immediately after booking in without passing through the booking out procedure. This may be due to an error in the event log rather than the simulation model, but this nonconformant behavior could be investigated further.

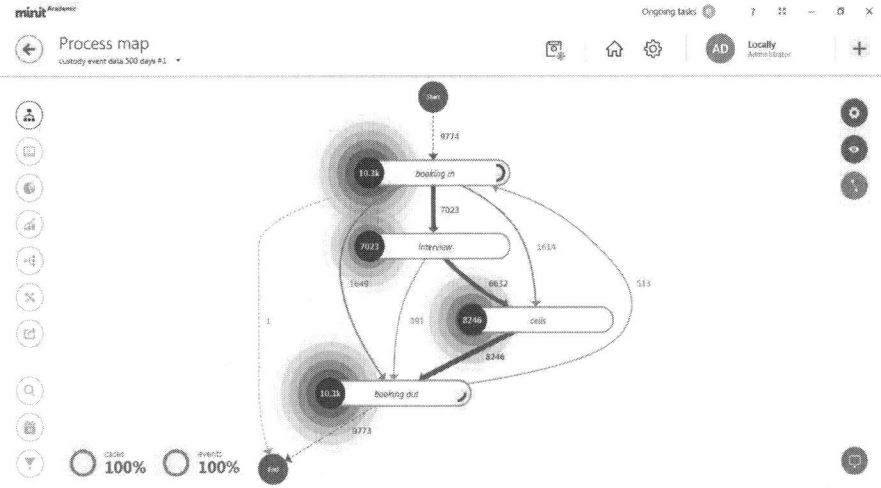

Figure 17.6: Discovered process map using process mining software (www.minit.io).

The process map can now be filtered by time and event attributes to investigate the state of the process in more detail. In addition, an animation facility allows for step-by-step observation of process flows within a specified timescale. The process map in Figure 17.7 shows an animated process map filtered for the date of October 1, 2019. An additional filter has been set to only show arrests of the type theft during this time period. This capability allows an in-depth analysis of process behavior at particular time periods of interest such as high waiting times.

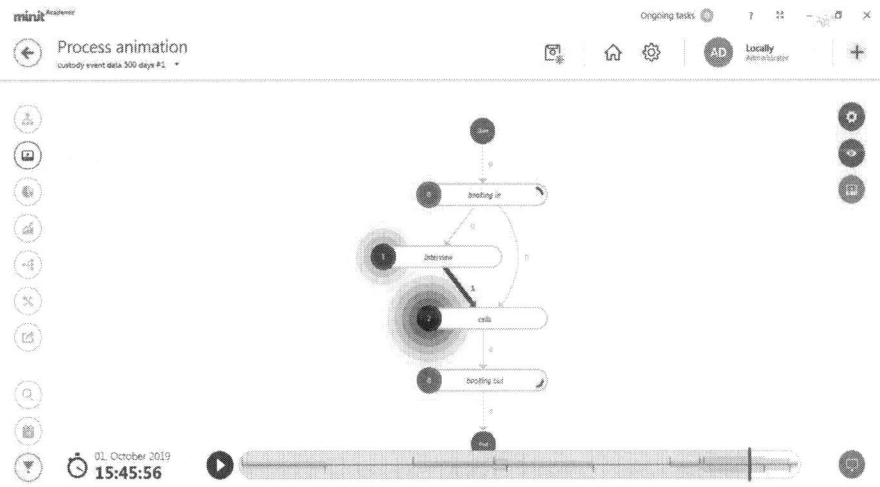

Figure 17.7: Process animation filtered for October 1, 2019 showing theft arrest process at 15:45:56 (www.minit.io).

Costing per activity (such as booking in, interview and cells) is provided by both the process mining (Figure 17.8) and simulation software. In terms of resource costs, these are available from the simulation, but because multiple resources are allocated to the booking in activity (PC and COF), resources costs for each resource can not be provided directly by the process mining software. Resource costs can be derived indirectly by multiplying each activity duration by the staffing cost per hour. Note for the booking in activity, the duration should be multiplied by both the PC and COF pay-rate to provide a total cost as both these resources are needed for this activity. The process mining is able to provide information on individual costing for an arrest type by employing the filter.

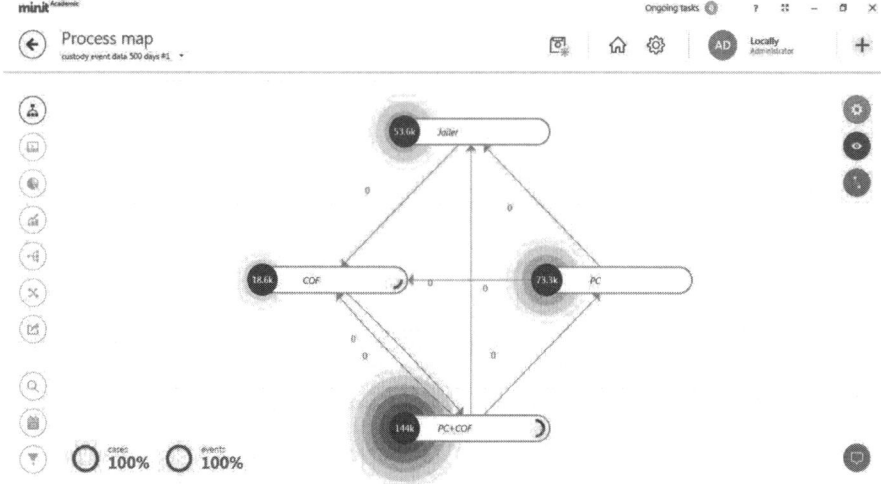

Figure 17.8: Process mining cost chart (www.minit.io).

Figure 17.9 shows the process mining Social Chart which shows the relationship and level of interaction between the resources, in this case people, in the simulation model. Because of the limitations concerning multiple resource allocation, the PC and COF resources are shown both as individual resources and as a combined PC+COF resource as used in the booking in process.

The process mining software also provides analysis of the different flow paths that individual customers take and groups them as case variants (Figure 17.10).

Case analysis can be filtered by time period and any attribute. Figure 17.11 provides a case active loading graph for October 1, 2019 showing only the arrests for theft. The screen provides detailed information on the timing, process duration and waiting time experience by the six arrests that occurred within the filtered set. The process mining software will report on waiting time if there is a time gap between the completion of a case event and the start of the subsequent event.

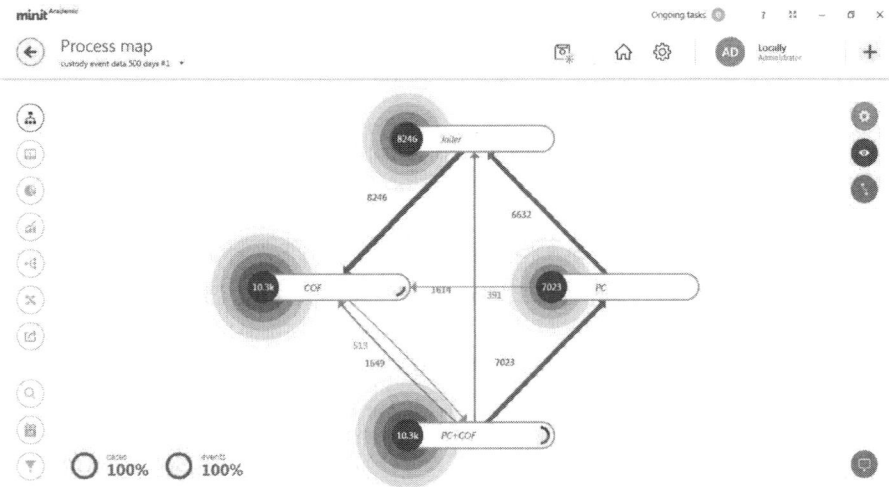

Figure 17.9: Process mining discovered social chart (www.minit.io).

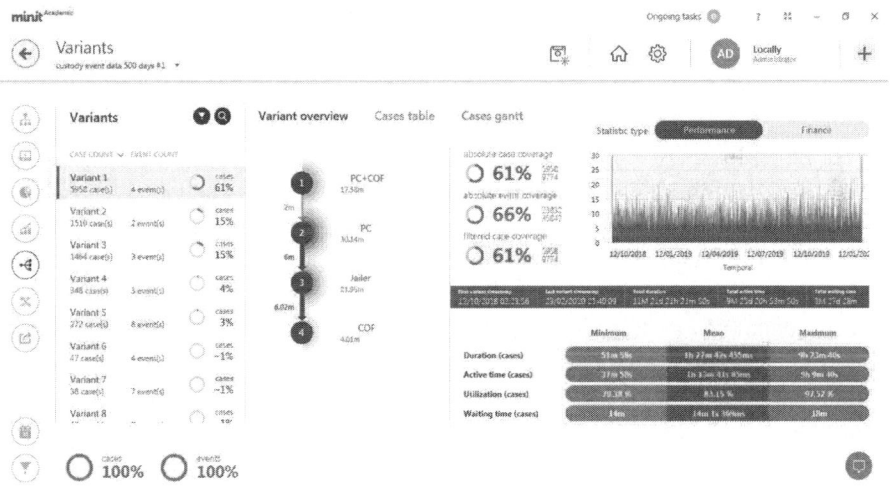

Figure 17.10: Process mining showing case variant analysis (www.minit.io).

Figure 17.11: Active cases occurring of theft type on October 1, 2019 (www.minit.io).

Conclusion

The ability of process mining to provide an alternative perspective of process performance is demonstrated by the case study analysis. Figure 17.3 shows the traditional simulation measures of long run averages and confidence intervals as reported by the Arena software. This type of report lacks a time-based analysis, which shows the sample path or entity flow for each person through the system. It is common practice to use the animation facilities to trace the movement of an entity through the system for validation purposes. However, an analysis of the effect of individual and aggregated entity behavior at a particular point in time is missing. This is provided in detail using the process mining software and can help identify risk points that are not uncovered by the long-run average performance reporting commonly used in simulation. For example, the long delays experienced by people for service at peak load times can be masked by averaging over a simulation replication. And in fact we may not be interested in the wait time of the person but the timing during the day when the wait time has occurred. The focus on case history and case variant history in the process mining software shows an approach that revolves around identifying individual process flows and investigating bottlenecks (high % variant common flows) and nonconforming flows (low % variant flows) of current operational performance.

There now follows an evaluation of the use of process mining to report process performance, outlining the benefits and limitations of the approach.

Benefits of Process Mining for the Reporting of Process Performance

In order to use the two tools requires the ability to share data between the simulation and process mining software. It was found relatively straightforward to generate event log data files in the CSV file format that could be imported into the process mining software. However, the use of the XES process mining file format may improve the ability to extract information and tools such as DISCO can be used to generate XES from CSV files.

Using the simulation model output to generate the event log used by the process mining software allows a focus on process performance rather than process discovery using a real event log with the attended issues around data quality and choice of process discovery algorithm.

It was found that the process flow time and process costing information provided by both methods gave near identical metrics, providing a useful validation between the simulation and process model developed by the process mining software.

A particular feature of the process mining software is the automatically generated graphical facilities of the software, which make the tool easy and quick to use for decision makers addressing operational decisions requiring a quick decision. This is useful as there are a growing number of people using simulation as part of an analytics toolkit who do not necessarily have in-depth knowledge and time to develop the model to produce sophisticated output reports.

Reporting of performance can be filtered by recognized attributes such as resource and cost and user assignable attributes such as arrest type. Reports can also be filtered by time period providing a powerful zoom-in tool for transient analysis for risk management.

Although the social chart is compromised in this case due to the need to allocate combined resources to a single process, the chart demonstrates the potential to use the process mining to map the nature of the interaction between people in the system. This shows one of the features of process mining, which is to provide an understanding of human behavior in the performance of system, in particular, the identification of nonconformant behavior that leads to reduced performance.

When using real event data, the process mining technique purely projects historical information and is not able to change the process design. However, the case study demonstrates the use of a simulation in a data farming mode to generate a synthetic event log. Logs can be generated to represent future scenarios that can be then be analyzed using the process mining software.

Limitations of Process Mining for Process Performance Measurement

The process mining software is unable to assign multiple resources to an event from the event log. Each resource allocation can be treated as a separate event (with a separate entry in the event log), but this will then generate multiple events for a single process, affecting the statistics reported by the process mining software.

In terms of waiting time analysis, the process mining software does not recognize queues. This issue of the incorporation of limited resources and subsequent queuing behavior in process mining has been addressed through the use of data mining and queuing theory methods under the term queue mining, although queue mining models are not yet available in commercial process mining tools. However as a case proceeds through the process, any time delays between the end of one event and the start of the subsequent event are treated as waiting time. This information allowed the reporting of case waiting time caused by the delay in availability of the PC, COF and jailer resources.

In summary, the facilities of process mining software can provide an extended and complementary capability to simulation output analysis. In particular, the ability to provide time-based analysis at the instance level can be used to identify when risks to system performance are taking place. The process mining software provides automatic and sophisticated graphical facilities that allow for quick analysis. From a process mining perspective, the methodology provides an extended use of the software from an analysis of historical event data to simulation-generated synthetic data that can be related to future performance of current systems or performance of systems that do not yet exist.

Chapter 18
Case Study: Using Simulation with Data Envelopment Analysis

Andrew Greasley

An example of a model-driven analysis technique is data envelopment analysis (DEA). This case study outlines the use of this technique in conjunction with simulation. The techniques are found to be complementary where each method can be used to improve the effectiveness of the other in decision making. DEA uses a linear programming approach to measure the potential for input reduction at a unit given its output levels, or the potential for output augmentation given its input levels. This study suggests that simulation can be used in order to offer practical guidance to improving the performance of benchmark operating units identified in a DEA analysis. This can be achieved by using sensitivity analysis of the benchmark unit using a simulation model to offer direct support as to the feasibility and efficiency of any variations in the operating practices to be tested. It will also be suggested that the simulation can be used as a mechanism to transmit the practices of the benchmark unit to weaker performing units by building a simulation model of the weaker unit to the process design of the benchmark unit. The model can then compare performance of the current and benchmark process designs.

Discussion

DEA assesses the comparative efficiency of homogeneous operating units, called *decision-making units* (DMUs), which are regarded as responsible for converting multiple inputs into outputs. Example DMUs include shops, hospitals, assembly plants and other manufacturing and service units, which can be characterized by input–output relationships. Each DMU is seen as consuming a set of resources (e.g., staff time, equipment) to deliver a set of outcomes (e.g., assembled products, serviced customer). The DEA analysis is able to determine a single "technical efficiency" rating for each DMU. The basic concept is that the efficiency of each member of a set of DMUs, the field, is evaluated against its own performance and that of each of the other members of the field. Those DMUs of which we can not identify other DMUs or combinations of DMUs that deliver the same output at less resource or alternatively more output for the same resource constitute a set of Pareto-efficient (benchmark) DMUs, which map out an efficient frontier. For the DMUs that are not Pareto-efficient DEA returns a measure of their efficiency, which reflects their distance from the efficient frontier. That distance, in turn, reflects their potential for resource conservation or output augmentation.

A method of using a combination of DEA and simulation analysis is suggested following a three-stage process (Figure 18.1). In stage one, it is necessary to obtain the data for the DEA and simulation analyses. In the case described in this study of the police force historical, data sets of published information of police performance were utilized. However, an aspect of DEA in the use of data from operating units is that an example may not exist or be available for each combination of input variables. Here a simulation model could be built, which could generate the output measures for a number of input variable scenarios.

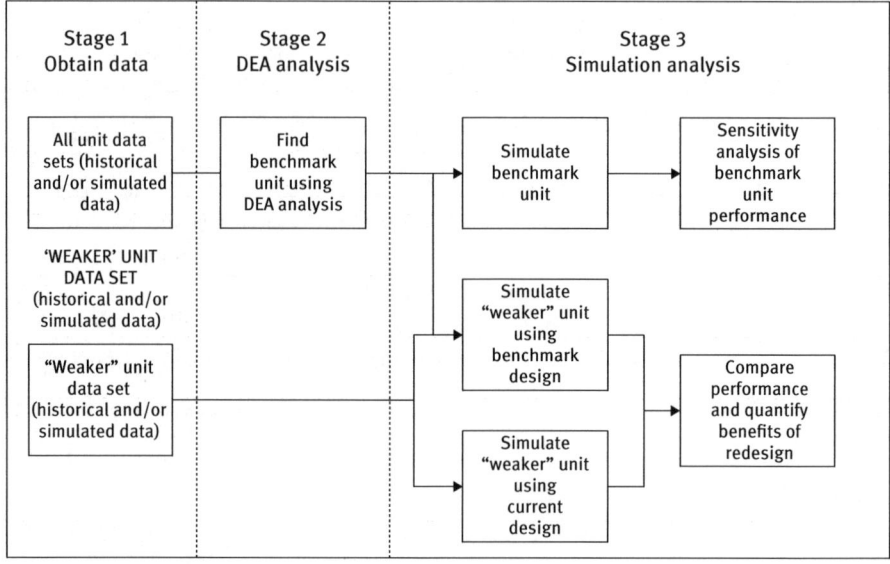

Figure 18.1: A three-stage model for the use of DEA and simulation.

The second stage is to analyze the operating units using DEA. This analysis would address a variety of aspects pertaining to each unit as well as to the particular industry from where the units are drawn. For example, the study could address issues of the comparative efficiency of resource utilization at each unit in terms of the scope for efficiency savings or output augmentation, any scope for efficiency improvements through changing the scale size of operations, any scope for cost reductions through a change in the mix of inputs used to better match prevailing input prices and so on. If longitudinal data are available, the analysis could also address the change in productivity over time of each unit and this could further be attributed to any changes in operating practices of the unit over time, including any changes in the mix of inputs (e.g., staff of varying categories) used.

In the third stage of analysis, simulation can now be engaged in order to offer practical guidance to operating units toward improved performance. In this regard, the fact that DEA offers performance information at operating unit level is particularly helpful. Any operating unit that is identified by DEA as Pareto-efficient (i.e., a benchmark unit) is likely to offer good operating practices in some aspect. DEA provides information as to the particular aspects of performance that underlie the characterization of a unit as Pareto-efficient. It is in those aspects that the unit is likely to offer particularly good operating practices. For example in the case of police forces, a Pareto-efficient force may be identified by DEA as offering especially strong performance in say clearing up burglaries. This type of information can be utilized in the context of simulation to map out the full range of procedures that constitute the operating practices in the area where a Pareto-efficient unit may be an exemplar to be emulated. In this framework, the simulation will not simply make it easier to codify and disseminate good practices that have been identified. Perhaps more importantly it offers the prospect of leading to still better operating practices. Pareto-efficient units are merely relative to the field of units used in the analysis. It is perfectly possible that even more efficient operating practices than those identified at Pareto-efficient units exist. The possibility of constructing such practices can be explored through simulation using the traditional "what if" type analyses supported through the simulation model, which answers as to their feasibility and efficacy. The recommendation here to design operating practices as variations on those identified as efficient through DEA bears some resemblance to the construction of unobserved operating units in the DEA framework albeit for a different purpose. If we rely on the user to provide trade-offs between the factors of production that are deemed feasible and desirable, the simulation model will offer direct support as to feasibility and efficiency of any variations in operating practices to be tested. Furthermore, the ability of simulation to operationalize change can be used as a mechanism to transmit the practices of the benchmark unit, identified by the DEA analysis, to weaker performing units. This is accomplished by the procedure of process mapping and building a simulation model of the weaker unit to the process design of the benchmark unit. The model can then compare performance of the current and benchmark process designs. Quantifying improvement in this way provides a useful driver to any process change initiative that is required to bring the performance of weaker units up to the best in class.

Conclusion

This study has outlined the mutually supportive ways in which simulation and DEA analyses can be undertaken. First, simulation can be used to generate some or all of the data sets needed for a DEA analysis. The use of DEA can guide us to the best of the observed practices, possibly identifying different units as exemplars for different aspects of operations. Simulation could then be used, modeled on the good practices identified, but offering the possibility of modifications to those practices that intuition and industry experience or other analysis suggests might be even more effective than those practices used hitherto by the Pareto-efficient units. In this regard it must be noted that where Pareto-efficient units offer good practice in different aspects of operation then simulation offers the prospect of combining these practices in a feasible manner to create even more efficient operating practices on a combination of aspects of performance. Furthermore by comparing the performance of a "weaker" business unit under current and benchmark process designs, the benefits of change can be quantified and used as a driver for the redesign effort.

Chapter 19
Case Study: Agent-Based Modeling in Discrete-Event Simulation

There has been an increasing interest in the use of agent-based simulation and some discussion of the relative merits of this approach as compared to discrete-event simulation. There are differing views on whether an agent-based simulation offers capabilities that discrete-event can not provide or whether all agent-based applications can at least in theory be undertaken using a discrete-event approach. This chapter presents a simple agent-based NetLogo model and corresponding discrete-event versions implemented in the widely used Arena and Simio software. The Arena version of the discrete-event model presented uses both a traditional process flow approach normally adopted in discrete-event simulation software and an agent-based approach to the model build. In addition, a real-time spatial visual display facility is provided using a spreadsheet platform controlled by VBA code embedded within the Arena model. The Simio version uses the object-oriented and spatial display facilities that are embedded in the software.

The Case Study

In order to investigate the feasibility of implementing agent-based systems using discrete-event software, a simple agent-based model "simple birth rates" was taken from the NetLogo software library. The model simulates population genetics with two populations of red and blue turtles. Each type of turtle has its own fertility and reproduces according to these birth rates. There is a limit to the population set by the carrying capacity of the "terrain" in which they are set and some agents will die if this population limit is exceeded. The model is used to show how differential birth rates can affect the ratio of red and blue turtles. After setup the code contains two main procedures for reproducing and killing turtle agents. The "reproduce" procedure interrogates each turtle agent and generates new turtles depending on the current turtle's fertility. The "kill" procedure destroys turtles if the population has reached the carrying capacity as set within the model. The NetLogo model display is shown in Figure 19.1. This incorporates buttons and sliders for setting up the simulation experiments, a time-based graph of turtle population and a spatial visual display of the turtle agents.

To establish if the simple birth rates model can be implemented in discrete-event simulation, an equivalent model was written using the Arena discrete-event simulation software to test the feasibility of this approach. The Arena model is shown in Figure 19.2.

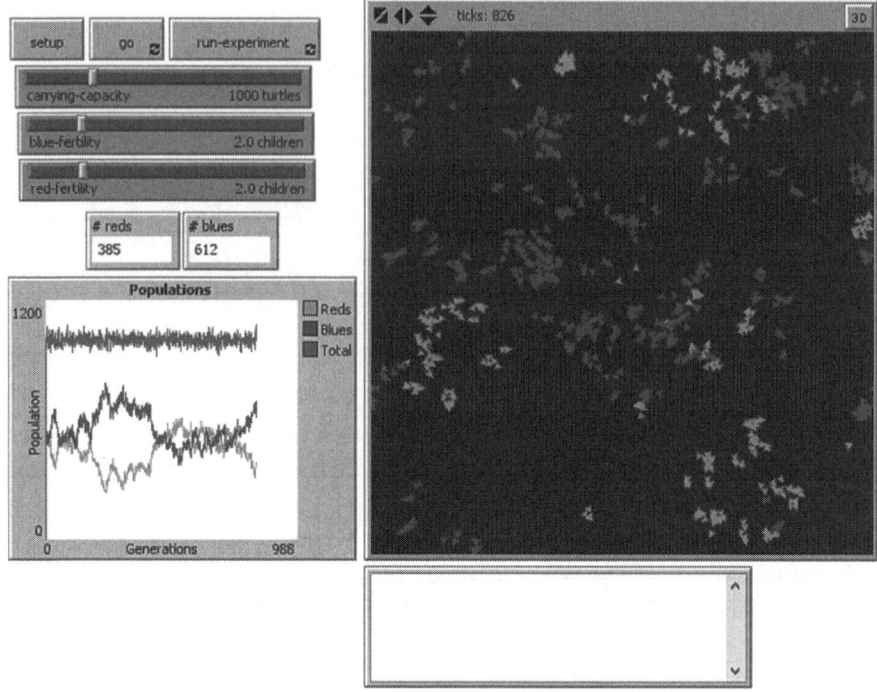

Figure 19.1: The NetLogo simulation display.

To implement the turtle model, only a simple Arena model is required. Blue and red turtles are created at the beginning of the model and then two sections of code implement the reproduce and kill procedures. The reproduce procedure generates new turtles depending on a probability held in the fertility variable set for red and blue turtles. The kill procedure destroys red and blue turtles depending on the capacity of the turtle population. Information on each turtle such as its color is held as an attribute value, which is a variable that is associated with each turtle entity. A graph was used in Arena to show the change in red and blue turtle population over time, but no spatial representation of the turtles could be provided using the Arena vector graphics.

The next stage of the investigation was to develop a model using Arena but using an object/agent-based approach and to provide a spatial display of turtle movement. Because of the limitations of the Arena graphics capability, this was implemented using the Visual Basic for Applications (VBA) facilities packaged within the Arena software. The VBA was used to provide a real-time spatial display of turtle movement in the Microsoft Excel spreadsheet application. The Excel spreadsheet was chosen for the display because each spreadsheet cell set at an appropriate zoom level could be used to hold the location of a turtle object. Also the ability to

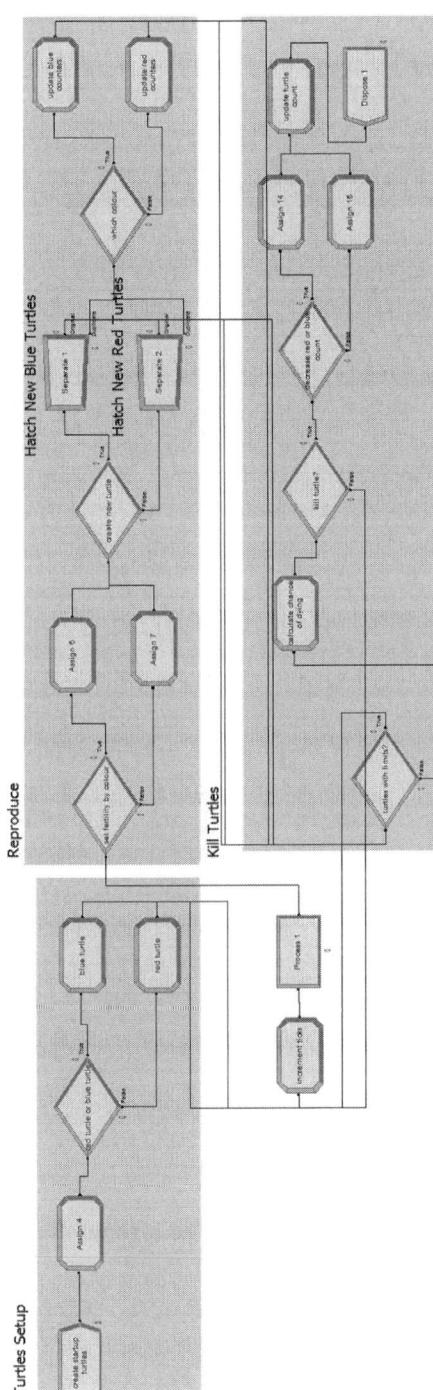

Figure 19.2: The Arena turtle model using a process flow approach.

execute VBA code to control Excel from within Arena allowed a real-time display of turtle movement as the simulation is running. The agent-based version of the Arena model is shown in Figure 19.3.

The VBA code is shown in Figure 19.4.

This version of the Arena model generates an initial population of red and blue turtles and then holds them in a queue for further processing. This is intended to mimic the internal mechanism of agent-based software where functions interrogate an object, rather than the traditional discrete-event approach of an entity moving through a process flow. The Arena program blocks are executed by a dummy entity that follows the process flow to generate and kill turtle agents as required. The reproduce procedure examines the attributes of each turtle in the queue in turn and generates new turtles based upon parent turtle properties. The kill procedure destroys red and blue turtles depending on the turtle population by removing them from the queue.

The next step was to provide a spatial visual display of the turtle population as the simulation is running. Currently, model results are provided using counters of red and blue turtle numbers and a time-based graph showing turtle population change over time. VBA code embedded within the Arena model was used to implement the spatial visual display in an Excel spreadsheet (Figure 19.5).

A VBA routine at the start of the simulation run opens the Excel application and sets the spreadsheet zoom level at an appropriate level for the display. During each cycle of the simulation, a VBA routine is executed from Arena that retrieves the current turtle object attributes from the Arena model. The attributes consist of elements such as turtle spatial location, turtle color and turtle direction of travel. The code then removes the turtle displayed at its current location, updates the turtle location and redraws the turtle at its new location. Finally the updated turtle attributes are copied back into the Arena turtle entity. Currently the display shows the turtle as either a red or a blue cell in the spreadsheet, but the coding is being developed to present the turtle as an icon within each cell with an indication of its current direction of travel. This would mimic the features of the NetLogo display shown in Figure 19.1.

The Simio Implementation

A third simulation was built using the Simio discrete-event simulation software. This software includes both an object approach to modeling and the ability to produce a spatial display of movement. Simio allows the use of object constructs in the following way. An object definition defines how an object behaves and interacts with other objects and is defined by constructs such as properties, states and events. An example in Simio is the ModelEntity or Server definitions. An object instance is an instantiation of an object definition that is used in a particular model. An example in Simio is the ModelEntity1 or Server1 instances. These objects can be

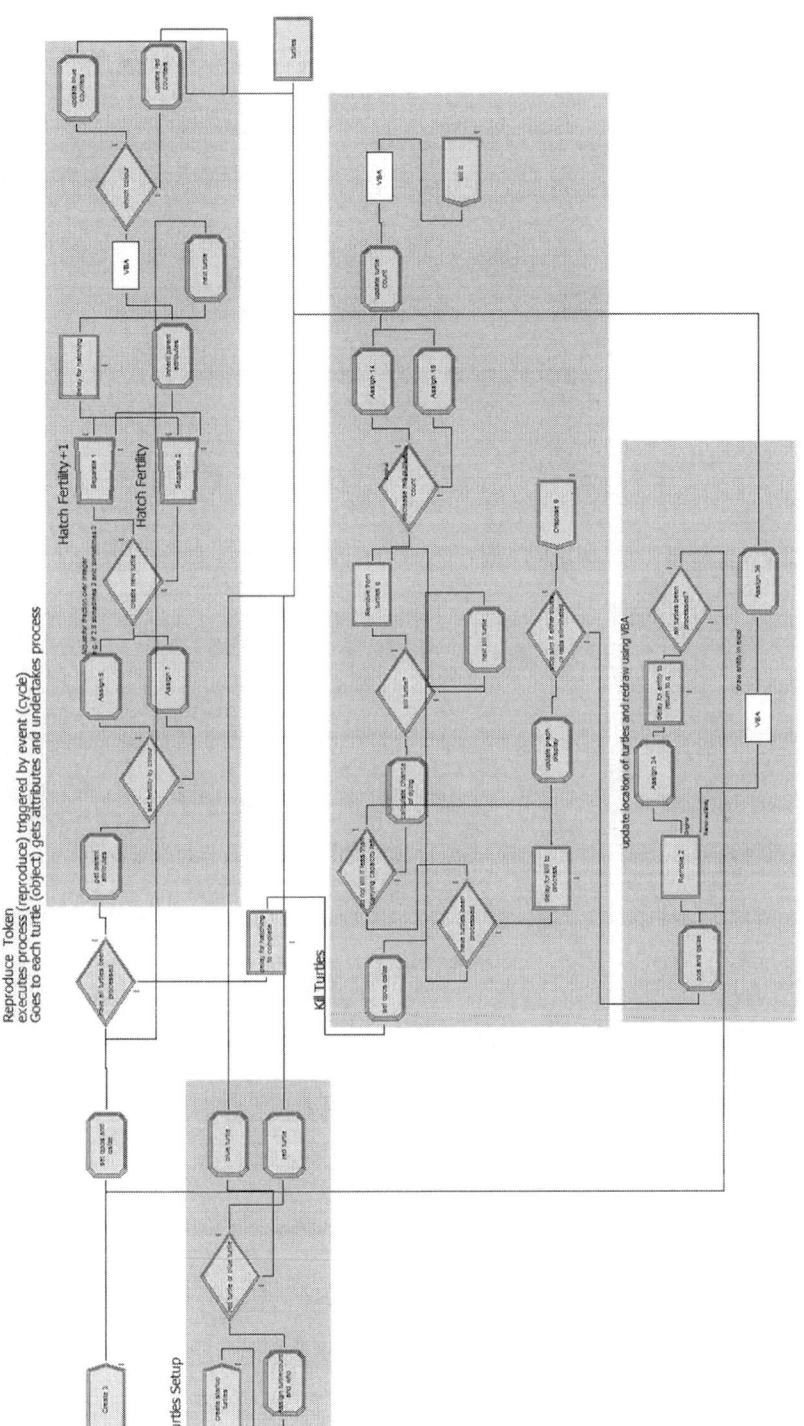

Figure 19.3: Arena turtle model using agent-based approach.

```
Private Sub VBA_Block_1_Fire()
Dim turtlexcoord, turtleycoord, turtlecol As Double
Dim turnby As Double
' get the current turtle attributes from Arena
turtlexcoord = g_SIMAN.EntityAttribute(g_SIMAN.ActiveEntity, g_turtlexcoord)
turtleycoord = g_SIMAN.EntityAttribute(g_SIMAN.ActiveEntity, g_turtleycoord)
turtlecol = g_SIMAN.EntityAttribute(g_SIMAN.ActiveEntity, g_turtlecol)
currentdegrees = g_SIMAN.EntityAttribute(g_SIMAN.ActiveEntity, g_currentdegrees)
'delete from current cell in Excel
oXLWorkSheet.Cells(turtlexcoord, turtleycoord).Interior.ColorIndex = 2
' rotate turtle
turnby = Rnd() * 8
'choose which way to move'
If turnby > 0 And turnby < 1 Then
turtleycoord = turtleycoord - 1
ElseIf turnby > 1 And turnby < 2 Then
turtlexcoord = turtlexcoord + 1
turtleycoord = turtleycoord - 1
ElseIf turnby > 2 And turnby < 3 Then
turtlexcoord = turtlexcoord + 1
ElseIf turnby > 3 And turnby < 4 Then
turtlexcoord = turtlexcoord + 1
turtleycoord = turtleycoord + 1
ElseIf turnby > 4 And turnby < 5 Then
turtleycoord = turtleycoord + 1
ElseIf turnby > 5 And turnby < 6 Then
turtlexcoord = turtlexcoord - 1
turtleycoord = turtleycoord + 1
ElseIf turnby > 6 And turnby < 7 Then
turtlexcoord = turtlexcoord - 1
ElseIf turnby > 7 And turnby < 8 Then
turtlexcoord = turtlexcoord - 1
turtleycoord = turtleycoord - 1
End If
'move to new cell in Excel
If turtlecol = 1 Then
oXLWorkSheet.Cells(turtlexcoord, turtleycoord).Interior.ColorIndex = 5 ' blue turtle
Else
oXLWorkSheet.Cells(turtlexcoord, turtleycoord).Interior.ColorIndex = 3 ' red turtle
End If
' put the cell coordinates and orientation back into the Arena turtle entity
g_SIMAN.EntityAttribute(g_SIMAN.ActiveEntity, g_turtlexcoord) = turtlexcoord
g_SIMAN.EntityAttribute(g_SIMAN.ActiveEntity, g_turtleycoord) = turtleycoord
g_SIMAN.EntityAttribute(g_SIMAN.ActiveEntity, g_currentdegrees) = currentdegrees
End Sub
Private Sub VBA_Block_2_Fire()
Dim turtlexcoord, turtleycoord As Double
' get the current turtle attributes from Arena
turtlexcoord = g_SIMAN.EntityAttribute(g_SIMAN.ActiveEntity, g_turtlexcoord)
turtleycoord = g_SIMAN.EntityAttribute(g_SIMAN.ActiveEntity, g_turtleycoord)
' delete from current cell in Excel
oXLWorkSheet.Cells(turtlexcoord, turtleycoord).Interior.ColorIndex = 2 ' blank cell
End Sub
Private Sub VBA_Block_3_Fire()
Dim turtlexcoord, turtleycoord, turtlecol As Double
' get the current turtle attributes from Arena
turtlexcoord = g_SIMAN.EntityAttribute(g_SIMAN.ActiveEntity, g_turtlexcoord)
turtleycoord = g_SIMAN.EntityAttribute(g_SIMAN.ActiveEntity, g_turtleycoord)
turtlecol = g_SIMAN.EntityAttribute(g_SIMAN.ActiveEntity, g_turtlecol)
' show at current cell in Excel
If turtlecol = 1 Then
oXLWorkSheet.Cells(turtlexcoord, turtleycoord).Interior.ColorIndex = 5 ' blue turtle
Else
oXLWorkSheet.Cells(turtlexcoord, turtleycoord).Interior.ColorIndex = 3 ' red turtle
End If
End Sub
```

Figure 19.4: VBA code for Excel agent display.

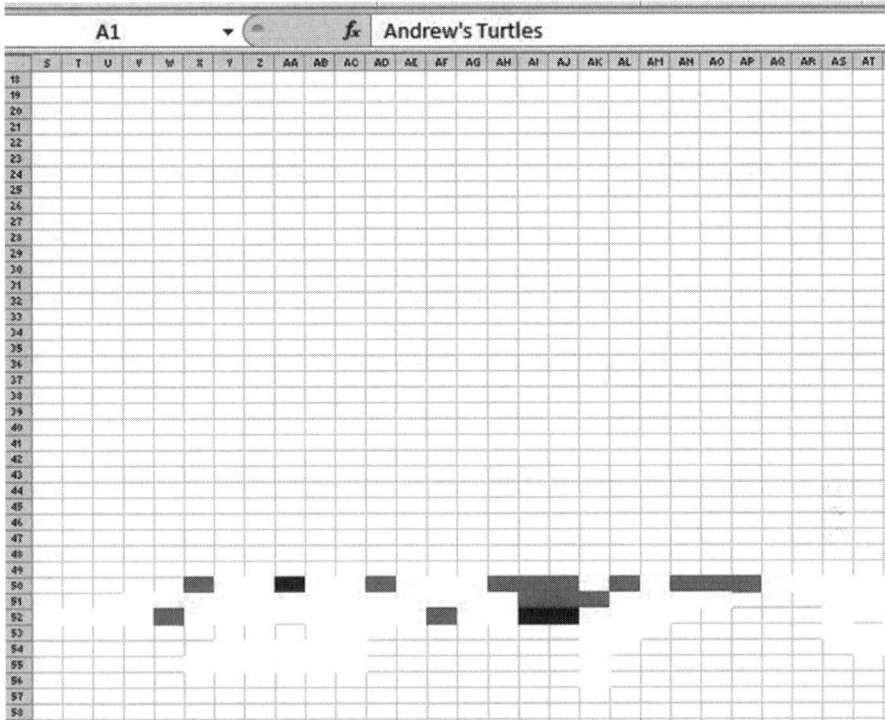

Figure 19.5: Spatial display of turtles in Excel.

specified by setting their properties in Simio. For example the Server1 processing time can be specified by setting the appropriate property parameters. An object runspace are objects that are created during a simulation run based on the object instance definition. An example in Simio is ModelEntity1[25] which represents the entity with an instance identification number of 25. In terms of a spatial display Simio allows entities to move in what is termed "FreeSpace." Here no pathways are defined but entities move between (X,Y,Z) coordinates at a defined heading, speed and acceleration.

In Simio the turtle agents are simulated using entities which are part of the object construct approach described above and so can have their own behavior and make decisions, be dynamically created and destroyed and move through 2D and 3D space. These capabilities are achieved with the use of entity token approach that was previously undertaken using Arena, but is explicitly supported in Simio. Here a token is created as a delegate of the entity to execute a process. Processes can be triggered by events such as the movement of entities into and out of objects. What Simio terms Add-on processes can also be incorporated into an object definition to allow the use of that object to insert customized logic into the "standard" behavior of the object.

332 — Chapter 19 Case Study: Agent-Based Modeling in Discrete-Event Simulation

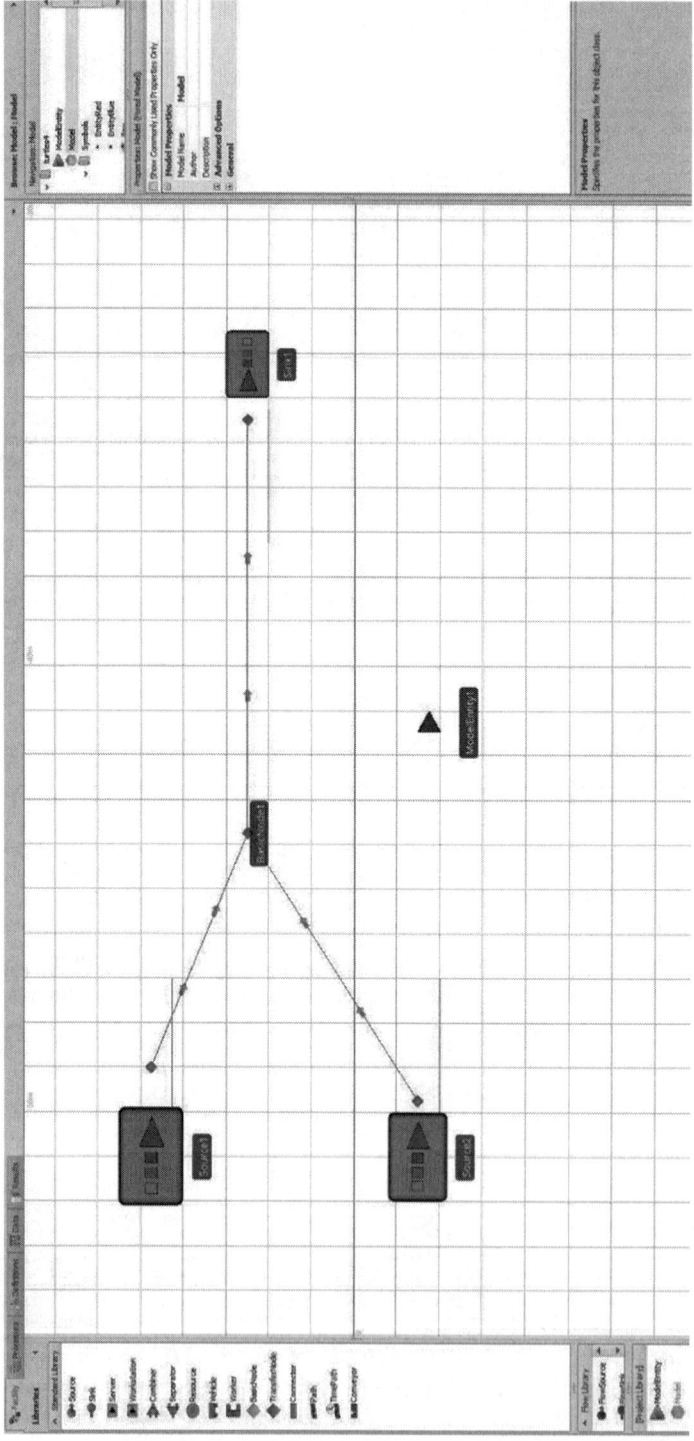

Figure 19.6: Simio turtles model.

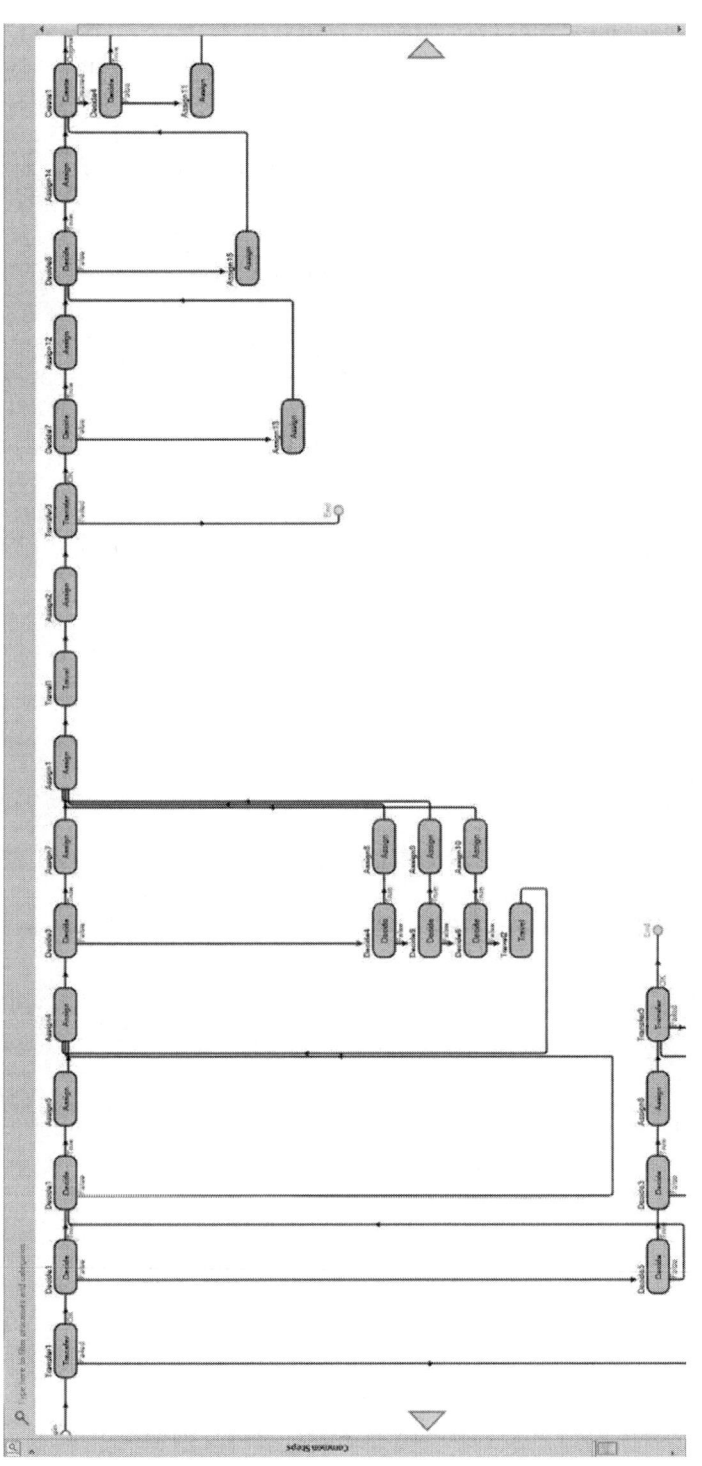

Figure 19.7: Process Definition for Turtle Model.

The Simio model for the turtles application is shown in Figure 19.6. This consists of 2 source nodes which are used to create the blue turtles and red turtles as separate arrival streams. An Entity object instance is also defined and named as ModelEntity1. One initial batch of turtles is created at the start of the simulation run and when they enter the BasicNode point an add-on process is triggered that defines the behavior of each turtle as it moves around the grid.

An exerpt from the add-on process definition is shown in Figure 19.7. This defines the actions of the token associated with the entity object that is represented as a turtle in the model. Actions here include placing the turtle on the screen display, moving the turtle from one coordinate to another and procedures for creating and destroying turtles. Turtles are created using the create block which creates an entity object instance which is associated with the entity object that triggered the process. These new turtles automatically inherit their properties from the entity (turtle) that is associated with them.

The turtle model implemented using Simio is shown in Figure 19.8. The display shows the model in a 3D view although only movement in 2 planes is defined in this case. The turtles move around the grid by the use of the Travel command which defines a subsequent random location in relation to the current coordinates.

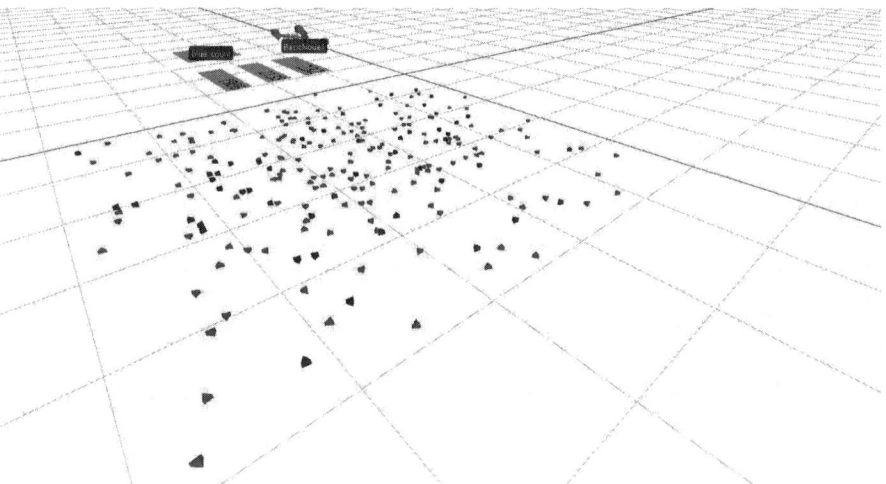

Figure 19.8: 3D Spatial Display of Turtles in Simio.

Conclusion

The presented models represent an initial investigation into the feasibility of incorporating an agent-based approach into a discrete-event simulation. Although a number of agent-based software applications exist such as NetLogo and even applications that create agent-based and discrete-event-type models, the barriers to current discrete-event simulation users are substantial in terms of the effort needed to become proficient in these software applications. It may be that many applications are developed in an approach that aligns with the modelers' background and expertise and this study has provided an indication that discrete-event-based systems could indeed be used to develop agent-based models. These results are relevant because implementing an agent-based model on a discrete-event simulation software platform provides a potential pathway for the established and very wide base of discrete-event simulation practitioners to develop agent-based models.

Appendix A

References

Greasley, A. (1998) "An Example of a Discrete-Event Simulation on a Spreadsheet", *SIMULATION*, 70(3), pp. 148–166.

Hill, A. and Hill, T. (2012) *Operations Management*, Third edition, Palgrave McMillan.

Kim, D. H. (1992) "Systems Archetypes: Diagnosing Systemic Issues and Designing High-Leverage Interventions," Toolbox Reprint Series: Systems Archetypes, Pegasus Communications, pp. 3–26.

Maani, K. E. and Cavana, R.Y. (2007) *Systems Thinking, System Dynamics: Managing Change and Complexity*, Second Edition, Pearson Education, New Zealand.

O'Neil, C. (2016) *Weapons of Math Destruction: How Big Data Increases Inequality and Threatens Democracy*, Penguin Random House

Pegden, C.D., Shannon, R.E., Sadowski, R.P. (1995) *Introduction to Simulation using SIMAN*, Second Edition, Mc-Graw-Hill.

Peppard, J. and Rowland, P. (1995) *The Essence of Business Process Re-engineering*, Prentice Hall.

Robinson, S. (2014) *Simulation: The Practice of Model Development and Use*, Second Edition, Palgrave Macmillan.

Senge, P. M. (2006) *The Fifth Discipline: The Art and Practice of The Learning Organization*, Second Edition Random House, London.

Slack, N, and Brandon-Jones, A. (2019) *Operations Management*, Ninth Edition, Pearson Education Ltd., Harlow.

Appendix B

Books for Simulation Modeling

Laguna, M. and Marklund, J. (2019) *Business Process Modeling, Simulation and Design*, Third Edition, CRC Press.
Zeigler, B.P., Muzy, A., Kofman, E. (2019) *Theory of Modeling and Simulation: Discrete Event & Iterative System Computational Foundations*, Third Edition, Academic Press.
Law, A.M. (2015) *Simulation Modeling and Analysis*, Fifth Edition, McGraw-Hill.
Robinson, S. (2014) *Simulation: The Practice of Model Development and Use*, Second Edition, Palgrave Macmillan.
Banks, J., Carson II J.S., Nelson, B.L., Nicol, D.M. (2014) *Discrete-Event System Simulation: Pearson New International Edition*, Fifth Edition, Pearson Education Limited.
Choi, B.K. and Kang, D. (2013) *Modeling and Simulation of Discrete-Event Systems*, John Wiley & Sons Inc.
Pidd, M. (2009) *Tools for Thinking: Modelling in Management Science*, Third Edition, John Wiley and Sons Ltd.
Greasley, A. (2008) *Enabling a Simulation Capability in the Organisation*, Springer-Verlag, London Ltd.
Leemis, L.M. and Park, S.K. (2006) *Discrete-Event Simulation: A First Course*, Pearson Education Inc.
Pidd, M. (2004) *Computer Simulation in Management Science*, Fifth Edition, John Wiley and Sons Ltd.
Harrington, H.J. and Tumay, K. (2000) *Simulation Modeling Methods: To Reduce Risks and Increase Performance*, McGraw-Hill.

Books for Model Building Using Arena

Rossetti, M.D. (2015) *Simulation Modeling and Arena*, John Wiley and Sons Inc.
Kelton, W.D.; Sadowski, R.P.; Zupick, N.B. (2015) *Simulation with Arena*, Sixth Edition, McGraw-Hill Education.
Altiok, T. and Melamed, B. (2007) *Simulation Modeling and Analysis with Arena*, Academic Press.
Seppanen, M.S.; Kumar, S.; Chandra, C. (2005) *Process Analysis and Improvement: Tools and Techniques*, McGraw-Hill.
Greasley, A. (2004) *Simulation Modelling for Business*, Ashgate Publishing Limited.
Chung, C.A. (2004) *Simulation Modeling Handbook: A Practical Approach*, CRC Press.
Seila, A.F.; Ceric, V.; Tadikamalla, P. (2003) *Applied Simulation Modeling*, Thomson Learning.

Books for Model Building Using Simio

Smith, J.S., Sturrock, D.T., Kelton, W.D. (2018) *Simio and Simulation: Modeling, Analysis, Applications*, Fifth Edition, Simio LLC.

Index

Activity-based costing 56–57, 200
Activity cycle diagrams 80–81
Activity driver 57, 200–202, 225–226, 240–242, 244–245
Advanced service provision 298
Agent-based simulation 12, 25, 31, 325
Aleatory uncertainty 51, 86
Analysis of variance 170, 173–174
Analytics
– descriptive 3, 5–6, 14, 67–68, 108, 154, 186, 200, 204, 244
– predictive 5–6, 14, 67–68, 108, 154, 188, 204, 247
– prescriptive 3, 5, 6, 14, 67–68, 154, 176, 188, 203
Analyzed data 18
Archetype 71–74
Arena modeling
– decisions 113–114
– entities 112
– processes 112–113
– resources 113
Arena modules
– assign 115
– create 115
– decide (chance) 116
– decide (conditional) 116
– dispose 115
– process (delay) 115
– process (seize-delay-release) 116
– resource 116
Arena reports
– discrete-change variables 122
– outputs 122
– tally variables 121
Arena statistics 123
Associations 5, 7
Association rules mining (arm) 8
Attribute (entity) 26–27, 76, 112, 114–116, 144

Balanced scorecard 54, 61–66
Bank clerk simulation 110
Benchmark 10, 52, 60, 66, 321–324
Big data 68, 86, 308
Black box 9, 106

Bootstrapping 91, 107, 109
Business process management (bpm) 3, 4, 52
Business processes 3, 4, 5, 14, 30, 52, 214, 217

Case studies 186–191
– advanced service provision 298
– ERP system 214
– food retail distribution 249
– logistics system 206
– police arrest process 239
– police call center 195
– process improvement at a UK police force 61
– proposed textile plant 259
– rail carriage maintenance depot 280
– rail vehicle bogie production facility 289
– road traffic accident process 271
– simulation analytics with process mining 308
– simulation with agent-based modelling 325
– simulation with data envelopment analysis 321
– snacks process 230
– systems thinking at a gas cylinder manufacturer 70
Causal dependencies 9, 312
Causation 9, 22
Cellular automata 25
Classification 7–9
Clustering 7–8, 69, 182
Cognitive 34, 91, 105–106, 109
Concept drift 155
Conceptual model 67–69, 79
Confidence intervals 156–157, 161, 163–165, 169, 171
Conformance 10, 108–109, 308
Context level 76, 79
Continuous distribution 92
Continuous systems 13, 31
Core manufacturing simulation data 86
Correlation 22, 101
Cost 56, 214, 280
Cost driver 57, 200–202, 225–226, 240–241, 245–246, 248

Dashboard 10, 182–183, 198–199
Data
– analyzed 17–18, 21–22

https://doi.org/10.1515/9781547400690-021

- raw 17–18, 21, 82, 91, 107
- sampled 17–18, 21, 108
- simulated 17–18, 308, 322
Data collection 83–88
Data-driven
- analysis 4, 7
- analytics 7, 17–18, 21–22, 148
- simulation 18–19, 21, 22, 68, 108
Data envelopment analysis 321
Data farming 11, 68
Data mining 7, 68
Decision-making unit (DMU) 321
Decision trees 8, 23, 106
Deep learning 8
Dependability 56, 207, 212–213
Descriptive model 5
Deterministic models 16
Digital twins 19–21, 44
Discrete-event simulation (des) 12–13, 25, 31, 70–71, 74, 80, 86–87, 102, 143, 269, 308, 325
Distribution center 249
Domain expert 12, 67–68
Dynamic mathematical models 13

Efficiency 53, 214, 223–224, 227–228, 250, 257–258, 295, 321–322
Empirical distribution 102, 104, 107, 109
Enterprise resource planning (ERP) system 214
Enterprise social software (ESS) 214
Entity (object) 26, 112
Entity (simulation method) 33
Epistemic uncertainty 51, 86
Estimation 91, 108
Event log 9–10, 91, 108–109, 182, 253, 308–314, 319–320
Events (systems view) 71
Externalize 31–32

Factorial designs 175–176
Feedback 11, 23, 72
Flexibility 56, 214, 225, 227–229, 238
Flow (simulation method) 31–32
Food retail distribution network 249

Geographical information system (GIS) 273

Half-width 123, 157, 161, 163–165
Hub-and-spoke 207–208

Hybrid simulation 30
Hypothesis testing 165, 170–174

Incompleteness 9, 83, 309
Individual (simulation method) 34
Information systems 3, 4, 43, 279
Interdependence 15
Involvement
- managerial 185
- operational 185–186

Last mile logistics system 206
Late drinking 240, 247–248
Less-than-truckload (LTL) 208
Level of usage 43–46
Linear regression 8

Machine learning 7, 68
Management science 3, 4
Manufacturing execution systems 18
Mathematical equation 6–7, 12, 14, 91, 102, 105
Mathematical model 3, 12–13
Mental models 71, 73
Model
- abstraction 31–32, 78, 83, 87, 153
- assumptions 33, 77–78, 84, 142, 14, 148, 153–154
- scope 22, 69, 75–78, 177
Model-driven
- analysis 5–6, 9, 11, 16–18, 21–22, 68
- analytics 17–18, 21, 68
- simulation 17–18, 21–22
Modeling
- areas 88–89
- human behavior 30–34, 79, 105
- input data 88–109
- methods 91

Neural networks 8, 9
Noise 9, 16, 83, 309
Nonstationary processes 101
Non-terminating simulation 154–155, 165–169

Operations management 3, 4, 52–54
Operations research 3, 4
Optimization 3, 4, 41, 176–181
Organizational
- ambidexterity 214

– context of implementation 184
– scope 19–20
Overfitting 16, 83
Out of scope 78

Pattern recognition 5
Patterns of behavior 71
People analytics 11
Performance measures 3, 52–57, 75, 89, 156, 211, 227, 308
Police arrest process 239
Police call center 195
Process discovery 9, 309, 314, 319
Process mapping 57–58, 79–81
Process mining 9–10, 41, 68, 82–83, 108, 182, 252–254, 308–320
Productivity 42–43, 53, 66, 75, 105
Product service systems (PSS) 298–300, 303, 306–307
– pay-on-availability 299
– pay-on-production 299
– pay-per-use 299
– product-oriented 299, 307
– result-oriented 298, 299, 307
– use-oriented 299, 307
Project
– implementation plan 184
– presentation 184
– report 183

Rail carriage maintenance depot 280
Rail vehicle bogie production facility 289
Reality
– digital 17–18
– farmed 17–18
– selected 17–18
– simplified 17–18
Reinforcement learning 8, 106
Resource (object) 26–27, 29, 33, 56, 76, 78, 89–90, 112–116
Resource driver 57, 200–201, 203–204, 223–226, 240–241, 245–246
Resources
– committed 240
– flexible 240
Retail delivery
– delivery point attributes 207
– location attributes 207
Road traffic accident process 271

Satisficing 177
Scheduling software 19–21, 40–41
Scorecards 10
Secondary distribution network 250–251, 253, 255–258
Sensitivity analysis 149–150, 152, 321–322
– Simio 150–152
Sensors 83, 85–86, 205
Sequences 5, 7
Service blueprinting 58
Service-level 208, 278, 280, 282
Services
– advanced 298–300, 307
– basic 298–299
– intermediate 298
Simplification 16, 31–32, 67–68, 77–79
Simplify (process design) 60–61
Simplify (simulation method) 31–32
Simulated data 18, 308, 322
Simulation 13
– benefits 36–37, 49–50
– costs 35–39
– hardware 38
– limitations 50–51
– project management 46–49
– software 37, 39–41, 55–56, 110
– sponsor 35
– training 22, 35–36, 38–40, 45–46
Skill sets 197–198
Snacks process production system 230
Software vendors 38, 40–41
Speed 56, 225, 237, 271
Spoke terminal 206, 208–210, 212
State space 9, 22, 79
Static mathematical models 12
Statistical analysis of non-terminating systems 165
Statistical analysis of terminating systems 156
Steady-state 154–155
Stochastic models 16
Stock keeping unit (SKU) 231
Supervised machine learning 8
Support vector machines (SVM) 8
System dynamics 12, 23–24, 87
Systems thinking 70–74

Task (simulation method) 33
Terminating simulation 154–155, 157–165
Test data 16, 22

Textile plant 259
Theoretical distribution 91–92, 99, 101, 108
Timestamp 9, 312
Trace (analysis) 143–144, 146–147
Trace (simulation) 91, 108–109, 150
Training (algorithm) 21, 106
Training (data) 8, 16
Transient 155–156, 165–166, 236–237

Underfitting 16, 83
Underlying structures 71–72
Unsupervised learning 8

Validation 148–153
– believability 148, 152
– conceptual 148
– operational 148, 149
Variability 14–16, 36–37, 75, 86, 154, 165, 268
Verification 142–147
– Arena 144
– animation inspection 143
– documentation 143
– model design 142
– Simio 146
– structured walkthrough 142
– test runs 143
– trace analysis 143
Visual analytics 10, 68, 182
Visual Basic for Applications (VBA) 106, 232–235, 325–326, 328, 330

XES 312, 314, 319